HOW FOOTBALL BECAME FOOTBALL

150 YEARS OF THE GAME'S EVOLUTION

TIMOTHY P. BROWN

JACK:

THANKS FOR YOUR SUPPORT.

I HOPE YOU ENJOY THE BOOK!

Tim Brown

BROWN HOUSE PUBLISHING

First printing: 2020

ISBN: 978-0-9995723-3-7 (eBook edition)

ISBM: 9995723-4-4 (Paperback edition)

Brown House Publishing, West Bloomfield, MI

Created with Vellum

To Carolyn, with all my love

CONTENTS

ACKNOWLEDGMENTS

Creating and publishing this book required me to gather information and images scattered in locations across the U.S., Canada, and the United Kingdom. Throughout the process, I benefited from the support of archivists and others at colleges, universities, and museums who located images or provided permission to use their images in this book. Without their assistance, this book would have far less flavor. While all were helpful, I particularly want to thank Tiffany Dogan, Alia Levar Wegner, and William M. Modrow. Each of them assisted me in accessing the Cradle of Coaches Archive in the Walter Havighurst Special Collections at Miami University.

I was particularly thankful for those with various commercial enterprises who provided pictures, granted permission, or spent time discussing their products and services with me. Chris Hornung of AntiqueFootball.com permitted the use of several images from his site. More important, his work in researching and describing early football equipment was an invaluable resource throughout this process. Nelson Kraemer, Director of Engineering, and Micheal Richards, Category Manager Riddell IQ, at Riddell Sports, took time from their workdays to help me understand the development processes and products offered by their firm. Eddie Ogden, Airship PR Specialist & Historian, with Goodyear Tire and Rubber Company, provided background on the history of the Goodyear blimps and directed me to additional resources. Others who provided support outside their regular duties included:

- Pamela Hollander, Vice President, Consumer Marketing at Allstate Insurance;

- Lindsey Naber, Director of Marketing at Rawlings Sporting Goods;
- Simon Hawkesley, Chief Executive Officer of Richard Lindon & Company; and
- Megan MacDiarmid, Manager of Marketing Services at Ricos Products Company.

Tom Lockney, Professor Emeritus at the University of North Dakota School of Law, provided insight into his father's background and motivations in conceptualizing and implementing the Lockney Lines that have helped everyone see football's gains and losses more clearly for the last sixty-six years.

Beyond those who provided input to this book were those who helped in its construction and design. Stewart Williams provided the cover design after rightfully rejecting my initial ideas. His quick and creative work is much appreciated. Mary Jewel (MJ) Brown created the diagrams that illustrate the various plays, formations, and field markings discussed throughout the book. Her excellent work and patience throughout this process were much appreciated.

Of course, I need to thank those who discussed my ideas and reviewed my writing at various development stages. Their feedback and encouragement were invaluable. Those lucky individuals included: Jim Mulcrone, Pat Brown, Phil Brown, Mary Jewel (MJ) Brown, and Carolyn Brown. I am thankful to each of you for your willingness to wade through reams of tiring text and otherwise spending many hours supporting me in this effort. Dave Pagnucco did not see fit to review any of this material but managed to provide friendly support along the way.

As with my first book, *Fields of Friendly Strife,* Erik Hane provided an editorial review that redirected my efforts, making the final product more coherent and, hopefully, enjoyable for the reader.

Thanks again to all of you!

PREFACE

Some folks watch football without thinking about the game's history and how football became football, how the sport evolved over the last 150 years. I am not one of those people, and neither are most who will read this book. Instead, this book is for people who are interested in the answers to the questions such as:

- Why are quarterbacks called quarterbacks, halfbacks called halfbacks, and fullbacks called fullbacks? Why do we call guards, guards?
- Why did American football eliminate the 55-yard line and add end zones in 1912? Where on the field did plays start before we added hash marks in 1933?
- Why do footballs have seams, while rugby balls, basketballs, and volleyballs do not?
- How did officials control the game before they had whistles, chains, and penalty flags?
- When did tackling dummies, blocking sleds, plastic helmets, and face masks arrive on the scene?
- Which schools had the first cheerleaders, marching bands, and mascots?

How Football Became Football answers those questions and more by examining how the game evolved and why it did so. Its focus is the pioneering players, coaches, schools, or fans who introduced particular elements to the game.

Readers will find that many elements of early football seem strange. Its rules and vocabulary are confusing, but it is that strangeness and confusion that illustrates how little early football has in common with the current.

To conduct this research, I reviewed a thousand books or college yearbooks and tens of thousands of newspaper articles. Other sources supplemented my need to identify how they played the game and what it looked like back in the day. Hopefully, this book succeeds in translating old-time football to readers who understand today's game. Despite my best intentions, however, I am sure this book credits some innovations to the wrong person. Other researchers can make corrections and additions, and that will make us all wiser.

Finally, as in the 1890s and early 1900s, football faces the need for dramatic reform today. Understanding football's history helps us recognize that football has adjusted to many pressures over the years. *How Football Became Football* is the story of how the game adjusted to those pressures in the past. It will not be easy, but I am confident football will make the needed changes again.

May 2020

INTRODUCTION

The first intercollegiate football game occurred on November 6, 1869, between Princeton and Rutgers. They played the game with a round ball, under rules resembling soccer, with twenty-five players per side. Over the next six years, East Coast colleges played similar matches under inconsistent rules with some games leaning toward soccer, others toward rugby, and with varying numbers of players per side. This inconsistency motivated representatives of several schools to gather at the Massasoit House in Springfield, Massachusetts, in 1876 to define a standard set of rules for future games.

The representatives at the meeting formed the Intercollegiate Football Association (IFA), and its members agreed to play a slightly-Americanized version of rugby. In organizing and outlining their rules, the IFA did not intend to create a new sport, but they tweaked the rules year after year, and the compounding effect was a game that increasingly diverged from its English parent. Similar rule changes came in the ensuing decades such that only three elements of the rules of 1876 remain in effect today, and the 12-page rule book from 1876 has morphed into an NCAA rule book 224 pages long.

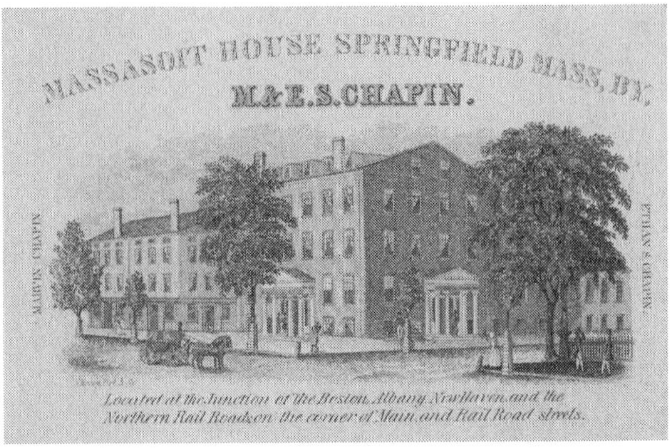

The Massasoit House in Springfield, Massachusetts hosted the first meeting of the IFA. (Trade card for Massasoit House, corner of Main and Rail Road Streets, Springfield, Mass., undated. Courtesy of Historic New England)

There have been several periods in football's history when changes in the game followed something akin to a plan, but those moments were few and far between. Far more often, football meandered, moving in one direction or another, based on the innovations of individual players, coaches, and officials. Similarly, inventors created new equipment, and commercial interests pushed the game in one money-making direction or another. Quite often, the game's rules did not set new directions; they only codified changes that had already occurred in the game.

Still, there have been consistent themes or paths along which the game has traveled. Some groups pushed football in one direction, other groups pushed for the opposite, with many of these arguments ending in compromise solutions. Decisions regarding a limited number of themes have shaped football's rules throughout its history.

Safety versus Toughness. Football is a rough game, and that is part of its attractiveness. The nineteenth-century advocates of Muscular Christianity admired the game for imbuing toughness in young men. Yet, the game became so brutal that numerous rule changes had to be made between 1894 and 1912 to bring the game back into line. Striking a balance between toughness and brutality has been at the center of many football rule changes and is the most important issue facing the game today.

Scientific Play versus Luck or Chance. Walter Camp pressed for rules that supported consistency, planning, and execution, and opposed those that favored luck. Camp's arguing for football's controlled scrimmage rather than rugby's scrummage is the classic example of his scientific thinking.

Team Play versus Specialists. The value of team play versus that of specialists underpins many conflicts in football. Changes in the point values awarded for touchdowns versus field goals and rules limiting or allowing substitutions reflect the different positions held on this issue.

Player versus Coach Control. The idea that players, not coaches, should control the game has mostly disappeared from football, but it was prominent for much of the game's history. The coach's job was to prepare the team in practice while leaving in-game decisions to the players. Prohibitions on coaching from the sideline are the reason quarterbacks called the plays for football's first one hundred years.

Kicking, Rushing, and Passing. The kicking, rushing, and passing games were promoted or discouraged over the years based on the preferences of the time. Before the forward pass, many football games were punting duels, and top punters received the acclaim now garnered by quarterbacks.

Of course, the history of football is more than a history of the game's rules. Understanding football requires us to step beyond the rules and examine the influence of its finances, fans, and the broader society in which football exists. Broader themes have influenced the direction and experience of football as well.

Amateurism versus Commercialism. Amateurism was a core belief among those who played football in its early days. Still, successful teams needed money for training, travel expenses, and the occasional inducement to encourage a top player to join their team. Money has been the root of many football evils, while also contributing much that is good about the game. It has been a fundamental force shaping football from the beginning.

Players versus Fans. As football grew in popularity, the game increasingly took the needs of fans and the media into account. Adding numbers to player jerseys was fiercely opposed by many coaches, yet the practice spread because it helped fans understand and enjoy the game. Schools and cities built stadiums that catered to the fans, and spectators' needs rather than those of the game's participants, drove many changes on and off the field.

Race and Ethnicity. Football and race have been strange bedfellows. The game was first played by white students at elite East Coast colleges. Carlisle Indian School played three or four Ivy League teams per year before WWI, yet the first game between an Ivy and a historically black college and university did not come until 1984. Quotas and segregationist policies kept African American players from substantial participation in mainstream football until the 1970s. Where would the game be today had those policies not changed?

These themes dominated football over the years, and the choices made about those issues have contributed to the game that exists today. Football has evolved due to external forces, the preferences of its leaders, and because little-known fellows in small towns came up with better ideas on a few occasions. The game could have evolved differently under other circumstances. Nothing about football's current state was inevitable or pre-ordained. Despite significant interplay between the two, one need only look to Canada to understand that American football could have taken different turns along the way.

Before exploring the game's history, it is worth making a few points about the editorial approach used in this book. *How Football Became Football* organizes the game's history into three eras and then uses a consistent set of topical chapters to focus the discussion of each era. The early era begins in 1869 and ends in 1905, with the substantial rule changes of 1906 separating the early and middle eras. The middle era, which lasted until 1959, is the period during which football became football as we know it. Football's modern era began in 1960 when ABC won the NCAA football contract and began revolutionizing football broadcasting. The early 1960s also saw the return of two-platoon football to college football, as well as the first nationally prominent teams that freely recruited and played black athletes in numbers. Multiple dimensions distinguish the modern era, but television and its money have been the primary drivers of change since 1960.

The book also focuses on college football rather than pro football because the game originated in the colleges, and much of football's innovation occurred there. For these reasons and simplicity's sake, the discussion focuses on college football. Both are discussed where the professional game was the source of innovation or differed from the college game in meaningful ways.

A final convention to note is that many colleges and universities experienced name changes over the years. Schools are generally referred to by their current, commonly accepted names, regardless of their formal names at the time of the historical events.

With that said, buckle your chin strap and follow along as we trace the history of the world's greatest game.

PART I

THE EMERGENCE OF THE GAME: 1869 TO 1905

1

THE EMERGENCE OF THE GAME (1869-1905)

Football, like life itself, began in an elementary form. The game lacked formal rules. There were conventional styles of play, but arguments and fights were common due to differences in the ground rules used from place to place. The football world needed order.

Among the early players of football-like games in the U.S. and Canada were university students. School teams were informal, student-run groups whose elected captains organized practices and taught the game to less-experienced teammates, many of whom arrived on campus without having seen a football game. During games, the captains dealt with the officials and determined who played when and where. Coaches did not yet exist, principally because no one knew more about the game than the active players. The modern concept of referees and other officials did not exist either. Instead, the referee was an associate of the players who had a working knowledge of the game and sufficient honor to apply the rules fairly. Last, the school teams did not fall under the school's official supervision beyond that which faculties exerted over students in general. All this would change during football's early era as the game became popular and substantially more institutionalized.

ORIGINS OF AMERICAN FOOTBALL

American and Canadian football descend from the kicking games of nineteenth-century England. The rules of the English kicking game varied from ground to ground, hence the term "ground rules," until 1863 when the London Football Association codified a set of rules that outlawed carrying the ball. That version of the game became known as the Association game, later shortened to soccer.

Others in England preferred a kicking game that allowed players to kick and carry the ball. Originating at The Rugby School, a prep school in Warwickshire, England, its adherents formed the Rugby Football Union in 1871, and their secession has separated rugby from soccer ever since.

Americans visiting England and vice versa brought the Association rules game across the water leading soccer to become the dominant kicking game played at East Coast colleges. Harvard was an exception; they played a folk game unique to Boston that was similar to rugby. The Princeton-Rutgers game of 1869, which is considered the first intercollegiate football game, was played under loose Association rules with twenty-five players per side. Other Association rules games followed in the next few years among a handful of East Coast schools.

Critical to the development of American football was a set of games played in 1874 between Harvard and McGill University of Montreal, where rugby was king. The teams alternately used the Boston and rugby rules in their games, and the Harvard boys enjoyed the rugby game enough that they began playing rugby back in Boston.

Harvard played McGill at Jarvis Field in North America's first intercollegiate game of rugby football. Cambridge, May 15, 1874. (Davis, Football, 1911)

As the number of games between colleges increased, differences in the rules used from one school to the next created to a desire for consistency. That led students from Columbia, Harvard, Princeton, and Yale to meet in 1876 to define rules, forming the Intercollegiate Football Association (IFA). A crucial decision at the 1876 meeting was whether to follow Association or rugby rules. Harvard and the rugby rules won the day, and that decision set the course for the combined rushing and kicking game that evolved into gridiron football.

The outcome of the 1876 meeting was a set of sixty-one rules that defined the game of football. Most rules were lifted word-for-word from the English Rugby Union rule book. Only a handful saw substantive change. Those included:

- The match winner was the team scoring the highest number of touchdowns rather than the highest number of kicked goals. (A kicked goal counted as four touchdowns.)
- The IFA standardized the field dimensions, whereas rugby set only maximum field dimensions.
- A referee and two umpires, each representing one of the teams, settled disputes rather than relying on the team captains to do so.
- Touching the ball down in the opponent's goal was called a touchdown rather than a try, but was otherwise unchanged.

The IFA rules (see Appendix I) are difficult to understand today, in part, due to the vocabulary of the time. Blocking was called "interference," out of bounds was "in touch," and kicking an opponent's shins was "hacking." Adding to the difficulty of understanding the rules is that many rules covered archaic elements dropped from football long ago. For example, Rule 30 reads:

> A punt on is a punt made in a manner similar to a punt-out, and from touch, if necessary, by a player who has made a fair catch from a punt-out or another punt-on.[1]

Few football fans today can make sense of Rule 30 or any number of similarly archaic rules. In addition to our struggle to understand the rules of 1876, the rules have been revised time and again so that only three of the sixty-one original rules are substantially unchanged today. Everything else about football has evolved since the game began.

Following the 1876 meeting was another in 1878 that was notable for the fact that Walter Camp was one of Yale's representatives. Camp became a dominant force in nearly every rule-making meeting of the IFA and its successors until his attendance at the 1925 meeting, during which he died. Camp consistently pushed for the "scientific" approach to the game that reduced the role of chance in favor of effective planning and team play. Among other achievements during his time, Camp was the architect of football switching from the scrummage to the scrimmage, the system of downs, and the creation of a point-based scoring system. For his many contributions, he is rightfully known as the father of American football. But saying Walter Camp is the father of American football is to understate his influence during the first fifty years of the game. Camp was the voice of college football to the nation when print was the only medium. He was widely published and syndicated. He was the football authority as a pioneering player, coach, and rule maker. He was Knute Rockne, Grantland Rice, Bud Wilkinson, Vince Lombardi, Paul Zimmerman, and Bill Belichick all rolled into one. His thinking and influence on football, for good and for bad, cannot be underestimated.

EASTERN DOMINATION

Walter Camp as Yale football captain, 1878-1879. (Edwards, Football Days. 1916)

The story of early football is the story of a game played at elite, East Coast colleges, particularly those that now comprise the Ivy League. (We use the "Ivy League" term to describe these schools, although the athletic conference did not form until 1954.) Yale, Princeton, Harvard, and Penn played particularly important roles in shaping early football, dominating opponents from other regions on the limited occasions they played. In games played against teams in states outside the Ivy League footprint through 1905, the Ivies went 54-5-1, including a 14-1-1 record against Chicago, Michigan, and Wisconsin, the top teams from the Midwest. They also held a 9-1 advantage over Virginia and North Carolina. Other games with opponents from outside the Ivy states came against Navy, Georgetown, and smaller schools that were not of the same caliber, but whoever they played, the Ivies dominated.

That domination was aided by playing almost all intersectional games at home. Yale did not play a game west of the Allegheny Mountains until 1931, and Harvard played its first game outside the East in the 1920 Rose Bowl. Its first regular-season game outside the region came during WWII. A similar pattern occurred on the West Coast in that the University of California did not play a regular-season game east of the Rockies until 1947. America, and football, were highly regionalized.

Some of the Eastern dominance off the field was pure provincialism. The All America teams, for instance, were comprised solely of Eastern players until a University of Chicago player achieved All America status in 1898. To believe the All America teams of the 1890s accurately represented the best players in the country is folly, but Easterners named the teams, and their newspapers dominated the national press.

The most critical element of Eastern dominance came through its monopoly over the game's rule-making bodies. The IFA was the primary rule-making body, and while it expanded its membership over the next two decades to variously include Columbia, Harvard, Pennsylvania, Princeton, Wesleyan, and Yale, it remained a wholly Eastern group. Initially run by players, the IFA added a Graduate Advisory Committee comprised of alumni and others that oversaw and funded college athletics. Ultimately, the graduates usurped the students' power as college football became too important to leave in the hands of the players.

In addition to creating the rules for the game itself, the IFA expanded its role to cover issues of player eligibility. While many of its core concepts remain in place today, disagreements over eligibility rules resulted in the IFA breaking up in 1893, which coincided with Midwestern and Southern schools becoming fed up with the Eastern rule makers ignoring their desire for input.

The IFA and East Coast schools established most of football's parameters, including positioning football as a sport played during the fall. Many Eastern schools greeted first-year students with hazing rituals that resembled folk football, and these rituals carried on with inter-class football matches. But football became a fall sport for other reasons as well. Crew and baseball already dominated the spring, students were not on campus in the summer, and Northeastern winters were too cold to play, so the autumn was the only option. Finally, football became institutionalized as a fall sport when the IFA established a championship game each Thanksgiving in New York. Those games proved hugely popular, and the schedule of fall games leading to the championship game became predominant.

THE THIRTY YEARS between 1876 and 1905 witnessed football's birth and its near demise. Radical change occurred in football during the early era. The shape of the ball was modified; the size and markings of the football field changed several times. Player outfits morphed from those worn in cricket matches to uniforms with school colors, striping, or symbols. The period also saw the addition of protective devices and pads to cushion the blows exchanged on the field.

Games played on campus greens and pastures watched by a handful of friends shifted to major-league baseball stadiums and football-only, on-campus stadiums seating tens of thousands. Newspaper reports of the games moved from brief notes on the society pages to front-page stories and detailed discussions warranting two to three pages in the emerging sports sections.

Football became a rallying point for students and alumni, expanded to the local public, and then on to state and national audiences. As the audience grew, so did the financial and emotional stakes tied to the game, which, in turn, led to wrestling over the game's governance within and across schools.

The following five chapters describe various elements of how the story unfolded. With that, our attention turns to the game and its evolution between 1876 and 1905.

2

THE BALL, THE FIELD, AND STADIUMS (1869-1905)

Every outdoor sport requires specific equipment and a configuration for the grounds upon which the game occurs. Many games have rigid rules while allowing for local variation. Baseball, for example, enforces the height of the pitching mound, the size of home plate, and the distance between the bases, but allows variation in the location of the outfield fences, their height, and the location of the grandstands in foul territory. Football has rigidly enforced selected rules, but allowed significant variation in other aspects of the field and stadiums.

THE BALL

The balls used in the early kicking games in England were inflated pig bladders; hence, football's pigskin nickname. In the old days, players tied one end of a pig bladder, inflated the bladder, and tied off the other end as well. Centuries later, cobblers made the balls more durable by inserting the pig bladder into a leather cover, inflating the bladder, and lacing the cover's open seam to seal the ball.

Early footballs varied in size, generally taking the shape of a plum. Richard Linton, a cobbler in Rugby, England, was the first to substitute a rubber bladder for the pig bladder in the mid-1850s. He also standardized the manufacturing process, which resulted in the balls he produced being nearly round. Linton's round ball proved popular among Association football players, but he continued producing an oval ball preferred by rugby players, which became the standard size and shape for rugby balls moving forward.

Although the IFA's original sixty-one rules provide specifications for the field and goal posts, the rules did not describe the ball, so teams used rugby balls of varying brands and sizes until the IFA formally adopted England's Lilywhite No. J in 1886.

The English Lilywhite ball remained the standard until the 1892 IFA meeting, which included a presentation by Julian H. Curtis of the A. G. Spalding Company. After Curtis outlined the benefits of their American-made ball, the IFA adopted the Spalding Model J as its official ball. Curtis left the meeting with contracts to supply balls to the attending schools and, since everyone playing football used the IFA rules, Spalding gained many future sales as well.

Richard Linton, a cobbler from Rugby, England, standardized the production of association and rugby footballs, thereby formalizing their size and shape. (Courtesy of Simon Hawkesley, Richard Lindon & Co., Rugby, Warwickshire, England)

Four years later, the gents at the 1896 IFA meeting established Rule 1c, which stated: "The football used shall be of heavy leather, enclosing an inflated bladder. The ball shall have the shape of a prolate spheroid."[2] The rule did not provide detailed specifications for the ball but introduced the term "prolate spheroid" to the vocabulary of generations of football players.

Despite the IFA not changing its rules in 1903, Spalding introduced the model J5, which had a 28-inch circumference along the major axis and a 23-inch circumference along its minor axis or midsection. The J5 was pointier and more aerodynamic than the model J and helped pave the way for the passing game that arrived in 1906. The J5 could be thrown more easily than its predecessors but was harder to handle than today's football. Today's ball is slimmer, easier to grip, and more aerodynamic, allowing for greater accuracy and distance in the passing game.

The Spalding Model J5 compared to an official NFL football from 2015. (AntiqueFootball.com)

THE FIELD

Early football was played on fields of varying sizes until the IFA defined the field dimensions in 1876 as being 140 yards long and 70 yards wide. The field was soon reduced from 140 to 130 yards in length and from 70 yards to 53 1/3 yards (160 feet) in width.

During football's first few years, the boundary lines were marked only by flags in the corners of the field, similar to pick-up football games that define the field boundaries using trees or lamp posts. The lack of boundary lines made it more difficult for players and the officials to ensure play remained in bounds, so they began marking the boundaries with chalked stripes.

A properly marked field had only five lines: the center or midfield line, two goal lines, and two touch lines (sidelines). Like today's Canadian field, the center line was the 55-yard line. The areas beyond the goal lines, what we call end zones today, were considered "in goal." The in goal areas were approximately ten yards deep but did not have an established depth or end lines. The lack of end lines seems odd today, but they were not necessary under the rules of the day. Before the forward pass became legal, offenses could score only by running the ball over the goal line or kicking the ball through the goal posts. The absence of end lines impacted play, however, because punts and kicks remained live after traveling beyond the goal line and onto running tracks, into the stands, or among people standing beyond the goal line, resulting in mad scrambles for the ball.

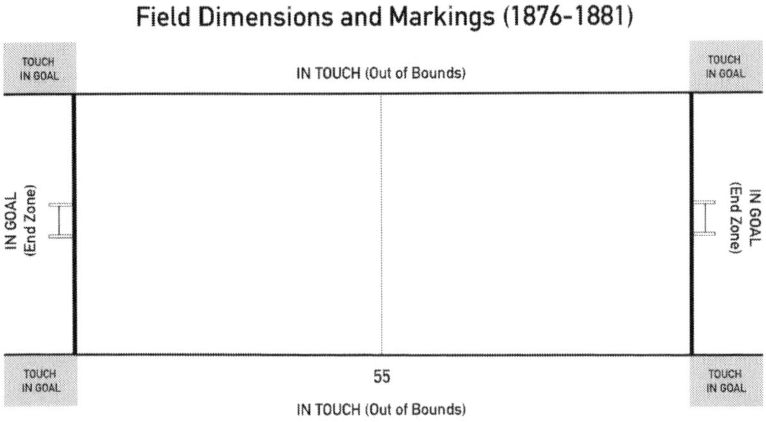

Diagram of pre-1882 football field illustrating the in goal (end zone), in touch (out of bounds), and touch in goal areas of the field.

Running the length of the field were "touch lines," now referred to as sidelines. The in touch areas were outside the touch lines and were analogous to today's "out of bounds" areas. Some fields had touch lines running ten yards beyond the goal lines to help identify the "touch in goal" areas, which sat in the four corners of the field behind the goal lines and outside the touch lines. The "touch in goal" areas no longer have a special status in football, but they served a purpose in the early game as described in later chapters. (Bits of the "in goal" terminology survive in Canada where the end zone is officially called the Goal Area, and the end zone sidelines are the Sidelines in Goal.)

Yard lines entered football with the introduction of the system of downs in 1882. Before 1882, the offensive team was not required by rule to give up possession of the ball, but an 1882 rule required teams to gain five yards in three downs or lose possession of the ball. During the discussion of this rule, Walter Camp proposed adding stripes every five yards to help the officials determine whether the offense had gained the necessary five yards. After Camp made his suggestion, a fellow committee member exclaimed, "The field will look like a gridiron," and the "gridiron" nickname has been tied to the game ever since.

Field Dimensions and Markings (1882-1902)

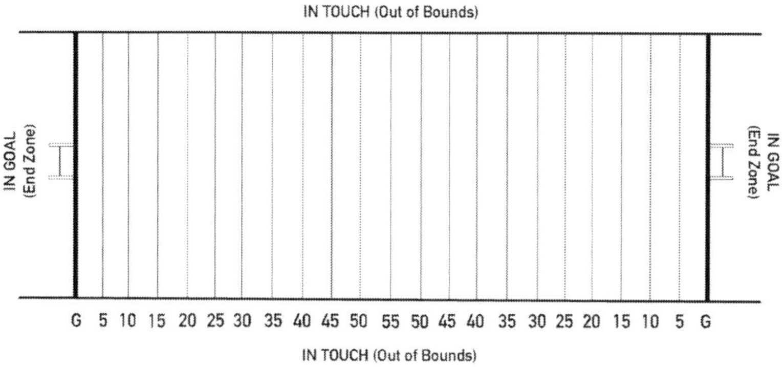

Introducing the system of downs resulted in the addition of yard lines spaced five yards apart.

After the addition of yard lines, the playing field remained unchanged for twenty-one years until the clamor for reform caused rule makers to attempt to open up the game. An 1885 rule had mandated that the offensive player receiving the snap from the center could not cross the line of scrimmage with the ball until another offensive player had possessed it, effectively eliminating the quarterback as a running threat.

A proposed rule change in the 1903 rule committee meeting would have allowed the player receiving the snap to run with the ball provided they crossed the line of scrimmage five yards to the right or left of the center. Schools playing a relatively open style game (e.g., Princeton) supported this rule, while those playing a power style (e.g., Yale) did not, so they compromised and applied the new rule only between the 25-yard lines. Stripes running perpendicular to the yard lines and five yards apart were added to the field markings between the 25-yard lines to assist the officials in monitoring this rule.

Field Dimensions and Markings (1903)

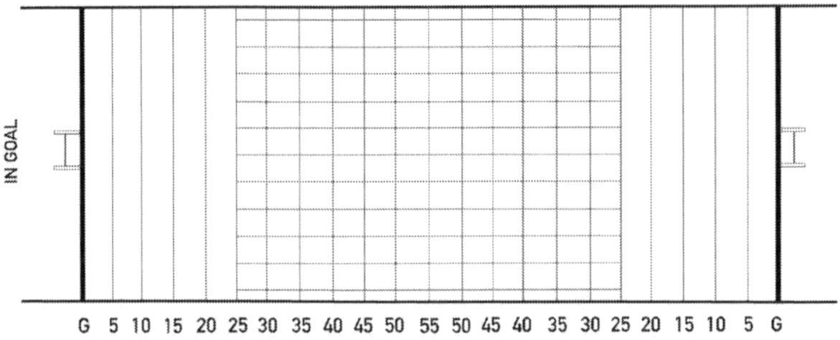

The 1903 season was the only one in which the field had transverse stripes only between the 25-yard lines.

The rule makers soon realized the compromise solution made little sense. The rules changed in 1904, so the five yards right or left of center requirement applied to the entire field, leading to the perpendicular lines extending the length of the field, making the field resemble a checkerboard.

Field Dimensions and Markings (1904-1909)

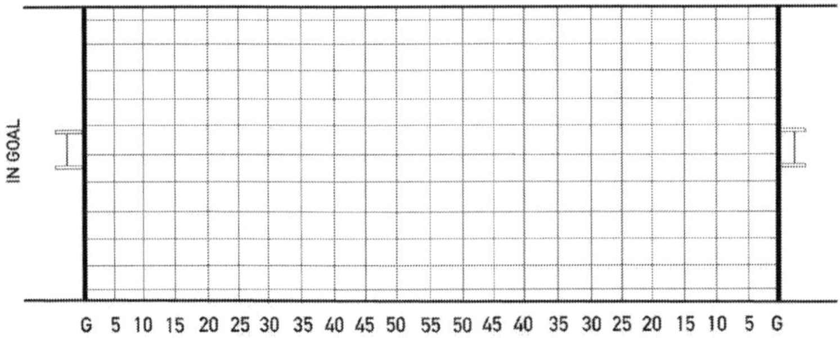

The football field had transverse stripes running the length of the field between 1904-1909.

To save chalk and application time, some fields of the checkerboard era did not have full perpendicular lines. Instead, they had short stripes intersecting the yard lines at five-yard intervals, akin to today's hash marks.

Princeton attempts to block a Cornell punt in 1907. Cornell's field is marked with long hash marks every five yards rather than the full checkerboard pattern. (Postcard, Unknown Publisher, Personal Collection)

Beyond field markings, the most prominent features of football fields were the goal posts, sited on each goal line. Early goal posts were rudimentary, with the uprights rising only a few inches above the crossbar. The need for the officials to accurately rule on field goal attempts led to several increases in the prescribed height of the uprights, which reached twenty feet by 1900.

Of course, having the goal posts located on the goal line was problematic when the ball was in play near the goal line. The posts could act as barriers to players on either side, affecting play on the field and causing injuries. To solve that problem, E. Manley, a Harvard graduate, invented the 'safety goal post' in 1900. Rather than position the goal posts on the goal line with the uprights shooting straight up, Manley moved the posts ten feet back from the goal line and used braces to position the crossbar and uprights above the goal line. The safety goal posts gained an audience but did not fully replace the traditional 'H' goal posts, though it proved to be a precursor of the modern "gooseneck" or "slingshot" goal post design that arrived in the 1960s.

A safety goal post on the field at Princeton in 1910. (Davis, Football, 1911)

STADIUMS

The first football stadiums were not stadiums at all, but open fields or college greens which spectators freely entered and exited. The desire to fund their uniforms, supplies and travel expenses soon led teams to fence off the grounds and charge admission. As interest in football and other sports grew, schools added wooden bleachers configurable for football, track, baseball, or other events to their athletic fields.

The crowd at the first Army-Navy game in 1890 stands several people deep around West Point's field. (Photograph NH 138, Archives Branch, Naval History and Heritage Command, Washington, DC)

The biggest stadiums used for college football games were cricket and polo grounds or, more frequently, major and minor league baseball stadiums, but bleachers and modest stadiums began appearing on campuses in the 1890s. Most campus stadiums were intimate structures until the 1920s. Few sat more than 5,000 fans, and almost all fans sat on simple wooden bleachers with the fanciest ones having a grandstand covering part of the home sideline.

A capacity crowd of 3,000 at Purdue's Stuart Field took in the 1904 game against in-state rival Wabash. (1905 Debris, Purdue yearbook)

Schools located in more remote locations and small stadiums often scheduled their most attractive games in cities with larger populations and stadiums. The biggest neutral site games of the era were the season-ending games between the top two IFA teams that occurred in or near New York City. Yale and Princeton played each other in this contest sixteen times between 1880 and 1899 when the two teams won or shared seventeen national championships. The game's crowd grew from 5,000 in 1880 to 43,000 in 1894 as the football frenzy took hold, and the capacity of the Polo Grounds or Manhattan Field increased.

Princeton driving on Yale at Manhattan Field on Thanksgiving Day 1893. Note the fans watching from Coogan's Bluff above the stadium. (Davis, Football, 1911)

Further west, the University of Chicago played the preponderance of their games at home, or at least, in Chicago. Visiting teams would have preferred hosting Chicago, but the visitor's share of the gate in Chicago exceeded the gate at home, leading the Maroons' opponents to bite the bullet and entrain to the Windy City.

Chicago also benefited from the availability of the Chicago Coliseum, which sat nearby on the south side of town. Chicago Coliseum was the largest indoor stadium in the world in the 1890s and could accommodate a regulation-size football field. Among the first football games played indoors was Chicago's Thanksgiving Day 1896 win over Michigan in the Coliseum. The Coliseum's many windows let natural light into the building, but a rainstorm during the game darkened the skies, requiring the use of the building's arc lights and making the game one of the first played under artificial lighting.

The second Chicago Coliseum hosted the Democratic National Convention shortly after opening in 1896. (WikiMedia)

The Coliseum hosted a Chicago-Michigan rematch the next year, as well as games featuring the Carlisle Indians against Wisconsin in 1896 and Indiana in 1897.

In addition to being substantially smaller than today's major college stadiums, early football stadiums were utilitarian. Constructed of wood, the bleachers of the early era required ongoing maintenance of the untreated and often unpainted wood. The cost of doing so was high enough to warrant separate line items in team budgets, and they were sufficiently fire-prone that Harvard and Yale had firemen patrolling the stands during home games.

Beyond those issues, wooden stands were subject to collapse, particularly the temporary stands installed for big games. Collapses occurred at numerous stadiums, but Wisconsin likely had more experience with bleacher collapses any other. The Badgers played Michigan at Chicago's Marshall Field in 1902, and to maximize the seating capacity, Wisconsin brought stands borrowed from a circus. They slapped the stands together on Friday night, the city inspected them in the morning, before the bleachers collapsed early in the game, with 500 people spilling to the ground. Three years later, the Badgers met Michigan on Ferry Field in Ann Arbor when a section of temporary bleachers holding 2,000 fans gave in. Finally, three sections of bleachers collapsed during the 1915 Wisconsin-Minnesota game at Camp Randall. Although few schools witnessed as many collapsing bleachers as Wisconsin, the fact that collapses occurred at three different Big Ten stadiums in thirteen years tells us they were not isolated incidents.

With the increased size of crowds attending big games, larger, safer, and more permanent stadiums came under consideration, but not much happened until a new method of construction emerged: reinforced concrete. Reinforced concrete allowed a new age of stadium building to dawn early in the twentieth century when several massive stadiums rose on the East Coast. First among them was Harvard Stadium.

Harvard Stadium is arguably the most important stadium in football history. (The Astrodome is its only competitor for the honor.) Built as a memorial to Harvard's Civil War dead, it opened in 1903 with 30,000 seats. Adding wooden bleachers at the open end of the U-shaped structure for big games increased the capacity to 42,000. It was massive for its day, more than doubling the capacity of the largest major league ballpark and dwarfing all college stadiums other than Penn's Franklin Field and Yale Field, both constructed of wood.

Harvard Stadium pioneered the use of reinforced concrete in the construction of large buildings. (Pictorial News Co., Library of Congress)

Architecturally, Harvard Stadium spoke of a connection to the ancient Greeks and Romans, but its lasting impact came from its physical permanence. Two years after it opened, the rules committee struggled during the crisis of 1905 and 1906 to find ways to make football safer. One option advanced by Walter Camp was to widen the playing field by forty yards to provide more space for breakaway runs. While schools could relocate wooden bleachers to accommodate a wider field, the concrete stands at Harvard Stadium were immovable and only 230 feet apart, making it impossible to widen the 160-foot wide field by 120 feet as Camp proposed. Since the field at Harvard could not be substantially widened, and the Crimson were not about to abandon their newly-built cathedral, Camp's proposal to widen the field became a non-starter.

The University of Pennsylvania increased Franklin Field's capacity by replacing its wooden stands with concrete stands between 1903 and 1905, reaching a capacity of 20,000 seats. Franklin Field expanded again as part of the post-WWI stadium boom with the addition of an upper deck. Also in the East, Syracuse announced in 1905 their plans for a 26,000 seat concrete stadium. Unlike Harvard Stadium, Archbold Stadium included a running track, baseball field, and Gothic-styled grandstand covering part of the stadium.

Syracuse's Archbold Stadium opened in 1907 with a capacity of 26,000. The field is marked in the full checkerboard pattern used from 1904-1909. (Postcard, Unknown Publisher, Personal Collection)

Despite these schools building massive stadiums using the latest technology, these new stadiums remained creatures of the previous century in that they lacked restrooms and permanent concession stands. Food was available from street vendors outside the stadium, but little was available inside the stadium. Stadiums were built to seat large numbers of people safely; comfort was secondary. As the first stadium constructed of concrete, Harvard Stadium opened with spectators sitting directly on the concrete slabs. Only after forcing fans to sit through a few cold November games did Harvard add wood planks atop the concrete.

Despite being spartan by today's measure, these stadiums were the first permanent stands on college grounds and foreshadowed the end of wooden construction for major stadiums. More important, they signaled that football was here to stay in one form or another and that football would find a solution for its ills.

ALTHOUGH THE FIELD markings of the 1880s differ from today, individuals from either period would immediately recognize one another's grounds as football fields. The stadiums surrounding the fields are another matter. Fans of the 1880s would feel comfortable in the confines of today's small-town high school football field, but the modern major college or professional stadium would be unrecognizable, particularly for games played at night.

Changes in the field dimensions were to come, and the introduction of hash marks in the 1930s would alter the game, but the football field has remained relatively stable in its dimensions. That might not be the case were it not for Harvard Stadium, and it is fun to speculate on how the game might have evolved had the field been widened. Football played on a wide field might have drifted back to its rugby origins by using the extra space for the laterals and sweeps of the horizontal game. Instead, without the wider field, football turned to the forward pass, which eventually evolved to the vertically-oriented passing offenses we know today.

The discussion now turns to the development of football's play and techniques as it moved away from rugby. While football remained rugby-like in many aspects, key elements of rugby were tossed aside as core elements of the separate game of football were conceived and implemented. By the end of the early era, football would be quite different from rugby, while remaining a distant cousin to the game played today.

3

PLAY AND TECHNIQUES (1869-1905)

The previous chapter described the ball, field, and stadiums of the early era and was a building block for understanding nineteenth-century football. However, little of that discussion described the on-the-field action; that is, how players battled on Saturday afternoons. Early era football was quite different from today's game. Many core concepts of modern football - the system of downs, blocking, the limited use of hands by offensive players, play design, signal calling, the game's scoring system, and more, came into being during the early era.

Football in the early 1880s was an open, free-flowing game that emphasized kicking the ball as much as rushing it, but it began transitioning in the late 1880s to a brutish game with masses of men running full speed into their opponents. Its danger came not from CTE suffered decades down the road, but from players dying on the field of crushed skulls, ruptured spleens, and injuries to other body parts. Saving the game required a public crisis and a Presidential intervention, but before discussing the crisis, let's review the game at its beginning and its evolution over the following four decades.

FOOTBALL BASICS

The IFA followed rugby in specifying there should be fifteen players per team, leading some to call football the "game of fifteens" during the 1870s. Yale and Walter Camp thought the playing field too crowded with fifteen players and advocated playing with eleven per side. Their view became the rule in 1880. (Camp's call to widen the field in 1905 also reflected his desire for more space.)

As in rugby, play began with the two teams forming a scrummage or scrum with the ball put in play by tossing it between the two teams. Both teams attempted to kick the ball back to a teammate who picked up the ball, ran with it, passed it back, or kicked it toward the opponent's goal.

Walter Camp and others considered the scrummage bad form because it gave both teams equal opportunity to gain possession of the ball, which was akin to a game of chance. Pushing for the scientific approach to the game, Camp succeeded in getting the scrimmage rule passed in 1880, which is among the building blocks of the sport. Starting play from a controlled scrimmage with one team maintaining possession of the ball allowed the development of structured play different from the free-flowing nature of soccer and rugby. In conjunction with the scrimmage was the "rule of possession," which teams to keep the ball for an unlimited number of downs, most teams punted if they did not move the ball after several plays.

Football in 1880 did not yet distinguish touchbacks from safeties. This meant that players on the team possessing the ball could carry it behind the goal line, take a touchback (originally called a safety touchdown), and then kick the ball to the opponent from their 25-yard line. (Today's rules distinguish touchbacks and safeties based on which team caused the ball to cross the goal line before being downed.)

The combination of unlimited downs and safety touchdowns led to several "block games" between Yale and Princeton, the latter of which had more than its share of less-honorable fellows. As it happened, after winning the IFA championship in 1879, Princeton needed only to tie Yale in their year-end game to retain the 1880 championship. (Teams kept the pennant if their opponents failed to take it from them.) Most of the game was played in open style, but Yale dominated, forcing Princeton to take multiple safety touchdowns. Late in the game and with the score tied, Princeton made no effort to advance the ball. Instead, they stalled and took additional safety touchdown, blocking Yale from earning the championship. It was poor sportsmanship on Princeton's part, but it was legal.

To close this loophole, Yale argued for an 1881 rule change that awarded one point to the opponent whenever a team took a safety touchdown. Unable to gain approval for this change, Yale settled for a rule that awarded a tie game to Team A if Team B took four or more safeties than Team A. Unfortunately for Yale, Princeton used another loophole when they met again in 1881. Rather than touch the ball down behind the goal line, Princeton touched the ball down in the "touch in goal" area, which, under the rules, did not count as a safety. This tactic allowed Princeton to stall and finish the game in another tie. Notably, Princeton left the field believing it had retained the championship banner, but their comeuppance came days later when the IFA voted Yale the champions for the 1881 season.

Beyond stripping Princeton of the championship, the IFA recognized the need for further rule changes. Walter Camp advocated for teams having three downs to either advance the ball five yards (or lose ten yards). That rule passed for the 1882 season. (Awarding a first down for losing ten yards followed scientific thinking because the loss of ten yards likely occurred due to a fluke.) The rule was later changed to award a first down when a team lost twenty yards and was eliminated in 1904 after teams stalled by deliberately losing twenty yards to gain a first down.

An early snapperback preparing to roll the ball back to his quarterback. All the players are in two-point stances.(Yale Athletics Photographs (RU 691). Manuscripts and Archives, Yale University)

Changing from the scrummage to the scrimmage did not immediately shift play to its modern form. Just as rugby players in a scrum kicked the ball back to a teammate, the controlled snap also relied on players rolling the ball backward *with their feet.* Since football did not yet have a neutral zone, defensive players sometimes kicked or swatted the ball as the snapperback prepared to roll it back. To counter such interference, snapperbacks began steadying the ball with their hands before snapping it with their feet. Over time, centers started using only their hands to snap the ball, a technique that became legal in 1892.

As in the scrummage, any football player on the line of scrimmage might snap the ball, and any of the backs might pick up the ball, but teams quickly formalized the position of each player, and the traditional T formation emerged. The traditional T had seven linemen with little or no spacing between them, and four backs. The designated snapper, "snapper-back," or "snap-back," later known as the center, aligned in the middle of the seven linemen. His teammates on either side protected him from the slaps of the defenders, so they became known as guards. The players outside the guards often made many tackles while on defense, so they became known as tackles. And, of course, those at the outermost positions on the offensive line were called ends.

Backfields often had one player aligned further back than the rest, and the role became known as the goal-tend or "full back." Other players set half as deep as the fullback were halfbacks. Finally, the player who received the snap from center and aligned partway between the halfbacks and the center became known as the quarterback. (The fifteen player per side teams had another back positioned between the halfbacks and fullbacks. He, of course, was the three-quarterback or the third-in-hand. We don't hear much about that position these days.)

Snapping by rolling the ball on its side to the quarterback. (Edwards, Football Days, 1916)

Another early rule prohibited the center from picking up the ball, even when snapping with his hands. Unable to toss the ball to the quarterback as they do in today's shotgun snap, the centers rolled the ball on its long side or tumbled it end over end. The switch to snapping the ball by lifting it off the ground and tossing it back came while John Heisman coached Buchtel College (now the University of Akron) in 1893. Heisman had a tall quarterback, and rather than have his quarterback bend over to pick up the rolling ball, Heisman instructed his center to toss the ball to the quarterback instead. Though technically illegal, no one stopped the center from picking up the ball during the snap, and the technique quickly became common.

Early line play was quite different from what we know today. Amos Alonzo Stagg, who played for Yale from 1885 to 1889, described play during the period, saying:

> In the early eighties, the lineman on offense stood erect with spread feet, extended arms and closed hands, while the defense stood opposite and sparred with their opponents in an effort to break down their barriers and get at the runner.[2]

As time passed, lineman began squatting at the line of scrimmage, much like the two-point stance used by offensive linemen today. The game transitioned to using three- and four-point stances after Pop Warner's Carlisle team pioneered the crouching stance in their 1899 victory over Columbia. Warner reasoned that if track sprinters started more quickly by using the three-point stance, then running backs would reap similar benefits. Soon after that, backs and linemen across the country used the crouching stance with most using a four-point rather than a three-point stance.

QUARTER-BACK TAKING THE BALL.

The rushers or linemen shielded the defense using techniques similar to basketball screens. (Johnson, The American Game of Foot-Ball, 1887)

Early football did not allow blocking because it violated rugby's onside rule. As Walter Camp noted:

> As soon as the snap-back [the center] has sent the ball behind him, he has really placed all the men in his side of the line off-side, that is, between the ball and the opponent's goal, and they, therefore, can theoretically only occupy the positions in which they stand, while the opponents have the legal right to run past them

> as quickly as possible. For this reason, and bearing in mind that the men "on-side" have the best claim to right of way, it has been enacted that the side having possession of the ball may not use their hands or arms, but only their bodies when thus off-side, to obstruct or interrupt the adversaries.[3]

Thus, offensive players gained the ability to interfere or block, but could not use their "hands or arms in any way to obstruct or hold a player who has not the ball."[5] Only the runner could stiff arm or otherwise use his hands and arms to ward off would-be tacklers.

Yale players practicing offensive line blocking and defensive rushing from standup positions. (Walter Chauncey Camp Papers (MS 125). Manuscripts and Archives, Yale University)

In addition to shielding defensive players at the line of scrimmage, some offensive players began running alongside or slightly behind the ball carrier to keep opponents from tackling him. Known as "interference," "guarding," or "warding," these schemes bordered on being illegal, but were accepted as part of the game. Soon teammates were running in front of the ball carrier, which made them offside, and initiating contact with defenders. Both actions were departures from rugby, but they also became accepted aspects of the game. The acceptance of blocking in the early 1880s had a profound impact on football in that it sent football further down the collision sports path. Rugby never accepted blocking, and its players never felt the need to pad themselves or wear helmets.

Football's acceptance of blocking opened the door to a series of increasingly dangerous schemes and techniques, beginning with Princeton introducing the "V" formation in 1884. Throughout football's history, coaches and teams have exploited situations in which specific acts were not explicitly outlawed. So it was that Princeton took advantage of a loophole in football's kickoff rules. At the time, the receiving team had to stand at least ten yards away from the kicker, but the kicking team was not yet required to kick the ball a specific distance before recovering it. This meant kickers dribbled the ball a few inches before picking it up and running with it. (As in soccer, the team starting play maintained control of the ball rather than kicking it deep.) Princeton extended this approach by lining up in a V formation behind the kicker. The kicker then dribbled the ball a few inches, picked it up, and handed the ball to a teammate positioned inside the V as it rushed downfield en masse.

Phil King tees the ball as his Princeton teammates align in the "V" formation in the early 1890s. (Davis, Football, 1911)

Harvard then adapted Princeton's V by introducing the flying wedge on kick returns. The key feature of the wedge was that players interlocked arms or put an arm around the back of the man preceding them in the wedge. This formation proved successful since it could be stopped only by opposing players throwing their bodies into or over the wedge.

Harvard's flying wedge formation preparing to attack Yale in a game in Springfield in 1892. (Davis, Football, 1911)

In addition, the transition from the scrummage to the scrimmage allowed the development of structured offensive plays, but that change did not occur overnight. Initially, the scrimmage was merely a controlled method of initiating action in a rugby-style game. Over several years, however, offenses recognized that coordinating each players' activities on plays from scrimmage could be more effective than simply winging it. For example, when punting on early downs, it was helpful for members of the punting team to know their team was punting so they could get downfield to cover the punt. Likewise, offensive linemen were better able to block on running plays when they knew the ball was going to the right or the left.

This realization led teams to develop structured plays called at the line of scrimmage via a system of coded "signals." Some team captains or quarterbacks used hand signals, such as placing his right hand on their hip or pulling up a sock to designate plays, but most used voice commands consisting of short phrases or sentences. "Play up sharp, Charlie," "Play up, Charlie," or "Charlie" might each indicate the next play was a punt, while other word combinations designated particular running plays.

Football folklore tells us that numerical signals supplemented the word phrases thanks to Chester County Military Academy, now Widener University. The legend tells us that new cadets arriving on campus were assigned a number, and were addressed by that number, rather than their name, during their time at school. At some point, confusion over the quarterback calling signals using the standard code words led them to use cadet numbers to call the plays: the first number identified the ball carrier, the second indicated the lineman who was the aiming point for the run. Though it is a nice, logical tale, the story also tells us the new signal system debuted in a surprise win over Princeton in 1888. However, Princeton's only loss that year was to Yale. We know Chester Military played Penn's freshmen team in 1888 and may have pulled off the trick against them. They might even have played and beaten Princeton's freshmen team, but they did not do so against the Princeton or Penn varsity eleven that year.

Whatever their origin, number, letter, and color codes became widespread, allowing quarterbacks to survey defenses and detect weaknesses before calling the signals. Of course, defensive players tried to decode the offense's signals, so the signals came to be encrypted with dummy and activation codes instructing the team to ignore or pay attention to subsequent codes. While the specific codes have changed over time, the fundamentals of signal calling remain the same today.

Calling signals at the line of scrimmage was consistent with the pace of play at that time. Offenses lined up in the same formation play after play and spent little time between plays. One play ended, they lined up for the next, called the signals, and snapped the ball. The rapidity in which teams ran plays did not result from rules requiring teams to do so. Instead, teams ran plays quickly because they had always done so when playing rugby.

A few teams huddled on occasion during the early era. Huddling is believed to have started in practices due to teammates on defense understanding the signals called by their teammates on offense. Paul Hubbard, the quarterback at Gallaudet from 1892 to 1895, is credited with calling the first huddle in a game. Gallaudet, a university for the hearing impaired, used American Sign Language (ASL) to call signals because they played most of their games against teams whose players were not hearing impaired. Gallaudet played another hearing-impaired team in 1894, and that opponent understood Gallaudet's ASL signals, so Hubbard called his team into a huddle before each play. A few other teams huddled from time to time, but it was not until the 1920s that teams huddled consistently.

RUNNING AND TACKLING

Football remained open and rugby-like through most of the 1880s, but began shifting to a power, inside running game as the 1880s progressed, primarily driven by changes in the tackling rules. The rule makers of 1884 clarified that tacklers could grasp the runner only between the waist and shoulders, but changed their minds in 1888 by legalizing tackling between the knees and shoulders. Since it was easier to tackle runners under the new rules, long gains from open-field running became less frequent. Moreover, tackling below the knees was seldom penalized, became an accepted part of the game, and was legalized in 1903.

7-3-1 Defense

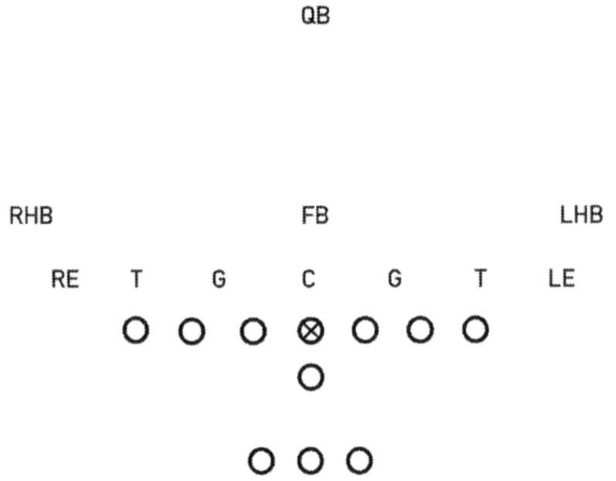

The 7-3-1 defense was typical of the early era with ten of eleven defenders close to the line of scrimmage. (Adapted from Yost, Football for Player and Spectator, *1905)*

Defenses adapted during the period by positioning their ends and halfbacks outside the offensive ends to limit sweeps, placed the quarterback or fullback twenty yards deep, and set the remaining six players between the ends.

A safety positioned 20+ yards deep protects against breakaway runs and punts during the 1908 Franklin-Hanover game. (Postcard, Unknown Publisher, Personal Collection)

With several defenders guarding against sweeps, runs to the outside met with limited success, so offensive play design shifted to penetrating the defensive interior front wall. Since football's rules did not yet require a specific number of offensive players to be on the line of scrimmage, teams aligned guards, tackles, or ends behind the line of scrimmage. Having those players in the backfield allowed offenses to more easily send men in motion before the snap and have them converge in one spot to lead the ball carrier through the hole. In addition to the mass of players that preceded the runner through the hole, one or more teammates followed the runner to push him forward. Some runners had handles stitched onto their pants so teammates could grab the handles and pull them forward. The combination of tactics resulted in players piling atop one another, finding little daylight, and gaining only one or two yards per play.

Mass Play from Ends Back Formation

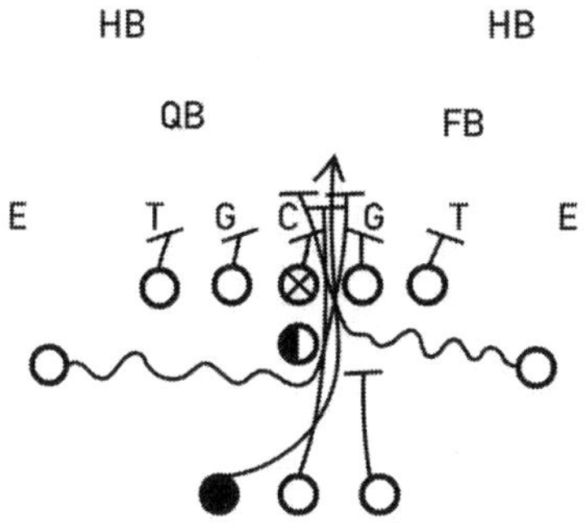

Both ends are in motion at the snap and lead the left halfback through the gap. Others push the ball carrier from behind. (Adapted from Stagg and Williams, 1893)

Pop Warner, who played his final season at Cornell in 1894, later described Penn's momentum plays during the period:

> The team lined up in a regular formation and on a signal the whole back field and the three lineman on the opposite side of the center from which the play was directed started on a run behind their own line and then the ball was passed to a running back in motion behind the mass of flying interferers who led him around the defensive end or tackle. It was a very effective method of advancing the ball.[4]

An 1894 rule restricted momentum plays by limiting the number of players in motion at the snap to three and allowing no more than three players to mass more than five yards behind the line of scrimmage. Through modern eyes, it is inconceivable that a rule intended to make the game safer still allowed three players to be in motion at the snap, but such was the mindset of the time.

Lafayette scrimmages during an 1890s practice. The offense (on the right) has six players behind the line of scrimmage. (Special Collections & College Archives, Skillman Library, Lafayette College)

Yale developed a variant of the guards back formation when it implemented the tackle back formation in 1900. The "tackle back" shifted a tackle from one side of the offense to the other, positioning him behind the offensive line. While the "tackle back" resembled other mass formations, Yale sometimes left a defender unblocked, who was then sideswiped by the tackle positioned behind the line of scrimmage. This tricky tactic became known as "mouse trap" blocking, later shortened to trap blocking, a more strategic alternative to brute force blocking.

Besides being responsible for numerous injuries, the tight formations and mass plays led to an unexciting game for spectators, much like modern teams running their goal line offenses and defenses the entire game. The traditionalists and open-game proponents could not agree on how to resolve this issue, so they compromised in 1903 by requiring seven men on the line of scrimmage between the 25-yard lines while only five men had to be on the line of scrimmage inside the 25-yard lines. (This coincided with the partial checkerboard field introduced the same year.)

Despite tweaking the rules, teams struggled to move the ball on first and second down, so they punted on third down. This pattern occurred over and over in games involving evenly matched teams. Successful punting and occasional breakthrough plays determined the outcome of many games. It was a brutal brand of football made worse by the number of injuries and deaths.

Early football also differed substantially from today in the way it handled the ball going out of bounds as well as in spotting the ball for runners tackled near the sideline. Balls fumbled "in touch" or out of bounds remained live, leading offensive and defensive players to scramble over benches, water jugs, band members, cinder tracks, and all manner of obstacles to grab the ball. An example of such a play occurred when Chicago traveled to Stanford in 1894, the first game between teams east and west of the Rockies. When the ball went "in touch" during a game in San Francisco, Chicago's Ad Ewing, a hurdler on the track team, used his hurdling skills to leap a picket fence surrounding the Haight Street Grounds and recover the ball while Stanford's men scaled the fence the old-fashioned way. Such out-of-bounds scrambles continued until a 1926 rule awarded possession to the player last touching the ball before it went out of bounds.

When a player ran out of bounds or gained possession of the ball out of bounds, the player capturing the ball had five options for bringing the ball back into play. The first option called a "fair" involved throwing the ball onto the field at a right angle from the sideline and between the two teams lined up across from one another. (The fair or "line out" remains part of rugby today.) The second method was to throw the ball back to a teammate who then ran or punted the ball. Third, the player putting the ball in play could enter the field of play himself and run or lateral the ball. The rule makers eliminated these three options in 1894.

A player puts the ball in play by throwing it back to another player on his side. (Johnson, The American Game of Foot-Ball, 1887)

The fourth option, an uncontested punt from out of bounds was eliminated in 1904, leaving only the fifth option. The fifth option allowed the player to walk onto the field and place the ball down five to fifteen yards from the sideline (after first announcing how far from the sideline he planned to walk the ball). The offensive team then ran a play from scrimmage. Of course, since the ball could only be walked five to fifteen yards from the sideline, many plays started close to the sideline until the introduction of hash marks in 1933.

Besides the five, now-obsolete options for bringing the ball back in bounds, different rules also applied on plays ending near the sideline. Back then, the next play started wherever the previous play ended, even when the ball was downed one foot from the sideline. On plays beginning close to the sideline, teams ran unbalanced formations with the offensive line and backs shifted to the side of the center away from the sideline. Although such plays seem odd to us today, they were wholly unremarkable at the time. Sideline plays were a normal part of the game; practicing these plays was part of normal practice routines.

A play from scrimmage near the sideline at Yale Field, c.1904-1909. (Postcard, E.P.J. Co., Personal Collection)

A final difference in running and tackling during the early era was that the concept of forward progress did not yet exist. Football plays ended only when the player possessing the ball was on the ground and yelled, "Down." A ball carrier who was stopped, but remained standing, could be pushed back and have the ball marked where he hit the ground and yelled, "Down." The same logic required runners to place the ball on the ground in goal to score a touchdown. This rule encouraged defenders to hold runners upright when in goal, push them back across the goal line, all while the ball carrier's teammates pushed or pulled the other way. These melees, called "maul-ins," resulted in frequent injuries and were eliminated in 1889, after which a touchdown required only that the runner possess the ball in goal.

Although the 1889 rule applied the concept of forward progress when scoring a touchdown, forward progress did not apply elsewhere on the field, so pushing runners backward remained widespread. The most famous example of such a play occurred in the season-ending game between Michigan and Chicago in 1905. Then bitter rivals, Michigan entered the game riding a 56-game win streak, having outscored opponents 495-0 in their first twelve games. Chicago had outscored its opponents by a mere 269-5 in its nine games to that point.

In the fourth quarter of the battle for the Western Conference championship with the score tied 0-0, Chicago's Walter Eckersall punted from the 55-yard line, sending the ball across the goal line. Michigan's return man, Denny Clark, caught the ball "in goal," raced left and, after breaking a tackle, crossed the goal line and entered the field of play. Clark was hit at the two-yard line by a Chicago player, whose hit lifted Clark into the air and sent the pair crashing to the ground behind the goal line. The play resulted in a safety and the only score of the game, giving Chicago a 2-0 win and the national championship.

While ball carriers were pushed back and tackled behind their point of forward progress in virtually every football game of the early era, the Denny Clark instance was among the last. One of the football reforms of 1906 was the decision to apply the forward progress rule to the entire field.

Chicago's Walter Eckersall, who later became a noted sportswriter and football referee. (Postcard, B.F. Newman & Co., Personal Collection)

SCORING

Football began with an equivalency-based scoring system in which a kicked goal was worth four touchdowns, and the team scoring the most touchdowns won the game. This system proved confusing and was eliminated in 1883 after Walter Camp suggested assigning point values to each scoring method.

	Touchdown	Goal from Field	Goal After Touchdown	Safety	Defensive Score on Try	One-Point Safety
1883	2	5	4	1		
1884	2	5	4	2		
1887	4	4	2	2		
1898	5	5	1	2		
1904	5	4	1	2		
1909	5	3	1	2		
1912	6	3	1	2		
1958	6	3	1 or 2	2		1
1988	6	3	1 or 2	2	2	1

Football's scoring system from 1883 to the present.

Kicking was the most valued part of the game in the new system. A goal from field (field goal) was worth five points, while a touchdown was worth only half as many points as the kick that followed it. (Touchdowns were worth two points, and the kicks that followed were worth four points.) Some called for increasing the value of touchdowns, arguing that the skills of individual kickers were over-rewarded compared to eleven players moving the ball downfield to score a touchdown. The latter opinion gained sway over time, and the value of goals from field and goals after touchdowns have decreased while the value of touchdowns has increased.

The push to reward consistent team play led some to argue for awarding style points. Specifically, they argued that teams should earn points for moving the ball inside the opponent's 25-yard line or for recording five consecutive first downs. Various proposals for awarding style points were proposed in future years as well, but they never moved forward. The standard of awarding points solely for penetrating the goal line on the ground or kicking it through the uprights remained in place.

KICKING

As a descendant of rugby, kicking was more central to football during the early era than it is today. Punting duels were common with teams booting the ball back and forth to gain a field position advantage. The kicking game also included several elements that have since disappeared and others that changed form.

Among the elements of the kicking game that changed form is the kickoff. Kickoffs initially occurred from the center of the field, which, on the 110-yard field, was the 55-yard or center line. As in rugby, the team just scored on kicked to the scoring team. Under the rules in place before 1894, the kicking team could dribble kick a few feet, recover the ball, and run forward with it, but an 1894 rule required kickoffs to travel at least ten yards before the kicking team could recover the ball. Kicking teams began booting the ball as far downfield as possible, so receiving teams aligned their men further downfield. That was the case when Pop Warner, Georgia's coach, scouted the John Heisman-led Auburn team before their 1896 Thanksgiving Day rivalry game. Warner noted Auburn's center positioned himself ten yards from the kicker, but all other Auburn players stood further back. To take advantage of Auburn's alignment, Warner's kicker practiced booting the ball short and toward the sideline as his teammates ran downfield to recover the kick. Warner employed this tactic to start the second half of the Auburn game, and the onside kick from placement was born.

Despite Georgia's success on the first onside kick, most kicking teams booted the ball far downfield, giving the ball right back to the team that had just scored. This was seen as appropriate because it gave the kicking team a field position advantage, but it did not work well in games between unevenly-matched teams since the lesser team spent much of the game on defense.

Acknowledging this problem in 1898, the Western Conference (Big Ten) gave the team that had been scored on the option to kick or receive the ball. The national rules committee approved the same rule in 1903. Even after teams received this choice, it was not uncommon for teams that had been scored on to choose to kick the ball in the hope the opponent would turn over the ball deep in their territory or, after running a few plays, shank their punt.

Kickers in the early era had to make do without artificial tees. Most kickers had a teammate hold the ball much as is done on a field goal attempt today. Others built tees by scooping dirt into a mound and placing the ball on the mound. The fact that there was enough loose dirt available on fields to create these tees gives us some indication of field conditions back then. Few fields had watering systems, they sustained beatings on rainy days, and many showed significant wear in spots. Even the fields in the best stadiums paled in comparison to those of today.

Harvard kicks out to Penn following a touchback in 1894. Note the Harvard player lying on the ground, holding the ball for the kicker. (Davis, Football, 1911)

Punting also evolved during the early era. Initially, players could punt at any point in a play and from anywhere on the field. That changed with the addition of downs and the line of scrimmage in 1880. Once offenses had three downs to make five yards, they commonly punted on third down just as they do today on fourth down. Teams also punted on first or second down, particularly when inside their own 20-yard line, and continued doing so until the 1920s when offenses developed that allowed teams to move the ball consistently.

Teams generally punted from the T formation. The center snapped the ball to the quarterback, who tossed it to the fullback, who then punted the ball. It was not until the late 1890s that teams began snapping the ball directly to the fullback in punting situations.

Rugby's onside rule significantly impacted the punting game. Rugby rules allowed the punter's teammates to recover the punted ball, provided were "onside" or behind him when he punted the ball. Those teammates who were behind the punter could run downfield and recover the ball, much like occurs on onside kicks today. In addition, the punter could run downfield and, by advancing beyond his teammates, place them back onside, making them eligible to recover the punt. Of course, the receiving team did not want the punter running downfield, so they commonly assigned a few players to knock him down, a tactic known as "roughing the fullback" or "roughing the punter."

Both to take advantage of this rule and to increase the effectiveness of mass and momentum plays, Penn's coach, George Woodruff, developed the "guards back" formation in 1892. Woodruff had his guards align behind the line of scrimmage, increasing their ability to shift and block on mass and momentum plays. When defenses moved their safeties and defensive halfbacks close to the line of scrimmage to defend the mass and momentum plays, Woodruff had the quarterback "quick" punt the ball short and toward a sideline, away from the deep safety. With both guards and three backs behind the quarterback, they were eligible to recover what became known as "quarterback kicks."

Penn's "guards back" formation helped the guards lead block on mass plays and recover quarterback kicks. (University Archives and Record Center, University of Pennsylvania)

Looking to make the game safer in 1903, the rules committee eliminated the punter's ability to make their teammates eligible to recover punt by running past them downfield. The new rule meant receiving teams no longer had a reason to knock punters to the ground, and punters received special protection with the creation of the "roughing the fullback" penalty.

The receiving team on punts also faced different rules in early football. The receiving team had the option to make a fair catch, which gave the signaling player unimpeded access to the ball and protection from being tackled. Until 1890, coverage teams could distract the man catching the ball by waving their stocking caps nearby, but they could not get in his way. The receiver's job was also more difficult because they signaled a fair catch by "heeling in" or marking the spot of the catch with their heel as they caught the ball. Given that the heeling signal came late in the process, coverage teams often hit the return man in the act of catching the ball. An 1894 rule addressed this problem by requiring the return man to signal his intention to fair catch by raising one arm above his head. After making a fair catch, the receiving team could attempt a free kick for a field goal, place the ball on the heel mark for a play from scrimmage, or punt the ball back to the other team.

The ball is in the air over the line following a Harvard drop kick versus Yale. (Davis, Football, 1911)

The process of kicking a "goal from field" or "field goal" differed from today in many respects. Among them was that players could drop kick a field goal when they were beyond the line of scrimmage. A famous drop kick from beyond the line of scrimmage occurred in the 1878 Harvard-Yale game when Walter Camp was in the midst of a breakaway run. While running downfield, Camp pulled up at the 35-yard line and drop kicked the ball through the uprights. Unfortunately for Camp and Yale, the whistle blew to end the first half while the ball was in the air, so the goal did not count. The rule allowing play to continue after time expired on the clock was enacted in 1894. You can bet that Camp voted in favor of that change.

On free kicks after a fair catch, drop kickers took the ball as far back from the heel mark as desired and, when ready, began their drop kick motion. The defense, aligned on the other side of the heel mark, could not charge the kicker until he began his kicking motion. Drop kick attempts were legal on plays from scrimmage as well, but the defense could rush and try to block the attempt immediately after the snap of the ball.

Wisconsin's Pat O'Dea drop kicked a 60-yarder against Minnesota in 1898. (University of Wisconsin Digital Collections)

Drop kicks were less accurate and did not travel as far as place kicks. Since drop kicks occurred as the ball bounced off the ground, the technique held the potential for a poor drop, a bad bounce, or limited bounce on a wet, muddy field. Drop kicks also had less power because the drop kicker's approach was shorter than that of a placekicker. Drop kicks longer than 40 yards were unusual, though Pat O'Dea, Wisconsin's Kangaroo Kicker, set the record in 1898 with a 60-yard drop kicked field goal.

Teams attempting a "free kick" field goal via place kick did not snap the ball either. The rules allowed the defense to rush the kicker as soon as the holder touched the ball to the ground, so holders used the "over-under" technique, which involved laying on their stomach perpendicular to the line of scrimmage. While on the ground, the holder extended both arms with the ball held upright between his fingertips until the kicker was ready. The holder then withdrew his lower hand, placed the ball on the ground, balanced by his upper fingers, and the kicker stepped forward to boot the ball.

Kickers also could attempt field goals via the placekick from scrimmage. Although the placekick is the only method used today, it was the last to be adopted because long snapping and holding techniques were underdeveloped. Recall that centers originally snapped the ball to the quarterback by rolling the ball backward with their feet or hands. Since centers rolled the ball back on regular plays from scrimmage, they did the same on long snaps, but with greater force, so the ball bounded unpredictably. Given the erratic bounces, teams attempting a placekicked field goal had their quarterbacks stand bent over like shortstops to catch the tumbling snap. After catching the ball, the quarterback fell to one knee, placed the ball on the ground, steadying the top of the ball with his fingertips as the kicker booted the oval. It was an inefficient process, but the best devised to that time.

Michigan players in 1902 demonstrating the placekick with the holder kneeling and using the over-under technique. (Bentley Historical Library, University of Michigan)

The technique changed in the mid-1890s through an innovation widely attributed to Princeton. More accurately, twin brothers at Otterbein conceived the idea of the center using a controlled toss to the holder. They wrote to Walter Camp to confirm its legality and implemented the technique in 1896. The boys from Otterbein taught the approach to Washington & Jefferson, who then passed it on to Princeton. Princeton used the controlled snap, and being Princeton rather than Otterbein, their "innovation" caught the eye of the Eastern press, and the technique became known as the "Princeton place kick." One team to make use of the technique was the University of Chicago, whose Clarence Herschberger became the first All American from a non-Eastern school in 1898. In an incredible feat of foot, Herschberger place kicked three field goals from scrimmage in Chicago's season-ending game with Michigan in 1897.

Having covered the various forms of goals from field, we can move to the goal after touchdown process. When a team scored a touchdown in early football, the official stood near the goal line, raised one arm in the air, and pointed with the other arm at the spot the ball crossed the goal line. Identifying that spot was critical because it was the location the scoring team received the ball for their goal after touchdown attempt. From there, teams had two options for attempting the goal after touchdown. First, the kicker could walk at a 90-degree angle from the designated spot on the goal line until he reached a location on the field that gave him a favorable angle and distance to attempt the kick. The kicker and holder then executed a free kick as the defensive side remained behind the goal line until the holder placed the ball on the ground. Walking the ball out was the preferred option when the touchdown was scored near the goal posts, but was less attractive for touchdowns scored near a sideline. On touchdowns scored near a sideline, the kicker could only achieve a reasonable kicking angle after walking thirty to forty yards down the sideline, making for a long kick at a less-than-ideal angle.

The scoring team's second option was to execute a convoluted process known as a puntout. Puntouts required a player on the scoring team to take the ball at the point the ball crossed the goal line on the touchdown. He then positioned himself behind the goal line and at least as far from the goal posts as the spot of the touchdown, even if doing so placed him out of bounds in the "touch in goal" area. The player then punted the ball onto the field. The linemen on the punter's team aligned near the 10-yard line to block the defense. The backs aligned behind the linemen in an attempt to catch the ball and run for the goal line, catch the ball and immediately attempt a drop kick, or fair catch the ball and attempt a free kick from the spot of the catch. Most teams fair caught the ball and attempted the free kick.

Puntout

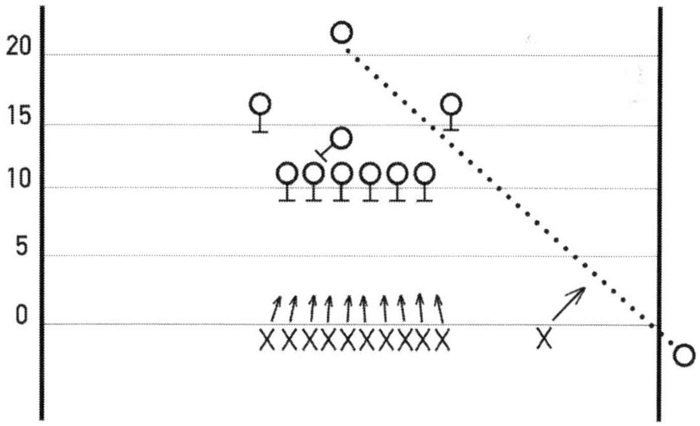

The illustration shows a puntout executed from the "touch in goal" area after a touchdown was scored close to the sideline. The defense aligned "in goal" and rushed after the ball was punted. (Adapted from Warner, A Course in Football for Players and Coaches, 1912)

The defense, meanwhile, aligned beyond the goal line, charging after the punt in an attempt to bat the ball before it could be caught. (The defense could not interfere with or touch the man making the catch.) Teams that failed to catch the punted ball lost the opportunity to attempt the goal after touchdown, and many close games were lost due to the failure to catch the puntout.

A final note regarding the puntout is that a five-yard penalty could be levied against the punter for feinting the punt in an attempt to draw the defense offside. Since the punter was already behind the goal line, the penalty moved the punter five yards further away from the goal posts, making it the only instance of a horizontal distance penalty in football's history.

FOOTBALL BEGAN in 1876 as an open, rugby-style game with sideline-to-sideline movement, but the shift to the scrimmage and allowing interference or blocking led to a substantive departure from rugby. Starting from controlled positions and allowing blocking increased the frequency and intensity of the game's collisions. In addition, the liberalization of tackling rules made open-field runs more difficult, and by 1905, the game had transitioned to one in which offenses played from tight formations and ran headlong into the opposition's line. The transition from a wide-open to a compact game led to players protecting their bodies with pads and other equipment. The nature of player equipment during the early era is the subject of the next chapter.

4

PLAYER EQUIPMENT (1869-1905)

After discussing football's rules and style of play, the focus now shifts to the equipment worn by players during the early era. The early era had few rules concerning player equipment, and those that existed generally prohibited the use of certain materials or equipment rather than requiring them. Still, player equipment evolved as football shifted from the open, rugby-style game to the closed, power game, and players added padding to protect themselves.

The IFA's first rule book had one rule concerning player equipment: "No one wearing projecting nails, iron plates, or gutta percha on any parts of his boots or shoes shall be allowed to play in a match."[6] Gutta percha, a hard latex made from the sap of a species of Indonesian tree, was outlawed to protect other players, not the wearer. This rule initiated a nearly eighty-year-long trend in which the equipment rules focused on protecting other players rather than protecting the wearer. Though accompanied by tremendous debate, it was not until the introduction of the plastic helmet in 1940 that the protective value for the wearer superseded that of other players in the game's rulemaking.

UNIFORMS

The first collegiate football game between Princeton and Rutgers was played by men in street clothes with some wearing school colors as part of their outfits. Shortly after that, teams began wearing outfits mirroring the rugby uniforms worn in England, Canada, and New Zealand, which consisted of flannel knickerbockers, light sweaters, stocking caps, and wool socks.

The 1878 Harvard football team poses in their light jerseys and stocking caps. (Harvard University Archives)

Since early football rules did not allow tackling below the waist, tacklers grabbed runners by the torso, often tearing their light jerseys. Ledru P. Smock of Princeton fixed this problem by having his tailor make a tight-fitting, sleeved canvas jacket that was difficult to grasp or tear. His teammates laughed at his outfit until they tried tackling him, and they soon began wearing similar jackets, tightly laced in front. His teammates also found that greasing the jackets made them a tad more slippery, but that tactic ended with the banning of slippery and "grippery" substances in 1894.

Smock's original jacket had long sleeves that restricted arm movements, so players switched to wearing canvas vests. Princeton wore their canvas vests for the first time against Harvard in April 1877, pairing them with orange striped black sleeves. Doing so earned them the first college nickname, the Tigers. Equipment manufacturers sold both the sleeved and vest styles that defined the standard football outfit for more than a generation.

The 1884 Yale team wore a mix of wool sweaters and canvas vests. (Manuscripts & Archives, Yale University)

Teams also wore wool sweaters as jerseys, often decorated with stripes or large letters identifying the school. In the East, the top football teams loaded their early schedules with lesser teams, saving their big games and best players for the end of the season. To recognize those who started the big games, Harvard allowed its starters to keep their jerseys at season's end, beginning the tradition of awarding varsity letter sweaters. The process of issuing formal letters came in 1902 when Amos Alonzo Stagg created the "Order of the C" letter winners' club at Chicago.

Another evolution in uniforms was the use of sturdier material for the player's pants. A report on the 1883 Harvard-Yale game described their pants, saying:

> (The Yale team) wore dirty white jerseys, fustian knickerbockers, and blue stockings and caps. ...The Harvard men appeared a moment or two later, also wearing dirty white jerseys. Their knickerbockers were of brown and their stockings, shirt-sleeves, and caps of crimson. The half-backs and back (sic) wore crimson shirts over their jerseys and the Yale occupants of the positions wore blue jackets.[5]

Yale's knickerbockers were "fustian," a family of heavy cotton fabrics that includes moleskin, velveteen, and corduroy, each being sturdier than flannel. Moleskin proved to be the fabric of choice for many elements of football uniforms and remained in use into the 1920s with canvas providing a lower-cost alternative in many cases. Moleskin became so closely identified with the game that "moleskins" became slang for football uniforms and football players generally.

A final note concerning early era uniforms is that they were often not uniform, particularly at the high school and small college levels. Many lower-level teams outfitted themselves in a mishmash of available equipment.

BODY AND LEG PROTECTION

Sturdier fabrics helped the uniforms withstand the wear and tear of the game, but they offered little protection until players began quilting fabric pads on the front of their pants. The early pants were baggy, and while streamlined versions became available before 1900, even the slimmest versions were bulkier than anything seen on a football field in the last century.

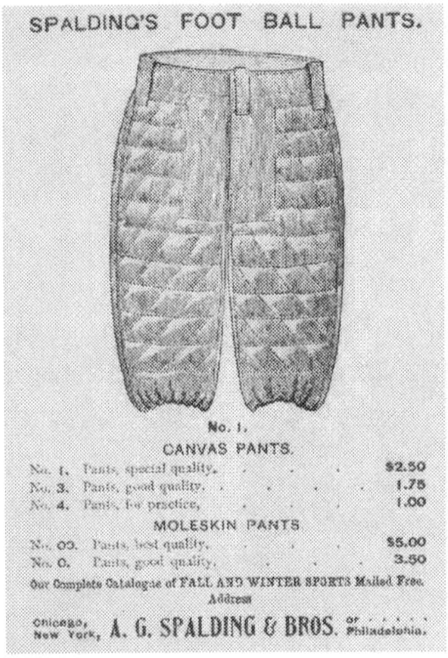

Spalding's foot ball pants advertisement. (1893 Spalding's Official Football Guide)

Another piece of equipment commonly worn during the early era was the shin guard. Typically made of chamois with encased cane running vertically, they appeared both over and under the players' wool socks. Shin guards had functional value in the rugby-style scrummage and protected against "hacking" (kicking opponents in the shin). Whether due to new styles of play or less hacking, shin guards largely disappeared after 1910. Sporting goods manufacturers continued offering them into the 1940s, but they were used only by players who had already suffered a shin injury.

Players began protecting their upper bodies in the 1890s with homemade pads of cotton batting stuffed with cotton or wool and then with commercially-produced, stuffed leather pads. The pads were sewn to the inside or outside of the jerseys with "shoulder pads" being most common. The number and location of pads depended on each player's position, injury history, and preferences, with some padding their sternum, elbows, or forearms.

1908 Huron College team union suit outfits with ribbed thigh pads. Some wore external shoulder pads and others did not. (Postcard, Unknown Publisher, Personal Collection)

Although we view the padding used in early football as archaic and know it provided limited protection, contemporary observers saw them as a significant advancement. As one observer in the late 1890s wrote:

> After the jacket came the system of padding, which to-day has been carried to such perfection that practically every point and vulnerable part of the body is shielded from violent contact with the earth during scrimmages and tackling falls.[6]

Shortly after the turn of the century, equipment manufacturers developed padding resembling current shoulder pads. Some were little more than a set of cloth pads connected by straps, while the most elaborate was Whitley's Foot Ball Armor, introduced in 1903. Whitley's product added caning to the exterior of the shoulder pads to distribute the force of blows and provide some level of mechanical protection.

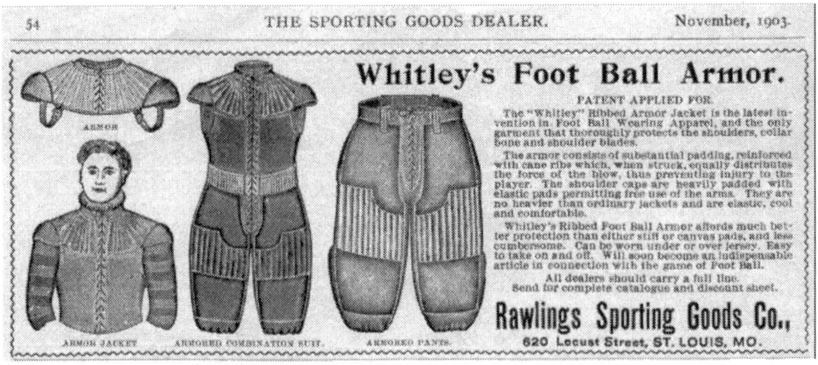

Whitley's Foot Ball Armor maximized the protection available at a time when metal and hard latexes were prohibited. (AntiqueFootball.com, Whitley's Foot Ball Armor advertisement, The Sporting Goods Dealer, November 1903)

The earliest football players wore heavy, leather street shoes or boots insufficient for running and dodging on grass fields. Baseball shoes were available on the market by then, but football's rules banned their metal cleats. The first shoes specifically marketed for American football came from Europe, where sporting goods manufacturers produced similar shoes for soccer and rugby. These shoes often had canvas or kangaroo skin uppers to keep them light, along with leather supports and soles for durability. Leather spikes and crossbars, the forerunners of cleats, were added to the soles in various configurations to provide traction. One problem with the leather cleats was that repairing or replacing the leather bars required a cobbler's expertise, making the process expensive and inconvenient.

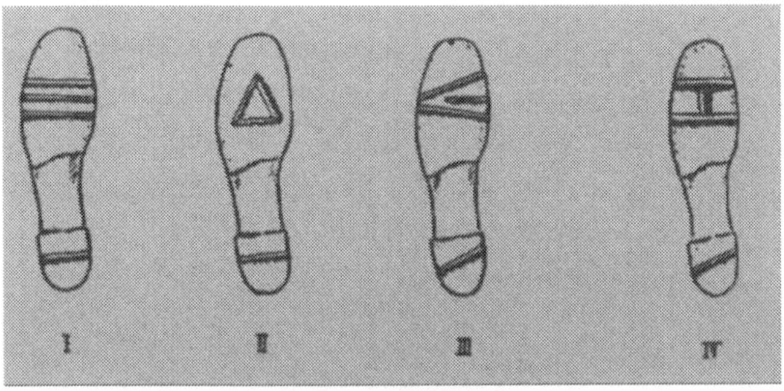

Illustration of the cleat designs for football shoes. (Camp, Inter-Collegiate Football in America, 1890)

HEAD AND FACIAL PROTECTION

The first known use of facial protection by football players came in 1889 when a Harvard player, John Cranston, was injured and rigged up a wire mesh mask to protect his nose. The mesh mask proved effective at protecting Cranston's face but was problematic for those he blocked since they often came away with cuts from the wire mesh. (Baseball catchers masks were in use by then, but their hard metal cages kept them off the football field.)

Cranston's teammate, Arthur J. Cumnock, a two-time Harvard captain and a top player of the era, developed a rubber nose guard his teammates used in 1890. After completing his eligibility, Cumnock patented the rubber nose guard and assigned it to John Morrill, a former big leaguer who operated a Boston sporting good store. Morrill modified Cumnock's design and began manufacturing and marketing the nose guard in 1891. The Morrill nose guard became the standard facial protection for the next twenty or more years, though action shots and team photos of the time suggest that only ten to twenty percent of players wore them.

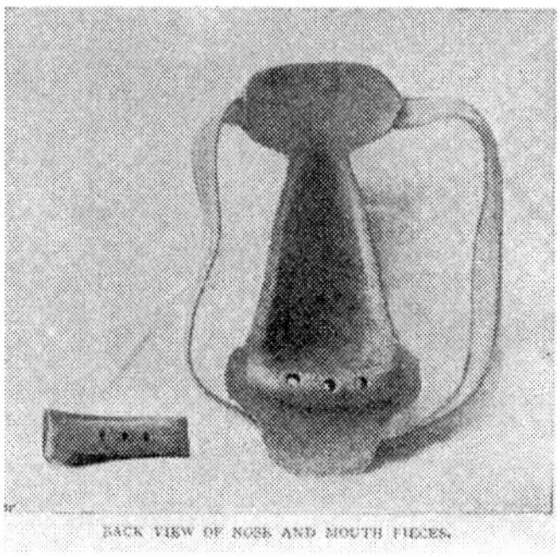

Nose guards or nose masks had integrated mouth guards that protected the teeth and kept the mask in place. (Cook, 'Football in Armour,' Strand, March 1897)

Morrill's nose guard was popular among those with nose injuries and a few seeking to avoid them. The devices had a top plate that rested against the forehead and was held in place by a strap encircling the head. Below the plate protruded a teardrop-shaped device covering the nose and mouth. Near the bottom, backside of the nose guard was a small shelf gripped between the teeth to keep the nose guard in place and protect his teeth.

Player wearing a head harness with combination nose and mouth piece.
(Cook, 'Football in Armour,' Strand, March 1897)

The football helmet is perhaps the most iconic symbol in the game, but the helmet, as we know it, did not exist in the early football era. Early football players wore stocking caps in school colors to distinguish friend from foe. While caps undoubtedly provided warmth and reduced some abrasions, they offered little protection. The earliest headgear used for protection focused on the ears. Players with injured ears and those concerned with developing cauliflower ear often wore bandages wrapped around their heads.

John Naismith, basketball's inventor, wrapped bandages around his head to protect his ears while playing center for McGill in the 1880s. (D. Hallie Lowry, Library and Archives Canada, C-038013)

The bandages often ripped off during games, leading to the development of leather head harnesses. Leading that charge was George Barclay of Lafayette, who had the local harness maker create a device similar to today's wrestling headgear. Barclay and several teammates wore head harnesses during the 1894 season, and the devices gained greater attention after they wore them during their upset of Penn in 1896.

George Barclay (far left) holds a head hardness, as do several other members of Lafayette's 1894 team. (Special Collections & College Archives, Skillman Library, Lafayette College)

Despite their utility, some players deemed protective equipment beneath them, believing it signaled a lack of manliness. Others spurned the equipment due to a belief that it was best to train the body to absorb football's punishment. The wearing of protective equipment among previously injured players was more widely accepted.

The first true football helmets came onto the market as the early era came to a close. Head harnesses and helmets differ in that head harnesses protect the ears or reduce abrasions but lack the helmet's characteristic hard shell that prevents skull fractures or similar injuries. Under that criterion, the first true helmet designed for football was the Spalding No. 60, which protected the top of the skull and forehead with a hard fiber shell.

FOOTBALL'S early era witnessed a transition from players wearing street clothes or unpadded athletic gear to equipment specifically designed for the rigors of the increasingly rough-and-tumble game. By 1905, a variety of leather and cloth pads covered players' bodies, while soft leather and cloth headgear protected some players' heads and ears from abrasions. Rubber nose and mouth guards offered facial protection.

Despite the widespread use of padded pants and shoulder pads, the majority of players went without head or facial protection. Players of the period understood the available equipment offered limited protection, but the desire to appear manly also limited its use. The latter sentiment manifested itself during the middle and modern eras as well.

5

COACHES AND OFFICIALS (1869-1905)

College football originated during an era in which many of the nation's elite took minimal physical exercise. Upper-class men increasingly held sedentary jobs, leading to concerns they were becoming physically and morally weak. One reaction to this situation was the Muscular Christianity movement that originated in Europe but took hold in the elite schools on America's East Coast. While its proponents saw football as a violent game, they justified participation because the game helped players build character by facing physical danger. Teddy Roosevelt encapsulated this thinking in an 1890 letter to Walter Camp:

> I am very glad to have a chance of expressing to you the obligation which I feel all Americans are under to you for your championship of athletics. The man on the farm and in the workshop here, as in other countries, is apt to get enough physical work; but we were tending steadily in America to produce in our leisure and sedentary classes a type of man not much above the Bengalee baboo, and from this the athletic spirit has saved us. Of all games I personally like football best, and I would rather see my boys play it than see them play any other. I have no patience with the people who declaim against it because it necessitates rough play and occasional injuries. The rough play, if confined within manly and honorable limits, is an advantage.[7]

The line of thinking expressed by Roosevelt at the end of the eighteenth century remains a part of football today.

COACHES AND COACHING

When football began, teams did not have coaches. Teams elected captains who managed the rosters, practices and coordinated with referees during games. The limited coaching that existed came from select alumni returning to practice for a few days to instruct and actively compete with the current team. Even the term "coach" was new, after being imported from Britain in the late 1880s. The first appearance of the term, football coach, in a U.S. newspaper occurred in 1889, while "baseball coach" appeared the previous year. However, as the game evolved to a more structured, scientific game and higher levels of honor and money were at stake, teams transitioned to the formal coaching model.

Many early coaches were recent graduates of Eastern college powers. They coached at smaller Eastern schools or headed to the hinterlands to teach the game for a year or two before moving on to more traditional careers. Bert Holden, Harvard's captain in 1887, returned in 1889 for a six-week stint with the team. Charles Gill, Yale's captain in 1889, took over the reins at Cal in 1894, the same year Walter Camp moved from Yale to become Stanford's head coach. Still, even the highest-paid coaches were seasonal workers for most of the early era. Pop Warner coached at his alma mater, Cornell, but went home in the offseason to practice law. Amos Alonzo Stagg was the exception to rule when he became a full-time faculty member at the University of Chicago in 1892.

Within a decade of schools first hiring professional coaches, virtually every school serious about football did the same, and many of the most successful and innovative coaches came from the Ivies including Walter Camp, Amos Alonzo Stagg, Pop Warner, H. L. Williams, John Foster Sanford, George Woodruff, and John Heisman. Eastern grads filled the second generation of top coaches as well. They included Andy Smith (Penn State), Perry Haughton (Harvard), Howard Jones (Yale), Red Blaik and Bob Neyland (Army), Wallace Wade (Brown), Jock Sutherland (Pitt), and Pappy Waldorf (Syracuse).

Other top coaches played at Midwestern or Southern schools under recent Eastern college graduates. Members of Eastern college coaching trees included:

- Bob Zuppke and Eddie Cochems played under Phil King at Wisconsin
- Gil Dobie and Bernie Bierman toiled under H. L. Williams at Minnesota
- Hugo Bezdek and Fritz Crisler were mentored by Amos Alonzo Stagg at Chicago
- Dan McGugin by Fielding Yost at Michigan
- William Alexander played under John Heisman at Georgia Tech.

By any measure, players from Eastern colleges and their coaching offspring dominated the sport of football during the game's first fifty years and much of its second.

Even as full-time coaches came to dominate the game, they played a more constrained role than today. Given the thinking that football helped developed young men, many wanted the game to test the players' brains and brawn, not that of the coaches. That thinking led to rules limiting the role of coaches during games. An 1892 rule called for a ten-yard penalty if instructions came from the sideline, whether those originated from coaches, teammates, or fans. Coaches could not call plays or otherwise influence the decisions of the players on the field. Even substitutes entering the game could not communicate with their teammates until they had been on the field for one play.

The coaching from the sideline rule was both widely supported and violated. Many coaches mouthed support for the ban, but like dirty recruiting, found ways to signal in plays from the sideline. Specific stances and movements indicated the quarterback should call a line plunge, a sweep, a punt, or attempt a field goal. In other cases, the coaching violations were more blatant.

The coaching from the sideline rule was difficult to enforce, given the limited number of game officials at the time. The rule makers considered placing the coaches and substitutes into fenced areas along the sidelines where they would be unable to signal in plays. Instead, they opted to limit the number of people that could stand on the sideline during games. The rules for 1900 allowed five people to stand on the sideline; all others had to sit or kneel. The number allowed to stand on the sideline ebbed and flowed through the years, but coaching from the sideline did not become legal in college football until the 1960s.

The modern system of offensive, defensive, and special team units shuttling in and out of games did not exist in football's early days either. Substituting for injured players became legal in 1882, and substitutions, in general, came at the captain's discretion beginning in 1897, but players that left the game for any reason could not return. One-platoon football required the starters to be in physical condition to play the 90-, then 70-, and finally, 60-minute game, and to have the skills to play offense and defense. And someone on the field had to handle the kicking and punting duties as well.

Despite being on the field the entire game, the pace of play was quite fast. The rules did not dictate the time taken between snaps, rather football's rugby origins drove the pace of play. Just as rugby scrums formed immediately after a tackle, football teams maintained the habit of aligning quickly after each play. (Readers can watch examples of the rapid pace in game films from as late as the early 1920s.)

Several other factors contributed to the fast pace. First, since the forward pass was not yet legal, the clock did not stop on incomplete passes, and no one took time retrieving the ball incomplete passes. Second, offenses aligned in tight formations with little variation, leaving players close to the ball at the end of most plays. Third, like soccer and rugby, the clock did not stop when the ball went out of bounds. It stopped only after scores and for several kicking situations. Fourth, teams seldom huddled, and the officials did not set the ball before each down; the center simply aligned on the ball wherever the previous play ended, and his teammates did the same. All this meant that after completing a play, the teams lined up quickly, the quarterback called his signals, and the center snapped the ball within fifteen seconds of the previous play ending. Teams maintained that pace the entire game.

The combination of one-platoon football and the pace of play drove differences in player size versus today. The starters in the Princeton-Yale game of 1880 averaged 154 and 165 pounds, respectively. Players weighing more than 220 pounds were relatively rare through the 1940s. Today's players are larger due to improved nutrition, disease control, strength and conditioning regimens, and the selection processes that come with college recruiting and the professional draft. They are selected and honed for their size, which has value in today's two-platoon game. However, many of today's two-platoon linemen would have difficulty maintaining the pace of play of the sixty to ninety-minute games of the early era.

PRACTICES AND EQUIPMENT

During football's early days, most players arrived on campus knowing little about the game. Prospective players learned the game's rules and techniques in practice while the captain determined who had the athletic skills to play various positions. While that assessment process continues today, few players arrive on campus today with little football experience.

Two signs of the game's development and institutionalization were the introduction of preseason camp and spring practice. The likelihood of holding preseason camp varied with the resources and the relative importance of winning at a given school. For those with sufficient funds, preseason practices took place in remote locations away from campus, hence the term "camp." Early preseason camps emphasized distance running and other aerobic conditioning to help prepare the team for their games. The first spring practice was organized at Harvard in 1889 by Arthur Cumnock, the inventor of the nose guard.

A natural element of camp and in-season practices were signal drills, which are familiar to all who have played organized football, though the process likely went by a different name. "Signal drills" was the early term for running plays against air (without an opponent) to assess alignment, understanding of the play calling, formation shifts, and play execution.

Of course, practices also provided opportunities for skill development, including blocking and tackling. The first piece of training equipment designed for football was the tackling dummy. Before its invention, varsity players practiced their tackling with objects called freshmen, so it was only natural they applied the term "dummy" when canvas and leather bags stuffed with sawdust and rags took the place of the frosh. Sources disagree on who created the first tackling dummy, but they agree it occurred in 1889. Some credit Yale's captain, Amos Alonzo Stagg, with creating dummies with rolled-up wrestling mats; others say Harvard's Arthur Cumnock did the same during his spring practice sessions. Though it is unclear who stuffed the first bag, tackling dummies were in use at colleges around the country by the turn of the century. The first tackling dummies were stationary or held by teammates, but inventive coaches soon rigged systems with dummies suspended from frameworks and swung in different directions to simulate a ball carrier's movements. None of the inventions simulating movement was ever worth much, but that did not prevent coaches from coming up with new designs.

Michigan's Fielding Yost, wearing a Lafayette sweater, oversees a player hitting the tackling dummy as another player pulls the rope to simulate movement. (University of Michigan Library Digital Collections. Bentley Image Bank, Bentley Historical Library.)

Another key invention was the "charging machine" or "plunging machine," devices known since the 1930s as "blocking sleds." By any name, these instruments of torture trace to Harvard in the waning years of the 1890s and quickly came into use by other teams. One was found north of Chicago in 1903 when Walter MacCornack's charging machine helped Northwestern push its way to a surprising 11-1-3 record. The next year Amos Alonzo Stagg added a charging machine to Chicago's practice equipment, which is notable because many credit Stagg with inventing the device.

Players pushing a wheeled charging machine during practice. (Edwards, Football Days, 1916.)

Several other coaches are cited as fathering the charging machine, and the questionable paternity likely stems from early charging machines being homemade. The typical charging machine used for defensive practice rested on wheels or skids, had a long, horizontal plank covered with padded leather into which linemen drove their hands. Comparable sleds with vertical pads spaced apart from one another allowed linemen to practice their offensive blocking. Princeton's version even had leather heads protruding from the pads to enhance the simulation. Generations of lineman toiled on these devices; their modern variations remain in use today.

Only one leading-edge coach at the end of the early era is known to have embraced the emerging technology of photography. Photography had little to contribute to the earliest coaches because the wet plate method used during the period required long exposure times. Most early football photographs were posed in studios that had controlled lighting. It is unclear who took the first photographs for use in coaching, but Camp and Deland's 1896 book, *Football,* notes that photography had limited use in coaching, so it likely had little value to that point.

This image of the 1895 Auburn-Georgia game at Piedmont Park in Atlanta is among the earliest game action photos of Southern football. (Fred L. Howe, Wikimedia Commons)

The technologies of still photography and motion pictures continued developing, however, and the first motion pictures of football games came in 1903 when crews from Thomas Edison's American Kinetoscope Company filmed the Princeton-Yale and Chicago-Michigan games. The films were shown in theaters far from New Haven and Ann Arbor, giving fans in other locations opportunities to see moving images of football players they had only read about previously. Despite their public viewing, it does not appear the teams' coaches made us the movies. The only known instance of football coaches using motion pictures in the early era came in 1905 when Harvard made an instructional film of alumni displaying proper football techniques.

CONDITIONING AND DIET

The desire to ensure the physical fitness of football players has been with the game from the beginning. Dr. Dudley Sargent, a graduate of Yale Medical School and director of the gymnasium at Harvard, was quoted in 1884 as saying:

> Last year there were men in the crew, in the base ball nine, and in the football team, who had no business there. They didn't keep the rules of training and were not manly enough to let people know about it until it was too late. I shall see that nothing of the sort happens again. Heretofore, I have examined the athletes two or three months before the various contests came off. Hereafter I shall examine them at short intervals up to the day of the games and races. If they are not in good condition they cannot take part in the contests.[8]

Sargent was a physical training pioneer, and like others of the early period, he prepared the team with early strength training, calisthenics, and running, and also had responsibility for the rehabilitation of injuries. While strength and conditioning staffs are separate from training staffs today, they were combined in one person or group early on. The better-financed training staffs had teams of rubbers -those who provided rubdowns or massages after practices and games- with the rubbers accounting for as much as ten percent of team expenditures.

Trainers or rubbers working on players in a locker room, c. 1899.
(Edwards, Football Days, 1916)

Conditioning was thought to have a hardening effect on the body that prevented injuries. Some took this to mean well-trained athletes did not need and should not wear pads because padding prevented the body from becoming conditioned for the upcoming games; pads only reduced players' speed and quickness. The same line of thinking countered criticism of the game's injuries and deaths. That is, the low number of injuries and deaths among the well trained and conditioned players at the top colleges showed football itself was not the problem. Instead, the problem was inadequate coaching and training. (They were onto something there since a substantial portion of period deaths attributed to football resulted from heat stroke or conditions not directly related to football's contact and collisions.)

The idea that a hardened body prevented injury was not the only bit of quackery floating in the football airs. The period's thinking about athlete's cleanliness and bathing habits were also suspect. Walter Camp, for instance, believed players should take a brief shower or sponge bath after morning practice and a slightly longer shower after afternoon practices, followed by a good rub down. Warm baths were advised fortnightly, much to the delight of local purveyors of cologne.

Training tables originated with the first intercollegiate sport, crew, and similar processes developed at schools pursuing football at a high level. Some schools limited the training table to the starters and a few substitutes, while others included up to fifty athletes. Training tables were controversial at times since many saw them as a form of payment to athletes, but that controversy dissolved as long as the players paid market value for the food.

Like some other elements of athletic conditioning, training table menus of the early era were constructed based on folklore. (Nutrition science had a long way to go, given the discovery of vitamins came in 1912.) Training tables of the early- and mid-1880s offered food aplenty, but limited selection. Most rejected rich foods, fruits, vegetables, coffee, and alcohol, while providing beef, mutton, potatoes, and oatmeal milk to make players lean. Odd ideas about nutrition included the prohibition of peas and fresh bread. Most problematic was the belief that water consumption should be limited.

The range of foods offered began to change in the late 1880s and 1890s when fruits were added to the training tables, though vegetables remained *verboten*. Even having a beer or two came into favor at Harvard in that "a few days before the Princeton game each man will have at dinner a glass of ale – the drinking of which goes far toward preventing any staleness in the men."[9] Although it is difficult to know exactly which symptoms of staleness were cured by consuming ale, the players surely toasted its return to their diets.

OFFICIALS

English rugby did not have an impartial referee to settle disputes. Contests between honorable men did not need one, but Americans recognized from the beginning that the referee was a pragmatic element of the game. Football officiating began with an impartial referee and two judges, each of whom was appointed by one of the teams. The judges, or umpires, ruled on scoring, out of bounds, and advocated for their teams when disputes arose. The referee settled disputes when the judges disagreed.

By 1883, the rules called for two impartial officials: a referee and an umpire. The referee was responsible for the ball. He judged where the ball was placed, ruled on out of bounds issues, and determined whether the ball crossed the goal line or passed through the uprights. The umpire took charge of the players, monitoring fouls and unfair tactics. With only one umpire monitoring twenty-two players, the umpire missed more than a few calls, leading to the addition of a second umpire in 1887.

Like the players who originally wore street clothes during games, the officials wore street clothes throughout the early football era. Officials were often former players chosen for their ability to keep their loyalties from influencing their on-the-field decisions. Officials commonly wore the letter sweater won during their playing days since they seldom officiated games involving their alma mater. Training programs for officials did not exist, and consistent rule interpretations were a challenge to deliver nationwide.

Princeton's Dana Kafer runs through the Cornell defense in 1903 as an umpire in street clothes looks on. (Edwards, Football Days, 1916)

To address concerns about the impartiality of the officials, the rules of 1892 required that the IFA Advisory Committee select the umpires, who could not be an alumnus of either school playing in the game, while the team captains selected the referee. These steps marked the first attempt to formalize the selection of officials. More substantial requirements and processes became the norm during the middle era.

Among the referee's responsibilities was clock management via a pocket watch or stopwatch. Football began with two forty-five minute innings or halves. The halves were reduced to thirty-five minutes in 1894, to thirty-minute halves in 1906, before shifting to four fifteen-minute quarters in 1910. The referee also warned each team as time was running out near the end of each half because scoreboards with running clocks did yet not exist. (Today's two-minute warning is a vestige of the pre-scoreboard clock era.)

Clock management was more straightforward in the early era since the clock stopped only while the ball was being readied for a kickoff, kick-out, or try at goal. The referee had the discretion to stop the clock for injuries, but the rapid pace of play and minimal clock stoppages meant games took less than two hours start-to-finish.

Another key duty for referees was to assess whether the offensive team earned a first down by gaining five yards in three downs. Doing so was not easy since the field had stripes every five or ten yards, while most first downs came at spots between the lines. To help make these judgments, referees dropped handkerchiefs on the field at the location of the first down. Of course, those handkerchiefs sometimes moved when play occurred atop the handkerchief, as well as when players deliberately kicked the handkerchief in the direction favoring their side. The confusion led to the addition of another official, the linesman, in 1894. His job was to mark the progress of each play and determine whether a first down had been earned. Linesmen continued dropping flags on the field until one of their smarter brethren connected two poles with a five-yard chain. Chains entered the rule book in 1898 when the home team was also required to supply the linesman with two assistants to help track the yardage gained in a series of downs. The assistants were to use "two light poles about six feet in height and connected at the lower ends by a stout cord or chain exactly five yards long."[10] Period photographs show the chains consisted of simple poles with no adornments and no down marker. More elaborate chains and down markers developed in time, primarily to aid spectators in the larger stadiums of the future.

Other than their striped shirts, no element of the football officials' kit is tied as closely to their role as the whistle, which was not in use when football began. One might wonder why football officials did not use whistles from the beginning, but the answer is straightforward: whistles did not yet exist. To clarify, there had long been low-volume whistles, but the modern whistle arose in response to a Scotland Yard request for a noise-making device to replace the hand rattles bobbies used to call for support. The request led Joseph Hudson to invent the first useful pea whistle, audible from one mile away. Scotland Yard adopted Hudson's Acme whistle in 1883, and they quickly came into use in England at soccer and rugby matches.

American football adopted whistles in 1887 both to stop play and to signal that a foul occurred, and that was the problem. Referees blew their whistles to stop play, while umpires blew their whistle to indicate that a foul had occurred. Of course, players could not tell one from another, so defenders sometimes heard a whistle, stopped play, only to watch the offense continued playing and score.

214 *Spalding's Official Foot Ball Guide.*

The rules specify that "The referee should use a whistle to indicate cessation of play on downs, fair catches and fouls, and the umpire (and linesman) should use a horn or bell of some kind, distinguishable from the referee's whistle, to indicate that a foul has been committed." For referees' use, two styles of whistles are shown herewith, either of which costs 25 cents, while for the umpires' and linesmen's use, two styles of horns are made, No. 1, of polished brass, costing $2.00, and No. 2, nickel-plated, $1.00. They make a loud sound and are not cumbersome in the hand.

No. 1.

No. 2.

No. 1.

No. 2.

Spalding's 1904 advertisement for referee whistles and umpire horns. The horns were touted as "making a loud sound and not cumbersome in the hand." (1904 Spalding's Official Football Guide)

The confusion continued until 1904 when the rule makers partially sorted the mess. The new rules called for the referee to use a whistle to signal plays dead. The umpire went whistle-less and used a bell or horn to signal penalties. The umpire's signal was supposed to be sufficiently different from the whistle that players could easily distinguish between the two. Nevertheless, it remained common for players to mistakenly stop play upon hearing the umpire's horn, leading to the other team gaining an advantage.

ALTHOUGH FOOTBALL COACHES are central to the game today, the game began without coaches because early contests were little more than pickup games. In short order, college football became too important to remain in the hands of the players or amateur coaches. Teams became eager to pay for coaches to improve their fortunes, and the football coaching profession began. Similarly, as the games became too important to leave the enforcement of the rules in the hands of classmates or friends, respected men in the athletic community took on the task. They received payment for their services, but unlike coaches, officials worked only one or two days per week, so officiating did not develop into a full-time job.

As with many aspects of society during the early era, the changes to the coaching and officiating roles reflected the increasing specialization and bureaucratization in the world, but neither group developed professional organizations to add their collective voices to debates about the future of football or to create standards for themselves. Both arrived as football developed further during the middle era.

6

OFF THE FIELD (1869-1905)

Most of the discussion thus far has focused on the events transpiring on the field or in training early football players. However, few of those events would matter today had others of the era not become fans of the game. Football and its history matter today because it mattered to the American public near the end of the nineteenth century and remained important to the present. Had the game developed differently and not attracted fans, you would not be interested in reading these words, and the author would not have bothered writing them. For better or worse, football is the most visible aspect of the American college and university system to the general public, so it is worth exploring how and why the American public embraced football.

Beyond fan behavior, the early era was the formative period for other elements of football's off-the-field identity. The organizations that managed football changed during the era with power shifting from individual teams, to several conferences, and on to the birth of a national organization. Football also existed in broader society, and some societal issues, such as the position held by African Americans, impacted their opportunities on the football field as well.

GAME ATMOSPHERE

Football's spectacle includes elements beyond the game itself. Pre-game music by marching bands, player introductions, the playing of The National Anthem, flyovers, cheerleaders, half-time shows, food vendors, scoreboards and video displays, and all manner of fan behavior are part of the football spectacle today. Each element developed over time, and most did so organically, making the origins of some difficult to trace. Of course, the beginnings of the football fan experience occurred on a cold November day in 1869.

Reports indicate that fifty Princeton fans traveled to Rutgers for the first intercollegiate game, but we have limited knowledge of fan behavior during football's first decade. The best-documented fan behavior during the early era occurred at the neutral site games played in New York City in the 1880s and 1890s. Played on Thanksgiving Day, the championship games were major social events as alums from far and wide descended on New York. Thousands of others without a school affiliation joined the festivities because the games were a place to see and be seen.

Princeton and Yale fans leaving their hotels for the drive up Fifth Avenue to Manhattan Field in New York, November 30, 1893. (Davis, Football, 1911)

As was standard at the time, New York's stadiums were not fully enclosed and had areas along the sidelines to park horse-drawn coaches. There, the best-heeled fans could comfortably watch the game while enjoying food and drink. The well-born and newly rich sat inside the stadium while the less fortunate sat on Coogan's Bluff, high above Manhattan Field. Betting was widespread, as was drinking by fans of the winning team. More than one undergraduate posted bail for the first time following a championship win.

The crowd sizes and extravagance in New York City were exceptions. Most games occurred before fewer, less well-to-do fans. At any number of college fields, fans stood along the sidelines or sat in simple bleachers. Even at the top football-playing schools, crowds below 10,000 people were far more common than those above, and less well-known school crowds numbered in the hundreds. However, because the attention and power rested with the elite

Eastern schools, their fans created many of the off-the-field traditions that continue today.

Like today, fans in the early era made road trips to support their teams playing in rival territory. For example, when Minnesota's undefeated team played at Northwestern in 1904, the number of supporters heading to Chicago pushed each of the five railroads serving the two cities to schedule extra trains, with a reported 1,000 students traveling to the game.

Trains played a part in another tradition of the era when fans gathered at the train station to hail teams returning from road victories. As played out on campuses across the country, teams were often met at the station by cheering crowds and a college band. The fans then paraded through the streets with the team in tow, blowing tin horns and shouting college cheers as they marched to a campus location to light a bonfire. That year's freshmen were responsible for collecting material for the bonfire, scouring the town for empty wooden barrels and crates, the odd sign, and other materials easily removed from their proper place. Speeches by college presidents, professors, coaches, and team captains preceded the lighting of the bonfire.

Touching the match to victory at Princeton. (Edwards, Football Days, 1916)

Princeton held bonfires on Cannon Green following IFA championship games, which meant they had a lot of bonfires. That tradition continues today with bonfire celebrations capping those seasons during which the Tigers beat Harvard and Yale.

Another manifestation of fan support was the development of cheerleaders. The first cheerleaders at football games were simply fans in the stands that encouraged others to join in cheering on the boys, often using published, school cheers. Princeton's Locomotive cheer picked up steam in the 1870s when stirring renditions of "Hurrah! Hurrah! Hurrah! Tiger! S-s-s-t! Boom! A-h-h-h!" filled the air at sporting and other events. Princeton had cheerleaders at some alumni events in 1895 and at football practices in 1897. The same year they held what would later be called a pep rally in advance of the Yale game, during which, official cheerleaders were named. Despite Princeton officially recognizing their cheerleaders, they were not universally popular. During the lead up to the same Yale-Princeton game for which they named cheerleaders, one editorialist called "Humbug" on the cheerleaders' artificial enthusiasm, arguing:

> Away with the special "leaders." They are illogical, they are superfluous, they are an excrescense, they mar the enjoyment, and at critical moments they become an annoyance and a peril to the players.[11]

Princeton's Scrouge-like fan notwithstanding, cheerleaders proved popular. They arrived at Minnesota in 1898 and soon jumped up at campuses around the country. Megaphones contributed to their noisy conversations by the following year.

Kansas cheerleaders prepare for an 1899 game. (University Archives, Spencer Research Library, University of Kansas Libraries)

All early cheerleaders were male, in part because many colleges had all-male student bodies. It was not until the 1910s that female cheerleaders first raised their voices to the crowd.

At the close of the season, when the din of the crowd had died, football fans of the early era were left with only one event worth anticipating: the announcement of All America teams. The idea for such teams arose in 1887 when football fans at Cornell suggested the IFA name All Eastern, All Western, and All America teams. It is particularly impressive that Cornell was the first to call for country-wide honors in 1887 because it was Cornell's first year playing intercollegiate football.

In any event, the first All America team was named in 1889 by Caspar Whitney, a top sportswriter of the era, best known for his work as editor of amateur sports for *Harper's Weekly*. Whitney named his first All America team in the publication, *This Week's Sports*. Every player named to the team played for Yale, Princeton, or Harvard (Cornell did not benefit from their great idea), establishing the trend of Eastern players dominating All America teams until WWI.

Beginning in 1890, the All America team transferred with Whitney to *Harper's Weekly*. Walter Camp took over naming the team from 1897 to 1924. Following Camp's death in 1925, Grantland Rice took on the task and held the reins until 1953.

Any number of other individuals and groups named All America teams. Most showed a decided bias toward players within their region. The teams became more representative when the groups expanded their selection processes and geographic reach following WWI.

MANAGEMENT AND CONTROL

When armies marched home at the end of the Civil War, the bulk of soldiers returned to family farms and small businesses. Enterprises of more than one hundred employees were rare and limited to the arms, textile, and railroad industries. Over the next several decades, industrialization took hold, and large, complex organizations became dominant forces in American society. Family-owned companies transformed into corporations led by technical experts and professional managers. Industrial forces created newly-rich owners, a burgeoning middle class, and a swath of lower-level employees that migrated to cities from the farms and overseas.

As with the rise of professional coaches, the business affairs of the student-run teams were increasingly taken over by professionals as well. Student athletic associations accepted alumni and faculty members on their boards for guidance and, in many cases, to help fund their efforts. Full-time trainers also came to supervise the teams, while bringing a level of expertise to the sport.

At the same time, the *Morrill Act of 1863* hastened the development of state universities focused on research and training students in agricultural, scientific, and mechanical skills. Traditional colleges increasingly abandoned the classical education model in favor of the university model with specialized curricula and graduate and professional degree programs.

Many traditional colleges of the second half of the nineteenth century had strong religious affiliations, and their faculties retained more control over student behavior than today. Faculties placed limits on team travel, the number of games played, and other aspects of intercollegiate athletics. For many faculty members, it was bad enough that students played or supported anything fun, but football's roughness made it a favorite target. Calls to ban football succeeded here and there. Still, school presidents and trustees often overruled faculties, allowing teams to continue because they brought interest, publicity, and were rallying points for alumni.

College football's commercialization began with rising ticket sales. Although the earliest football games had several hundred spectators or fewer, 7,000 fans attended the 1879 Princeton-Harvard game. In 1905, the Harvard-Yale game attracted 43,000 fans, the Chicago-Michigan game drew 26,000, and the Harvard-Penn game set a Philadelphia record with 22,000 attendees. Other schools drew smaller, though still impressive crowds: 12,000 saw Stanford beat Cal and 10,000 attended the Princeton-Cornell game. At the lower end, 7,000 attended Harvard's game with a lesser opponent, Maine, and only 1,000 saw North Carolina beat Davidson. These crowds pale in comparison to today's top games, but compare favorably with Major League Baseball crowds of the same year when only four of the sixteen major league teams averaged more than 5,000 fans per game.

In addition to drawing spectators, college presidents used football to bring publicity to their schools. No school did more in the early era to promote itself via football than the University of Chicago. Whereas the Ivies were founded in the 1600s and 1700s, Chicago began operations in 1892 following John D. Rockefeller's donation to create a research-driven American university. William Rainey Harper was the president of the new university, and he stocked the Midway campus with top faculty members hired away from other schools. Among those was a former student, Amos Alonzo Stagg, who received a hefty salary as a tenured professor of physical culture and head coach of Chicago's athletic teams. Among his instructions from President Harper was to "develop teams which we can send around the country and knock out all the colleges."[12] Stagg was more than happy to bring publicity to Chicago by playing well-known schools within and outside the Midwest. In their third year of play, Stagg took his team to California to face Walter Camp's Stanford team over Christmas break. Chicago traveled East for three Ivy games and one with Army between 1898 and 1905. They also hosted five Ivy games and one with Texas. Only Carlisle, which played intersectional games and traveled to the West Coast twice during the early era, had a schedule of comparable geographic scope.

Increased media coverage reflected college football's rising popularity as newspapers competed in the 1880s and 1890s to differentiate themselves. Some did so with their political slants, others through a new concept: sports pages targeted at fans of horse racing, cricket, baseball, and college football. The growth of sports sections coincided with the formation of the Associated Press and, later, the United Press. Syndicates connected newspapers in every pocket of the country to the news emerging from the centers of those networks. Centered in New York, news that made the sports page there was published everywhere, and newspapers across the country filled their columns with reports on Eastern football. Big city and small-town newspapers across the country reported on their local teams but filled much space with coverage of Eastern football games and heroes.

As the battles among schools on the field took on increased importance, questions arose as to who should represent schools in intercollegiate athletics. The answer had multiple dimensions, with the first being the amateur-professional divide. America's college elite accepted the British concept of amateurism, and few wanted professional athletes competing on college teams. The amateur-professional divide led to debates about the use of inducements such as free tuition or room and board to attract athletes. Those arguing publicly for inducements were few; those coordinating such inducements were more common.

Few schools had clean hands when it came to using questionable players, but among the more audacious examples was an unpaid ringer named Fielding Yost, who later became a prominent coach at Michigan. Despite playing for West Virginia throughout his senior season, Yost managed to slip out of town one weekend to play for Lafayette in their game against Penn, which Lafayette won to break Penn's three-year win streak.

A second example was Edward Wagenhurst, who played football and baseball at Princeton, graduating in 1888. Wagenhurst played professional baseball in the months after graduation but left baseball to become the football coach at Penn. Wagenhurst received money to coach, as well as tuition-free law school, but played on Penn's 1888 football team nonetheless. In the lead up to the Princeton-Penn game of 1889, Princeton protested Wagenhurst's eligibility, leading to a hastily-called IFA meeting to rule on the matter. Walter Camp submitted an IFA constitutional amendment that, in modified form, passed to became the IFA's first statement on eligibility. The amendment addressed the core issues over which college eligibility arguments continue to this day:

> Section 1. No man shall be allowed to play more than four years upon a team

> representing any of the colleges in this association, or of the team of more than one college.
>
> Section 2. No man shall be allowed to play on a team representing any of the colleges in this association unless he be an undergraduate of said college.
>
> Section 3. No student in the department of law, medicine, or theology of any of the colleges in this association who has previous to his membership therein play upon a team representing any other college in this association shall be allowed to play on the team of said college in which he is a student.
>
> Section 4. No man shall be allowed to play in a team representing any of the colleges in this association if he in any way, directly or indirectly, receive any pay for doing so. Any inducement of pecuniary value shall be included in the meaning of the word "pay" as used in this section.
>
> Section 5. All questions of eligibility arising under this section must be investigated and decided by the advisory committee on application of any college.[13]

Section 3, which barred graduate and professional students from playing, targeted Harvard and Penn, both of which had graduate and professional schools. Arguments over this issue would lead the two and Cornell to leave the IFA in 1894. Despite the splintering of the IFA, a broader desire existed among many school faculties to align with other schools that agreed on eligibility rules and the place of athletics within academic settings.

This desire led to the formation of the Intercollegiate Association of the Northwest (IAAN), which formed in 1892 to coordinate football, baseball, and track competition at Michigan, Minnesota, Northwestern, and Wisconsin. The conference granted eligibility to former professional athletes. Still, it required all competitors to be bona fide students who had attended the school for at least two months before participating in athletics. The IAAN folded after only two years.

Next up was the Southern Intercollegiate Athletic Association (SIAA). The group's overly ambitious plan to cover multiple sports across much of the South failed in 1893. It became a reality in 1895 with Sewanee (University of the South), Alabama, Auburn, Georgia, and Vanderbilt joining as charter members. The group quickly doubled and more in size, forming the core of the current Southeastern Conference, many southern ACC schools, and some members of the Big 12.

The SIAA's constitution included provisions mirroring the IFA amendments of 1889, but added or expanded on several others:

- Game officials could not have prior affiliation with either of the contesting colleges [the opposite of the IFA stance]
- Defined a professional athlete as a man who "... at any time received money to play on a team, or for his athletic services as a coach, trainer, athlete, gymnasium instructor, or who has competed for a money prize or portion of the game money in any contest, or who has competed for any prize against a professional"[14]
- Eliminated training table in excess of normal board
- Barred faculty or instructors from playing for teams in the association.

Further north, similar provisions gained approval with the formation of the Intercollegiate Conference of Faculty Representatives (Western Conference, now the Big Ten) in 1895. The Westerners agreed on many of the same provisions as the SIAA, adding a requirement that students spend six months in residence as a full-time student before being eligible for intercollegiate athletics. This provision was the forerunner of rules on freshman ineligibility and the one-year wait period for transfer athletes.

Other conferences formed with each ratifying different combinations of these rules, resulting in incompatibilities across conferences. The incompatibilities meant that contracts for games between teams from different conferences had to spell out which eligibility rules applied for each game. Some conferences, such as the SIAA, barred members from playing teams from conferences with less stringent rules.

While the formation of conferences brought order at the region level, the more important long-term impact was the shift of power from the individual institution to the conference. Conferences, rather individual schools, became the primary force in college football for the next fifty years. The National Collegiate Athletic Association (NCAA), which formed early in the twentieth century, did not gain substantial power until its role expanded with the negotiation of national television contracts in the 1950s.

A final point about player eligibility concerns the treatment of Native American and African American athletes. The Carlisle Indian School was founded in 1879 and served as a model for similar schools formed by the Bureau of Indian Affairs. Football and other sports were seen as tools to teach American values to the Native Americans that poured in from tribes across the land. Carlisle, Haskell, Perris/Sherman, Chemawa, and a few other Indian schools regularly played predominantly-white college and athletic club teams in their area. Teams from the historically black colleges and universities (HBCUs) could not schedule such games.

However, one scholar estimated that thirteen black men played college football before 1900 at predominantly white schools. The earliest known black college football players were William Henry Lewis and William Tecumseh Sherman Jackson, who played for Amherst from 1889 to 1891. Lewis became the first black player to be named All America when he played for Harvard during law school. Another early pioneer was George Jewett, who played for Michigan in 1890 and 1892, and for Northwestern in 1893.

The 1891 Amherst football team included William Henry Lewis (holding the ball) and William Tecumseh Sherman Jackson (top row, third from left), the only African Americans known to play college football at the time. (Amherst College Archives & Special Collections)

With one or two exceptions, every predominantly white college with black athletes on their rosters was in New England or the Midwest. Given the highly regionalized schedules of the time, teams from the North and the Deep South seldom played one another and avoided arguments about racial issues. Such was not the case at some Northern schools and those in states bordering the Mason-Dixon Line. Schools that did not want to face black players instructed upcoming opponents to either leave their black player(s) at home or cancel the game.

Black players also faced discrimination off the field. Matthew Bullock of Dartmouth was refused accommodation at the Princeton Inn before their 1903 game, and Princeton players were overheard discussing their plan to target Bullock. Three plays later, Bullock suffered a dislocated shoulder and left the game. A similar incident occurred when Harvard played Yale the following year when Harvard substituted William Matthews into the game.

Matthews was punched and kicked by his opponents to the point that he left the game within ten minutes.

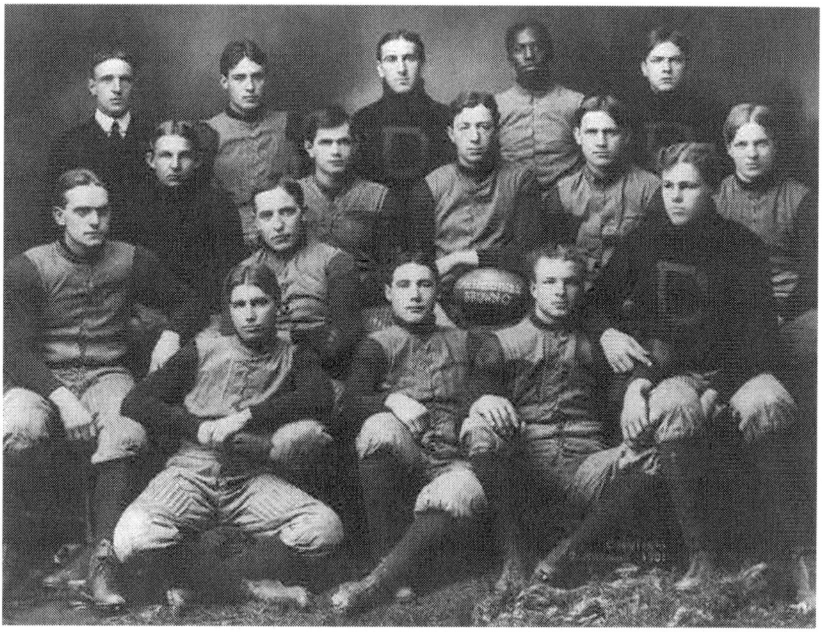

Matthew Bullock was the first black player at Dartmouth as a member of the 1901 team. He was subjected to abuse on and off the field when playing Princeton in 1903. (H.H.H. Langell, Library of Congress)

The following year, Springfield started a black player against Worchester Polytech. Springfield's man was knocked out by a punch near the beginning of the game, resulting in the ejection of his assailant. However, Worchester Polytech had only eleven players, so the assailant returned to the game and played the remainder of the contest.

Such was the state of affairs at the turn of the century, and the situation did not improve substantially during football's middle era. There would be pockets of success, and attitudes began to change in the 1940s and 1950s. Still, neither college nor professional football made a significant dent in their discriminatory practices against African American players until the 1960s and 1970s.

RULES COMMITTEE AND THE LOOMING CRISIS

Most football fans have at least a passing familiarity with the football crisis of 1905 to 1906, during which President Theodore Roosevelt intervened, threatening to ban the game unless its rules saw substantive changes. Less recognized is the fact that the demand for change did not arise suddenly in 1905; it was there from nearly the start. It was there in 1883 when the Harvard faculty ended the football season prematurely due to the brutality accepted within the game's rules. (Players could be ejected from the game for "slugging" or punching only after their third offense.) The move toward mass and momentum plays made the problem worse, and newspapers widely publicized football injuries and deaths in the decade leading up to 1905.

Football's rule makers were slow to act because they did not see football itself as the problem. In retrospect, some of the football deaths cited by the newspapers did not result from football per se (i.e., deaths from infections that began with a cut sustained playing football). More directly, they failed to act because they believed most football deaths resulted from inadequate coaching and conditioning, combined with inexperienced players. A summary of the 1898 rules meeting noted that additional rules were not required to eliminate mass plays.

> "The committee took notice of the fact that in the big games played by the University of Pennsylvania, Harvard, Yale, Princeton, Cornell and Brown not a single member of any of these team was seriously injured by mass plays, so-called, but that there were some accidents in games played by minor institutions where the elevens lacked both physical strength and skillful knowledge of the fine points of play."[15]

In effect, the rule makers watched as the kettle boiled, only to spill over in 1905 when Teddy Roosevelt called representatives from Harvard, Princeton, and Yale to the White House. Although Roosevelt lacked formal authority in the matter, the meeting brought needed focus to the call for rule changes to create a more open, less violent game.

As the need to change the game became apparent in late 1905, members of the football community bandied about potential rule changes. Most rule changes that would be enacted in 1906 had been raised, discussed, and rejected in previous years. For example, legalizing the forward pass, which had the most significant long-term impact of the 1906 rule changes, had been under discussion for at least a decade. In the terminology of the time, passing was the generic term for all laterals or pitches to teammates. While the rules required passes to travel parallel to or backward from the passer, it was reasonably common for players to inadvertently or deliberately lateral the ball forward to teammates. Hundreds of newspaper game reports written before 1906 mention penalties for forward passing.

The first known argument for legalizing the forward pass came in 1894 when Samuel J. Elder published an article in the *Boston Globe* suggesting several rule changes. Elder played baseball, not football, at Yale, but was one of three students Walter Camp credited with forming the Yale Football Association in 1872. Elder remained involved with football after graduation and, as a prominent Boston lawyer, played a central role in Yale's athletic relationship with Harvard. Elder published an article following the 1894 season when the rule makers tried to restrict momentum plays by restricting the number of men in motion at the snap. Although the 1894 rule was technically effective, teams found alternate ways to run mass plays between the tackles, such as the tackle back formation. Elder believed the game could be opened up not by restricting mass and momentum plays, but by giving offenses an attractive alternative. In advocating the forward pass as a new method to advance the ball, Elder argued:

> The change would have several salutary results. Lightness and swiftness would be chosen in place of mere weight and brute force. Massing of men for interference around the end would be a thing of the past, and we should constantly see as brilliant passes as that in the Princeton-Yale game last fall, which startled every one by its unexpectedness.[16]

Similar arguments were made by former Yale football player and Dartmouth coach Wallace Moyle several weeks later. In both cases, however, they envisioned the forward pass as relatively short laterals or pitches to a man a few yards forward of the passer. They did not conceive of the long downfield passes that developed after the legalization of the forward pass.

The following year, John Heisman, then Auburn's coach, witnessed a forward pass while scouting the Georgia-North Carolina game. A North Carolina runner, while being tackled, tossed the ball forward to a teammate who went seventy yards for a touchdown. The referee did not see the play, so the North Carolinians received credit for what turned out to be the game's only score, much to the displeasure of the Georgians. Of more long-term importance, Heisman recognized the potential of the forward pass and became an advocate of its use.

Following the 1899 season, Princeton and Yale advocated for several rule changes, including legalizing the forward pass. That suggestion met with opposition from their counterpart at Penn, George Woodruff, who summarized the argument against the forward pass, saying:

> The only one of the proposed changes which would radically affect the game is the allowance of the forward pass. ...That would be inadvisable, because it would completely change the character of the game. The adoption of the forward pass would tend to make kicking much less frequent than at present, and would altogether do away with the quarter back kick. If indiscriminate forward passing were allowed, one of the most fundamental and characteristic principles of Rugby foot ball would be abolished. The change is unnecessary and

> too radical. The quarter back kick was allowed in order to favor the open game as much as possible. This made no vital alteration in the style of play, but forward passing would go too far in this direction.[17]

Woodruff's argument that the forward pass would reduce the role of punting illustrates a key difference in perspectives on football then versus now. Punting was appreciated as a central part of the game, not a symbol of failure or an act of last resort. Fans appreciated punters and enjoyed a good punting duel at a level incomprehensible today to anyone other than a punter's Dad. Woodruff's second point about the impact of the quarterback kick goes to the heart of the matter in terms of the failure of previous attempts to open up the game. Woodruff, the originator of the quarterback kick, argued that his baby forced defenses to spread out, but the quarterback kick had not had enough impact to open up the game and significantly reduced the game's brutality.

An attempt to make football safer came from the 1903 rules committee. They required seven men on the line of scrimmage between the 25-yard lines (changed to the entire field in 1904), barred roughing the punter, and attempted to open up the game by allowing the first man receiving the ball from center to run with it, assuming they did so five yards right or left of the center. Unfortunately, those rule changes had little immediate effect on the number of football deaths, so the pressure for change mounted. Due to both the external pressure and the openness of some football insiders to further change, substantial rule changes arrived before the 1906 season. How the rule makers struggled to find solutions to the football crisis, the choices they made, and the impact of those changes is central to Part II of this books.

PART II

FROM CRISIS TO ASCENDANCY: 1906 TO 1959

7

FROM CRISIS TO ASCENDANCY (1906-1959)

Football in 1905 was an archaic game that retained many elements of rugby, but dramatic change occurred during the middle era, during which football became football as we know it. The rule changes that preceded the 1906 season were the most important in the history of the sport. Only the rule changes of 1880 and 1882, and the acceptance of blocking that occurred outside the rules, that occurred during football's formative years were comparable in their impact. The sport was new in the early 1880s, and few cared about those changes. By 1906, however, the game was hugely popular, and the mid-course corrections required balance. Too many changes might destroy football's essence, but too few could threaten its existence. In seeking a balance, the changes proved inadequate, keeping the rule makers busy the next six years, tweaking some rules, and making more dramatic changes to others.

THE RULE CHANGES OF 1906 TO 1912

By 1905, football had evolved into a brutal game focused on smashing the ball into the middle of the opponent's line. It had lost the artistry and the relative safety of the more open rugby match, leaving the nation's newspapers to track the number of deaths and serious injuries resulting from football. Although rule changes had eliminated momentum and mass plays, the rules and thinking of the time did not offer alternative methods of moving the ball. More radical surgery was required.

The issue came to a head in October 1905 when Teddy Roosevelt called a meeting with representatives from the Big Three -Harvard, Yale, and Princeton- and threatened to abolish the game if they did not reduce its violence. (The President did not have the authority to ban football, but understood the symbolism of the threat.) Roosevelt had not played football himself, but believed the game developed manly virtues. He encouraged young men to play, including those in his own family. His second cousin, William Roosevelt, broke his leg playing for Stanford in the first Rose Bowl in 1902, while Teddy's oldest son broke his collarbone playing for Harvard's freshman team shortly after his father met with the Big Three. Despite issuing the ultimatum, Roosevelt continued enjoying football, as evidenced by his attending the season-ending Army-Navy game, hosted by another football fan, Princeton's president, Woodrow Wilson.

President Teddy Roosevelt watching the Army-Navy game at Princeton in 1905. (Theodore Roosevelt Collection, Harvard College Library, Courtesy of Stephen and Maria Balch)

Despite the presidential nudge, the Big Three initially showed little willingness to make significant changes in the game, and they lost control of the situation following the late November death of a New York University (NYU) player in a game against Union College. The tragedy motivated NYU's Chancellor, Henry McCracken, to call meetings to discuss the abolition or reform of football. Sixty-two schools, none of them football powers, participated in these meetings, leading to the formation of the Intercollegiate Athletic Association of the United States (IAAUS), which, in 1910, was renamed the National Collegiate Athletic Association (NCAA). The IAAUS had several meetings to discuss rule changes before agreeing to merge with the remnants of the IFA.

The IAAUS discussed potential rule changes that departed significantly from the past, making both their supporters and detractors eager to assess the impact of these changes. To test some of the rules, Washburn and Fairmont (now Wichita State) agreed to play a test game on Christmas Day. John Outland, a former Penn player and namesake of the Outland Trophy, was Washburn's coach while Willis Bates, a former Dartmouth player, coached Fairmont. Each brought a valuable Eastern pedigree to their Western teams.

The test game rules allowed the forward pass, required the offense to gain ten yards in three downs, and gave the officials the authority to disqualify players for unnecessary roughness. The teams met six weeks earlier with Washburn winning 11-6, so neither team was an offensive juggernaut. The test game ended in a 0-0 tie, with only seven first downs between the two sides. Afterward, both coaches roundly criticized the rule giving teams three downs to gain ten yards, arguing it was too challenging a standard in games between evenly-matched teams. The teams made several forward pass attempts, and while both coaches believed the play had potential, neither had thought deeply about how to employ the pass strategically or tactically. In fact, in a precursor to the Single Wing offense, Washburn opened play without a quarterback, snapping the ball directly to the runner, hoping the faster snap would allow him to get outside on sweeps. It didn't.

More broadly, while the game received nationwide press coverage as the sole test of the potential rule changes, it was not a fair test and could never have been one. Other than using the direct snap, neither team fundamentally changed their offense. While they threw seven forward passes, it was not clear whether the play designs or passing techniques differed much from the past. Neither was a straightforward change. No one had ever designed football plays that deliberately used forward passes or spent the time to determine how best to throw a forward pass, so neither was done particularly well in the test game. While the game was inconclusive for assessing the forward pass, the primary takeaway among football observers was that football would not be made more open by tinkering with one or two rules. More drastic surgery was needed.

Despite the efforts to change the game, some college leaders remained unconvinced that reform was possible. Stanford and Cal, the top football-playing schools west of the Rockies, dropped football in favor of rugby and convinced a range of other California colleges and high schools to do the same. Columbia was the most significant Eastern school to drop football, while Northwestern filled that bill in the Midwest. The rest of the Big Ten conference agreed to limit their seasons to five games. Football's future and trajectory remained uncertain heading into the 1906 season.

In April 1906, the IAAUS published new rules with many substantive changes. In terms of long-term impact, the most significant change was the legalization of the forward pass, but the forward pass had a limited impact during its first few years of use, in part, because some saw it as a temporary measure. As a rules committee member commented in 1910:

> "The forward pass was not approved...through any notion that it of itself would prove a good ground gaining play. On the contrary it was passed for the sole purpose of opening up the defence (sic). This need is still imperative and the play should be left intact. Within another year the game may have opened up sufficiently for us to restrict or eliminate the forward pass altogether."[18]

That a rules committee member saw the forward pass as a temporary measure four years after its legalization points to a lack of vision on his part, but also points to the limited impact the forward pass had during its first few years of use.

A second reason coaches did not embrace the forward pass was the restrictions on its use and penalties for ineffective use. Like the 1903 rule prohibiting the first player touching the ball from running with it until they were five yards to the right or left of the center, passes could only be thrown from at least five yards right or left of the center. This rule eliminated the opportunity for quick passes and virtually required the passer to rollout before throwing the ball. Third, incomplete passes that did not touch a player before hitting the ground resulted in the loss of possession, with the ball given to the defensive team at the spot the pass was thrown. Fourth, forward passes that bounced or flew over the goal line resulted in a touchback. These restrictions and penalties made coaches leery of using the forward pass since most had not yet figured out how to use it effectively, so using it brought much risk and little reward.

The next year saw the penalty for an incomplete pass reduced from a turnover to a fifteen-yard penalty, but the passing game remained uninviting. A companion rule in 1907 awarded a ball thrown out of bounds on the fly to the defensive team at the spot the ball crossed the sideline. A side effect of this rule was that teams with strong-armed players used them in punting situations to heave the ball downfield and out of bounds. "Thrown punts" became so common they eliminated the rule in 1915, making balls thrown out of bounds just another incomplete pass.

The relative lack of use and continued opposition led to a near-death experience for the forward pass when three factions emerged on the rules committee after a high number of player deaths in 1909 brought pressure for further rule changes. One, led by Amos Alonzo Stagg, wanted to open the game by removing most restrictions on the pass. A second, led by Lt. Horatio Hackett of West Point, argued for limiting passes to those caught behind the line of scrimmage, while a third, led by H. L. Williams of Minnesota, sought to eliminate the forward pass. In May 1910, the rules committee approved the second option to require passes to be caught behind the line of scrimmage, while also reducing the number of yards needed to gain a first down from ten to eight. Both changes would have sent the game careening backward, but neither lasted. Stagg marshaled the supporters of the forward pass and succeeded in switching the vote two weeks later. In the horse-trading required to save the downfield pass, they eliminated the requirement that passes had to be thrown from five or more yards right or left of the center. Replacing it were rules requiring passes to be thrown from at least five yards behind the line of scrimmage and no more than twenty yards downfield. The twenty-yard limit remained in effect for only one season, while the requirement to throw passes from at least five yards behind the line of scrimmage remained in the game until 1945, thereby delaying the development of the quick passing game for thirty-five years.

While the restrictions on the forward pass limited its ability to open up the game, other safety-oriented rule changes arrived during that period. The reader will recall the earlier discussion of the quarterback kick, which allowed the quarterback/punter and players behind him to recover a punted ball. Seeking to spread out defenses, the rule makers of 1906 liberalized the quarterback kick rule by creating the "onside kick from scrimmage," which made every player on the punting team eligible to recover the ball, not just those positioned behind the punter.

In some respects, liberalizing this rule made more sense than legalizing the forward pass. Whereas teams already used this play and had the skills to execute it, virtually no one was skilled in throwing forward passes. The result was that the onside kick from scrimmage received relatively wide usage in 1906 and the next few seasons. It was made more challenging in 1910 when punts had to travel at least twenty yards downfield to be recovered by the punting team, and the 1912 rule book removed all versions of the onside kick. The old "quarterback kick" was reestablished in 1913 and survived until 1923 before its elimination from the American game. (The onside kick from scrimmage or onside punt remains legal in the CFL.)

A third 1906 rule change intended to enhance player safety came by redefining the downing of a ball carrier. Under the old rules, a ball carrier who was tackled or otherwise fell to the ground could crawl forward until he was physically stopped or yelled, "Down," leading defensive players to pile on ball carriers that crawled forward. The new rule considered the ball carrier down when any portion of his body other than his hands or feet touched the ground, a definition that remains in place today.

Two other new rules targeted mass and momentum plays. One required the offensive team to have six players on the line of scrimmage. If a seventh player was not on the line of scrimmage, he had to align outside one of the offensive ends. (The 1907 rule requiring seven men on the line of scrimmage still stands.) Further, offensive players could not be in motion at the snap unless they were moving away from the line of scrimmage. Another vestige of momentum plays was eliminated in 1910 when it became illegal for teammates to push or pull the ball carrier to assist his forward movement.

Another 1906 rule introduced a neutral zone equal to the width of the football. (The offensive center was the only player allowed in the neutral zone before the snap.) This rule gave the head linesman a clear line of sight to assess offsides and other pre-snap fouls. With the creation of the neutral zone, football technically gained a second line of scrimmage. One was the defensive line of scrimmage at the front of the ball, behind which defensive players must remain. The other was the offensive line of scrimmage at the back of the ball, the boundary for offensive players. The fact there are two lines of scrimmage is the reason the officials return the ball to the previous "spot" rather than the previous line of scrimmage.

The rule changes of 1906 also allowed teams to decline penalties. The value of this rule seems obvious, but it took almost forty years for football's rule makers to recognize that teams could benefit from declining a penalty. Yet another rule prohibited tackling below the knees, making sweeps and open field runs more effective.

Finally, the rule makers doubled the yardage needed to gain a first down (from five yards in three downs to ten yards in three downs). Since traditional plays run up the middle often resulted in gains of only one or two yards, it was thought that doubling the yardage to gain forced teams away from such tactics and toward new plays and formations.

Despite the rule changes of the previous six years, most teams' tactics had not changed by 1912, and they struggled to gain ten yards in three downs. Some argued for requiring teams to gain only eight yards in three downs. Others argued the opposite, thinking that innovative, open offenses could be spurred by requiring teams to gain twenty yards in three downs. Still others promoted a field position game in which teams had five plays to gain whatever yardage they could, after which they would turn the ball over to the opponent. In the end, the 1912 rule makers opted to give teams four downs to gain ten yards, a rule that became a fixture of American football.

The 1912 season also saw a revision to football's scoring system. Since many teams struggled to move the ball, even comparatively successful drives often stalled inside the 30-yard line, at which point the offenses attempted field goals. With the outcome of many games turning on the accuracy of kickers' legs, a scoring system that gave greater value to two field goals (six points) than a touchdown earned through the efforts of a full team (five points) seemed inappropriate. To reward team play, they increased the value of a touchdown to six points.

An additional suggestion for bolstering the forward pass in 1912 came when H. L. Williams of Minnesota argued for making all offensive players eligible receivers. Williams' idea proved too radical, but the committee removed the rule limiting passes to twenty yards downfield. The immediate justification for this change was the difficulty the three-person officiating crews faced in judging whether a catch had occurred nineteen, twenty, or twenty-one yards downfield. While this rule change had the immediate effect of simplifying officiating decisions, its real impact was to allow the ball to be flung far downfield. Few took advantage of the rule in the next few years, but it opened the door to the downfield passing game that revolutionized football in the 1960s.

The final rule change in 1912 was to legalize passes thrown over the goal line. Previously passes had to be caught in the field of play and carried over the goal line. The new rule change forced the elimination of the amorphous "in touch" area, which was replaced by a formally-bounded end zone. This change is covered further in the discussion of changes to the playing field in the next chapter.

FOOTBALL, as we know it, emerged during the middle era as the game transitioned from its archaic to modern form. The rule changes of 1906 through 1912 took time to blossom, but the period of radical rule change came to an end. For more than a decade, the rule changes were less substantive, before restarting after WWI. Rule changes and tactical adaptations would bring a substantial change to football by the end of the middle era.

The introduction of the forward pass and the other rule changes made between 1906 and 1912 set the stage for that transition. The Single Wing offense was the first significant innovation to emerge under the new rules, but many other elements had to change for the game to take on its modern form.

Football's growth in popularity, first with the colleges and then with the professional leagues, brought money and expertise to the game. The professionalization and growth of coaching staffs during the middle era allowed the development of a more sophisticated game, particularly after the introduction of two-platoon football. Very little of the sophistication that exists today could have occurred without unlimited substitutions. The next five chapters detail how that process took place during the middle era.

8

THE BALL, THE FIELD, AND STADIUMS (1906-1959)

Football's middle era saw reductions in the size of the football itself and the field on which the games were played, but witnessed extraordinary growth in the size, if not the sophistication, of its stadiums. Changes in the size of the football and field markings significantly affected the nature of play. At the same time, the transition from simple stadiums seating thousands to massive stadiums holding tens of thousands redefined the game's economics. The eagerness of fans crowding into large college stadiums raised the possibility of commercial opportunities outside the colleges as well. Professional football grew in fits and starts during the middle era, with more leagues failing than succeeding. Still, professional football ended the middle era positioned to rival the college game for America's attention.

THE BALL

Until 1912, the rules describing the football itself were underspecified; they simply required the ball to have an internal rubber bladder, a leather cover, and have the shape of a prolate spheroid. John Heisman described the problems with those rules, noting:

> ...so far as the rule was concerned, a team could have brought out a football as big as a barrel had they chosen to do so, and one that weighed a ton, or an ounce, and the other team would have been unable to pull a rule book to back up [their protest], so long as the blooming thing had the right shape.[19]

The 1912 rules had more detail, specifying a ball 28 to 28 1/2 inches around the length and 22 1/2 to 23 inches around the midsection. These specifications made the ball slimmer, so it was more aerodynamic and easily grasped by players without large hands.

The rules required a single ball to be used the entire game, which was problematic given the poorly drained fields of the day. Balls used in rainy games became waterlogged and muddy, interfering with passing, kicking, and general handling. A 1922 rule finally gave the referee the discretion to replace the ball at halftime during games played in wet conditions.

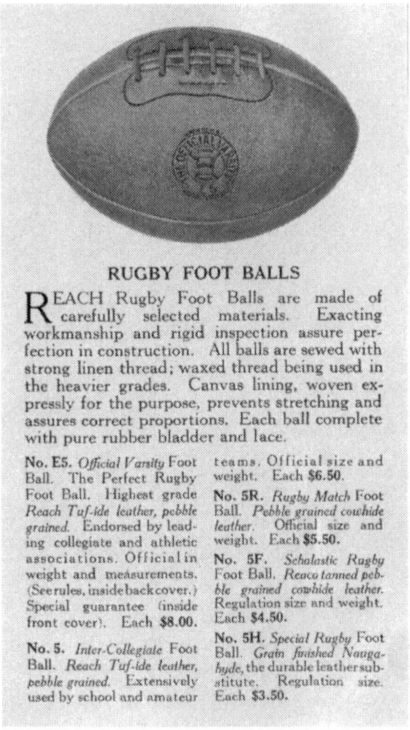

RUGBY FOOT BALLS

REACH Rugby Foot Balls are made of carefully selected materials. Exacting workmanship and rigid inspection assure perfection in construction. All balls are sewed with strong linen thread; waxed thread being used in the heavier grades. Canvas lining, woven expressly for the purpose, prevents stretching and assures correct proportions. Each ball complete with pure rubber bladder and lace.

No. E5. *Official Varsity* Foot Ball. The Perfect Rugby Foot Ball. Highest grade *Reach Taf-ide leather, pebble grained.* Endorsed by leading collegiate and athletic associations. Official in weight and measurements. (See rules, inside back cover.) Special guarantee (inside front cover). Each **$8.00.**

No. 5. *Inter-Collegiate* Foot Ball. *Reach Taf-ide leather, pebble grained.* Extensively used by school and amateur teams. Official size and weight. Each **$6.50.**

No. 5R. *Rugby Match* Foot Ball. *Pebble grained cowhide leather.* Official size and weight. Each **$5.50.**

No. 5F. *Scholastic Rugby* Foot Ball. *Reaco tanned pebble grained cowhide leather.* Regulation size and weight. Each **$4.50.**

No. 5H. *Special Rugby* Foot Ball. *Grain finished Naugahyde,* the durable leather substitute. Regulation size. Each **$3.50.**

Footballs or Rugby Foot Balls listed in a 1918 Reach catalog. (Reach Athletic Goods for Fall and Winter, B.H. Days Co., Los Angeles, 1918)

Beyond the size and shape of the football, a significant innovation came in the 1920s when valves became the preferred means of inflation. The internal bladders had been inflated and tied off like balloons until metal valves, similar to the air stems on bicycle inner tubes, were integrated into the bladders in 1923. The valve allowed the bladder to be inflated with a pump, keeping the bladder inflated longer, but the valve still sat under the leather cover, requiring the ball to be unlaced and relaced during the reinflation process.

Thankfully, the world has its share of Frank Buechners, who identify a problem and create a solution. Old Frank owned a tire shop in Grand Rapids, Michigan, and filled his spare time making inflatable toys for his grandchildren using old tires and inner tubes. Frustrated with having to unlace and relace the toys to reinflate them, Buechner designed an internal valve that mounted flush to the toy's surface, allowing for its inflation using a needle and pump. Buechner patented his invention in 1925 and marketed it to sporting goods manufacturers for use with inflatable balls. Inflatable balls with Buechner's valves hit the market in 1927, eliminating the need to unlace and relace balls and, by implication, the need for lacing. Manufacturers soon removed the laces from basketballs, soccer balls, volleyballs, and even rugby balls, but they remained on footballs due to their role in throwing forward passes.

Although the laces remained on footballs, they changed in number and form. Most pre-internal valve footballs had six laces, but most shifted to seven or eight laces with the eight-lace ball becoming the standard. The pre-internal valve footballs had thin, leather laces that did not rise substantially above the surface of the ball. Once the laces did not need to be pliable, their purpose shifted to helping quarterbacks throw tighter, longer, and more accurate spirals, so the laces became thicker and stiffer. That change eventually led to the disappearance of leather laces, the introduction of reinforced cotton laces, and now, polyvinyl chloride laces.

Beginning in the late 1920s, some manufacturers produced footballs that were thinner than specified in the rules, and passing-oriented teams began using them in games. This caused a bit of a hubbub until a nationwide survey of coaches revealed that most preferred the slimmer ball. Shortly after that, the 1934 rules reduced the circumference of the ball's midsection by 1 1/4 inch. The slimmer ball impacted the game in three ways. First, it was easier to grip and throw accurately. Second, the slimmer ball made the direction of the bouncing ball more erratic, making the path of fumbled balls less predictable and more amusing. Third, and sadly, the slimmer, pointier football caused the demise of the drop kick because the pointy ball bounced off the turf more erratically. The drop kick, which was being challenged by advancements in long snapping and placekicking techniques, fell into disuse.

In addition to changes in the football's shape and lacing, the ball went through a series of cosmetic changes during the middle era, primarily driven by the arrival of night games. Thomas Edison filed his first patent related to electric light bulbs in October 1878, two years after the IFA met to define football's first set of rules. Surprisingly, it took only fourteen more years to play the first college football game under the lights. More accurately, it took only fourteen years to play half of a football game under the lights since they stopped the 1892 Mansfield State Normal- Wyoming Seminary game at halftime due to poor lighting and fog. The 1890s and early 1900s saw a handful of games played under the lights, but outdoor games played under the lights did not occur on a semi-regular basis until the 1920s.

For no apparent reason, football games traditionally started at 2:00 P.M. or 2:30 P.M. Because games lasted only two hours, artificial lighting was not needed unless the match started late or lasted longer than usual. Things changed a bit after the introduction of Daylight Saving Time in 1918. A few years of late-season games ending at dusk led to a 1922 rule allowing referees to confer with the team captains at halftime to shorten the second half if needed. Some schools opted to start their games an hour earlier, a few lit their fields, and others painted their footballs white to make them more visible. Whoever first painted a football white is unknown, but we know Harvard practiced with a white football in 1922, and Washington did the same in 1924. Between those events, Cincinnati hosted Kentucky Wesleyan in a season-opening night game in 1923 using a white ball under primitive lighting conditions.

Advances in lighting technology and the building and renovation of stadiums led to an increased number of lighted fields by the end of the 1920s. Of course, the lighting was not up to current standards, which is why teams used a white ball. The rules committee formally approved white footballs in 1930 and mandated the addition of black stripes on either end of the white balls in 1941. White footballs remained in use well into the 1950s when the quality of stadium lighting improved to the extent that white balls were no longer needed.

Drake's Joe Makarewicz, holding a white ball with black stripes, hurdles a defender in a 1949 victory over South Dakota. (1950 Quax, Drake University yearbook, Drake University Archives & Special Collections)

An alternative to using a white ball with black stripes for night games was a brown or tan ball with white stripes. The first known use of white striping on the standard ball came in a 1935 night game between BYU and Northern Colorado. It seems that Northern Colorado objected to using a white ball because BYU wore white away jerseys. At the same time, Northern Colorado wore brown pants, so BYU objected to using a brown ball. Ultimately, the coaches agreed to use a brown ball painted with white stripes, allowing the game to carry on.

A Drake player runs with a double-striped ball in 1950. (1951 Quax, Drake University yearbook, Drake University Archives & Special Collections)

As with other elements of the game, the football world did not immediately settle on a single approach to striping the football. Some footballs had double stripes, and many had single stripes positioned closer to the laces than is standard today. Any of these alternative striping options might have become the norm, but they did not, and the football aficionados of the early 1950s settled on the striping pattern we know today.

THE FIELD

An earlier chapter described the 1903 rule change that allowed the player receiving the snap to advance the ball if he moved five yards right or left of the center. Similarly, a 1906 rule required players to be five yards right or left of the center before throwing a forward pass. The checkerboard field markings that supported those rules disappeared when the rules committee dropped both rules for the 1910 season. As a result, the field returned to its earlier markings with sidelines, goal lines, and stripes every five yards between the goal lines.

Field Dimensions and Markings (1910-1911)

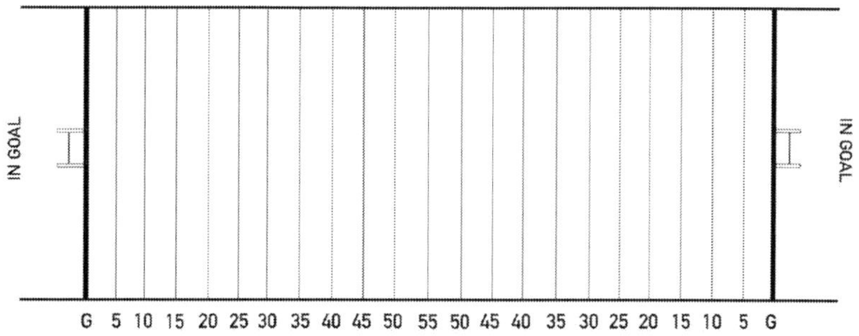

After the checkerboard era, the football field returned to the form used from 1882 to 1902.

The field markings used in 1910 mirrored those of 1882 to 1902, reflecting the fact that offenses had two ways to score: they could run the ball across the goal line or kick the ball through the uprights rising above the goal line. These markings remained appropriate after the introduction of the forward pass because offensive players had to catch the forward pass in the field of play and carry the ball across the goal line for a touchdown. Forward passes that crossed the goal line without first touching a player resulted in a touchback. That meant the "in goal" area did not yet need an end line because it would not have served a purpose.

The situation changed in 1912 when the rules changed to allow forward passes to be caught "in goal." The rule makers could have retained an "in goal" area of indeterminate depth or established an end zone twenty yards deep, but they opted for an end zone ten yards deep with an end line running parallel to the goal line.

Fans at the Polo Grounds in 1903 stand behind the goal line in the unmarked, "in goal" area. The Polo Grounds was among the locations that could not support the 130-yard field. (Leslie's Monthly, November 1903)

Just as the rule makers chose not to widen the field in 1906 due to the reinforced concrete stands at Harvard Stadium, similar constraints affected the field design in 1912. Adding two marked end zones as extensions on the 110-yard field would have made the marked field 130 yards long, a length some stadiums could not handle. The solution was to eliminate the 55-yard line, allowing the marked end zone to fit within almost any facility that handled the previously-sized field. The change in field length also moved kickoffs from the midfield line to the kicking team's 40-yard line.

Field Dimensions and Markings (1912-1926)

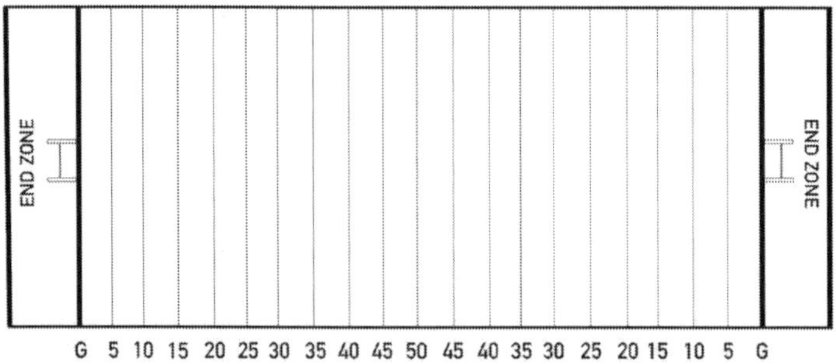

The field dimensions first used during the 1912 season have remained unchanged, though the goal posts have since been moved to the end line.

The 1912 rule that allowed receivers to catch forward passes thrown into the end zone also called for incomplete passes that crossed the goal line to result in a touchback. That rule affected play calling near the end zone until 1934 when it was changed to award a touchback only on the second incomplete pass thrown over the goal line in one set of downs. The rules committee eliminated that rule in 1938, so incomplete passes crossing the goal line were treated like incompletions anywhere else on the field.

A big change in the field markings came with the 1933 introduction of hash marks, which have played a significant but under-appreciated role in football's evolution. Before hash marks existed, each play started wherever the previous play ended (unless the previous play ended out of bounds). If the previous play ended one foot inside the sideline, the next play started from that spot.

The quarterback (#12) calling a play from scrimmage along the sideline in the 1922 Hamilton vs. Rochester game. (Postcard, Unknown Publisher, Personal Collection)

Having the ball spotted close to the sideline presented offenses with two choices. The first choice was to align in an unbalanced formation and run a play seeking to gain yardage. (Teams devoted portions of their playbooks and practices to running and defending sideline plays, so they were well prepared to do this.) The problem with sideline plays was that defenses also knew that offenses generally ran away from the sideline, and the defenses overplayed to that side. As a result, offenses commonly ran or passed the ball out of bounds, which caused the ball to be spotted fifteen yards infield for the next play, albeit at the cost of a down. (Deliberately running or throwing the ball out of bounds was a wasted play, much like spiking the ball today, but it gave offenses more flexibility on the next play.)

The lack of hash marks constrained play calling near the sidelines, but it did the same in the middle of the field. Without hash marks, sweeps and outside passes brought the risk of the runner being tackled near the sideline. That affected play calling, especially in the red zone, where teams had to consider the angle on potential field goal attempts.

After a 1932 study showed teams deliberately went out of bounds plays an average of fourteen times per game, college coaches recommended new methods for spotting the ball when play ended near the sideline. Shortly after the college coaches made their recommendations, the NFL had their championship game in Chicago. Due to frigid weather, the Bears moved the game from Wrigley Field to Chicago Stadium, an indoor basketball and hockey arena. The indoor field was 80 yards long and 45 yards wide rather than the standard 120 yards by 53 1/3 yards. Playing inside on a smaller field led to several rules adjustments, one of which was to spot the ball ten yards from the sideline when the previous play ended within ten feet of the sideline. While hash marks were not painted on the field, the 1932 NFL Championship game was the first in which the ball, by rule, was never spotted close to the sideline.

Both the college and NFL rule committees implemented hash marks for the 1933 season. Both started with hash marks ten yards infield, though the distance crept toward the center of the field over time. Today, the NFL hash marks align with the goal posts at 23 yards, 1 foot, and 9 inches infield; college hash marks are 20 yards infield; and high school hash marks are 17 yards and 8 inches infield, splitting the field into three equal zones.

Moving the hash marks further infield gave offenses a realistic option to each run play to the right or the left. The introduction of hash marks encouraged offensive formations that shifted ends out as wide receivers. Later, flankers replaced one of the running backs and so on. Each move required defenses to spread out, opening more options for the running and passing games.

It is now largely forgotten that the hash marks added in 1933 consisted solely of short stripes intersecting each chalked yard line, leaving playing fields of the 1930s to the mid-1950s barren compared to today. That remained the case until John Lockney laid down additional stripes in 1954. Lockney was a football fan from Waukesha, Wisconsin, who was frustrated by how frequently chain gangs came onto the field for measurements as well as the number of times officials incorrectly spotted the ball when the down marker was on the opposite side of the field. Unlike most fans who become frustrated with the officials, Lockney did something about it. Lockney's idea was to add short stripes parallel to and between the yard lines in the area of the hash marks, as well as adding short stripes outside the sidelines. (The outer Lockney Lines were painted outside the sidelines until the late 1960s. Why they moved inside is a story for a later chapter.)

Fenway Park marked for a Boston Patriots game on October 10, 1963. Note that the outer Lockney Lines are marked outside the sidelines. (Photo by Russ Adams, Boston Herald. Courtesy of Boston Public Library)

After Lockney added his lines on the local high school field, his frustration level dropped because the officials brought the chains onto the field less often, and their spotting improved. The lines also proved popular with fans and announcers who were better able to judge the yardage gained or lost on a play. First used for a Friday night game at Waukesha High School, the first college game on a field with Lockney Lines occurred the following day on the same field when Carroll met UW-Whitewater.

Lockney then convinced the University of Wisconsin to add his lines for a nationally televised game against Rice early in the 1954 season. Since there was only one college game televised each week at the time, the game between the #3 Badgers and the #11 Owls drew a large audience. Television viewers, announcers, and others praised Lockney's innovation and the word spread. The Badgers used Lockney Lines the remainder of the season, while the Green Bay Packers adopted Lockney Lines in 1955. Soon they were popping up elsewhere, and the college rules committee made them mandatory for the 1956 season. Unfortunately, John Lockney's contribution is largely forgotten, and the NCAA rule book refers to Lockney Lines only as "short yard-line extensions."

Just as Lockney Lines help fans and others determine the ball's location on the field, so do the various forms of yard markers (the numerals indicating which yard line is which). Yard markers are under-appreciated today, but imagine a world without these little gems. Without yard markers, fans would have to count the number of stripes between the nearest goal line and the ball to know where the ball is on the field. Yard markers also help officials control the game, particularly when respotting the ball as teams change directions between quarters.

The Stanford student card section executes a routine during the 1941 Rose Bowl, while yard markers sit quietly along the near sideline. (Unpublished Snapshot, Personal Collection)

The earliest yard markers were signs hung along stadium walls, bleacher fronts, or on posts near the sideline. Most appeared every ten yards (e.g., the 10-, 20-, 30-yard lines), but some stadiums placed them every five yards, as they did at Franklin Field in 1901. Others placed metal or wooden pedestals and placards placed along the sidelines. These proved problematic when players were injured falling into them, leading a South Dakota judge to patent yard markers made of spongy rubber in 1931.

The final step in the evolution of the yard marker came in the 1930s when schools in the East began chalking or painting field numbers directly on the field. Field numbers have grown larger over the years, and directional arrows were added in the 1980s, but have otherwise changed little because they were highly effective from the start.

Despite field numbers working well, Mike Casteel, Arizona's head coach from 1939 to 1948, came up with a better or, at least, a different idea. Casteel was a member of the AFCA rules committee in 1946 when he proposed numbering the yard lines from 0 to 100 rather than from 0 to 50 and back. As Casteel argued:

> ... the offensive team would always be going progressively up the field from the lower yardage numbers to the higher figures. It would help the spectators a great deal in following the game and be far easier for newspaper men and radio announcers. They could tell in a second that a pass from the 40 to the 70 yard line would be good for 30 yards.[20]

Casteel's idea never went anywhere, so frustration levels remain high among mathematically-challenged fans more than seventy years later.

Another aspect of field markings and equipment that changed during the middle era resulted from relocating the goal posts in the 1920s. Like rugby, football goal posts were on the goal line from the beginning, though that location proved problematic at times. Players ran into the posts when crossing the field on pass plays, and the posts obstructed rushing plays near the goal line. They interfered when punting out of the end zone and presented difficult kicking angles on many field goal attempts from inside the 20-yard line.

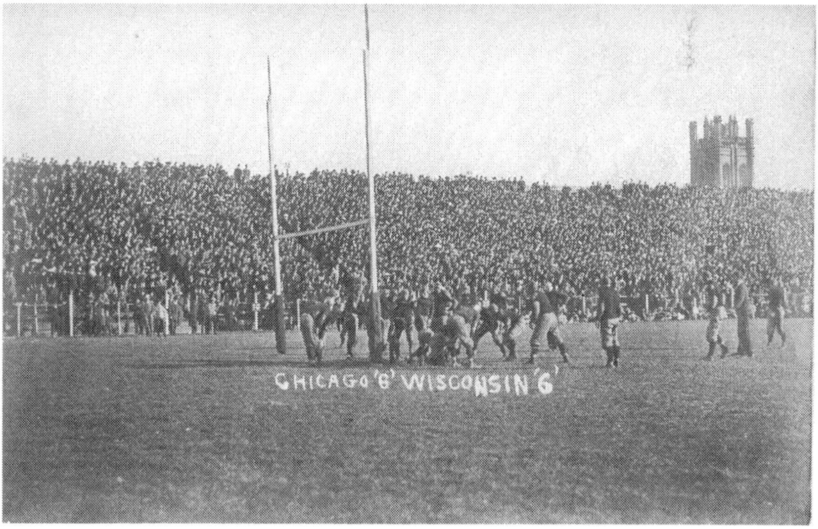

After fielding a Wisconsin punt in 1909, Chicago prepares to snap the ball while positioned immediately in front of the goal post. (Postcard, O.E. Nadeau, Personal Collection)

These issues lead to the goal posts being pushed back to the end line in 1927, which then created a new problem. With everyone accustomed to the goal posts being on the goal line, many thought the players and fans would confuse the goal line and end line. Some suggested visually demarcating the goal line with a second stripe, but the more popular option was to decorate the end zones to distinguish them from the rest of the field. Harvard painted diagonal stripes in the end zones, while several Southern schools added checkerboard patterns. Yale marked their goal lines by chalking the letter "G" on the turf; Princeton did nearly the same by stenciling a zero.

The engineers at Georgia Tech took a different path by placing "cushions," the forerunners of today's pylons, at the intersection of the goal line and the sidelines. Still others marked the intersection with a flag mounted on a taut spring, leading the NCAA to mandate the use of flags in 1940. (The goal line flags are the reason today's corner route was known as the flag route back in the day.)

The 1946 Wisconsin-Cal game program shows a Cal player scoring just inside the goal line flag. (Harry Bonath, Associated Students, University of California, Personal Collection)

Since the NFL used the college rule book through the 1932 season, they moved their goal posts to the end line in 1927 as well, but that changed when the NFL adopted a separate rule book in 1933. Twenty percent of NFL games during the 1932 season ended in ties, and, looking to increase scoring opportunities, the NFL returned the goal posts to the goal line in 1933, where they remained for more than thirty years.

THE STADIUMS

Harvard set the standard for college football stadiums in 1903, but Princeton's Palmer Stadium (45,745 seats) topped them in 1914, as did the Yale Bowl with permanent seating for 64,025 (expandable to more than 70,000). Most games did not fill those houses, but the return of their loyal sons for games among the Big Three filled them to their capacities. The stadiums of the Big Three and a few others were exceptions. Almost all major college football stadiums built before the 1920s remained simple wooden structures. A few other schools discussed building permanent stadiums, but no one moved ahead. It was as if university leaders were waiting for something big to happen.

The crowd at the less-than-opulent Georgetown Field watched their team suffer their only loss of the 1912 season to Jim Thorpe and Carlisle. (Harris & Ewing, Library of Congress)

America entered WWI in 1917 and left the war as the world's economic power, leading to an economic boom in the 1920s, a time during which the popularity of college football ballooned. Increased enrollments, expanded newspaper coverage, the beginnings of radio, and tremendous increases in the number of automobiles and paved roads resulted in increased interest in and accessibility to college football games. While reformers at the beginning of the century sought to limit the commercialization of football by restricting off-campus games, football's popularity in the 1920s caused schools to invest heavily in on-campus stadiums, many of which were dedicated as memorials to the WWI dead. Some were massive, with Michigan Stadium topping the heap at more than 84,000, followed by California Field at 73,000. A number exceeded 60,000, and many topped the 40,000 mark.

The stadiums of the 1920s continue to impact college football with twenty-eight of the sixty-four stadiums used by Power Five teams constructed that decade. Outside the campuses, stadiums built for civic pride or in pursuit of Olympic dreams included the Rose Bowl, Los Angeles Coliseum, Chicago's Soldier Field, San Francisco's Kezar Stadium, and Baltimore's Veterans Stadium.

The 66,210 seat Ohio Stadium was under construction when it served as a backdrop for a 1922 fraternity baseball game. (The Ohio State University Archives)

A second, smaller building boom occurred in the 1930s as part of Depression-era, federal works programs with the construction of the Alamo, Citrus, and Orange Bowls. Smaller-scale improvements and new stadiums were built at many other colleges and high schools as well.

The rise of these stadiums meant that fans were increasingly distant from the playing fields, which was particularly problematic in poorly-designed stadiums. The Yale Bowl, for example, was the model for many future stadiums, but only thirty-five percent of its seats were between the goal lines and fans at the top of the end zone stands were more than 200 yards from the playing field. The large stadiums also drew audiences more varied in their knowledge of the game, particularly as the rule book increased in complexity. The combination left fans in the stands wondering what the heck was going on down on the field. Thankfully, football's middle era witnessed changes in the game's customs, rules, and facilities to make the game more fan-friendly; one of those was the development of loudspeaker systems.

Before loudspeaker systems, speeches or announcements made in large facilities required a booming voice, a megaphone, or a good ear. There simply were no effective methods of amplifying sound until commercially viable loudspeaker technologies emerged in the 1910s. The first installation of note in the sporting world was the placement of sixty-three "enunciators" in Chicago's Comiskey Park in 1913. That system produced low-quality sound, made male voices sound higher than most men preferred, and did not transmit music well.

In the football world, the first college games to use loudspeakers to introduce the teams and provide play-by-play were USC games played at the year-old Los Angeles Coliseum in 1924. Loudspeakers became common at big stadiums in the late 1920s and early 1930s before trickling down to small college and high school fields in the late 1930s and 1940s.

Another communication technology that changed the in-stadium experience was the scoreboard. Most football stadiums of the early era did not have scoreboards; their first documented use came at Penn's home games in 1892, but that scoreboard, and most others used in the early years, was likely designed for baseball. Scoreboards designed for football came into prominence during the middle era as teams increasingly played in facilities purpose-built for football. Like baseball scoreboards, early football scoreboards were hand-operated and displayed the score and some combination of the quarter, down, distance, and ball location.

Regardless of the amount of information displayed, it was a challenge for scoreboard operators to ensure they displayed the correct information because they lacked the communication technology we take for granted today. Consider the 1909 Yale-Princeton game played before 35,000 fans in New Haven. Yale Field had scoreboards atop either end of the stadium whose operators did not have a means of communicating with people on the field. Early in the game, Yale blocked a Princeton punt to record a safety, but neither set of scoreboard operators could determine whether Princeton or Yale recovered the ball, so they did not post a score. (Referees of the time did not consistently signal touchdowns, safeties, and penalties to the press box and fans.) The operators did not correct the error the entire game, so many attendees did not know the game's score when they left the stadium, though they knew Yale won because the final score was 17-0.

Harvard solved the scoreboard accuracy problem by having a man on the sideline use arm motions and body contortions to signal information to the scoreboard operators. (He continued in this role until at least the mid-1920s.)

By the mid-1920s, major stadiums began connecting the sidelines and scoreboard operators by telephone. California Field was on the cutting edge of communication and scoreboard technology when they had two men wearing telephone headsets trail the plays along the sideline. One provided information to the scoreboard operators, the other to the press box. That was fancy stuff, but it was nothing compared to the advance the Californians made when they solved an issue that had dogged football fans since 1869.

From the beginning, fans, coaches, and players had a simple question that often went unanswered, "How much time remains on the clock?" By the 1920s, timekeeping was the responsibility of the field judge who, besides monitoring the game itself from his position in the defensive backfield, also tracked timeouts, delays of game, and other clock stoppages. By rule, the field judge had the responsibility to warn the team captains of the time remaining when there were between ten and five minutes left in the half. (The team captains could inquire about the remaining time three times in the last five minutes of a half.) Although this process worked for those on the field, it did not help the fans. The situation led some stadiums to place a timekeeper on the 50-yard line to monitor the game and control the scoreboard clock. The folks at Harvard Stadium claimed to be the first to pull off this feat in 1930, but our friends at California Field were ahead of their time by synchronizing the two in 1927.

A game clock was added to Wisconsin's Camp Randall scoreboard in 1927. Operated from the sideline, the clock moved in half-minute increments. (University of Wisconsin Digital Collections, 2017s00611)

Scoreboard clocks gave players on the field and fans a better sense of the time remaining in a game, and by the mid-1930s, their accuracy improved such that some conferences made the scoreboard clock the official game clock.

In addition to falling short on the fans' information needs, stadiums of the time often failed to meet fans' biological needs. The football stadiums built during the 1910s often did not have restrooms or permanent concession stands. Restrooms became standard elements of stadium construction and renovation plans in the 1920s, though their number remained limited by today's standard.

Spectators buy Cokes, candy bars, and cigarettes from a temporary stand outside the stadium during the 1939 Duke-North Carolina game. (Marion Post Wolcott, Library of Congress)

Similarly, even after stadiums added permanent concession stands, they sold a limited selection of food. Few menus included items beyond hot dogs, sandwiches, candy bars, and fruit washed down by soft drinks, coffee, and hot chocolate.

THE FOOTBALLS, fields, and stadiums all changed size and shape during the middle era. Some changes were driven by rule changes, while others arose organically and entered the rule book after significant use.

The ball became thinner and turned white as passing and night games became more common, with both entering the rule books only after periods of organic use. Changes to the playing field resulted both from direct rule changes and organic adaptations. The checkerboard field entered the game in 1903, disappearing in 1910 due to a rule change. Similarly, revisions to the forward passing rules brought the addition of the end line and the elimination of the 55-yard line in 1912, and the relocation of the goal posts resulted from explicit rule changes. Decorated end zones and flags came in reaction to rule changes, but did not enter the rule books until they were already widely used. Lockney Lines, on the other hand, were an innovation so simple and useful that they went from the idea stage to nationally mandated within fifteen months. It is unclear that Lockney Lines affected play on the field to any extent, but they provided an assist to game officials and made the game more enjoyable for fans.

The most visible symbols of the growth in popularity of football during the middle era were the massive stadiums built on college campuses and in major cities across the country. The rule makers did not order the building of those stadiums. Instead, stadiums rose in response to the desire of local fans to attend games, all while their experiences were upgraded by new-fangled loudspeakers, scoreboards, and game clocks that provided fans with additional information during games.

9

PLAY AND TECHNIQUES (1906-1959)

The most significant change to the rules of football in 1906 was the addition of the forward pass. In many respects, the approval of the forward pass was football's final break from rugby in that allowing players to throw and catch forward passes was football's most significant violation of rugby's "on side" rule. Throwing, catching, and defending forward passes had no correlates in rugby, so football with the forward pass became a substantially different game.

The forward pass ultimately proved successful in opening up football, but it took years, even decades, to do so. It took decades for teams to consistently align in passing-oriented formations with split receivers to spread the defense horizontally, and the downfield passing game we know today took another decade or two to arrive on the scene. Part of the delay resulted from limitations embedded in the rule book. Still, the more significant delay was due to coaches being unable to conceptualize a different style of game, to envision how to employ the forward pass. It is perhaps the best example from football's history of ideas and concepts needing to steep for a period before significant innovation could occur.

THE EARLY PASSING GAME

The rules of 1906 hobbled the passing game, but the greater restriction on its initial use was the lack of techniques and concepts needed to use the forward pass. In the forty years leading up to 1906, forward passes were common but illegal. Players lateraled more often than today, and a portion of those laterals went to players forward of the passer. The 1906 rules allowed forward laterals (aka passes) only if the passer was behind the line of scrimmage and five yards left or right of the center. An incompletion resulted in a loss of possession unless the ball contacted another player before hitting the ground. As a result, coaches were motivated to identify reliable methods of passing the ball and were unwilling to risk its use without a high likelihood of success. At least, that was the case for most coaches.

The standard offensive set in 1906 was the traditional T formation. Seven linemen aligned immediately next to one another; the quarterback stood a few feet behind the center; the fullback several yards behind the quarterback; with halfbacks on either side of the fullback or slightly in front.

Colorado's 1909 team aligned in a traditional T formation. The linemen are in four-point stances with tight splits, while the backs form a T. (Postcard, Unknown Publisher, Personal Collection)

The quarterback's role in 1906 was far different than today. Centers delivered the ball via a short toss to quarterbacks who stooped behind them or to their side. The rules allowed the quarterback (or whoever received the ball from center) to cross the line of scrimmage with the ball only after moving five yards left or right of the center. That meant quarterbacks were not inside running threats, and the odd snapping technique lessened their ability to run outside.

The center-quarterback exchange derived directly from picking up the ball from a rugby scrum. (Spalding's Official Foot Ball Guide for 1908)

Under those conditions, the quarterback's primary role was to take the snap and quickly lateral the ball before joining others in blocking for the runner.

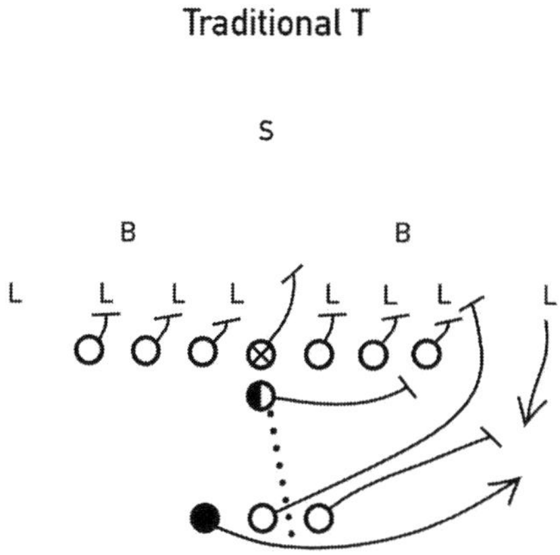

Illustration of a sweep from the traditional T formation. The center snaps the ball to the quarterback, who laterals to the left halfback before joining the other backs blocking to the right.

The forward pass was a challenge in 1906 because no one had ever thrown a legal forward pass, and the best techniques for doing so were not yet clear. We now know the overhand spiral is the most effective technique for passing a football -we struggle to conceive of alternatives- but that was not apparent in September 1906. Some held the ball in the flat of their hands, tossing the ball with a straight arm like one might toss a grenade. Others gripped the ball in one hand while the ball rested along the forearm and flung it end over end toward the receiver. The two-handed basketball set shot technique was used as well, particularly in the East. Swarthmore's coach, George H. Brooke, recommended passing the ball as follows:

> This [the following image] illustrates the correct method of making a long pass.

> The point of the ball is held in the palm of the hand with the fingers spread around it. The ball should be made to sail flat in the air. In passing the ball while on the run it should be thrown almost always with two hands, very much like a basketball player throws and passes.[21]

Before the 1906 season, a well-known coach thought the best passing technique was to fling the ball downfield as shown above. (Brooke, George H. 'How to Play Football Under the New Rules,' New York Tribune, September 23, 1906, Library of Congress)

During the 1906 season, most teams pitched the ball forward only a few yards or threw the ball high into the air to an intended receiver surrounded by teammates that kept defenders from hitting the receiver. (Neither offensive nor defensive pass interference existed until 1909.) Another common tactic had the passer shout a code word to his receiver as he threw the ball, indicating the receiver should turn around and look for the ball.

As most coaches and players sorted out these soon-to-be-forgotten techniques, Bradbury Robinson had already found the best one. Back in 1903, Robinson was practicing punting at Wisconsin when a teammate fielding his punts threw the ball back using the overhand spiral technique. Robinson, who had the large hands needed to grip the plump ball of the day, became intrigued and learned the technique before transferring to St. Louis University. He joined the St. Louis football team in 1904, and it was Robinson's good fortune that Eddie Cochems became the St. Louis coach in 1906.

Cochems spent the summer of 1906 thinking of ways to take advantage of the forward pass before taking his team to training camp in Wisconsin to escape the heat and humidity of St. Louis. While there, the team worked on passing plays with Robinson throwing overhand spirals, which Robinson, normally an end, threw after dropping into punt formation. Before returning to St. Louis, Cochems scheduled a game with Carroll University in early September, during which Robinson threw the first legal forward passes, leading his team to a 22-0 win. St. Louis went on to dominate its schedule, making regular use of the forward pass.

Pop Warner was another passing pioneer. His Cornell team threw eight passes in the first game of the 1906 season, his 1907 Carlisle team completed 8 of 16 passes against Penn in 1907, and he later integrated it into his new Single Wing offense. Most teams only toyed with the forward pass or used it in desperation. They had neither the players who could throw the ball accurately nor the concepts to design effective passing plays. Instead, they used the same old running attack as in previous years but now had to gain ten yards in three downs rather than the five yards of old. It was not a winning formula. In the 1906 Harvard-West Point game, for example, each team earned one first down the entire game, with Harvard winning 5-0 by blocking an Army field goal attempt and running it back for a touchdown. The frustration resulting from the game was voiced in the *New York Times* two days later.

Saint Louis quarterback, Bradbury Robinson, throwing an overhand spiral forward pass in 1906. (Courtesy of Saint Louis University Libraries Archives & Digital Services)

> If it is possible to devise auxiliary plays, onside kicks, and forward passes that can be practiced until a team is sure of short five-yard gains by certain handling of the ball, without the liability of losing it at least 50 percent of the time by fumbling or interception, then it is possible to build up a real attack under these rules, and the game will become scientific and worth while, but the experts, coaches, players, tacticians, and others who make a study of play are not yet convinced that this can be done-that the game will not become a mere kicking duel, decided by luck.[22]

In general, Midwestern teams developed more sophisticated passing attacks than those in the East, but the limited intersectional play meant the Eastern press did not see many Midwestern teams in action. That changed on November 1, 1913, when little-known Notre Dame traveled to West Point to take on undefeated Army. Led by senior team captain and end, Knute Rockne, the Irish completed 14 of 17 passes for 243 yards and complemented the passing attack with a strong ground game. The way Notre Dame tossed the pea around the field on the way to a 35-13 victory astounded the New York sportswriters, particularly because that was Army's only loss that year. The polished Notre Dame passing game demonstrated the power of the forward pass when given time and imagination. More important, it moved the forward pass from a game element whose permanent presence was in doubt to one that became cemented in the game of football.

The Notre Dame-Army game also brought exposure to the Notre Dame Box, one of the two main offensive systems that arrived on the scene during the

1910s. The other key system was the Single Wing, popularized by Pop Warner at Carlisle and Pitt. The Single Wing was the product of the football rule changes and Warner's creative genius encountering a generational athlete.

OPENING UP THE GAME

The rule forcing the player who received the snap to be five yards from the center before crossing the line of scrimmage was dropped in 1910. Many saw this move as providing greater possibilities for T formation quarterbacks and, while that was true, Pop Warner took the opportunity to create a new offense based on a direct snap to a deep tailback. Warner's Single Wing, so named because one of the halfbacks aligned just outside an end, positioned the quarterback and fullback on the same side of the formation as the wing. The tackle on the weak side often shifted to the strong side as well, so the formation was unbalanced in both the line and the backfield.

Single Wing

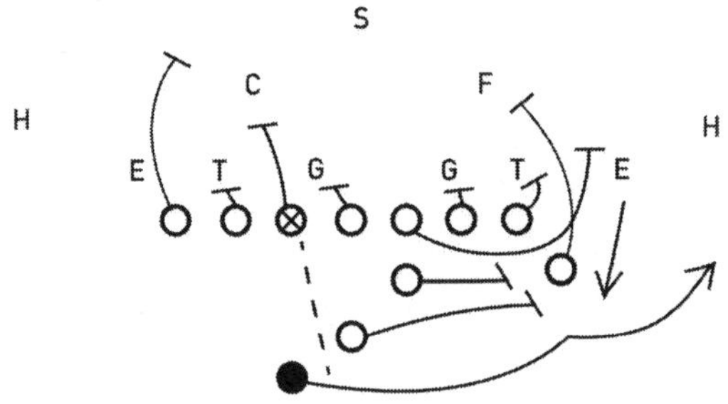

Illustration of a sweep from the Single Wing. The center snaps the ball directly to the deep tailback, leading him as he begins his motion to the right. (Adapted from Warner, A Course in Football for Players and Coaches, 1912)

Like its predecessors, the core of the Single Wing was a power running game that used blocking backs, but it also used angle or down blocking, pulling linemen, and "mouse trap" blocks. ("Mouse" fell out of use, leaving us with trap blocks.) The focus of the offense was the tailback who, ideally, was a triple threat, able to run, pass, and punt at a high level. Warner had such a player in Jim Thorpe. The direct snap from center enhanced the speed of sweeps, which, in turn, increased the effectiveness of reverses to the wing. The wing's positioning also made it easier for the wing to release into pass patterns with the ball generally being thrown by the tailback on a fake sweep. The Single Wing became football's most widely used offense, supplemented over the next fifty years with deceptive elements such as spinners. (The quarterback received the snap and spun 180 or 360 degrees while handing off or faking and running).

Warner also created the Double Wing formation, which placed backs in wing positions on both sides of the formation. Other than the offset quarterback, the Double Wing was balanced, threatening defenses on either side of the ball and was highly effective for misdirection and passing plays. Passing from the Double Wing typically involved a direct snap to the fullback (set deep behind the center), who then dropped back a few steps to pass the ball. Although Warner introduced the Double Wing in 1912 with the Single Wing, it attracted limited attention until Warner made it his focal formation in the 1920s when Ernie Nevers was his All American fullback at Stanford.

Warner's Single Wing had staying power. The Pittsburgh Steelers were the last NFL team to use the Single Wing when they abandoned it in 1952. Princeton's Dick Kazmaier was the last Single Wing tailback to win the Heisman Trophy, earning the award in 1951, but major college teams continued running the Single Wing into the late 1950s.

Whereas the Single Wing emphasized power, the core of the Notre Dame Box was deception. Its origins lay in sets and shifts used by Amos Alonzo Stagg when Jesse Harper played at Chicago in 1905. Harper adapted the offense at Notre Dame, and Rockne extended it further after taking over for Harper in 1918.

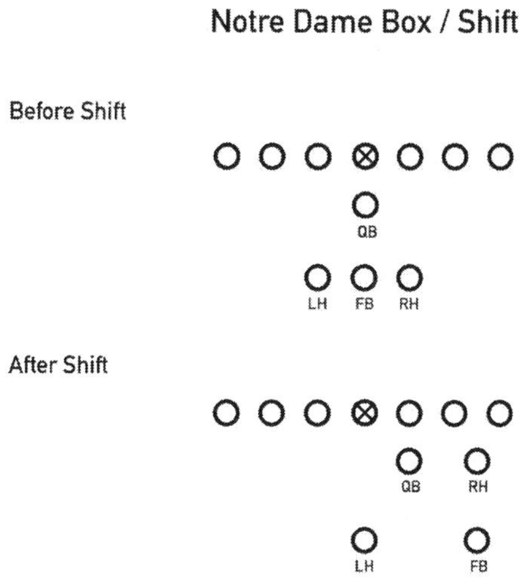

The Notre Dame Box had all four backs shift positions shortly before the snap to create a box that was strong right or left.

Teams running the Notre Dame Box aligned in the traditional T with the backs shifting to one side of the formation shortly before the snap. The shift happened quickly enough that defenders struggled to realign, resulting in an offensive numbers advantage to the strong side. When snapping the ball to the deep tailback, the Notre Dame Box mirrored mass and momentum plays in that it overwhelmed defenses with numbers. But they also snapped the ball to the offset quarterback and used misdirection to keep defenses from overplaying to the strong side. In addition, teams using the Box often had the backs switch positions from play to play to match players' strengths with the play call. The ability to leverage the strengths of different backs separated the Box from the Single Wing, which was less effective without a top triple threat. In that respect, Jim Thorpe epitomized the Single Wing, while Notre Dame's Four Horsemen of the Apocalypse -Harry Stuhldreher, Don Miller, Jim Crowley, and Elmer Layden- became the quintessential Notre Dame Box backfield.

The Notre Dame Box also took baby steps in stretching the defense horizontally by sometimes flexing the ends a yard or two outside the offensive tackles. Creating a gap between the offensive tackle and end forced defenses to move their defensive end further out, pull another man from the line of scrimmage to back up the line, or suffer the consequences. The wider splits also allowed the end to release downfield more easily on passing plays.

Notre Dame became dominant in the 1920s running this offense, as evidenced by Rockne having the highest career winning percentage among major college coaches. The Box was also widely used in the early NFL. Curly Lambeau, who played at Notre Dame in 1918, used the Box to win three NFL championships from 1929 to 1931. He extended the Box in the 1930s and 1940s after drafting end, Don Hutson. Hutson was difficult to defend one-on-one, so Lambeau sometimes positioned him well outside the offensive tackle, pioneering the split end or wide receiver position. Ends that remained aligned near the offensive tackles became known as tight ends, and, over time, the different end positions became specialized with the physical requirements of the positions diverging.

One complaint lodged against the Notre Dame Box was that its late shift gave an unfair advantage to the offense, much like the momentum plays of the 1880s and 1890s. This complaint reached a crescendo in the 1920s when another innovation arrived on the scene: huddling. As discussed earlier, teams seldom huddled during the early era. As each play ended, teams immediately lined up, the quarterback reviewed the defense's alignment, called his signals, and the center snapped the ball. It was a continuous game, like rugby. Huddling, as we know it, came into use when Bob Zuppke, who won four national championships coaching at Illinois, had the Illini huddle regularly in 1921. Huddling allowed teams to settle down between plays, and ensured the quarterback's teammates heard the play call above the noise of the increasingly large crowds. Huddling also simplified play calling because quarterbacks did not need to use fake or dummy calls as they did when calling signals at the line of scrimmage.

The primary benefit of huddling for the Illini was that huddling caught defenses off guard. Like Notre Dame's pre-snap shift, Zuppke's Illini broke the huddle, quickly moved to their final pre-snap positions, and snapped the ball shortly after getting aligned. Critics charged the Illini gained an unfair advantage by not stopping before the snap, the same criticism levied against teams that used pre-snap shifts.

The "tea partiers," as sportswriters derided them, were also criticized for slowing down the game, though a study or two showed huddlers snapped the ball as quickly as those calling signals at the line. Since football did not have a rule against huddling or a requirement that teams snap the ball within a set time after the previous play, the real issue was that huddlers broke the long-standing convention of calling signals at the line of scrimmage. Among those who did not like the break from the convention were some game officials, who had the discretion to penalize teams for delay of game. A few in the East choose to apply that discretion when Rutgers was penalized six times for huddling against Penn early in the 1922 season. Although each infraction cost them a measly two-yard penalty, it was enough for Rutgers to abandon the tactic.

The criticism of huddling, combined with concerns about pre-snap shifts, led to a 1927 rule requiring players to stop for one second before the snap (extended to "at least" one second in 1930). The 1927 committee also established rules of thumb that huddles last no more than fifteen seconds, and plays start within thirty seconds of the ball being made ready. The rules for making the ball ready for play became increasingly specified -it was during this period that the officials took responsibility from the offensive center for setting the ball- and the 30-second rule of thumb became a formal rule in 1939.

Well into the 1930s, the forward pass remained more of a threat than a reality. Defenses had to align and be prepared to counter the pass, but offenses mostly ran the ball, and defenses focused on stopping the run. In 1932, the first year the NFL kept official game statistics, the average team completed four of twelve passes thrown per game. Similarly, when consistent game statistics came to the colleges in 1937, the average offense completed five of thirteen pass attempts for 64.5 yards per game. Teams rushed for nearly 139 yards, meaning they had 198 yards of total offense, which yielded an average of 10.1 points per game. Football was not yet a high-octane game.

The halfback or fullback who received the direct snap from the center handled most of the passing, though teams relying on misdirection spread the passing load a bit more. Pass routes remained primitive and included combinations such as sending both ends downfield to force the single deep safety to defend one or the other. The short passing game was similarly rudimentary with wings or other backs running into the flats while the ends ran in or out routes.

Teams could be highly successful despite having inaccurate and ineffective passing attacks. The Chicago Bears won the 1933 NFL Championship during a 13-game season in which they completed 74 of 212 passes. Eleven players threw at least one pass for the Bears, with five throwing twenty-five or more. The eleven passers threw a combined twenty-nine interceptions, second highest in the league. By comparison, Ben Roethlisberger led the NFL in interceptions thrown in 2018 with 16 interceptions on 675 attempts. That means Roethlisberger threw slightly more than half as many interceptions as the 1933 Bears while attempting three times as many passes and completing six times their number.

Poor pass blocking contributed to the ineffective passing game, forcing most to rely on play-action passing. In addition to halfback passes thrown off sweeps, Pop Warner developed a new form of play-action pass off the Statue of Liberty play in 1927. The Statue of Liberty play typically involved a direct snap to a tailback who held the ball high as if intending to pass. Instead of passing the ball, he pulled it down, holding it behind his back in his non-throwing hand while a teammate ran behind him, took the ball, and ran it around end. Pop Warner's 1927 Stanford team ran variations of the Statue of Liberty throughout the year, but they saved a special version for their Big Game with Cal. Leading 7-6 with the ball inside Cal's 10-yard line midway through the fourth quarter, Stanford ran what appeared to be a Statue of Liberty play. Instead of giving the ball to the back sweeping to the left, Stanford's Biff Hoffman kept the ball, concealed it on his hip, and ran around the right end for a touchdown. Nicknamed the "bootlegger" by the Stanford players, the concept of the passer rolling opposite the run action became a standard part of most teams' passing attacks. (It is worth noting that Stanford's bootleg and other backfield trickery upset Eastern sportswriters when used against Army the next year. Tactics viewed as unsportsmanlike and contemptible then are seen as quite ordinary now.)

Pass blocking also suffered, in part, because the rules did not restrict ineligible receivers from going downfield. Rather stay on the line in pass protection, offensive linemen went downfield as blockers or decoys. (That changed a bit in 1939 when ineligible receivers could only be downfield on passes caught behind the line of scrimmage.) Offensive linemen were useful decoys because most were the same size as the backs, the pre-snap shifts confused the defenders, and few teams wore numbers on the front of their jerseys.

Even teams that wore numbers on the front of their jerseys did not assign them based on position, but despite the challenges facing defenders, few passing attacks were effective.

Harvard's receiver catches a screen pass against Centre (wearing striped jerseys) in 1920. The location of the chains on the opposite sideline show the offensive linemen and receiver are beyond the line of scrimmage at the time of the catch. (Haughton, Football and How to Watch It, 1922)

Pass protection improved when the concept of cup or pocket protection arrived in the mid- to late-1940s. Paul Brown often receives credit for devising cup protection while coaching the AAFC's Cleveland Browns despite Dana X. Bible describing cup protection in his 1947 *Championship Football*, so the originator of cup protection remains in dispute. Whereas offensive linemen had typically attacked their assigned defenders in a straight line across the line of scrimmage, cup protection had the center and guards give ground grudgingly. At the same time, the tackles dropped a step or two before taking on defenders rushing from the outside. The protection also improved because coaches began teaching quarterbacks to stay in the pocket and throw more quickly.

When the forward pass was in its infancy, defenders hit passers after they threw the ball, but a 1920 rule introduced the roughing the passer penalty. It was a controversial rule because it afforded protection to one player and not another. The Big Ten eliminated the roughing the passer rule in 1922, reasoning that it was the passers' responsibility to protect themselves and the existing unnecessary roughness rule protected all players. By 1928, the Big Ten's view won the day, and passers lost their special protections nationwide.

By 1938, the NFL, which openly acknowledged they were in the entertainment business, reinserted the roughing the passer penalty to protect Sammy Baugh and other passers whose skills put butts in the seats. The NCAA continued its wishy-washy stand and inconsistent enforcement until 1979 when an explicit roughing the passer rule returned to the college game.

PASSING OFFENSES

The evolution of football offenses did not stop with the Single Wing and Notre Dame Box. The rules requiring players to pause for one full second before the snap deflated the offenses based on tricky shifts and led coaches to seek alternative ways to gain ground. Many coaches looked to the Short Punt formation, which preceded the forward pass but provided one formation from which teams could threaten to run, pass, or punt on any down.

In traditional punt formations, the ends aligned wide, much like the gunners in punt coverage today. In the Short Punt formation, the ends aligned two yards wide of the tackles on every play. One back took a position one yard behind the line of scrimmage between the strong-side tackle and end. A second, on the weak side, was two yards off the time between the guard and tackle. A third aligned two yards back behind the tackle, while the tailback, the key to the offense, stood five yards behind the center. Their positioning allowed ends and backs to release into their routes quickly, while the center could snap the ball to multiple backs for inside runs, reverses, and sweeps. And as the name of the formation indicates, the tailback's ability to punt forced defenses to keep at least one defender deep at all times.

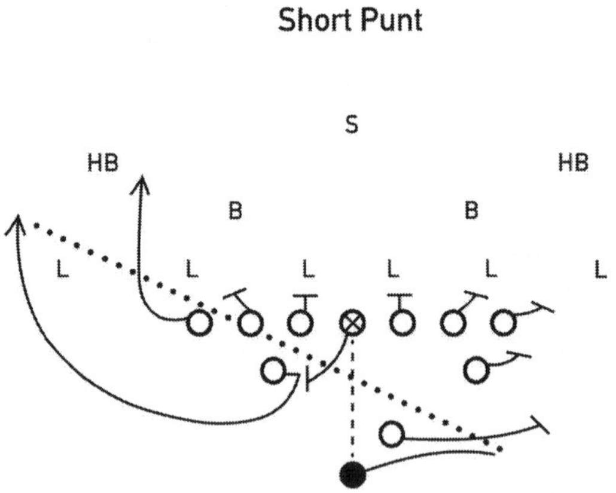

The short punt formation offered rushing, punting, and passing options, including the throwback pass.

Like the Single Wing, the Short Punt formation was difficult to stop when it had a triple threat tailback, but it differed from the Single Wing in valuing the tailback's arm over his legs. Michigan executed the offense best, starting with Benny Friedman in the mid-1920s and ending with Forest Evashevski in the late 1930s. Edward Dooley, a sportswriter and 1924 Dartmouth All America, commented on Michigan's short punt formation in 1934, saying:

> ... the formation is splendidly adapted to forward passing and Michigan has made much of that in recent years. Many old-time coaches feel that no formation has ever been invented which is as strong, as dangerous, as deceptive and as easy to run from as the short kick formation. It gives the elusive runner a good chance to get into the open field. It gives the line bucker an opportunity to show his ability. It makes possible hidden ball plays, end sweeps and criss-cross plays. And it gives the aerial game all that can be desired.[23]

In some respects, the Short Punt formation was a forerunner of today's spread, but it lacked key elements of modern offenses, including wide receivers, passing trees, cup protection, and option plays.

Football's evolution continued thanks to Ralph Jones, who recognized that the Single Wing, Notre Dame Box, and Short Punt formations had a common weakness. Every play started by snapping the ball four to six yards behind the line of scrimmage, sacrificing space and wasting time. Jones was Illinois' basketball coach and an assistant football coach from 1912 to 1920, before taking over as the coach and athletic director at Lake Forest College near Chicago. He had success at Lake Forest until George Halas, who played basketball and football under Jones at Illinois, hired him as the Chicago Bears coach in 1930. Jones began using the modern T formation, which differed from the traditional T in that the linemen took wider splits, and the quarterback aligned immediately behind the center, hands in the center's crotch, taking the snap via a direct handoff.

Taking the snap by direct handoff was a revolutionary technique affecting both the running and passing games. The quarterback received the ball quickly and consistently, allowing him to reliably hand the ball to a halfback on dive plays that hit the hole faster than any in football to that time. The linemen's wider splits and the speed in which the halfback hit the hole enabled brush blocking, that only required the offensive line to shield defenders from the hole rather than driving them from the point of attack.

The success of the modern T and the passing game also gained an assist from a rule change resulting from a controversial play in the 1932 NFL Championship game. Fullback Bronco Nagurski had taken the ball for a plunge up the middle but saw his path blocked by Portsmouth defenders, so Nagurski jumped into the air and threw the ball to Red Grange for the game-winning touchdown. Portsmouth supporters contended that Nagurski was within five yards of the line of scrimmage at the time of the throw, which would have made the pass illegal by the rules of the day, while Nagurski claimed he had backed up before throwing the pass.

The controversy resulted in the NFL changing its rules in 1933 to allow forward passes to be thrown from anywhere behind the line of scrimmage. While the jump pass itself largely faded from use, the Nagurski Rule ultimately opened up the quick passing game. Every bubble or slip screen to a wide receiver; every pass from a three-step drop; every rollout, bootleg, or scramble pass thrown from within five yards of the line of scrimmage descends from that rule change. It was a big deal and allowed for quicker, more accurate pass plays that did not require extended pass blocking.

The modern T formation continued morphing during the 1930s when Jones returned to Lake Forest after winning the 1932 NFL championship. Critically, Halas regularly consulted with Clark Shaughnessy, who had succeeded Amos Alonzo Stagg at the University of Chicago in 1933. Shaughnessy had success during his first few years at Chicago with Jay Berwanger running the ball and winning the first Downtown Athletic Club Trophy, renamed in 1936 after John Heisman's death. However, the University of Chicago's president had other ideas about the value of football, starving the team of resources and talent before abolishing the sport after the 1939 season.

Despite a 6-23-2 record in his last four years at Chicago, Shaughnessy remained a top football strategist which led Stanford to hire him to revive its moribund program in 1940. Shaughnessy implemented his version of the T formation, and went undefeated his first year, including a 1941 Rose Bowl win. One tactic popularized by Shaughnessy was to send a halfback in motion across the formation to spread out his offense and the defense. (In the 1950s, it became popular to forego the motion and simply position the back between the tight end and the sideline, creating the flanker position.

Modern T

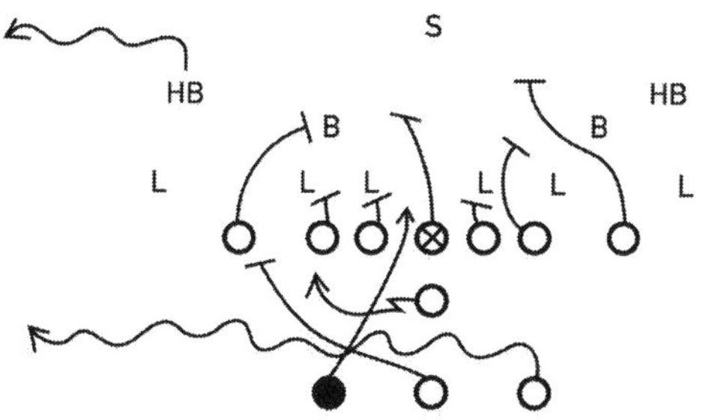

The right halfback motions across the formation before the left halfback dive versus a 6-2 diamond defense. Note that the motion man causes a defensive back to follow him outside.

However, the most significant contribution of Shaughnessy's modern T was the transformation of the quarterback from a glorified blocker to the central figure in the offense. After handing off or faking to the dive back, the quarterback turned his back to the defense and dropped back from the line of scrimmage, all while hiding the ball or executing fakes. After completing the drop back, the quarterback was in position to throw to the right, left, or center of the field. Those movements became a central element of the passing game for the next eighty years.

Stanford's Gallarneau (#29), in motion on the 50-yard line, draws the Nebraska defensive halfback to the outside during the 1941 Rose Bowl. (Unpublished Snapshot, Personal Collection)

Linebackers quickly learned to drop into coverage upon seeing quarterbacks drop back. During one Packers-Bears game in the early 1940s, Buckets Goldenberg, a Packers linebacker, spotted a tell or difference in Sid Luckman's stance on plays in which he dropped back to pass. Every time Goldenberg noticed Luckman in that stance, Goldenberg immediately dropped into pass coverage. In turn, the Bears center, Bulldog Turner, picked up Goldenberg's tendency and suggested the Bears show the dropback fake before giving the ball to fullback Bill Osmanski on a delayed handoff. The play proved successful and was the origin of the draw play, adding to the cat-and-mouse game played by offenses and defenses.

Halas, Jones, and Shaughnessy were not the only source of innovation in football at the time. One year after Shaughnessy implemented the modern T at Stanford, Don Faurot began running the Split T at Missouri. The offenses differed from one another in two key respects. First, Faurot put horizontal pressure on defenses by using even wider splits in the line than those used with the modern T. The splits among the backs also widened.

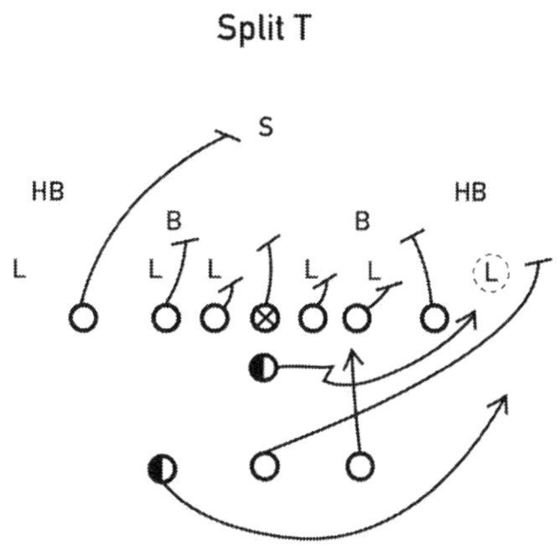

Faurot's Split T added horizontal space between the offensive linemen, faked to the dive back, and optioned the last defender on the line of scrimmage.

Second, and more important, the Split T introduced the option running attack to football. As in the modern T, the quarterback aligned under center, and his first movement post-snap was to give or fake a quick-hitting halfback dive. The Split T's dive play was predetermined, meaning the quarterback called the give or fake in the huddle; it was not an option read. After faking the dive, the quarterback continued moving to the outside and parallel to the line of scrimmage, reading the defensive end who was left unblocked by the offensive line. If the defensive end penetrated the backfield or moved to the outside, the quarterback kept the ball and turned upfield. On the other hand, if the defensive end attacked the quarterback, the quarterback pitched to the sweeping halfback. (Unlike the one-handed, thumb-under pitch used in later forms of the option, the Split T quarterback tossed the ball underhand using both hands.) Since the quarterback ran directly behind the line of scrimmage on the base series, he was within five yards of the line of scrimmage and could not legally pass the ball until the college rules changed in 1945. Even after the rule change, Split T quarterbacks remained too close to the line to pass effectively, so the halfbacks handled the passing, as they did in the Single Wing.

Like many innovative coaches, Faurot's coaching tree included several assistants who themselves played significant roles in the game of football. Faurot interrupted his tenure at Missouri to coach the Navy's Iowa Pre-Flight team in 1943 where his assistants included Jim Tatum and Bud Wilkinson, both of whom used the Split T as head coaches during the 1940s and 1950s. Tatum won the 1953 national title at Maryland, while Wilkinson won three national titles at Oklahoma and still holds the major college record of forty-seven consecutive wins. Whether influenced by Shaughnessy or Faurot, the majority of major college and professional teams ran some variation of the T formation by the late 1940s. Other variations of the modern T soon followed, including the Wing T.

The Wing T was developed by Dave Nelson while coaching Maine from 1948 to 1950 and Delaware from 1951 to 1965. Nelson was a Single Wing halfback under Fritz Crisler at Michigan and used the Single Wing at the start of his coaching career before becoming frustrated with its reliance on a great tailback. His Wing T put the quarterback under center (as in the modern T) while borrowing heavily from the Single Wing through its use of a wing, double teams, pulling lineman, and backfield fakes. Although teams could pass effectively from the Wing T, it was a run-first offense emphasizing deception through series plays. For example, in the Buck Sweep series, the line movement and backfield action appear the same to the defense regardless of whether the ball goes to the dive (fullback), sweep (halfback), or waggle (quarterback). The ability to spread the carries across multiple backs was another attraction of the Single Wing, much like the old Notre Dame Box.

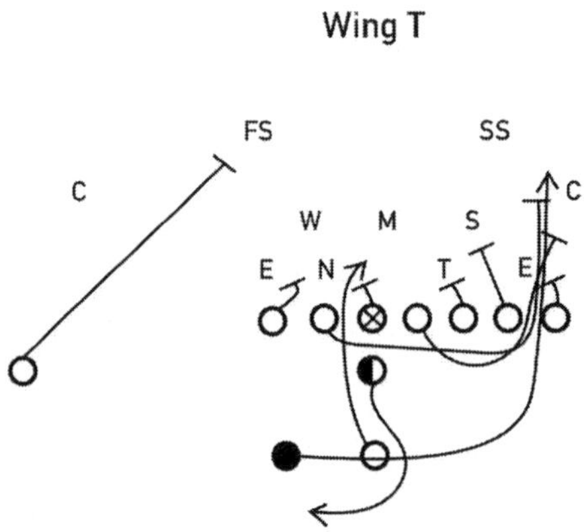

The Wing T's Buck Sweep Series shows the same look regardless of whether the ball goes to the dive, sweep, or quarterback waggle.

Although the originators of the Modern T and Wing T began with tight formations, both could spread the field by sending a back in motion or aligning an end wide. These ultimately transitioned into the pro or split back formations with a flanker and wide receiver.

KICKING GAME

Football during the middle era marched away from its kicking roots, only to see the kicking game reinvigorated during the modern era thanks to innovations in kicking techniques.

Kickoffs saw little change during the middle era. Besides shifting the kickoff from the 55-yard line to the kicking team's 40-yard line in 1912, the primary difference involved the use of tees. Since kickers could not use artificial tees, they either had a teammate hold the ball, or they built tees from dirt and scraps of sod lying around the playing field. Some kickers supplemented the on-field materials by keeping a bag of dirt on the sideline and bringing a double handful onto the field to form their tee. Others got around the ban on artificial tees by using molded clay tees, though a 1917 rule put a stop to that approach. Of course, the search for materials and the building of tees took time, which made the building of a tee a potential stalling tactic, so the rule makers banned all tees in 1924.

Tees had a return engagement in 1944 when one-inch artificial tees were approved for kickoffs. One-inch tees for field goals and extra points became legal in 1948, and two-inch tees became legal in 1958.

Punting only saw a few changes during the middle era as well. Recall that an 1894 rule required players to raise one hand in the air to signal their intention to fair catch. The rule worked well until 1905 when some return teams had one player signal for the fair catch while another player caught the punt and returned it. Other teams had multiple players signal for a fair catch. Though neither action violated the letter of the law, they violated its spirit, leading to a 1907 rule change that allowed only one player on the receiving team to signal for a fair catch with that signal applying to the entire receiving team.

One other event worth mentioning occurred in punting during the middle era, and that is due to its being an example of a dumb idea. As we all know, punting is a simple act in which the punter takes a step or two, drops the ball, and kicks it before it hits the ground. Not satisfied with snapping the ball to a back who punted the ball as God intended, a few coaches over thought the process and snapped the ball to an up back, who held the ball a few feet off the ground for the punter. To ensure the technique was kosher, its developers asked the rules committee to redefine the punt in 1934 to allow a second player to join the action. After that, the rule read: "A Punt is made by a player holding or dropping the ball and either he or another player kicking it before it touches the ground."[24]

Photographs of this folly show the punting team in a Single Wing formation with one back a few yards behind and to the offensive right of the center. Upon receiving the snap, the back swiveled left toward the punter, holding the ball at the desired height and angle until the punter booted the oval. The whole process made little sense other than for teams with one-armed punters. Since most teams had two-armed punters, however, the two-person punting technique disappeared as quickly as it came upon the scene.

More substantive changes occurred with extra points and field goals.

Entering the middle era, the extra point attempt was a free kick. The kicker and holder were the only kicking team players involved in the play; their teammates stood or sat on the field behind them. The defenders, meanwhile, positioned themselves behind the goal line and could legally rush the kicker only after the holder touched the ball to the ground. Finally, the referee stood, squatted, or laid on the ground near the holder to monitor the placement of the ball, raising his arm once the ball touched the ground to signal that the defense could rush the kicker.

Oregon's Bill Steers attempts an extra point against the charging Idaho defense, while his teammates sit on the ground behind him. (1921 Oregana, University of Oregon yearbook)

The extra point process changed in 1920. The rule makers sought to make the extra point process easier to increase the likelihood that teams scoring touchdowns would earn more points than teams making two field goals. They did so by eliminating the puntout and allowing the scoring team to attempt the extra point from anywhere on the field. In addition, the defense could not rush the kicker.

Missouri attempts an extra point while the Oklahoma defense relaxes in the end zone in 1921. (University of Missouri, 1922 Savitar)

The point-after rules were changed once again in 1922 with the scoring team receiving the ball at the five-yard line. From there, they had the choice to attempt the extra point via place kick, drop kick, run or pass with the defense contesting all four options. Offensive penalties on the attempt resulted in the offense losing the opportunity to score the point, while defensive penalties resulted in a point being awarded to the offense. The ball was placed on the three-yard line starting in 1924 and has shifted between the two- and three-yard lines ever since.

The next big set of changes in the try after touchdown came in 1958 when the rules committee sought to reduce the number of tie games and, trying to pique fan interest, compete with the NFL's more exciting style of play. Their big move was to award two points for converting the try by running or passing the ball; an approach the NFL adopted in 1994.

The point values and process of attempting field goals changed substantially during the middle era as well. The field goal's value dropped from four to three points in 1909 following a shift in thinking about the relative merits of individual versus team play. Those supporting the reduction in the field goal's value believed that the eight points earned for two field goals should not exceed that of one touchdown and an extra point. They considered a team's ability to score a touchdown to be the ultimate sign of team play, while successful field goals meant the team failed to score a touchdown and relied on the skill of one player to score points.

Although the center snap for placed field goals arose in the 1890s, the process remained anything but automatic, and many teams continued using the drop kick. In seeking a more consistent snap, George Foster Sanford, the Rutgers coach and College Football Hall of Fame inductee, devised a process for snapping and holding on field goal attempts even more bizarre than the two-person punt mentioned earlier.

Sanford's multiple kick began by snapping the ball to the quarterback who knelt in a position comparable to today's field goal holder except he had a teammate lying prone, between his legs. The player lying between the quarter-back's legs faced a teammate laying the ground as well. When the quarterback received the snap, he placed the ball between the hands of the two players lying on the ground, and they held it for the kicker.

An illustrated version of the steps involved in George Foster Sanford's multiple kick. (Taylor, James F. 'The Five-Man Kick – Football's Newest Play,' Times (Shreveport, LA), December 3, 1916.)

An initial benefit of the multiple kick was that the holders kept it slightly off the ground, elevating it like the tees of later years. However, a 1917 rule required the ball to touch the ground during the field goal attempt, so Foster's multiple kick went away until he brought it back in 1923 to show, once and for all, its true ineffectiveness.

The middle era also witnessed the demise of the drop kick. Although it remained a common method for attempting field goals well into the 1930s, the technique fell into disfavor due to improvements in long snapping and holding techniques, which allowed for greater accuracy and distance. Drop kicking also faltered due to the reshaped football, which was made slimmer and pointier in 1934 to enhance passing. The pointer ball bounced more erratically off the turf, reducing drop kicking's accuracy and distance. Although drop kicking remains legal in college and professional football, it has all but disappeared from football since the early 1940s.

The last substantive change in field goal kicking came near the end of the era when college football battled the NFL for the attention of football fans. Looking to increase scoring, the nation's coaches supported returning the goal posts to the goal line. The last thing football needs nowadays are more field goals, but it was a different world in the late 1950s. As of 1958, a major college player had never kicked more than six field goals in a season (the current record is thirty-one), and there were only 53 made field goals in major college football in 1956 (compared to 1,229 in 2017). To increase scoring, the colleges widened the goal posts in 1959 from 18 feet 6 inches to 23 feet 4 inches, before returning to their original width in 1991.

The final element of the kicking game in which change of note occurred during the middle era involved the kick-outs following safeties and touchbacks. Recall that after Princeton took safeties to stall their way through the block games in the early 1880s, the rules changed to distinguish safeties from touchbacks. Teams taking a touchback kicked out to their opponent from the goal line. Dissatisfaction with that rule led to a 1909 change giving the team taking a touchback the option to kick-out or put the ball in play from scrimmage on the 25-yard line. With the elimination of the 55-yard line in 1912, the rule changed slightly by giving teams taking a touchback the ball on the 20-yard line. Since teams overwhelmingly chose to put the ball in play rather than kick-out to their opponent. The kick-out following a touchback became functionally obsolete, so the committee eliminated it in 1914.

Similarly, teams taking a safety could kick-out or put the ball in play at the 20-yard line (changed to the 30-yard line in 1921 so fans could distinguish touchbacks from safeties). While teams tended to keep the ball after touchbacks, they generally kicked it after safeties. That was, until the 1925 Iowa State-Drake game. Iowa State, the underdog, scored an early touchdown and spent the rest of the game holding on to their 7-0 lead. Three times Iowa State's defense stopped Drake on downs deep in Iowa State territory. Three times Iowa State failed to move the ball and faced a decision. The Cyclones could punt from inside their 10-yard line, or defy convention by taking an intentional safety, followed by taking the ball at the 30-yard line rather than kicking out. Taking the safety cost two points, but it allowed Iowa State to kill time by running a few plays and, even if they did not move the ball, punt from around the 30 rather than from inside 10. Three times Iowa State took the intentional safety and punted after running plays from scrimmage. When the gun sounded, their strategy had paid off as Iowa State won the game 7-6.

Later that season, Northwestern took an intentional safety late in a game against Michigan. By keeping possession of the ball, Northwestern hung on for a 3-2 win, the Wolverines' only loss on the season. Although Iowa State and Northwestern acted within the rules, many saw the approach as devious, and the rules for the 1926 season removed the choice, requiring teams taking a safety to kick-out from the 20-yard line.

DEFENSE

Other than the requirement for the players to remain onside, football's rules have never placed limits on the positioning of defensive players. Instead, defensive alignments have generally mirrored the offenses they faced. Since defenses did not need to concern themselves with the forward pass before 1906, their job was to stop the run and field punts coming from tightly-bunched offenses, so defensive alignments were similarly bunched.

Early defensive football did not involve the many adjustments that occur today. Playing good defense largely relied on the team being in the correct initial alignment and then relying on individual players to beat the man in front of them. In the days of one-platoon football, players generally held the same position on defense as they did on offense and spent the entire game facing the same opponent on both sides of the ball. The primary adjustment in most coaches' quiver was to vary the defensive alignment. As Dana X. Bible wrote without a note of irony:

> The best defensive arrangements that have been found most effective are: 6-2-2-1, 5-3-2-1, 7-1-2-1, 7-2-2, 6-3-2, 5-4-2. (And on the goal line, such line-emphasizing formations as 7-4 and 8-3.) [25]

Since most offenses aligned with both ends tight and all backs inside the ends or in a wing position, defenses commonly aligned in the 7-3-1 or similar. The defensive ends aligned outside the offensive ends and, at the snap, took several steps into the backfield, to force sweeps back inside. The interior linemen ensured the ball was not run over their position, often submarining the offensive linemen to create piles.

7-1-2-1 Diamond Defense

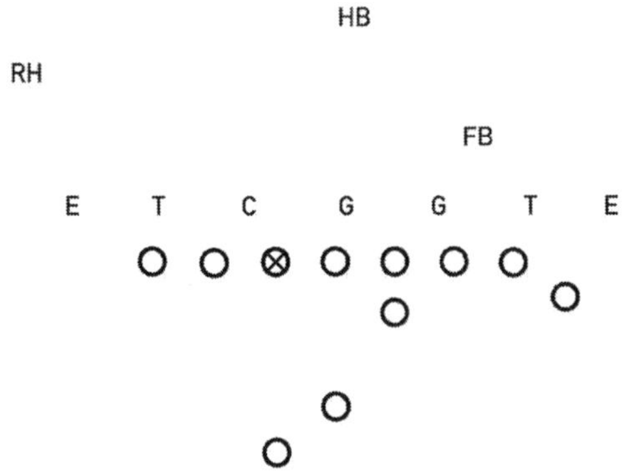

7-1-2-1 Diamond defense with the fullback shifted to the strength of the Single Wing offense. (Adapted from Clark, Football - A Book for Players and Football Fans, 1935)

The fullback played several yards behind the line. His role in supporting the front line led to a new term, "line-backing," in the late 1920s. Other teams used six-man lines that covered each offensive linemen other than the center, who was covered by the defense's "roving center" several yards off the line. With only six men on the line of scrimmage, the 6-2-2-1 was well suited for passing situations, whether the defense was in zone or man coverage. Eddie

Casey, a 1919 Harvard graduate and coach, described zone coverage in 1920, writing:

> In the middle of the field, the best defense against the pass is the so-called zone system. Every backfield man on the defensive has a certain territory to protect. ....The short zones, which defend against the short passes, should be taken care of by the defensive fullback and the centre (sic). The deep zones to protect against longer passes are covered by the two halfbacks. And an exceedingly long pass, which is a rarity now, is usually taken care of by the quarterback, which can come up from his position very quickly as he sees the play develop. [26]

As the passing game increased in sophistication and offenses began throwing deep with some regularity, defenses shifted toward using two players as "safeties." The diagram below shows the 6-3-2 defense used by Potsy Clark's Detroit Lions in 1935.

6-3-2 Defense

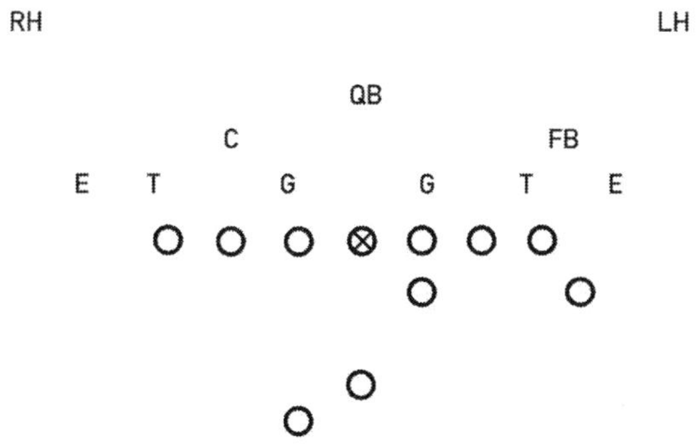

In the 6-3-2 defense, the center moves off the line and becomes a linebacker. (Adapted from Clark, Football - A Book for Players and Football Fans, 1935)

Pro football offenses relied on the passing game more than the colleges, leading to pro defenses orienting themselves to handle the passing game. With professional football also using the two-platoon system consistently, they began emphasizing players with speed who could cover more territory. The same period saw defenses increasing their aggressiveness with the introduction of "red dogging," now known as blitzing. Don "Red" Ettinger, an All-Pro as a rookie guard for the New York Giants in 1948, is often credited with being its pioneer. Athletic enough to play guard on Kansas' basketball team, the Giants leveraged Ettinger's quickness by having the defensive tackles slant outside while Ettinger red dogged inside. As with other stories, the problem with crediting Ettinger with inventing the blitz and, especially with inventing it in 1948, is that Dana X. Bible describes "red dogging" in his book published a year earlier:

> [Rushing the passer] must be done by the defensive men on the line of scrimmage, with occasional assistance from a line-backer slicing through as the ball is snapped.[27]

While it is unclear when teams first blitzed, the strategy appears to have started with the onset of six-man fronts in the 1930s, while the tactic took on the name 'blitz' only after WWII.

Defenses continued transitioning at the pro level due to the greater use of split receivers and flankers. Greasy Neale, coach of the Philadelphia Eagles, devised the 5-2-4 or 52 Eagle in 1947 by swapping the middle linebacker in the 5-3-3 for a fourth defensive back. Neale's version of the 52 had three down linemen inside the offensive tackles while the linebackers aligned just outside the offensive tackles.

The addition of the fourth defensive back provided flexibility for secondaries, but made life difficult for the men up front. Whereas a 53 or 62 defense with eight men in the box allowed each man to be responsible for one gap, defenses with only seven men in the box had more gaps than defenders. Something had to change.

A solution to this problem came from Oklahoma's defensive coordinator Gomer Jones and head coach Bud Wilkinson. Their version of the 52 defense (the Oklahoma 52 or Okie) aligned the defensive tackles over the offensive tackles while placing the linebackers over the offensive guards. Critically, they made the nose guard responsible for the gaps on either side of the center (known as two-gap responsibility).

62 Gap Responsibilities

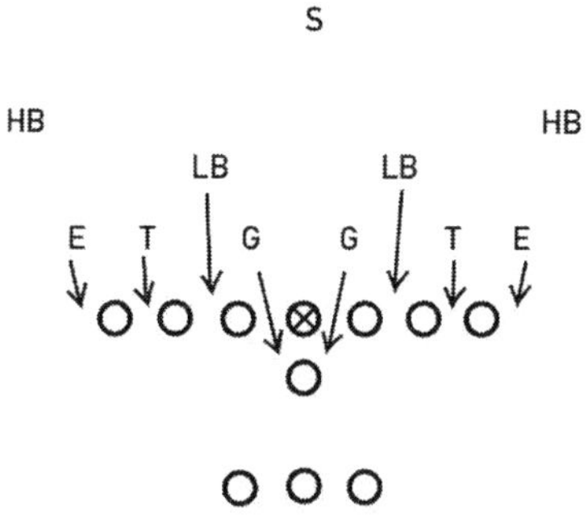

52 Gap Responsibilities

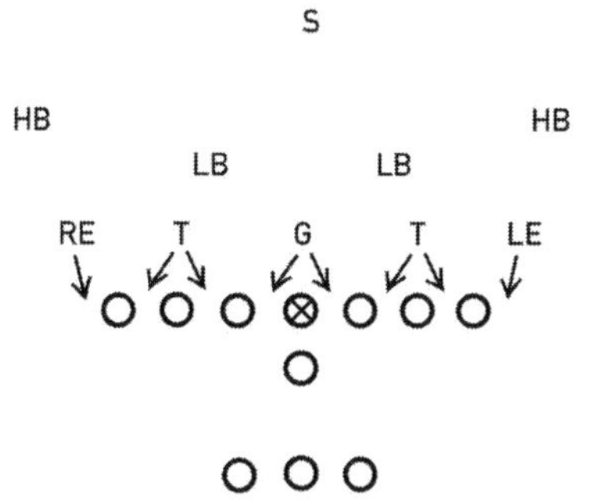

The eight defenders in the 62 defense are responsible for individual gaps. In the Okie 52 defense, each interior defender had two-gap responsibility, freeing the linebackers to flow to the ball.

Two-gap responsibility was later extended to the defensive tackles, giving the three interior linemen on defense primary responsibility for six gaps. The scheme freed the linebackers to roam behind the defensive line, read the offensive backfield action, and react to the ball, including dropping into coverage when the offense showed pass. Two-gap technique became a building block used by almost every defense moving forward. Of course, not every team possessed defensive linemen with the power and athleticism to play two-gap defense, but almost everyone tried to do so at some level.

During the same period in which Oklahoma devised the 52, the New York Giants under Steve Owen developed a different solution. The story goes that Owen scouted Paul Brown and the Cleveland Browns when they played the Philadelphia Eagles in 1950. Owen saw the Browns devastate the Eagles' state-of-the-art 52 defense with sideline routes by the receivers and flare routes by the back.

Owen's base defenses were the 61 or 52 alignments with his defensive backs in the "Umbrella" formation: two defensive backs aligned wide and shallow covering the split end and flanker and two aligned deep and tight. To handle the Browns' passing attack, Owen aligned in a 61, but dropped his defensive ends into pass coverage, creating an early version of the 43 defense. Owen described the Umbrella formation in the early 1950s, saying:

> ... we use the umbrella most often in a 5-2-4 and work eight changes off it.
>
> 1. We can red-dog the backers-up through the line, with the Ends holding to protect the outside.
>
> 2. We can send in an End from one side and a backer-up from the other, with the backer-up on the end side sliding off to cover and the End on the backer-up side dropping a few yards to protect the vacated area.[28]

Owen's use of the term "backer-up" for linebacker tells us the linebacker terminology remained in transition at the time, but the second adjustment describes the essence of the zone blitz (i.e., blitz with a linebacker and drop a defensive lineman into the area vacated by the blitzing linebacker) which would become popular several decades later. These movements, combined with the other stunts made the position of defensive players post-snap less predictable. In turn, that forced offensive lines and offenses, in general, to adapt, accelerating the movement toward advanced rule and zone blocking.

The last step made by the New York Giants defensive staff occurred when Tom Landry, a cornerback in their Umbrella formation, became a player-coach and then the full-time defensive coordinator. In 1956, his final season as a player-coach, Landry modified the 52 defense by eliminating the defensive lineman aligned over the center, replacing him with a middle linebacker. The three linebackers and four down linemen formed the 43 defense, which dominated football over the next several decades. Landry made only one mistake in creating the 43, and that was his decision to use female names for the three linebacking positions. Landry called them Sarah (strong side), Meg (middle), and Wanda (weak side), a naming convention quickly rejected by others. The following year the Los Angeles Rams called their middle linebacker Mike. We assume that Sam and Will soon followed.

A final point on the naming of defensive positions is that the 1955 Green Bay Packers appear to have been the first to differentiate two types of defensive halfbacks on their roster. Those playing shallow and wide were listed as cornerbacks, while those in the middle of the field were called safeties.

THE MIDDLE ERA covered the first fifty-eight years of the passing game, which began with players and coaches trying to figure out the best techniques for throwing forward passes. It took time and numerous rule changes for coaches to develop the formations and plays that opened up the game, but those came in time, and football became a far more dynamic game as a result.

New offensive formations and philosophies emerged that leveraged the forward pass, misdirection, and the direct snap. The combination led to the quarterback's role changing from that of gutty blocker who sometimes ran the ball to the key player on the field who led through smart play calling, and the accuracy and strength of his arm. Although the running game remained primary during the middle era, the rise of the quarterback continued in the modern era until the position came to dominate the game. This transition is reflected in the college game by the shift in positions awarded the Heisman Trophy. Only four of the first twenty-six Heisman Trophy winners (1935 through 1961) played quarterback, while only eight of the last twenty-seven (1992-2018) did not.

Defenses transformed during the period as well. In addition to evolving away from tight, line-oriented formations as offenses spread the field vertically and horizontally, defenses became aggressive with blitzing and other tactics. Over time, two-platoon football and specialist, full-time defensive coaches combined to develop the tremendously sophisticated defenses that have emerged since the 1950s. Defenses in the 1970s became sufficiently dominant that rule changes were made to put offenses back on even footing and, once again, open up the game.

10

PLAYER EQUIPMENT (1906-1959)

Although later periods brought improvements in the materials, weight, and protective capabilities of football equipment, all essential elements of today's uniforms and padding were in place by the early 1950s. Some types of equipment worn in the early era disappeared, never to return, while others faded from use only to reappear in a different form. As the equipment morphed, so did the materials used in their manufacture. Wool, canvas, and moleskin shifted to cotton, silk, and satin, before transitioning again to nylon, rayon, and other artificial fabrics. Such changes generally provided functional benefits for the players, but a few of the more visible changes in uniforms during the middle era occurred to enhance the experience of fans in the stands and those watching at home.

Other equipment changes reflected modifications in football rules and style of play. For example, with the rule changes of 1906-1912, football became a more open game that placed increased emphasis on speed. The need for speed complemented a perception that manly players wore few or no pads, and players responded by shedding all equipment they did not consider vital. As Steve Farrell, Michigan's athletic trainer, noted in 1913:

> The only thing we know of that will prevent ALL such injuries is a feather bed, and a football player would not be able to travel at quite his usual speed if he had a feather bed bound around him. Moreover, it has been noticed that the fellows who wear the most armor –shin guards, nose guards, head gears, pads, etc.- generally are the worst players. On the best team of its size that we can recall all the members wore unpadded pants, jerseys, and vests ...Nary a headgear, nary a nose guard, nary a pad, and yet this team went through two

> seasons without a single serious or even severe injury. Talk about the fearful brutality of football; if all the teams would keep in as good physical condition as the bunch in question did, there would a very few names on the so-called "casualty lists."[29]

Although the attitude voiced by Steve Farrell remains a part of football, the wearing of protective equipment returned to being the norm, in part because the equipment became increasingly protective as well as lighter and less bulky. Part of these advances occurred because sporting goods manufacturers began coordinating their product development efforts with football insiders. The 1920s saw numerous sporting goods manufacturers work with leading coaches and teams to design new equipment. In the 1930s, the rule making committee began working directly with manufacturers to coordinate new equipment and rules.

Football also began using formal studies to drive equipment development. Multiple studies conducted by state high school athletic associations and the American Football Coaches Association (AFCA) assessed the nature and causes of football injuries. Among their findings were that:

- A high percentage of injuries occur early in the season and early in each half of games, suggesting the need to improve early season conditioning, reduce early preseason contact, and enhance warm-up procedures.
- Serious injuries often occurred among players who returned to games after earlier injuries, pointing to the need to better monitor injured players.
- A higher percentage of injuries occurred in open play than line play and tacklers were more prone to injury than ball carriers or blockers.
- "Bird cage" face masks were the highest single cause of injury. (Bird cage face masks were forerunners of today's multi-bar or full face masks.)

The studies were less conclusive regarding how specific types of equipment related to injuries, but anecdotal evidence suggested that increasingly hard equipment players protected the wearer, but put other players at risk.

BODY AND LEG PROTECTION

Body protection saw several significant transitions during football's second era. One significant change was the move from pants and jerseys with integrated pads to the pads being distinct, interchangeable units. Shoulder pads that began as stuffed leather pads sewn on the outside of the jerseys switched to multi-layered plastic units worn under jerseys. Similarly, football pants with pads quilted into the thighs, knees, and hips changed to those with distinct pads inserted into pockets on the thighs and knees.

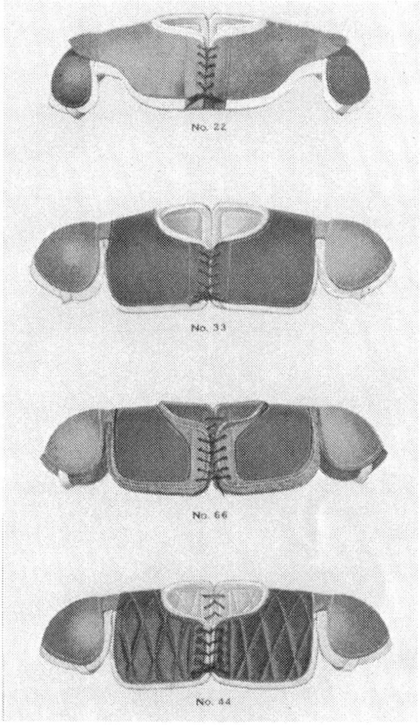

Shoulder pads with varying amounts of leather outer protection, reinforced fibre shell, and felt padding. (1918 Reach Catalog)

The original shoulder pads worn by footballers were stuffed leather or cloth pads sewn on the jersey exterior, making them easy for opponents to grasp. Primitive shoulder pads worn under the jersey began appearing during the transition between the early and middle eras. Through the WWI era, the typical interior shoulder pads covered the shoulders and upper torso with a fiber shell that provided mechanical protection and had leather and felt underneath to cushion blows.

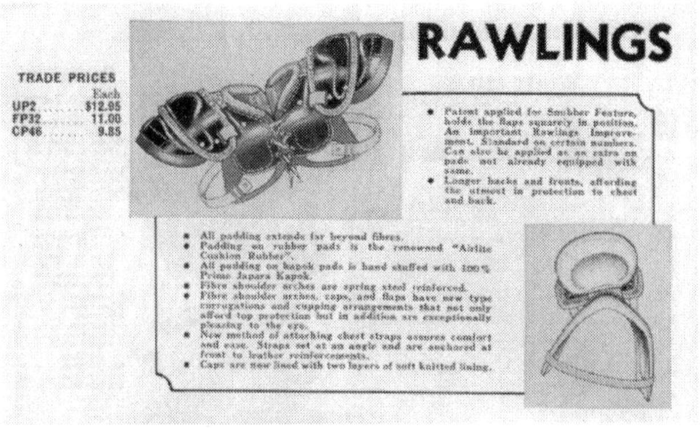

Cantilevered shoulder pads spread the force of impact across the shoulder. (1941-42 Rawlings Sporting Goods Co., Catalog 95)

Shoulder pad design progressed during the 1920s as manufacturers added epaulets stacked in cantilevered fashion to distribute the force of impact across the shoulder area and reduce the likelihood of broken collar bones. Player safety also improved through better methods of securing the shoulder pads to the body. Shoulder pads initially had armlets or straps that looped around the upper arm through the arm pits. The newer shoulder pads shifted the straps to the torso, connecting the back plate to the chest plate near the rib cage. Following those changes, the fundamental design of shoulder pads remained unchanged through the remainder of the middle era, though hard plastic replaced the leather and fiber materials used in the past.

Pants with high hip pads were a common sight when Oregon swept around Penn in the 1917 Rose Bowl. (Tournament of Roses, New Year's Number 1917, Pasadena Star-News*)*

Further down the body, the earliest hip pads were reeded or cushioned pads integrated into the pants, but their form evolved several times during football's second era. By the mid-1910s, pads extending well above the belt line were integrated into pant designs to protect the hips, lower ribs, and kidneys. These were replaced in the late 1920s by separate hip pads that cinched around the waist, covering the tailbone and hips with hard fiber plates over rubber padding. While bulky and comparatively heavy, they provided improved protection due to the protective shell. Wrap around hip pads remained in use for several decades until a few manufacturers introduced step-in hip pads during the 1950s that functioned as a pair of padded shorts.

Early football pants were made of heavy moleskin or canvas and were relatively loose with integrated quilted or reeded padding on the thighs and knees. Starting in the 1910s, the integrated pads shifted to removable fiber and felt pads that inserted into pockets on the interior of the pants.

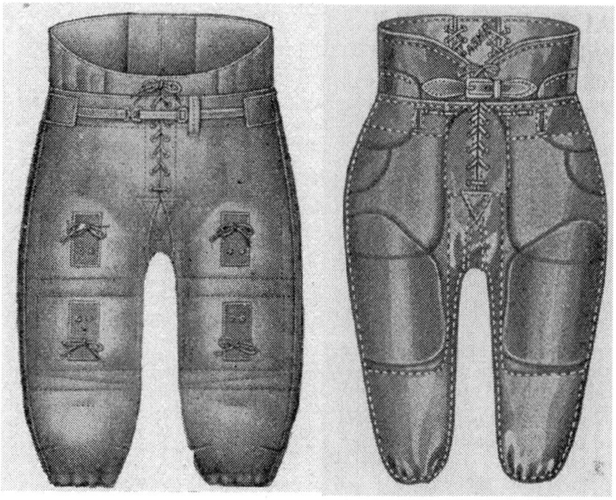

The loose-fitting pants of the 1920s with drawstrings to keep the thigh pads in place (left) were replaced by streamlined, closer fitting pants (right). (1926 Spalding and 1928 Rawlings catalogs)

Many brands used drawstrings to keep the thigh pads in place. These often had leather patches on the front of the thigh to reinforce the area where the drawstrings were tied. More tailored pants without drawstrings arrived in the late 1920s, but these were more expensive, and it took time for the older style pants to work their way out of athletic department inventories.

Some schools, like Georgia Tech, addressed the loose pants issue by having the pants tailor-made for each player. Ensuring the proper fit protected the wearer from bruised thighs and knees, but the primary rationale behind the 1932 rule requiring players to wear knee pads was the concern about unpadded knees striking another player's head.

The fabrics used for football pants also evolved during the middle era. Moleskin and canvas pants weighed several pounds in dry conditions, and their cotton construction meant they became waterlogged and heavy when wet. Well-funded teams changed pants at halftime of rainy games. Pop Warner tried to solve the waterlogged pants problem by having his Pitt team wear rubber pants versus Penn State in 1921, but few, if any, teams followed Warner's lead.

Among those that did not follow Warner's lead were Jimmy Phelan's Purdue Boilermakers, the first to wear silk pants. Phelan's silk pants came about due to his concern over Purdue's season-opening game with Navy in 1926, when the Midshipmen finished the season as national champions. Seeking all possible advantages in the first trip East by a Purdue football team, Phelan asked his uniform supplier to provide pants the same color as the football. The supplier investigated and found the best color match came with pants made of silk airplane cloth, which also weighed much less than moleskin pants. Phelan placed the order, and the pants must have done some good since Purdue came within four points of tying Navy. Up the road, Knute Rockne heard about Purdue's pants and immediately placed an order himself, allowing the Irish to sport silk pants by mid-season. Other teams followed Notre Dame's lead and, despite Purdue having worn silk pants first, the sporting world came to believe silk pants were a Rockne and Notre Dame innovation.

The choice of fabric also affected football aesthetics since the traditional moleskin and canvas football pants were sold only in earth tones. One manufacturer's 1928 catalog showcased their top-of-the-line canvas pants as coming in earth tones such as Olive Drab, Dead Grass, Steel Gray, or custom colors, and the custom colors were where things got exciting. Long Island University, playing football for the first time in 1928, was the first team known to wear vibrantly-colored knickers when they appeared in blue pants. Stanford, under Pop Warner, wore silk pants the first year they were available but waited until 1929 to break out red pants for the Big Game with Cal.

Stanford wore white jerseys and red pants in their 1929 Big Game with Cal. Though the image is black and white, Stanford's pants are clearly darker than Cal's earth-tone pants. (Stanford Historical Photograph Collection (SC1071))

Notre Dame was not the first team to wear silk pants, but they rightfully claim the title as the first to wear nylon pants, which they premiered at their November 1941 game with Army. Nylon, among the first artificial fabrics, was lighter than natural fabrics and provided a snug fit. Once again, other schools took Notre Dame's cue and tried to order nylon pants, but it was too late. By then, nylon was unavailable to sporting goods manufacturers due to restrictions established by the War Department. Polyester was invented during this period as well, and synthetic fibers became the predominant materials used for football pants after the war.

HEAD AND FACIAL PROTECTION

The middle era witnessed the disaggregation of body and leg protection as the integrated pads on pants and jerseys became separate. The opposite occurred with head and facial protection as helmets with face masks replaced nose guards and head harnesses. Although sometimes referred to as helmets, almost all pre-1906 football equipment that protected the head were simple head harnesses made of leather, canvas, and moleskin. Like rugby, football's rules forbid equipment with exposed hard materials with the result that football's headgear lacked the hard shells that provide mechanical protection against skull fractures. The typical head harness covered the top of the head and neck, had separate ear flaps, and was held in place by elastic chin straps that wrapped under the jaw, near the neck.

Head harnesses with molded crowns and separate 'dog ear' flaps. Nose guards were also available. (1918 Reach Catalog)

The early helmets covered the fiber shell with soft leather with various brands and models placing extra padding on the forehead, often covered with the pad stylized to form a wing pattern. Many had leather bands in transverse or longitudinal patterns on top of the helmet. The remnants of this style helmet remain in the painted wing and striped helmets worn by Princeton, Michigan, and Delaware today.

The leather bands atop the helmet took on added importance due to a 1930 rule prohibiting elbow pads, jerseys, and headgear in the same color as the ball. The 1930 rule required that head gear have:

> ... the solid color be broken by at least two stripes of markedly contrasting color at least two inches in width, and that the solid color of such jerseys (or attachments) be definitely broken up by stripes or numbers of markedly contrasting color.[30]

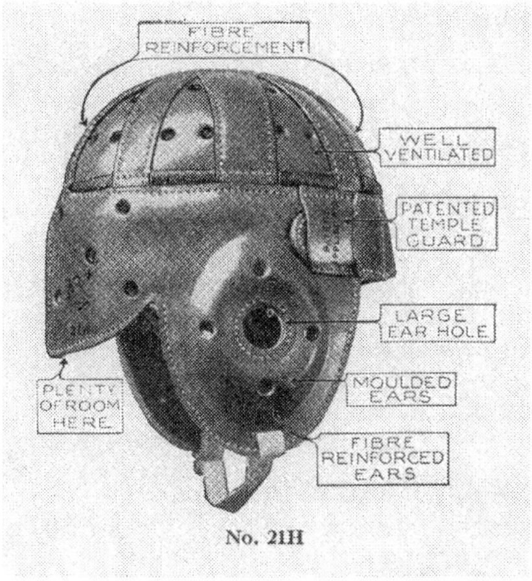

The leather straps atop the helmet were painted a team color distinct from the rest of the helmet. (1928 Fall 1929 Winter D&M Athletic Goods Catalog, Model 21H)

With the requirement to add color to their helmets, most teams painted their helmets in school colors, making the uniforms more vibrant and distinctive. In addition to being attractive, the colored helmets helped passers distinguish friend from foe as well.

Two important changes in the helmet department came shortly before America's entry into WWII. First, the NCAA finally required players to wear helmets in 1939 and added rules specifying the proper thickness and materials used in other pads. The more significant change in head protection before WWII came with the introduction of helmets made of hard plastic. Designed by Riddell to prevent skull fractures, the plastic outer shell of the early helmets was transparent, with the team colors painted on the inside of the helmet. Northwestern was the first team to wear them in their 1940 season opener against Syracuse. Other colleges tested them during the 1940 season, before the plastic football helmet revolution took a hiatus due to wartime shortages of plastics.

Northwestern's Ike Kepford, wearing a plastic helmet, runs with the ball during their 1940 game at Syracuse. (Courtesy of Northwestern University Archives)

Riddell's plastic helmet had an innovative web suspension system on the interior to keep the wearer's head from hitting the plastic shell. That system included the first chin strap that wrapped tightly around the chin rather than looping under the jaw and proved so useful that Riddell licensed the combination to the U.S. military for use with the twenty-two million M1 helmets produced during WWII. Riddell also developed plastic helmets worn by paratroopers during the war.

The first plastic football helmet included Riddell's innovative suspension system. (Courtesy of Riddell Sports Group)

Plastic helmets returned to football after the war and were adopted in sufficient numbers to spur the demand to ban them. The opposition to plastic helmets centered on injuries caused to other players when hit by the hard plastic shell. For example, Harvard's quarterback broke his leg in 1948 when struck by a plastic helmet, and their Athletic Director, William Bingham, called for a ban on their use. Bingham, who chaired the NCAA rules committee at the time, announced a plan to ban plastic helmets by the 1950 season. However, the rules committee never approved the ban because most believed the value of plastic helmets to the wearers outweighed the potential harm they inflicted on others. The battle over leather versus plastic helmets continued into the early 1960s, with teams often wearing one or another based on the head coach's view on the matter.

The evolution of football helmets enabled a similar evolution in facial protection. The primary method of protecting the face during the early era were nose guards, which were problematic because they required clenching the lower bar between the teeth, restricting the ability to breathe through the mouth. Since many of those wearing nose guards had broken noses, forcing those players to breathe through the nose was not a good thing. In the post-1905 trend to shed equipment, the uncomfortable nose guard fell victim, and its popularity faded, though sporting goods manufacturers continued selling them into the 1940s.

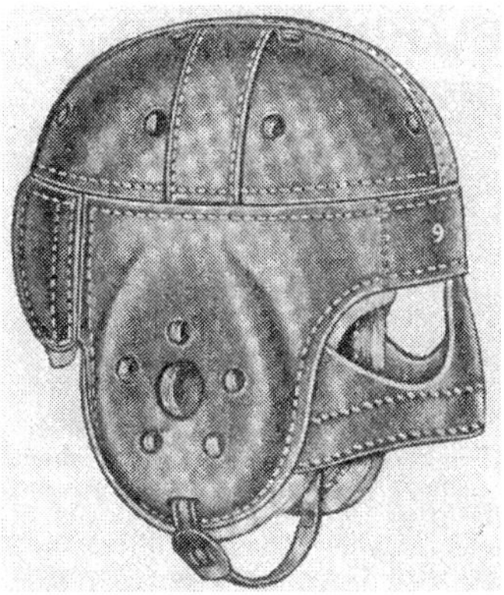

Rawlings offered the Nose Protector Helmet with a sole leather mask reinforced by steel that could be molded to the wearer's face. (Rawlings 1928 Winter 1929 Spring Catalog)

A side effect of reinforced helmets gaining popularity during the 1920s and 1930s was the ability to attach devices that protected the face to the sturdier helmets. Among them were contoured masks covering the face, save the holes for the eyes and nostrils. The executioner style masks are the reason we call such devices "face masks" and were available as a permanent part of the helmet or as add-ons to existing helmets. Although they offered robust protection, they were uncomfortably hot and limited the player's peripheral vision, so most preferred the new face masks constructed of bars. Often referred to as "bird cages," they consisted of one or more rubber-coated metal bars that protruded from the profile of the helmet. Besides protecting those with eye and nose injuries, bird-cage face masks allowed players to wear eyeglasses on the football field. (Contact lenses were not yet commercially significant.) Among the earlier wearers of a bird-cage mask was Jay Berwanger, who wore one throughout his career at Chicago.

Chicago's Jay Berwanger, nicknamed The Man in the Iron Mask, begins a 61-yard touchdown run versus Dartmouth. (1934 Cap and Gown, University of Chicago yearbook)

A 1948 study by three state high school associations, conducted when most players wore leather helmets, and few wore face masks, found that 52.2% of football injuries involved the face and teeth, and 97% of the injured were not wearing mouth or nose protection when injured. Findings like these put football authorities between a rock and a soft face. Like the plastic helmet, wearing a face mask put others at risk, while not wearing one led to more work for plastic surgeons and orthodontists.

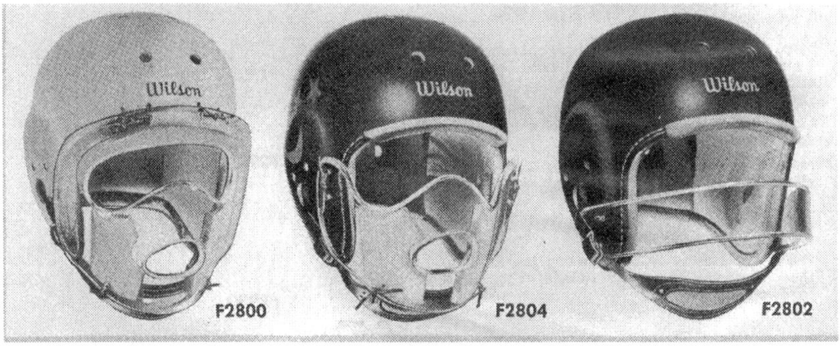

Wilson's transparent face guards for 1956. (Wilson Fall Winter Catalog, 1956-57 Trade Price Edition)

The 1950s saw the sporting goods manufacturers create several alternatives to "bird cage" masks, with some geared to minimizing injuries to others. One was a flat, clear bar made of Lucite and approximately two inches wide. The Cleveland Browns' Otto Graham wore one in 1953 after suffering a facial injury that required stitches. (Graham is often incorrectly credited with being the first player to wear a face mask. He was not, though he contributed to their increased popularity.) Others covered the face more broadly.

Several manufacturers created designs with clear plastic exteriors molded to the contours of the face with interior pads that rested against the wearer's cheeks. These designs did not hurt other players and dramatically reduced the likelihood of being face masked. The Rawlings Safe-T-Vue Face Protector and the Wilson Grid-Gard attached to the helmet with a standard chin strap and a second, higher strap similar to those used today.

In addition to the designs that did not survive the decade, a range of bird-cage face masks became available by the mid-1950s as well. These ranged from single bars, to half-masks that covered the eyes and nose only, to the full-frontal cages that became popular in the 1960s and are now universal. The growing popularity of face masks also meant that ball carriers were increasingly tackled by defenders grabbing their masks, leading to the introduction of the face masking penalty in 1957.

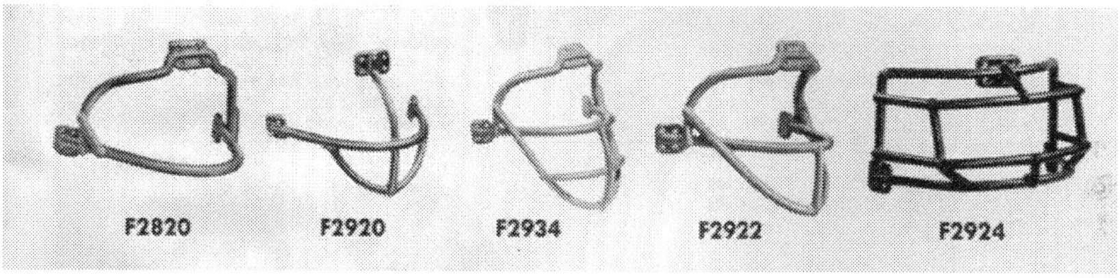

Wilson's plastic-covered steel face guards for 1956. (Wilson Fall Winter Catalog, 1956-57 Trade Price Edition)

As noted earlier, players kept the old nose guards in place by clenching the lower part of the device between their teeth. While doing so made breathing more difficult, the rubber device provided a minimum level of protection for players' teeth. Although separate rubber mouth guards were available through several manufacturers since early in the century, their usage was low, resulting in numerous football players losing a tooth or three during their careers.

Several Purdue football players celebrating their victory are missing teeth, presumably due to prior gridiron action. (Purdue University Archives)

Oral protection entered the modern age in 1947 when Rodney O. Lilyquist, a Los Angeles dentist, created a molded acrylic mouth guard for use by athletes in multiple sports. He published a report on his work in the *Journal of the American Dental Association* in 1948, the same year the ADA began sponsoring research on mouth guards. By 1960, the ADA recommended mouth guards for all contact sports, and their research led to the development of the now-ubiquitous molded latex mouth guard. All high school players nationwide were required to wear mouth guards starting in 1962, the same year the NCAA recommended mouth protectors for all players. The NCAA made mouth guards mandatory in 1973.

Beyond the functional value provided by the evolution of the helmet, face mask, and mouth guard, football headgear evolved along aesthetic lines as well. At the beginning of the middle era, almost all headgear retained the color of tanned leather (brown or black), though some teams, such as Tufts and Oregon State, painted their helmets white as early as the mid-1910s.

Oregon State brought their white headgear east in 1915 when they scored three touchdowns in their 20-0 victory over Michigan State. (Michigan State University Archives and Special Collections)

Headgear aesthetics advanced when the rules required the painting of the straps atop the helmets, and more so when padded wings became part of helmet designs. Ohio State was the first team to wear helmets with stylized front pads in 1930, but they soon dropped their wings. Others picked up the winged headgear, with Indiana and Purdue having a small block I or P carved into the front pads in 1933. Michigan State followed in 1934 with a green S on their forehead wings. A few schools painted players' numbers on the front of the helmets.

William Bell wearing Ohio State's winged helmet in 1930. (The Ohio State University Archives)

While the small letters on the helmet wings arguably constituted instances of helmet logos, the first team to apply a full logo on their helmet was the NFL's Los Angeles Rams in 1948. Their logo came about because the Rams' left halfback, Fred Gehrke, majored in art at Utah and thought the Rams' plain leather helmets were boring. For grins, Gehrke painted a helmet dark blue with yellow horns and showed it to the team owner. The owner immediately approved the design, and the rest, as they say, is art history.

Jack Banta, Bob Waterfield, and Bob Hoffman of the Los Angeles Rams rest on the bench during a 1948 game. Banta wears a leather helmet painted with the Rams' logo. (Steve Banta, Wikimedia Commons)

Some credit Gehrke with two other football innovations, but only one of those stories is true. Let's cover the bad news first. Gehrke broke his nose during the 1946 season and wore a custom executioner's mask, leading some to credit him with inventing the face mask, but such masks were around for at least fifteen years before Gehrke's injury.

Gehrke rightly deserves credit for an innovation he developed in the 1960s when he was the Denver Broncos director of player personnel. Besides his front-office role, Gehrke did part-time duty as the team's kicking coach. During the 1968 preseason, Gehrke noticed the Broncos' kicker, Bob Humphreys, kicking into a net hanging from a goal post crossbar. Although designed for quarterback drills, the net allowed Humpreys to practice kicking without having to shag the balls. The scene caused Gehrke to think about the type of net that would be most useful to kickers. Gehrke then designed and built a portable kicking net for Humphreys that he could also use to warm up on the sidelines during games. The Broncos obtained league approval to use the net during games, with the result that millions of television viewers must now watch kicker after kicker use that silly net when warming up for game-winning kicks.

SHOES AND CLEATS

A few pages back, we mentioned Riddell as having invented the plastic football helmet in the late 1930s, but the company got its start producing products for the other end of the human body. John T. Riddell, was the football coach at Evanston (IL) High School from 1913 to 1927, and was frustrated by the difficulty of switching between short and long cleats based on weather conditions. (Players wore long cleats in wet conditions and shorter cleats on dry fields.) Since the cleats of the time were laminated leather and tacked to the shoe soles, teams needed cobblers to make the switch. Riddell's problem was that Evanston's cobbler prioritized Northwestern University's football team over Riddell's high school team, causing the prepsters to be short cleated when they should have been long and vice versa.

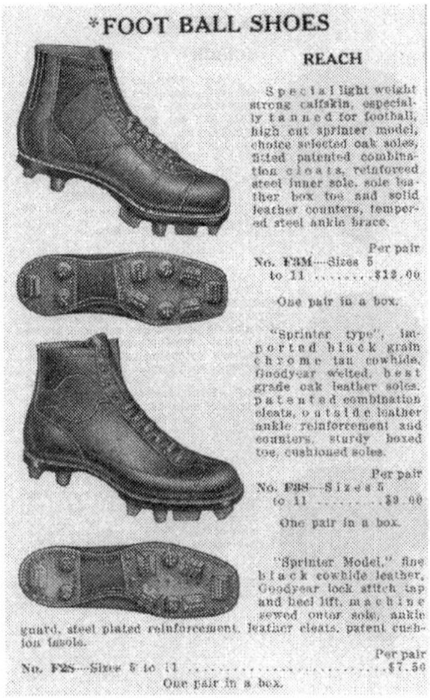

Prior to Riddell's invention, football cleats were laminated leather tacked to the shoe sole by a cobbler. (1922 House-Hasson Hardware Company Catalog)

Riddell's solution was the interchangeable cleat, which could be quickly screwed on or off by players and managers. When his interchangeable cleats grew in popularity, Riddell left teaching to form his namesake company and expanded his line to include interchangeable track spikes and, later, football helmets and other gear.

Interchangeable cleats addressed the key disadvantages of leather cleats, though Riddell's original cleats had a female configuration rather than male, so cleats that came unscrewed left a bolt sticking dangerously from the shoes. Riddell switched the configuration in later versions.

Long, pointy cleats gripped the turf better than short, blunt cleats, but they presented a greater danger to others, leading to a 1939 rule limiting cleats to one-half inch in length and requiring them to be truncated cones in shape. Cleats were further limited to 3/8 inch in 1940, though the NFL still allows cleats up to 3/4 inch in length.

Another innovation during the middle era was the low-cut shoe. Football players wore high-top shoes when football began because boots were the norm for streetwear, and high tops helped avoid ankle sprains. However, high-top leather shoes were heavy, leading Duke and Mississippi to experiment with low cut shoes in 1937.

Players talking on the field following the 1937 Duke-Georgia Tech game. The player closest to the camera is among those wearing low-cut shoes. (Duke University Archives)

Most football players also wore socks, though the 1925 Alabama team abstained from that pleasure during their Rose Bowl season. During the early era, heavy wool socks covered players' lower legs and were often the same dark color as their jerseys. A problem with those heavy socks was that the dyes in use were not colorfast. Nap Lajoie, a major league baseball player, sat out most of the 1905 season due to blood poisoning that was incorrectly attributed to the dyes from his socks seeping into a spike wound. The belief caused Lajoie and others to wear white "sanitary" socks beneath their colored socks. ("Sanitary" socks are so named because they can be disinfected by boiling and bleaching them.) To ensure their shoes still fit, many players cut the heel and toe from the colored sock, resulting in the sock becoming a stirrup. Manufacturers soon produced purpose-made stirrups.

Football teams began wearing stirrups as well, but football players tended to wear white crew socks over the stirrups rather than having the sanitary socks under the stirrups. Some teams opted not to wear knee socks, others sported crew socks only, and the knee sock versus crew sock controversy has raged among collegians ever since. The NFL took a different stance when Elmer Layden, the NFL commissioner, mandated the wearing of knee-high socks in 1945. Layden had a longstanding affinity for knee-highs paired with crew socks, wearing the combination during his days as one of the Four Horsemen and as Notre Dame's head coach from 1934 to 1940.

Elmer Layden coaching his 1937 Notre Dame team while wearing football pants, stirrups, and crew socks. His players were not so refined. (Acme Newspictures)

The NFL still enforces its knee-high sock rule, regularly fining players for exposing their calves in public. Similarly, the Canadian Rugby Union (CRU), a forerunner of the CFL, moved in 1956 to require those playing in the Grey Cup to wear socks. Of course, if you are playing in the last football game of the season in Canada without socks, you likely have issues that a pair of socks will not solve. The NCAA added a sock rule in 1997 when it first required team members to wear either white or team-colored socks of uniform length.

UNIFORMS

Football uniforms took their modern appearance by the end of football's middle era. Although the materials, colors, and some styling elements have since changed, little distinguishes the silhouette of a post-WWII player from his current counterpart. Still, there were substantial changes to players' uniforms during the middle era that provided little benefit to the players; instead, the benefit accrued to the fans and press.

The most important change to football jerseys during the era was the addition of uniform numbers. As football became more popular at the end of the early era, an increasing percentage of fans did not personally know the players on the field and had difficulty distinguishing one from another. Players increasingly wore headgear, executed shifts, and ended plays in large piles. Even those fans who knew members of the home team well had difficulty distinguishing opposing team members.

Sportswriters had similar difficulties, despite the assistance of spotters. Game reports in competing newspapers commonly contained differences in who ran or caught the ball and which substitutes entered games. Penn went so far as to install telephones near the team benches so spotters on the field could inform the press box as to who made a run or tackle, and who substituted for whom.

The fans were not so lucky in the days before loudspeakers, but they had a friend in the Windy City in the person of Amos Alonzo Stagg, the foremost advocate of adding numbers to player uniforms. (He also argued briefly for players wearing different hues of their team color based on their position, but we forgive him that indiscretion.) Stagg wanted to implement uniform numbers in 1900, but opted against doing so because he believed it would have been a competitive disadvantage and he was pessimistic about his team's prospects that year. How did uniform numbers create a competitive disadvantage? In the days before game film, Stagg understood that wearing numbers would make it easier for opposing scouts and players to identify his team's top players, plays, and shifts. Others opposed numbering players believing it promoted individualism over team play. At the same time, the engineers in the crowd argued that players on the line of scrimmage were aligned at right angles to the fans in the stands, so fans often could not see the players' numbers anyway.

Harvard took a slightly different approach when they opened the monumental Harvard Stadium in 1903. Rather than place numbers on players' jerseys, Harvard sold scorecards listing each Harvard player along with a number between 1 and 50, while the opponent's players had numbers between 51 and 99. Following each play, spotters on the field used hand signals to inform the scoreboard operators who had run with the ball, made a tackle, or the like. The operators then posted the relevant player numbers on the scoreboard.

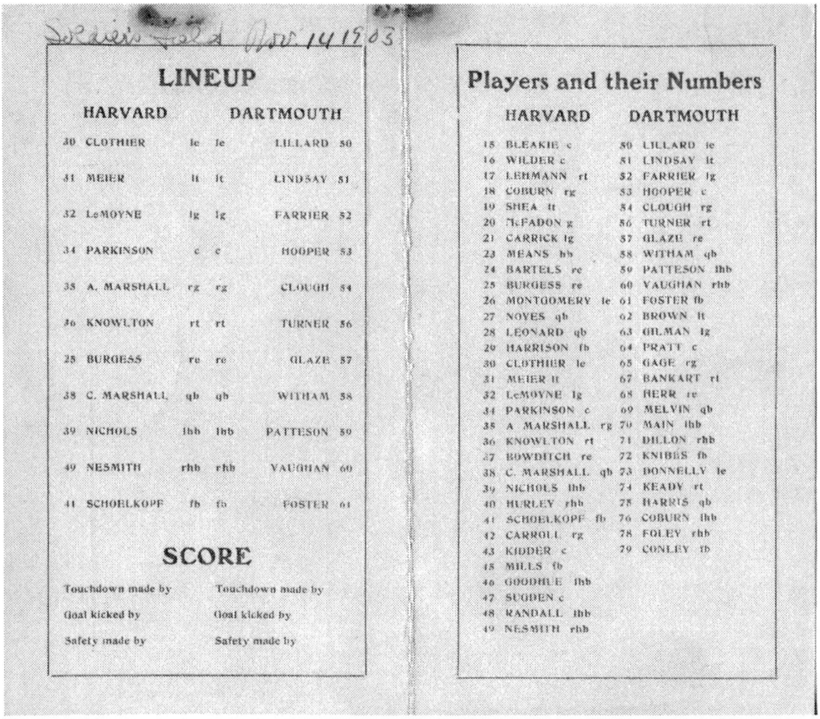

LINEUP

HARVARD			DARTMOUTH	
30 CLOTHIER	le	le	LILLARD	50
31 MEIER	lt	lt	LINDSAY	51
32 LeMOYNE	lg	lg	FARRIER	52
34 PARKINSON	c	c	HOOPER	53
35 A. MARSHALL	rg	rg	CLOUGH	54
36 KNOWLTON	rt	rt	TURNER	56
25 BURGESS	re	re	GLAZE	57
38 C. MARSHALL	qb	qb	WITHAM	58
39 NICHOLS	lhb	lhb	PATTESON	59
49 NESMITH	rhb	rhb	VAUGHAN	60
41 SCHOELKOPF	fb	fb	FOSTER	61

SCORE

Touchdown made by	Touchdown made by
Goal kicked by	Goal kicked by
Safety made by	Safety made by

Players and their Numbers

HARVARD	DARTMOUTH
15 BLEAKIE c	50 LILLARD le
16 WILDER c	51 LINDSAY lt
17 LEHMANN rt	52 FARRIER lg
18 COBURN rg	53 HOOPER c
19 SHEA lt	54 CLOUGH rg
20 McFADON g	56 TURNER rt
21 CARRICK lg	57 GLAZE re
23 MEANS hb	58 WITHAM qb
24 BARTELS re	59 PATTESON lhb
25 BURGESS re	60 VAUGHAN rhb
26 MONTGOMERY le	61 FOSTER fb
27 NOYES qb	62 BROWN lt
28 LEONARD qb	63 GILMAN lg
29 HARRISON fb	64 PRATT c
30 CLOTHIER le	65 GAGE rg
31 MEIER lt	67 BANKART rt
32 LeMOYNE lg	68 HERR re
34 PARKINSON c	69 MELVIN qb
35 A MARSHALL rg	70 MAIN lhb
36 KNOWLTON rt	71 DILLON rhb
37 BOWDITCH re	72 KNIBBS fb
38 C. MARSHALL qb	73 DONNELLY le
39 NICHOLS lhb	74 KEADY rt
40 HURLEY rhb	75 HARRIS qb
41 SCHOELKOPF fb	76 COBURN lhb
42 CARROLL rg	78 FOLEY rhb
43 KIDDER c	79 CONLEY fb
45 MILLS fb	
46 GOODHUE lhb	
47 SUGDEN c	
48 RANDALL lhb	
49 NESMITH rhb	

The scorecard for the 1903 Harvard-Dartmouth game, the first played in Harvard Stadium, shows the numbers assigned to the players on both teams. (Personal Collection)

Although Harvard did not wear uniform numbers during the period, their numbering system inspired the first known game in which players wore numbers on their jerseys. In 1905, Drake's athletic director, W. J. Monilaw, proposed that Drake and Iowa State wear numbers for their Thanksgiving Day game, and the Ames boys agreed to do so. Leveraging Harvard's idea of each team using a string of numbers, Drake wore numbers between 1 and 25, while Iowa State wore numbers between 26 and 50. (Rugby teams in New Zealand and Australia in the late 1890s, the first to wear uniform numbers, used similar systems.)

Drake's Tom Burcham scores a touchdown against Iowa State in the only known image of players wearing numbered jerseys during the 1905 Drake-Iowa State game. (Des Moines Register, newspapers.com)

Since the wearing of numbers was an experiment, Drake and Iowa State painted the numbers on canvas shields and sewed the shields to the backs of the jerseys. These temporary attachments were typical for the next decade when uniform numbers remained uncommon, and, being temporary, they were often poorly attached and tore off during games, adding to the argument against their use.

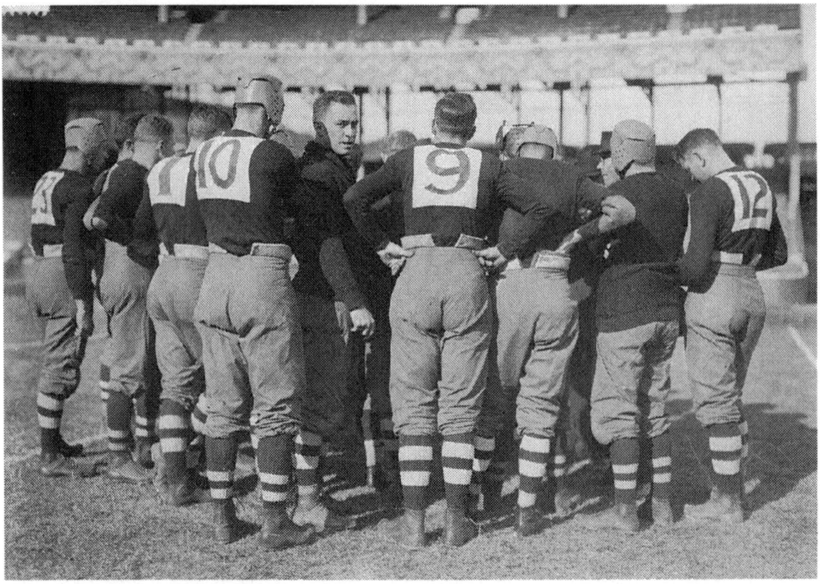

Brown players in conference prior to their 1914 game with Cornell at the Polo Grounds. #10 is left guard Wallace Wade, who later coached Alabama to three national titles and took Duke to two Rose Bowls. (George Grantham Bain Collection, Library of Congress)

The Big Ten recommended its teams wear uniform numbers starting in 1914, but not every team did so. Minnesota's coach, H. L. Williams, a pioneer of pre-snap shifts, sent his teams onto the gridiron numberless until 1921 when a new conference rule required their use. But Williams had one last trick up his sleeve or, rather, a trick on the back of his players' jerseys. Williams sent his Gophers onto the field for their early-season game against Northwestern in uniforms with four-digit numbers, which made it more difficult for opposing players, coaches, and scouts to track which Minnesota player shifted where.

Minnesota quarterback Arthur Gilstad, wearing number 2335, lies on the ground after a teammate scored against Northwestern in 1921. (1923 Gopher, University of Minnesota Archives)

The rules committee recommended that all teams use numbered jerseys in 1920, and the practice soon became nearly universal. Still, every party has a pooper, and Furman's coach, Dad Amis, claimed that title in 1929. Following in H. L. Williams' footsteps, Amis sent his team on the field for their game with Erskine wearing Roman numerals rather than Arabic numerals.

Despite some reluctance to adopt uniform numbers, it did not take long for fans and others to associate specific numbers with particular players. The first to have his jersey number become part of his national identity was the Galloping Ghost, Red Grange, of Illinois. Grange made such an impression that Illinois framed his jersey after his final game in 1925 and pledged that no one else would wear the number 77 at Illinois. That made Grange the first player in any sport to have his number retired.

Notably, few teams wore numbers on the front of their jerseys during the 1920s; almost everyone wore them on their backs only. The NFL's Rock Island Independents wore numbers on the front in 1924, but the use of "friction strips" on the front of many football jerseys delayed wearing numbers on the front. Readers may not be familiar with the term, friction strips, but most recognize them from photographs of football players from the mid-1910s to the mid-1930s as they were all the rage.

Among the best-known images in football history is this 1925 photograph of Red Grange in a Chicago Bears jersey with friction strips. (National Photo Company Collection, Library of Congress)

Friction strips, also known as "stickem" or "stickum" cloth, were leather or moleskin pieces sewn onto the front and sleeves of jerseys that kept the ball from slipping from the wearer's grasp. Sporting goods manufacturers sold friction strip jerseys in standardized patterns, with the most common having vertical stripes on the torso. Teams also created an array of custom patterns, while others featured oval patterns dyed to match the color of the football, a practice outlawed by rule in 1931.

Some teams have targets on their backs. The 1925 Furman team had targets on their fronts. (Courtesy of Special Collection and Archives, Furman University)

All good things come to an end, and the end for friction strips came in the 1930s. Some teams stopped using them for stylistic reasons, moving to cleaner designs that set the stylistic trend for the next seventy-plus years. Others, like UCLA, used strips the same color as the jersey to obtain the functional benefit while achieving the desired clean look. A 1936 NCAA recommendation that teams place 6-inch tall numbers on the front of their jerseys sounded the death knell for friction strips, as did the NCAA rule requiring jersey numbers on the front and back starting in 1937.

Four years later, the rules committee took the big step of recommending the numbering of players by position. Doing so was expected to help officials identify players committing fouls, including ineligible receivers downfield. Since teams had invested in their current stock of jerseys and some players were emotionally invested in their jersey numbers, the committee positioned the first season or two as a test. The test period required schools to choose one of the alternative numbering systems and to update their jerseys accordingly. The fun part of the story, of course, is the alternative numbering systems devised at the time.

One numbering system, which became the norm, had the first digit of the player number correspond to their offensive position such that quarterback numbers started with a 1, halfback numbers started with a 2, and so on. Some took this idea a step further by having players on the left side of the formation use odd numbers as the second digit, while those on the right side wore even numbers. A second approach went the opposite direction, calling for the second digit of the player number to correspond to the player's position. That meant centers' numbers ended with a 2, and guards ended with a 3, and so on.

A third approach touted by Duquesne's Buff Donelli and Arizona's Miles Casteel (the latter also proposed having the field numbers run from 0 to 100) called for alpha-numeric combinations rather than two digits. Each player was to wear a letter corresponding to their position (e.g., guards wore a G, while halfbacks wore an H), followed by a number indicating whether they played on the left or right side, and whether they were first or second string. Thus, the starting left end would wear E1, the second-string left end would wear E3, while the starting right tackle would wear T2 and his backup would wear T4. Neither Duquesne nor Arizona used the alpha-numeric combination, though Lehigh used a similar system in 1929, and Penn did so in 1930, but the two-digit system became the standard. Due to minimal rule changes made during WWII, the two-digit system did not become mandatory until 1947.

While the football world settled into the system in which the first digit of the uniform number designated the player's position, evil minds remained at work down on the bayou. Thinking that the frequent substitutions of the new two-platoon football confused fans, LSU gained permission from its 1952 opponents to give the alpha-numeric system another try. (Kentucky and UCLA used the system for some games that season as well.) Since LSU's defense shifted between five, six, and seven-man fronts, and those shifts wreaked havoc with the system's alpha logic, they used the alpha-numeric system only for their offensive players. As it turned out, the rules committee repealed the substitution rules that allowed two-platoon football after the 1952 season, so LSU and others returned to the two-digit numbering system used today.

The 1952 LSU offense aligned in formation and showing their alpha-numeric jerseys. (1952 Gumbo, LSU yearbook)

If the addition of numbers was the most important change to jerseys during the middle era, the move to using white jerseys on the road was the second most significant change. Football teams commonly wore white uniforms in the 1870s and early 1880s but shifted to darker jerseys in their school colors in the 1880s.

So it was in 1910 that Clyde Williams, Iowa State's coach, took the unusual step of dressing his team in white jerseys because Williams believed the white jerseys helped his passers spot open receivers in the new forward passing game. Whether it was the jerseys or his coaching in general, something worked because Iowa State won the Missouri Valley Conference title in 1911 and 1912. Unfortunately, Williams stopped coaching football after the 1912 season, and the use of the white jerseys left with him. So did winning football. The conference championships won during the 1911 and 1912 seasons remain Iowa State's only conference titles in football to date.

White jerseys remained rare until money, and better weather lured Pop Warner from Pitt to Stanford in 1924. Warner dressed the Stanford Cardinal in white jerseys for an away game at Idaho because both teams wore red jerseys at the time. The move so confused the Stanford fans attending the game that they believed the team in red, who they thought was Stanford, had lost the game. The white jerseys became something of a Stanford trademark, and their invitations to the 1925 and 1927 Rose Bowls made them a team to be copied.

Stanford scores against West Coast Army during a transition time in uniforms and equipment. Both teams have numbers on the front of their jerseys, though Stanford wears modern white jerseys, and Army bears friction strips. Two Army players are without helmets, and the officials still wear plain white shirts. (1933 Quad, Stanford University yearbook)

Oregon State took up the white jersey in 1925, as did Northwestern in 1928, and Duke in 1929. Other teams used white jerseys only when playing a school with similar colors, but which team wore which color remained unsettled. Elmer Layden was coaching Duquesne in 1929 when he advocated for home and away uniforms, suggesting that football follow baseball's lead with the home team in light-colored jerseys and the visiting team in the dark. Not much happened until the NCAA ruled in 1949 that opposing teams wear colors that contrasted with the home team, which left open the possibility of one team wearing blue and the other red.

The All American Football Conference, a professional league that rivaled the NFL between 1946 and 1949, was the first to require away teams to wear white jerseys. Still, the road-team-wears-white system did not become standard until television changed the dynamic. While fans sitting in the stands could easily distinguish blue and red jerseys, fans watching on black-and-white televisions could not. Having signed a major television contract with CBS in 1956, the NFL instituted a rule for 1957 requiring visiting teams to wear white jerseys. College football established a similar rule in 1983 but, by then, everyone wore white on the road anyway; the rule simply codified the standard practice. Even high schools followed the road white fashion trend despite few high school games being televised during the black-and-white era.

The final changes in football jerseys during the middle era were refinements rather than new practices, with the first involving the typeface used for the uniform numbers. The NCAA mandated six-inch numbers on the front and eight-inch numbers on the back of jerseys in 1937. They updated the rule in 1946 to require at least eight and ten-inch numbers, respectively. Moreover, they required block-style numbers with 1 1/2 inch wide stripes, making the digits 3, 5, 6, 8, and 9 difficult to differentiate in certain conditions.

Frustrated with the block numbers, Ralph Douglas, an art professor at the University of New Mexico, developed an alternate typeface with slimmer, contoured numbers that were easier to read from a distance. Since the typeface made it easier for spotters to identify players, the typeface became known as "spotter numbers." Various college and high school teams adopted them, as did the Chicago Bears, who added them in 1957 and have retained the spotter number typeface to this day.

New Mexico end, Dick Drake, being tackled by a New Mexico State player in 1954. Note the spotter number typeface on Drake's jersey compared to the opponent's block numbers. (1955 Mirage, University of New Mexico yearbook)

Besides the changeover to white road jerseys, television, with a boost from the National Photographers Association (NPA), changed football uniforms in other ways. Early in 1955, the NPA suggested that conferences require teams to add player numbers on jersey shoulders or helmets to make it easier to identify players in photographs or on television.

Miami's Whitey Bouviere attempts to avoid multiple Georgia Tech defenders during the first game in which a team wore TV numbers on their shoulders. (Courtesy of the University Archives, University of Miami Libraries, Coral Gables, Florida)

Whether or not the NPA influenced the decision is not known, but Georgia Tech opened the season against Miami wearing TV numbers on their shoulders, making them the first football team to do so. Appropriately enough, that game was also the first football game televised in color.

West Virginia opened the season a week after Georgia Tech sporting numbers on their helmets, and the New York Giants added numbers on their sleeves in 1956. Others caught the wave when Big Eight coaches agreed that all teams add numbers on their helmets in 1957. (Kansas received an exception because they already had numbers on their sleeves.) Among the schools caught in the TV number tide was Alabama, which added numbers on the sides of their helmets in 1957, the year before Bear Bryant returned to Tuscaloosa.

PLAYER EQUIPMENT EVOLVED SUBSTANTIALLY during the middle era along both functional and aesthetic lines. Many functional changes resulted from advances in the material sciences that saw plastics and synthetic fabrics enter everyday life. Plastics allowed for sturdier and harder equipment that better protected the wearer, at the cost of increasing the risk to others on the playing field. Some challenged the use of harder materials, but the desire to prevent catastrophic injuries (e.g., skull fractures) led to an acceptance of those costs. Similarly, the addition of face masks and mouth guards dramatically reduced the incidence of broken noses, orbital sockets, and jaws. Broken noses and missing teeth went from an ordinary mark among football players to one seldom seen.

The movement from moleskin and wool uniforms to cotton and silk and then to nylon and rayon made uniforms lighter, less water absorbent, and more form-fitting. The more form-fitting uniforms also helped keep players' thigh, knee, and other pads in their proper place.

Beyond the safety-related changes in equipment, uniform aesthetics changed dramatically during the middle era to become more fan-friendly. Player numbers on the backs of jerseys, then the front, and later on the helmet and shoulders made it easier for spectators and fans watching on television to identify the players on the field. The movement to the road team wearing white jerseys also helped fans distinguish teams on black-and-white televisions.

Other changes to uniforms and equipment would come in the modern era as teams opted for more vibrant colors and the integration of multiple fabrics in one jersey -a phenomenon presaged by friction strips- that altered the look-and-feel of uniforms once again.

11

COACHES AND OFFICIALS (1906-1959)

The last vestiges of the amateur coaching model disappeared during the middle era as college football coaching became a full-time, year-round job for which experience counted. In the late 1910s, major colleges still hired as head coaches individuals only a year or two removed from playing college football, but the increasingly sophisticated nature of the role led schools to hire as head coaches those with track records as assistant coaches. The more complex game also led to an expansion in coaching staff size from one coach to four or five. The founding of the American Football Coaches Association in 1922 was another marker of the professionalization of coaching. On the other hand, the desire to keep elements of the game in the hands of the players remained widespread, so rules against coaching from the sideline remained in place until the easing of the game's substitution rules late in the middle era.

Football officials followed a similar path in terms of the increased complexity of their roles, but officiating did not evolve into a full-time job. It remained a side gig, albeit an increasingly demanding one. Most notable to spectators during the middle era was the shift in the officials' appearance and the signaling of their decisions to the players, press, and crowd. Those innovations began with individual officials, before being adopted by their peers, and then becoming national standards.

COACHES AND COACHING

Before WWII, the college football season began in early October and ended by Thanksgiving. The coaches also played a more limited role in recruiting -

which was not supposed to occur anyway. Some head coaches were not directly involved in spring practice. Even in the 1920s, a few top football coaches, such as George Foster Sanford of Rutgers, were volunteers who had independent wealth or business interests that allowed them to forego payment for their services. Others received payment for their services but earned their primary income through business interests, sometimes in cities far from campus. In effect, football coaches could be seasonal workers because the game and coaches' off-the-field responsibilities were much simpler than today.

Some of the most mobile coaches were highly successful. Hugo Bezdek coached Oregon's football and basketball during the fall and winter of 1913 through 1918, coaching Oregon baseball through the 1917 season as well, before taking over as manager of the Pittsburgh Pirates from 1917 to 1919. Pop Warner had a similarly odd arrangement during the 1922 and 1923 seasons after he accepted the Stanford job following the 1921 season at Pitt. When Pitt did not release him from the last two years of his contract, Warner facilitated Stanford's hiring of Andy Kerr, then Pitt's freshmen coach, as Stanford's interim coach, so Kerr could implement Warner's system. Beyond that, since Pitt did not allow spring practice and Stanford did, Warner traveled west to coach Stanford each spring before returning to Pitt for the fall. Such an arrangement would be unthinkable today, but the relationship was cozy enough that Warner also arranged a holiday game between Pitt and Stanford following the 1922 season.

Even those coaches that were full-time university employees frequently had duties beyond coaching football; many coached multiple sports, taught physical education classes, or had other assignments. John Heisman was Georgia Tech's baseball coach most of his time there and coached basketball for two seasons as well. Dick Romney coached Utah State's football and basketball teams from 1919 to 1941 before focusing on football another eight years. On the flip side, Phog Allen, who won three national titles as Kansas' basketball coach, spent eight seasons as a college football head coach, including one at Kansas. As the middle era progressed, however, the head football coaching role increasingly became a full-time job.

Coaches in big-time programs were well paid, often making as much or more than full professors, but only a few earned superstar money. Much as coaches now appear as panelists on network television shows, coaches of the era wrote magazine and syndicated newspaper articles. Rockne wrote weekly columns during the season summarizing the national football scene and identifying the best teams, Zuppke published daily articles discussing plays and techniques, and John Heisman expounded on the broader role of football in the colleges. Many top coaches wrote books revealing the secrets of their success. Coaches also made money as product spokesmen. Knute Rockne purportedly received the highest salary of any football coach in the nation but made far more money endorsing products for Wilson sporting goods, Barbasol shave cream, and Studebaker automobiles.

In the professional leagues, head coaches did not need a second job, but assistant coaches, like players, held other jobs in the offseason into the late 1940s and early 1950s. Paul Brown was the first head coach to insist on having a full-time coaching staff when he took over the AAFC Cleveland Browns. Others soon followed.

Despite the professionalization of coaching, the desire for the players to control the game remained strong, as reflected by rules prohibiting anyone, including substitutes or fans, from coaching players during a game. In 1906, only five people were allowed to walk on the sideline; all others sat on the bench. Similarly, only one person could care for an injured player on the field and only after gaining permission from the umpire.

A 1912 rule allowed only one person to stand on the sideline. The 1914 rule makers forced everyone to sit or kneel. That rule remained in place until 1949 when coaches, trainers, and substitutes could stand in the bench area but not "*walk up and down* (italics in original), or needlessly approach, either sideline."[31] The restrictions on sideline behavior were eased substantially in 1957 when players gained unrestricted access between the 35-yard lines. Still, the various rules limiting or prohibiting players and coaches from standing on the sidelines explains why period pictures show nearly everyone seated on the bench.

Nebraska players seated on the bench during the 1941 Rose Bowl. (Unpublished Snapshot, Personal Collection)

Some coaches violated the rules against standing on and coaching from the sideline. Coaches or the backup quarterback might sit or stand in certain positions, cross or uncross their legs, or hold items in their hands to transmit basic instructions to their quarterback. Dr. John R. Richardson, Wisconsin's coach in 1920, was accused by Ohio State of writing instructions on the bottom of the team's water bucket scoop, leading some to consider Wisconsin the ladle of coaches. (Apologies to Miami of Ohio.) A common violation of the rule against standing on the sideline came on opening kickoffs. Although some officials strictly enforced the sideline rule, many allowed both teams to stand on the sideline during the opening kickoff to show support for their teammates. Post-kickoff, the teams were sent to the pines.

Both teams stand on the sideline as the home team, Brown, prepares to kickoff to Colgate in 1952. (Unpublished Snapshot, Personal Collection)

One whacky suggestion to eliminate coaching from the sideline came from Jack West, who won eleven conference championships coaching South Dakota State and North Dakota from 1919 to 1945. In the mid-1930s, West suggested adding a twelfth offensive player on the field whose sole duty was to call the signals, after which they would step away and not participate in the play. West also suggested having the twelfth man stand on the opposing sideline while his team was on defense to ensure he did not receive instructions from his coaches. Even the NFL, comprised of professional players led by professional coaches, did not allow coaching from the sideline until 1944, and that was limited to the players receiving instructions on the sideline during timeouts.

One effect of coaches increasingly running the show was a change in the role of the team captain. Whereas captains formerly held functional responsibility for the team on the field, their role became increasingly ceremonial, and the need to name a single captain disappeared. Back in the day, teams elected their captain for the next year and announced their choice at the awards banquet concluding each season, and it was in that situation that Baylor named co-captains for the 1925 season. However, one of the elected captains did not return to school for the 1925 season, so only one captain served that year. The next year, Notre Dame announced they would have co-captains, and at least five other schools followed. Electing separate offensive and defensive captains became popular after two-platoon football came around.

The idea that coaching from the sideline was unsportsmanlike remained widespread into the early 1960s when the rules allowed the substitution of one or two players per play. Red Blaik, who coached Dartmouth and Army from 1934 to 1948, made the old-school argument against using substitutes to send in plays, saying:

> If the coach has worked properly with his quarterback, he knows more about running the works than does the coach. Interfering with the quarterback destroys his confidence. He loses faith in his coach when the bench falters.
>
> The continuous shuttling of players for the purpose of communication makes a bad impression on spectators. They get the feeling that the men in the field are nothing more than pawns for the geniuses on the bench, most of whom are horrible chess players.[32]

Although coaches had surreptitiously called plays from the sideline, doing so overtly began with Paul Brown and the Cleveland Browns in 1954. The NFL allowed unlimited substitutions by then, so Brown used messenger guards to shuttle in plays. (One of those guards was Chuck Noll, who later won four Super Bowls coaching the Pittsburgh Steelers.) The shuttled players sometimes mixed up the play calls, and the entire process took precious time, so Brown was open to new approaches. One came in 1956 when a pair of Ohio inventors approached Brown with a radio headset that fit inside his quarterback's helmet. The Browns used the system in an exhibition game and four regular-season games, despite the unit sometimes picking up the local taxi dispatcher's calls, before the NFL banned all electronic methods of communicating with players on the field mid-season, shelving such units for a few decades.

A major contributor to the easing of restrictions on coaching from the sideline was the similar easing of substitution rules. Liberal substitution patterns are now the norm, but that was not the case for most of football's history. For years, having separate offensive and defensive units in football would have seemed as odd as having distinct units in baseball, one to bat and the other to play the field. In 1906, a player leaving the game could not re-enter the contest. This affected player safety because those who had their "bell rung" or who suffered injuries that temporarily kept them from playing, did not leave the field. Recognizing this was a safety threat, a 1910 rule allowed substituted players to return to the game at the beginning of a subsequent quarter. Later rule changes allowed players to substitute at any time during a subsequent quarter or at clock stoppages. Still, there were relatively few substitutions in competitive games. Some coaches with deep rosters substituted entire units at the beginning or end of a quarter. Knute Rockne was known to start the game with his second unit in an attempt to wear down the opposition. Even when substituting full units, however, whoever was in the game played both offense and defense.

The substitution rules might not have changed if not for WWII. With draftees and volunteers leaving campuses, concerns arose about the likely depth of college football rosters. To give coaches the flexibility to substitute for an injured or fatigued starter, the 1941 rules committee approved unlimited substitutions. Under the new rules, players could enter and reenter whenever the ball was dead, and substitutes could immediately communicate with their teammates.

The committee anticipated coaches would use the new rule as intended: substitutes would enter the game one at a time due to injuries or fatigue, and that is how coaches used the rule from 1941 through most of the 1945 season. While the letter of the law allowed coaches to substitute players freely, no one used the rule for mass substitutions, until one of them finally did.

Fritz Crisler was Michigan's coach and the president of the AFCA in 1941. As AFCA president, Crisler presided over the rules meeting that approved unlimited substitutions, but even he did not fully appreciate how the new rule could be applied. In 1945, however, Crisler's team was composed mainly of freshmen who were not yet of draft age and 4-Fs (men rejected by the draft board for physical reasons). Faced with a late-season game against West Point, a team that included future Heisman Trophy winners, Doc Blanchard and Glen Davis, Crisler created separate offensive and defensive units, swapping them with each change of possession. Though Michigan lost 28-7, Crisler's strategy caught the attention of coaches nationwide, and others copied it the next year. One was the opposing coach, Army's Red Blaik, who gave two-platoon football its military name. Blaik found the two-platoon approach helpful because his team had only one hour and fifteen minutes to practice each day, so the two-platoon system allowed him to focus each player on a limited set of responsibilities.

Two-platoon football was widely adopted by 1950. It was an advantage for players who had the skills to play offense or defense or to kick, but not all three, so the impact of specialized players increased. Two-platoon football also ensured players were less fatigued, and more players saw action, both of which were positives. Some coaches used their best players on offense one game and defense another or switched them during games based on the tactical situation.

Despite the advantages of the two-platoon system, it ran counter to the long-held ideal of the all-around athlete and sixty-minute man. More important, two-platoon football required larger rosters and more coaches, so college administrators were less supportive due to the increased costs. Many colleges that suspended football during WWII struggled to restart their programs at competitive levels after the war, and the increased cost of two-platoon football added to their burden. When fifty small colleges dropped football for cost reasons in the early 1950s, the NCAA eliminated free substitution in 1953.

The NFL also liberalized substitutions during WWII by allowing three players to substitute at a time whenever the ball was dead and allowed mass substitutions between quarters. The NFL moved to unlimited substitutions in 1950 and has retained that rule ever since. Thus, during most of the 1950s, the NFL had unlimited substitutions while the colleges played one-platoon football. Oddly enough, the NFL abided by college substitution rules for the College All-Star games during that period despite every participant being a professional.

The NCAA slowly liberalized its substitution rules between 1954 and 1965 when full two-platoon football returned to the college game. Although it took a convoluted path, Fritz Crisler's innovation proved to be among the most profound in football history. Two-platoon football led to specialized offensive and defensive players, as well as specialist kickers. As Sean Lanham noted, two-platoon football removed the need for versatility and shifted the emphasis to specialization:

> [Before two-platoon football], your starting quarterback had to be quick enough to play safety, your running backs tough enough to play linebacker. The downside to this approach was that a player with one specific skill – say blazing speed – might not be enough of an all-around player to crack the starting lineup. With free substitution legalized, specialization became the norm.... Free substitution helped the passing game immensely because it allowed coaches to use quick players at offensive end who weren't big enough to play defense. Their speed could be used as a weapon, and many teams moved to formations that featured three ends and just two backs.[34]

The move to two-platoon football also meant teams needed specialist coaches for their offensive and defensive units, and eventually, special teams. Those coaches focused on more specific aspects of the game, teaching more specialized techniques and concepts to their players who, playing only one side of the ball, could absorb them.

The two-platoon system was reflected in the naming of All America teams. The first AP All America team to name separate offensive and defensive units came in 1950, five years after two-platoon football began. The AP All America team returned to naming a one-platoon team with the 1953 rule change and switched back to the two-platoon format in 1964, one year before the return to unlimited substitutions. Punters and kickers were another story. Specialist punters and kickers became common in the late 1960s and early 1970s, but the AP All America team did not include spots for punters and kickers until 1981.

Among the aids to the increased specialization of coaches was the development and increased access to game and practice film. The football world genuflects to coaches and players who study copious volumes of film, so it is not surprising that film study may be the element of the game with the highest number of claims to its fatherhood. Paul Brown, Sid Gillman, George Halas, Frank Leahy, Bob Neyland, and Carl Snavely all receive mention as the father or, at least, a pioneer in using motion pictures as an aid to coaching football. However, none of those claims are true. Instead, it appears the father of football film study was Cornell's Albert Sharpe, who, in his first year coaching a poor Big Red team in 1909, had a moving picture camera brought to practice one day. Afterward, Sharpe claimed he learned more in one day than he had in a month of watching his team by the naked eye. Sharpe shared his insight with Andy Smith at Penn, who made use of moving pictures, as did Logan Cunningham at Princeton.

Although he was not the father of film study, a kind uncle who advanced the art and science of film study was Bill Hayward, Oregon's famous track and field coach and trainer from 1904 to 1947. Hayward was an amateur photographer who used photographs and film to teach athletic techniques in a range of sports. After acquiring a moving picture camera in 1913, Hayward filmed Oregon's football games, which the team reviewed with coach Hugo Bezdek. As the 1910s progressed, an increasing number of schools filmed their games, with some teams showing them at local theaters to recoup their expenses.

Oregon's 1917 Rose Bowl champion team. Trainer Bill Hayward stands on the far left and Coach Hugo Bezdek stands on the far right. (1917 Oregana, University of Oregon Yearbook)

The use of film and photography for scouting opponents became an issue by the mid-1920s, so the NCAA formed a subcommittee to investigate the matter. The subcommittee sent questionnaires to the 230 NCAA-member institutions, with 98 returning the questionnaire. Two schools "admitted" to filming opponents as part of their scouting, seven used still photography, and forty strongly condemned the use of either. After hearing the study results, the 1924 NCAA convention banned filming or photographing athletic contests not involving your school. Supporters of the ban argued that filming opponents increased costs and, more concerning, it pushed football in the direction of a business controlled by coaches, not players.

The following year there was talk of abolishing scouting altogether, but the AFCA convention chose not to act on the issue, and neither did the NCAA. Selected schools and conferences developed agreements not to scout one another, but these fell apart within the next few years. Ultimately, teams and conferences moved in the direction of exchanging films with upcoming opponents and the need for in-person scouting of opponents all but disappeared.

PRACTICES AND PRACTICE EQUIPMENT

Although Harvard held the first spring practice in 1889, spring practice did not become widespread until after WWI and, even then, was primarily focused on conditioning. That changed in the 1920s as football increased in complexity, and coaches used spring practice to teach skills and evaluate talent. The 1930s saw the addition of full scrimmages and practice games at the end of spring practice at many schools, while others called for eliminating spring practice due to its exemplifying the overemphasis of football. The call went unheeded until the Ivy League and Southern Conference did so in the early 1950s. The Ivy League held that stance for six decades, while the decision sharpened the differences among Southern Conference members, leading a group of larger schools to leave the conference to form the Atlantic Coast Conference in 1953.

Whether in spring or fall practice, coaches have long created practice equipment that allowed players to gain football skills without risking injury by hitting one another. Some practice equipment has stood the test of time, and others have not. One such device is the bucking strap, which had several waves of popularity. (Bucking is an old-school term to describe backs running between the tackles with the ball.) Running into the line was a skill worthy of improvement, so Fred G. Folsom designed and gained a patent for the bucking strap in 1906 when he was in the last of his four years coaching his alma mater, Dartmouth. Folsom coached Colorado before and after his Dartmouth stint and had enough success that Colorado's football stadium, Folsom Field, is named in his honor.

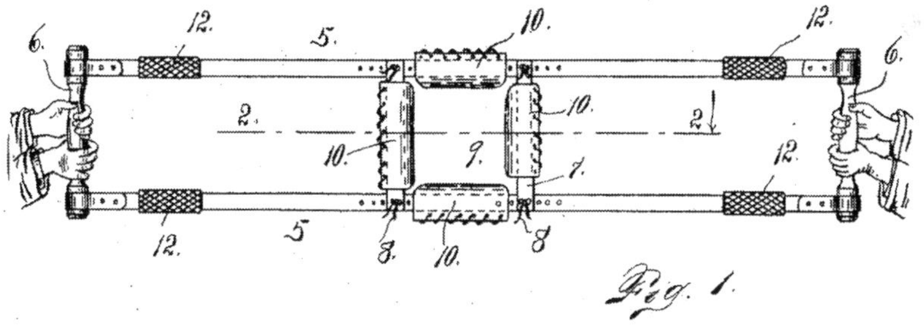

Illustration from Fred G. Folsom's 1906 patent for the Foot-Ball Bucking-Harness. (U.S. Patent No. 829,590)

The original bucking strap was a leather and canvas contrivance with two long belts, between which was a padded leather, square harness. The straps were held parallel to the ground by two or more teammates such that the harness presented a target for a running back. The back charged at the bucking strap, inserted his head through the opening, and continued charging as his teammates offered resistance.

A Dartmouth player bucks the strap as his teammates offer resistance in 1926. (Acme Newspictures, Personal Collection)

Bucking straps were popular when first introduced and remained so from the 1920s through the 1940s. They enjoyed a resurgence in the late 1950s when Woody Hayes used a bucking strap hung between posts, rather than held by teammates. Bucking straps disappeared after that, but its cousin, the pull sled, became a favorite of strength and conditioning coaches in the 1990s.

Another piece of practice gear that fell from use was the blocking or padded apron. It faded so fully that few football aficionados are aware they ever existed. Had these pads been used only by a few oddball coaches, they would not warrant mention here, but their users included legendary coaches such as Biggie Munn, Red Blaik, Sid Gillman, and Vince Lombardi.

Columbia University players wearing blocking aprons in practice in the early 1940s. (Mechanix Illustrated, December 1941)

Like aprons more generally, blocking aprons hung from the neck and tied around the waist, but most came with leggings that tied around the calves. The pads protected the wearer while allowing them to move somewhat naturally, but they appear to have disappeared in the late 1960s, presumably due to their retaining heat.

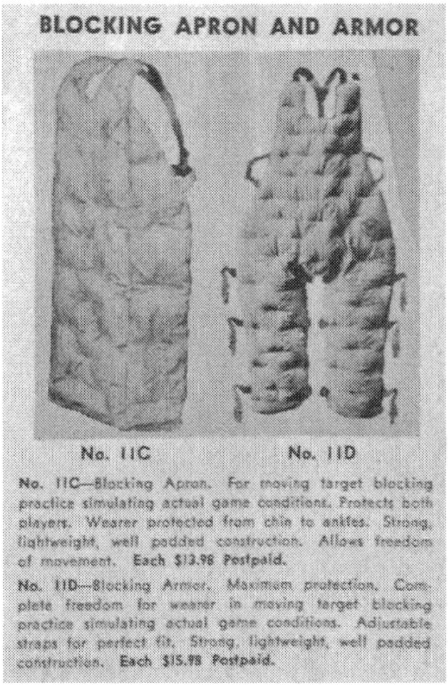

An advertisement for blocking aprons in both the full curtain look and the traditional two-legged version. (1950-51 Central States Basketball Headquarters catalog. Courtesy Paul Lukas, Uni Watch)

A different piece of practice gear that has stood the test of time is the practice vest, which visually distinguishes offensive and defensive players during practice scrimmages. In the old days of one-platoon football, there was more separation between the varsity's first and second teams, and the reserve or "scrub" team, so coaches often had the reserves wear red jerseys for practice while the varsity wore another color. (The "red shirts" worn by reserve players later took on a second meaning, as covered in the next chapter.)

Harvard players wearing a mix of crimson and white jerseys during spring practice in 1925. (Harvard University Archives)

Having the varsity and reserve teams wear separate colors worked fine as long as the units remained distinct. However, the advent of liberal substitution rules in the 1940s led to players switching between the reserve and primary units. References to "scrimmage vests" begin to appear in the 1940s, and because the blousy vests looked like pinafores, people began calling them "pinnies" or "pennies."

TCU coach Abe Martin gives advice on the T formation to quarterback Ronald Clinksdale. The pinnied players on defense eagerly await the action. (1954 Horned Frog, TCU Yearbook)

Outside their use on the practice field, the vests found a second use when more restrictive substitution rules returned to the college game in the early 1950s. Under those rules, players taken out of the game could not return until the next quarter. To avoid inadvertently reinserting those players, some coaches had substituted players don scrimmage vests until the next quarter began.

Beyond practice equipment, core elements of football practice are the drills. Football has borrowed any number of military terms, but one that might surprise many as having a military background is the "skeleton drill." Early in conflicts when countries were in the process of raising armies, regiments sometimes had their full complement of officers, but a limited number of enlisted men, and these units were known as "skeleton regiments." Since those armies marched into battle in formation, it was critical for officers to practice their commands despite having a limited number of enlisted men, so the men at the corners of the formations held ropes to represent the full size of the unit. These were known as skeleton drills.

The same concept applied to football practices when teams had insufficient men or, more often, wanted to separate the training of the backs from the linemen. Skeleton drills were in use by 1915 at the University of Detroit and by Penn State while preparing for the 1923 Rose Bowl. Walter Eckersall of the *Chicago Tribune* reported that "Bezdek put the men through a long, grueling practice, which consisted of blocking and charging by the forwards and skeleton signal drills by the back fields."[34] Although skeleton or "skelly" drills continued in use for practicing signals and running attacks, they became increasingly associated with the passing game as that part of football developed.

The Oklahoma Drill, also known as the Nutcracker and a few other names, is football's most storied drill. The drill evolved or devolved into a tool for evaluating toughness and desire and, in doing so, became part theater, a right of passage, and a team-building exercise. More recently, its use receded due to concerns about concussions and other injuries, as well as its association with the brutal side of football.

Still, the drill originated for all the best reasons in 1947 when Bud Wilkinson became Oklahoma's head coach and installed his Oklahoma 52 defense. Wilkinson saw the 52 as a means of defending the increasingly popular Split T, an offense he ran himself. Given the Split T's wider splits and option attack, Wilkinson wanted to free his linebackers to pursue the ball rather than be responsible for a specific gap. To do so, Wilkinson gave each down lineman responsibility for the gaps to their right and left (i.e., "two-gap" technique), a technique they needed to learn by drill.

One of Wilkinson's bedrock coaching philosophies was to simulate game situations in practice. As Wilkinson said in 1955:

> Another thing I believe -and I got this from Henry Iba, basketball coach at Oklahoma A&M- is, 'your measure of a coach is based on how well he creates in practice the situations the player will face in a game, and keeps repeating it until the player reacts properly from memory.' That sounds a little fancy, but it isn't. Most of us coaches are adapters and copycats. There really are very few original ideas. Missouri Coach Don Faurot's idea of splitting the lineman -that's the Split-T- was an original contribution.[35]

To combat Faurot's original idea, Wilkinson created a drill mirroring the defensive lineman's new responsibilities. The drill positioned an offensive lineman across from a defensive lineman, both of whom were in a narrow alley created by two tackling dummies lying on the ground. Upon a simulated snap, the defensive lineman tried to shed the blocker and tackle the running back running through the alley just as they would need to do in a game. Offensive and defensive linemen had long battled in one-on-one drills, but creating the alley and adding a running back to the drill simulated game conditions, so the drill spread rapidly and became a staple of football practices nationwide.

CONDITIONING AND DIET

Full-body movements was not a term thrown around football practice fields in the early 1910s, yet a classic full-body exercise arrived during the period, thanks to Dartmouth's Frank Cavanaugh, who had the following to say about his innovation:

> "...this exercise leads to perfect muscular co-ordination through movements arduous but interesting, because involving both mental and physical effort besides an intense spirit of competition. The drill demands and teaches immediate response to the word of command. It has the priceless value that the test of endurance which it provides takes place under the direct supervision of the coach."[36]

Cavanaugh, of course, was referring to grass drills that require teams to run in place while periodically being ordered to lift the knees higher or faster or to fall forward or backward. Once on the ground, commands for other movements follow until its victims are allowed to stand and return to running in place. (Up-downs or down-ups are similar exercises stripped of the ground movements.) Regardless of the coach, the frequency of commands instructing the team to hit the ground and then stand bears an inverse relationship to the quality of the team's recent performance.

Selected members of Canavaugh's 1922 Boston College team perform grass drills. (1923 Sub turri, Boston College yearbook)

Cavanaugh left Dartmouth at the onset of WWI to become an officer in the 26th Division. During training, he introduced grass drills to his company, which led to their adoption by the rest of the division, and then by other parts of the U.S. Army. (Grass drills remain a part of U.S. military training programs to this day.) After the war, Cavanaugh coached at Boston College and Fordham, leaving the latter the year before Vince Lombardi's freshman year. Fordham continued doing grass drills under their new coach, Jim Crowley, and it appears that Lombardi took them to heart since they were a mainstay of his Green Bay Packers practices in the 1960s. Lombardi's status in the game and his endorsement of grass drills ensured that another generation or two of football players suffered or benefitted from Cavanaugh's creation.

Other efforts to improve the agility of football players included numerous forms of obstacle courses that often emphasized the need for high knee action from runners. Boxes and tires laying on the ground were common until Joe Paupa, former coach of DePaul and Chicago's Navy Pier team during WWI, patented a rope system in 1944 that became ubiquitous on football practice fields.

The 1922 Kansas State team under Charlie Bachman improved their agility by weaving through a series of wooden boxes. (1923 Royal Purple yearbook, Courtesy Morse Department of Special Collections, Kansas State University Libraries)

Exercise science was in its infancy when the Carnegie Foundation Report of 1929 devoted one of its twelve chapters to medical and training issues in college football. Although the overall report came from interviews at 180 schools, the medical and training chapter focused on twenty-two relatively well-heeled colleges and universities. Still, only half those schools conducted baseline physical exams of varsity athletes and only two tracked concussions or other injuries from year to year. The investigators were troubled by the influence and use of trainers who lacked scientific training, the failure to regularly clean equipment and wash athletic gear, and the use of communal buckets for drinking water and rinsing bloody towels. It was a different world back then.

Harvard's 1923 football team warming up for practice. The group furthest left performs the duck walk, which likely damaged more knees than it strengthened. (United Newspictures, Personal Collection)

Little scientific attention was given to the training of football players and athletes generally, leaving the door open to fads, like isometrics, which came on the scene in the late 1950s. A published study or two and anecdotal reports from prominent athletes suggested that isometrics were highly effective in building strength and mass, and did so in less time and using less equipment than other methods. The combination of effectiveness and ease of administration proved irresistible to many football coaches and trainers, leading professional, college, and high school teams across the nation to implement isometric exercise programs in the early 1960s.

As it turned out, the early "studies" on isometrics were poorly designed. They lacked the experimental controls needed to separate the contributions of isometric exercise, mental or visualization routines, or the anabolic steroids administered to some study participants. Like many things that seem too good to be true, isometrics proved useless for athletic training and quickly disappeared from football training regimens.

OFFICIALS

During the early era, schools negotiated with one another when selecting game officials. A shortcoming of this system was that officials who made controversial calls sometimes did not work another game involving the coach or school that suffered from the call. The middle era saw the informal system disappear at the process of selecting and training officials became systematized. In the first few decades of the era, each conference or region of the country developed organizations to select, train, and assign officials. These groups also assigned neutral observers to monitor the officials and asked coaches to rate the performance of the officials handling their games. All or most of these elements were in place with associations across the country by 1940.

Interestingly, while the processes for managing game officials became highly organized, many of the most visible elements of the officials' role in football games did not. Instead, they arose through the innovations of individual officials and grew organically. Only later were they codified by the rules committee or the various officials' organizations.

One aspect of the officials' duties driven by both rule changes and local innovations was clock management. From early on, the officials managed the game clock using handheld watches. In 1906, that meant keeping tracking of each 35-minute half. A 1907 rule change shortened the halves to 30 minutes before the halves were split into 15-minute quarters in 1910. Justified as tripling the number of times team physicians could assess the players' physical condition during the game, breaking the game into four quarters has remained the same since then.

Since 1910, however, there have been periodic challenges to using a clock to control football games. For example, concerns about teams huddling as a means to stall resulted in a 1920 suggestion to have each quarter comprised of forty plays, regardless of the time taken to execute the plays. Walter Camp became convinced of the system's merits, leading the rules committee to approve the 40-play quarter system for test games. Brown and Boston University played a 40-play per quarter test game that year and, while all feedback on the game was positive, the time had not yet arrived for eliminating the game clock.

The same idea popped up in 1942 following Minnesota's tenth consecutive victory over Michigan. It seems the Gophers benefited when the game clock was improperly stopped during a substitution late in the second quarter of the game. The clock stoppage allowed Minnesota to kick a last-second field goal, and those points made the difference in the Gopher win. To avoid such timekeeping mishaps, Bernie Bierman dusted off the 40-play quarter system and recommended its use. Bierman was an appropriate advocate since he coached Minnesota to five national championships in the 1930s and 1940s, though he was a somewhat disinterested observer in 1942 because he was coaching Iowa Pre-Flight, not the Gophers. Bierman returned in Minnesota in 1943 and convinced the Big Ten coaches to recommend the 40-play quarter system to the rules committee. The idea again went nowhere. Neither did a similar proposal in 1946, and the 40-play quarter system has not been heard from since.

The "down box" was actually a box during an earlier period in football's history. (Postcard, Unknown Publisher, Personal Collection)

Besides keeping time, the game officials also were responsible for tracking downs and distances, and their lives were made easier in 1898 when the lineman's chain entered football by rule. Initially, the chains were a simple set of poles connected by a ten-yard long chain or rope supplemented by a third pole, the down marker, that marked the spot of the ball following the most recent play. The plain poles proved functional for the game officials, but they were difficult to see from across the field and from the stands. The plain poles also did not communicate the down, only the distance to gain. The 1920s saw the introduction down markers that were rectangular boxes atop a pole with each of the sides indicating first, second, third, or fourth down. These were known as "down boxes," a name that remains in use today despite down boxes no longer having boxes.

Rectangular down boxes remained in use for another twenty years, but the 1920s also saw the development of the "flip" down marker, whose numbered plates flipped to display the correct down on the front and back (unlike the down box). Flip markers were in almost universal use before being supplanted by the louvered Dial-A-Down marker, which came on the market in 1987.

Down markers were one of several methods game officials used to better communicate with the teams and crowd during the middle era. Of course, the most significant change in their visibility came when football officials transitioned from wearing street clothes to standard uniforms. For the first forty years of football, game officials wore street clothes, which typically meant a dark wool jacket, pants, white shirt, and bow tie. Some wore their college letter sweaters because it reinforced their neutral status.

Georgetown captain Dap Dailey and Virginia captain Joe Wood shake hands before their game in 1911. The field judge, Emory S. Land, wears his Navy letter sweater. (Photo by Harris & Ewing, Library of Congress)

By the late 1910s, many football officials copied their basketball brethren by wearing white shirts and pants, along with a bow tie. Their white outfits visually set them apart from the players who almost universally wore dark jerseys in their team colors.

Enter Lloyd W. Olds, who graduated from Eastern Michigan in 1916 and returned there after earning his Ph.D. Olds began officiating high school football and basketball games in 1912, handling major college football games from 1921 to the 1940s. Like other officials dressed in all white, Olds experienced players inadvertently passing him the ball, but Olds was determined to fix the problem. As Olds noted years later:

> When I started officiating, the customary garb for a basketball referee was a white shirt and a little black bow tie and white duck pants. Trouble was that many players wore white, or mostly white tops.
>
> All very confusing. Out of the corner of his eye a player would see a blur of white that might be a guy on his team. Or it might just be a referee. Which is why referees kept dodging or catching or ducking. It got pretty lively at times.
>
> I finally decided I needed an outrageously distinctive costume. And what's more distinctive than the stripes of a zebra? So I went to [a clothing shop] and had

> them order me a couple of long-sleeved wool shirts with black and white stripes. ...And they did the job. Oh yeah. I took a lot of ribbing. But there was no question as to my identity.[37]

Olds reportedly wore his striped shirt for the first time at a 1921 high school basketball tournament and soon wore it for football games as well. While the shirts were unusual and ugly, they worked, and Olds' design proved popular among individual officials before becoming the required uniform for high school officials in select states in the early 1930s. They appeared at college games as well, with the Big Ten requiring football officials to wear striped shirts beginning in 1937.

Three officials signal a Stanford touchdown during the 1928 Big Game with Cal. Referee George Varnell is the sole crew member wearing an early version of the striped shirt. (Courtesy Stanford University Archives.)

The NFL adopted the striped shirt in 1941, but took the idea to another level under the belief that fans wanted to differentiate the officials by role. Referees wore black-and-white stripes, umpires wore red-and-white stripes, field judges wore green-and-white stripes, and head linesmen adorned themselves in orange-and-white stripes. The NFL returned to the black-and-white shirts in 1947, and that was the last of the color variations until the American Football League (AFL) arrived on the scene in 1960 with their officials sporting red-and-white striped shirts.

The North Carolina and Texas captains meet with the stripe-shirted referee for the coin toss before their 1948 game. Tom Landry is the Texas captain wearing #32. (Hugh Morton, North Carolina Collection, University of North Carolina Library at Chapel Hill)

Officials in black-and-white striped shirts are now universal in football, hockey, wrestling, and basketball below the professional level. And it all occurred because some guy in Ypsilanti had a better idea.

The now universal practice of football officials wearing distinctive uniforms was not the only common officiating practice that started with one individual. So it was with the referees' practice of signaling penalties to the press and spectators. We have all seen football officials conference on the field, after which the referee steps to the side and performs a set of arm and leg movements indicating the nature of the infraction. In earlier times, referees did not signal the nature of penalties. Instead, they informed the captains of their calls, assessed the penalties, and instructed the teams to resume play. Often, that left everyone in the press box and crowd wondering what had occurred.

Members of the print press could interview the officials, coaches, and players after the game about key penalties, but the lack of information about penalties became increasingly problematic when radio broadcasts became common. The announcers wanted to understand the reasons for penalties in real-time so that they could describe the infraction to their listening audience.

It is against that backdrop that many sources credit Ellwood Geigas as being the first referee to use penalty signals. As the legend goes, before the 1929 Syracuse-Cornell game, Geigas was asked by Ted Husing, CBS' top sportscaster of the day, to signal the press box to indicate the nature of each penalty. Geigas quickly suggested four different signals and used them in the game that day.

The Geigas-Husing account is attractive because it coincides with the period in which radio broadcasts of college football games became popular, but there are problems with the account. First, Syracuse and Cornell did not play one another in 1929 or any other time between 1901 and 1933. Syracuse played Colgate and Columbia each year during the period, so the supposed event might have happened against Colgate or Columbia, with the Cornell reference being a case of mistaken identity. Moreover, Husing called the 1929 Syracuse-Columbia game in New York City during the last week of the season, but there is another problem or two with the Geigas-Husing story.

It turns out that the National Association of College Football Officials recommended the use of a standard set of referee signals before the 1929 season, and newspaper articles appeared at the beginning of the season included illustrations of those signals. Hence, the signals were in place before the season, not cobbled together by Geigas and Husing before a game at season's end. The 1929 season also saw a raft of newspaper articles crediting the development of "penalty codes" to Elmer Layden. Layden devised a set of signals late in the 1928 season and promoted their use in 1929, but Layden had a Duquesne cheerleader signal the penalties, not the referee.

FOOTBALL SIGNALS

Code of Signals Used to Indicate Various Fouls

Signals.	Fouls.
Grasping of wrist	Holding
Shaking fists	Unnecessary Roughness
Crossed legs	Tripping
Sifting of hands	Illegally in motion
Hands on Hips	Off-side
Arm aloft	Refusal of Penalty
Arms extended sidewise	Incompleted F. Pass
Arms folded	Interlocked interference
Both arms aloft	Score
Military Salute	Loose-ball foul

NOTE—These signals will be given to the press-stand by the referee from behind the offensive team.

FRANK BIRCH, Referee.

A list of referee signals used by Frank Birch, as published in an 1918 book about sign language. (Seton, Sign Talk, *1918)*

In the end, the real problem with crediting Geigas or Layden with creating referee signals in 1929 is that Frank E. Birch started signaling penalties in 1910, when Birch also started providing a list of his penalty signals to members of the press before each game. Birch frequently handled Big Ten and Missouri Valley games and had a long run working the annual Notre Dame-USC game, so he was a well-known and well-regarded referee.

Some of Birch's signals remain in the game today: he grasped one of his wrists to indicate a holding penalty, and he put his hands on his hips to indicate offsides. Other signals developed by Birch were modified or dropped when their corresponding penalties became obsolete. The NCAA published its first set of referees' signals in the 1934 rule book.

Frank Birch, in all white, referees Iowa's victory over Nebraska in 1919. (Postcard, Unknown Publisher, Personal Collection)

Frank Birch was not the last person to enter the pantheon of officiating innovation during the middle era, and the next person also helped reduce confusion surrounding the calling of penalties. As previously discussed, confusion reigned when officials tooted their horns to signal that a penalty had occurred during play. Minnesota's H. L. Williams suggested the use of a flag-based system in 1917 to signal penalties as they occurred and to communicate the nature of the penalties to spectators after the play. His system borrowed from the flags used by soccer referees as well as the semaphore system used in the military, and it is unclear whether Williams' flag system ever saw use in a game.

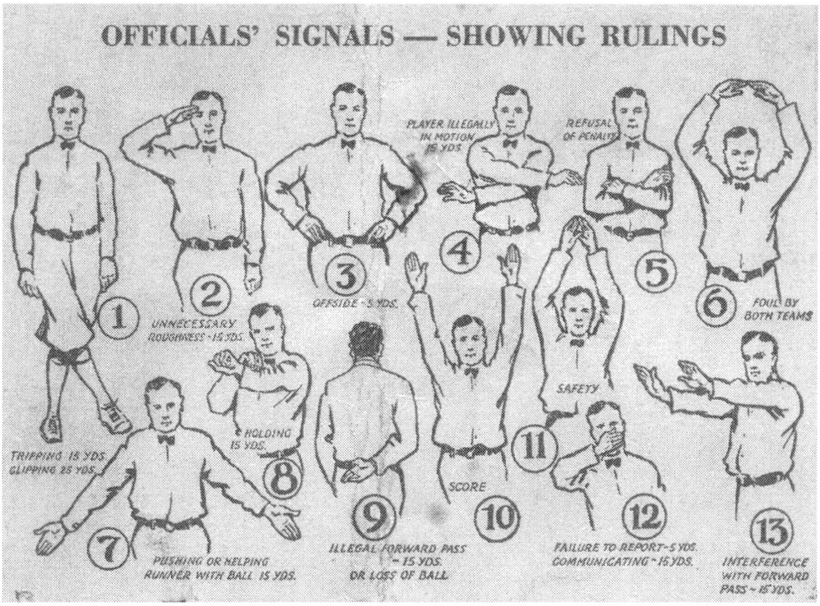

This 1931 illustration of referee signals includes the now obsolete signal #12 indicating coaching from the sideline or the failure of a substitute to check in with the referee. (1931 Brown-New Hampshire Official Foot Ball Score Card, personal collection)

The use of dropped or thrown flags to signal penalties popped up a few decades later. A former high school official from Pennsylvania claimed he used flags in games beginning in 1935, and we know penalty flags were used in Florida by 1940 since a newspaper columnist editorialized about the frequency in which officials dropped their handkerchiefs in games played that weekend.

Despite some earlier use, the thrown flag landed on the national scene due to Dwight "Dike" Beede, Youngstown State's longtime coach. Like others, Beede wanted to remove the confusion between the officials' horns and whistles, so his wife sewed a handful of small, weighted flags. Using red fabric from an old Halloween costume, white fabric from a bedsheet, and drapery weights, football's Betsy Ross created a set of striped penalty flags. Beede then convinced the opposing coach and the officiating crew to use the flags in Youngstown State's game with Oklahoma City University in 1941.

Everyone seemed to like the flags, including one of the game officials, Jack McPhee, who kept his flag and continued using it. McPhee was a Big Ten official and used the flag in prominent games, including the 1948 Rose Bowl. The NCAA officially adopted penalty flags in 1948, recommending that officials drop the flag toward the offending team's bench. Later rule makers considered but did not adopt the use of different colored flags for offensive and defensive penalties, which was likely a good thing. We have all seen plays in which it is clear the offense or defense committed a penalty. There are also plays for which the teams and crowd are uncertain which team committed the foul. That uncertainty brings drama, as evidenced by the groans and cheers that follow a referee's announcement of those penalties.

A final comment about on-the-field officiating relates to the period during which the referee alone used a whistle; the other officials signaled fouls by ringing a bell or blowing a horn. Bells never caught on, but period photographs show umpires holding bulbed horns similar to those on bicycles. Most umpires, however, used small horns mounted on wristwatch-like straps. Despite the kazoo-like sound being unlike a whistle's tweet, some players still hesitated or stopped play when they heard the tooting of the horn, so the confusion lessened but did not disappear.

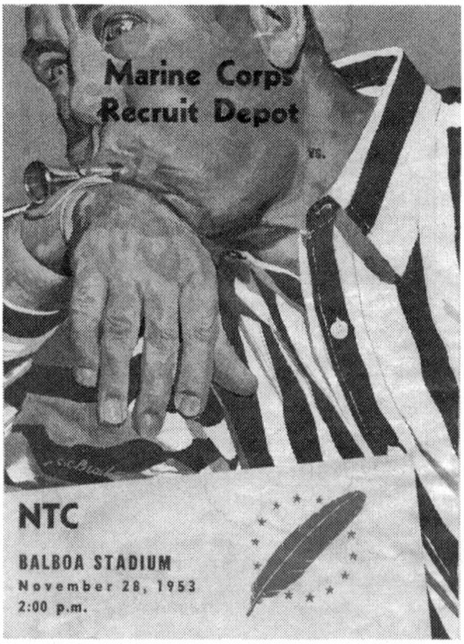

The cover of the 1953 U.S. Marine Corps Recruit Depot vs. Naval Training Center game program shows an official blowing a horn attached to a wristband. (November 28, 1953 Marine Corps Recruit Depot-NTC game program. Unknown artist. Personal Collection.)

The kazoo-like horns also were problematic because they were not very loud. At times, referees did not hear the field judge's horn signaling the end of the quarter due to the din of the crowd. Seeking a louder signal to designate the end of a quarter, some officials turned to the starter's pistol, which, along with gongs, had signaled the end of periods in intercollegiate basketball since 1911. The NCAA never required the use of pistols, but made them optional in 1924, the same year the Big Ten required home teams to provide the field judge with a starter pistol and holster. References to the optional pistol remained in the NCAA rule book until 1947 when it disappeared without fanfare, and the timing of its actual disappearance from use is muddied.

The NFL, which used the college rule book when pistols first came into use, continued using pistols when they switched to their own rule book in 1933 and only dropped the pistol in 1994. While the final gun no longer sounds on the football field, it remains a frequently-used metaphor among sportswriters looking to add poignancy to their writing.

Having covered several steps in the evolution of on-the-field officiating, we turn to an important change that occurred off the field. Through the 1936 season, college football lacked consistent rules for tracking game statistics and systematically collecting them from the schools. The rules for calculating game statistics differed from school to school and newspaper to newspaper. Some included punt return yardage in rushing statistics; others tracked yardage on inside runs separately from sweeps. Disagreements existed on whether to calculate punt and field goal yardage from the point of the snap or the kick. Others argued whether to award first downs on long touchdown runs or when first downs resulted from defensive penalties. Any number of other differences existed, but no one took on the challenge of standardizing football statistics until Homer F. Cooke, Jr. stepped forward.

Cooke was a sportswriter for several newspapers and part-owner of a semi-pro football team in the Northwest during the early 1930s. He tired of news articles touting various players as the greatest in the nation, given that the game lacked the statistics to compare one against another. To help address the issue, Cooke convinced the semi-pro Northwest Football League to track game statistics using a system he developed, and Cooke agreed to summarize those statistics.

Cooke later asked various major college programs to use his system and report their statistics. Joseph H. Petritz, sports publicity director at Notre Dame and Fielding Yost, Michigan's former coach and then a member of the NCAA Football Rules Committee, supported his efforts and argued Cooke's case in their various committees. Within several years all major college teams provided their statistics to Cooke, the Associated Press began using his numbers, and Cooke's *American Football Statistical Bureau* became the official source of NCAA football statistics. In 1959, Cooke sold his reporting bureau to the NCAA, which absorbed it, with the result that the official NCAA statistical records for football begin with those gathered by Homer Cooke, Jr. in 1937.

THE PROFESSIONALIZATION of football coaching resulted from the importance placed on football success and the increased demands placed on those responsible for achieving it. During the middle era, coaches became accountable for recruiting athletes, for managing larger squads and expanded coaching staffs, and the game itself became more complex. Scouting and film study to dissect the play of upcoming opponents became the norm. Those direct football tasks and the ancillary public relations roles could no longer be performed only during the football season or by individuals with substantial obligations outside the athletic department.

The role of game officials also evolved during the middle era. The increased number of rules required monitoring more game elements, and forward passing required the coverage of more territory. Those tasks could only be accomplished by increasing the number of officials and spinning off some duties (e.g., timekeeping) to others. Like coaching staffs, the number of officials working games increased from four to five with a sixth optional official.

In many respects, however, the most visible changes in the role of officials were the expanded duties aimed at helping the press and spectators understand the actions on the field. The equipment used by chain gangs became more visible, the referee signaled the nature of penalties to the press and crowd, and penalty flags provided an immediate visual cue that a penalty had occurred. Each change was an innovation dreamed up by an official or coach hoping to improve the game, and each proved effective.

While the most visible change in the role of the officials was their signaling of penalties, the most noticeable change to their appearance was the adoption of the black-and-white striped shirt. More important, the consistency of their selection, training, and scheduling increasingly matched the uniformity of their appearance. Officials who had previously been chosen based on the agreement of the competing teams were now trained and assigned by the teams' conference or similar organization. This standardization of officiating was an example of larger organizations taking control of the game of football. Far more significant changes in the control of college football occurred as the NCAA was redefined and became the most powerful authority in American sports. That is the overarching story of the following chapter.icial

12

OFF THE FIELD (1906-1959)

Most of what we now consider to be the core fan traditions in college football developed during the middle era as the game extended its reach to a broader swath of the population. College enrollments grew more than tenfold from 1906 in 1959, and more general societal changes led to football's popularity extending to those without direct affiliation with their state or other colleges. Immigrants and America's rural population poured into the cities as America transitioned from an agricultural country to one in which half its people lived in urban areas by 1920. The country's workforce increasingly made things rather than grew them, shifting toward a five or six-day workweek that left time for leisure activities, including spectator sports.

Technological advances also impacted how fans experienced football. The emergence of commercial aviation meant that teams increasingly played intersectional games, and select fans followed them there. The majority that could not attend games in person listened to radio broadcasts and, in later years, watched their team's play once or twice per year on television.

As all this happened, the stakes to run a top-level college football program increased. Fielding a football team required inducements to athletes that increasingly came out of the universities' pockets rather than those of boosters, and the resources committed to facilities and coaches became significant as well. Some schools determined the costs were too high and left the race, while others poured greater and greater resources into their athletic endeavors.

All these changes ultimately led to a different governance model for college athletics. National trends buffeted schools that had banded together in regional conferences, particularly the emergence of television programming. When televised games threatened attendance at games, schools and conferences used the NCAA to negotiate TV contracts to limit the number of games broadcast. This ceding of power to the NCAA was a significant turn in the evolution of college athletics, and set the stage for many events that came to pass during football's modern era.

GAME ATMOSPHERE

Much of what makes college football unique is the pomp and tradition surrounding the games, yet all the traditions we hold dear are less than 150 years old; most are substantially younger. Many of football's finest traditions are unique to particular campuses, but this chapter covers those that flowered during the middle era and became widespread, including one or two that have faded into obscurity. Most college football traditions emerged organically on one campus, spread to others through informal mechanisms, and were tweaked to fit their new locations.

One college football tradition that emerged early in the middle era was the homecoming celebration. Homecoming is among the traditions most closely associated with college football, but it did not originate on college campuses. Instead, the first homecoming events were fairs that encouraged former city residents to return home for a weekend or week of concerts and other activities.

Identifying the first college homecoming depends on identifying what makes homecoming, homecoming. For our purposes, a college homecoming is an annual event that includes a football game, and other activities that vary by region. The first homecoming-like event that included a football game occurred in Austin in 1908. Texas and Texas A&M played on Thanksgiving Day as part of a homecoming event wrapped around the university's 25th anniversary. The purpose of the event was to celebrate the university's 25th anniversary, and the failure to hold similar events in subsequent years means Texas cannot claim to have started homecoming.

The situation gets stickier when considering Baylor's homecoming in 1909. That event was positioned solely as a social or fraternal activity for alums - and Baylor played TCU in football that weekend- but Baylor's next homecoming did not occur until 1915, so they are out of the running as well.

That brings us to Illinois' campus in 1910 where Clarence Foss Williams and W. Elmer Ekblaw had the idea to hold a homecoming event each fall to bring former Illinois students back to campus. The two worked for several months building support with campus organizations and the administration, and they succeeded in holding the first school-sponsored homecoming the weekend of October 15, 1910, capped by a win over Chicago.

Illinois students create the Block I during the first homecoming game, a 3-0 win over Chicago. (Courtesy of the University of Illinois Archives)

Unlike their brethren from the Lone Star state, Illinois hosted a homecoming event each year from 1910 to the present day other than when the Spanish Flu pandemic forced its cancellation in 1918. Following Illinois' lead, homecoming became nearly universal at the university and high school levels across the United States.

The topic of returning to campus leads to a question of how alumni and other fans traveled to games. At the beginning of the middle era, local fans went to home games by foot, horse-drawn carriage, or local trolley. Visiting team fans and others more distant from the stadium used rail systems until the first decade of the 20th century when wealthy alumni also could drive their electric or internal combustion vehicles to the big ball game.

With few exceptions, visiting teams and members of their traveling parties used the same transportation methods as fans. Exceptions occurred with a few teams associated with the military. Since the military has an interest in getting people or weapons from one location to another, they have long invested in emerging transportation technologies. Such was the case during WWI when the U.S. Army's Air Service created training bases across the American South and West. Like other training bases during the war, the flight schools formed football teams to compete with colleges, athletic clubs, and all other comers in the area. So it was only natural that the first team known to have flown to their football games were the airmen from California's Mather Field during the 1918 season. Not only did they fly to their games, but many team members were air cadets that piloted the two-seater planes themselves.

(Late in the same season, the team from San Pedro Submarine Base in the Port of Los Angeles traveled by submarine and submarine tender to San Diego to play Rockwell Field to a 3-3 tie.)

It was a different world among civilians for whom commercial air travel remained in its infancy, but there are a few stories of fans riding in Air Mail planes or chartering flights to away games during the 1920s. Futuristic newspaper articles trumpeted the day when football teams would fly to intersectional games, speeding the travel process and minimizing the number of missed classes.

Dartmouth, which is located well off the beaten path, made plans for an airfield in 1929 to allow teams to fly in and out, but those plans never took off. Instead, the first instances of college football teams flying to games occurred not in the Northeast, but the Southwest. The first instance of a college football team flying to a game appears to have been when New Mexico hopped aboard a Transcontinental Air Transport (TAT) flight to Los Angeles on October 10, 1929, for a game with Occidental in the Rose Bowl. (As airline aficionados know, TAT morphed into Trans World Airlines (TWA), which became part of American Airlines in 2001.) An estimated 15,000 to 20,000 people saw Occidental defeat the flying New Mexicans in one of the first games played under the lights on the West Coast. A month later, Nevada's football team took to the air for the three-and-one-half-hour flight from Reno to Los Angeles for their game with USC.

Oklahoma's football team arriving by plane for the 1946 Gator Bowl. Coach Jim Tatum, wearing the hat, is at the bottom of the airstair. (Photo by Robert E. Fisher, State Library and Archives of Florida)

Although these and other teams flew to games before it became common, travel by rail remained the norm for teams and fans alike until after WWII. Well into the early 1950s, Midwestern teams had to decide whether to travel by rail or air when playing games in Florida or California.

While the transportation methods for teams and fans traveling to games have evolved, traveling to away games was and remains expensive. Nowadays, fans can watch away games on television, but in the old days, the only way to monitor a big, away game in real time was to attend a simulated or reenacted game. Game simulations began in the 1890s and relied on local newspapers to establish a direct telegraph or telephone connection with a reporter at the game. The reporter transmitted play-by-play results to the home office, where they displayed key information for the local audience. Big-city newspapers often had scoreboards on the exterior of their buildings showing the score, possession, down and distance, and other game facts. Some had representations of football fields with lights or figures indicating the progress of the battle waged on the faraway gridiron. Announcers with megaphones might supplement the information at these events, which saw hundreds or thousands of fans standing on the sidewalk, in the street, or in the gym to monitor the big game.

Oregon State's varsity 'O' organization spent $1,000 on this electric scoreboard in 1924. Fans paid 50 cents to watch the Oregon State-Whitman game. (Ball Studio, Historical Photographs of Oregon State University)

Similar gatherings took place when radio first came on the scene and before many households had their own radio set. Technically, the first radio broadcasts of football games were sent by engineering students and hobbyists to limited gatherings listening to these broadcasts. The first commercial broadcast came when a Westinghouse radio station, KDKA, handled the Pitt-West Virginia game in 1921. KDKA broadcast every Pitt home games that year using a play-by-play announcer at Forbes Field connected by telephone to the KDKA station. From there, KDKA broadcast his voice on radio. Students on the campuses of some Pitt opponents gathered at local auditoriums or similar venues to listen to the games.

Having covered how fans traveled to or monitored away games, our attention turns to home games. Then, as now, the majority of fans traveled a short distance to attend games, and, as the middle era progressed, most traveled by car, and many arrived hungry. It is impossible to know when tailgating began, but if we define tailgating as eating and drinking in or near a vehicle before a football game (or another sporting event), then the first tailgaters were those whose carriages or buggies lined the sidelines at football games in the late 1800s and early 1900s. Newspaper accounts of the IFA championship games in New York City describe carriages filled with fans who arrived well in advance of the game. The passengers sat atop the carriages and "brought out their hampers as soon as they arrived on the field and those seemed to be amply provided with good things."[38]

Parking carriages along the sideline stopped being an option as stadiums grew larger and more formalized, yet the desire among fans to arrive early and have a bite to eat before the game remained. In some settings, fans had their fill at local restaurants or taverns, but stadiums more distant from commercial areas generated a tailgating culture. Yale Field, which preceded the Yale Bowl, was surrounded by open fields when Harvard visited Yale in 1906. It was a perfect spot for tailgating fans who, by then, traveled to the game by automobile rather than horse-drawn carriage. The tailgaters proved the envy of those arriving by train, as noted in the *New York Times* the following day:

> The train crowd came principally about noon. ....Each trainload as it reached the station quickly hurried away down Church Street to the campus in a mad rush to get cars to make the journey to the field. ...Few were able to get luncheon on the way, and these gazed with envious eyes as they neared the field at small parties of automobilists eating tempting viands that had been brought in hampers spread out in picnic fashion on a table cloth laid upon the ground.[39]

The above is the first published reference to tailgating at a football game, but it is worth noting that one did not "tailgate" at the time; one took a "football picnic." Tailgating replaced football picnic as the common name for this activity only when station wagons became popular in the 1950s. The station wagon's tailgate served admirably as a table for serving food, and the name transferred to the broader activity. Tailgating received a boost from the invention of portable charcoal grills in the 1950s, allowing fans to prepare hot food onsite rather than depend solely on picnic fare.

After the tailgaters ate and drank their fill, they waddled into the stadium for the game and encountered the sights and sounds of their college band. It is hard to imagine the atmosphere of college football games without fight songs played by school marching bands. Almost every fan recognizes fight songs such as Michigan's *The Victors,* the *Notre Dame Victory March,* and USC's *Fight.* Despite their popularity, none have the honor of being the first college fight song. That honor is often credited to T. J. Hurley's, *For Boston,* composed in 1885 for his alma mater, Boston College. Hurley was a busy boy since he also headed the committee that selected maroon and gold as Boston College's school colors. Recent research shows Hurley did not write *For Boston* until several decades later, so the honor appears to reside with the Ann Arborists and *The Victors.*

It is also not clear when the first college band marched on a football field, but we know that America's oldest, continually operating college band belongs to Notre Dame. It has played at every home football game since the first, an 1887 clash with Michigan. The sport so new in Northwestern Indiana at the time of the game that Michigan had to teach the Irish the rules and techniques of football before kickoff, an act of charity the Wolverines have come to regret.

Marching bands as we know them originated as military or cadet bands after the turn of the last century with Army, Navy, Minnesota, and Purdue having active bands by 1907. The popularity of college marching bands boomed after WWI via the many veterans with military band experience and the inclusion of music in high school curricula. According to the bandies at Purdue, their marchers were the first to break ranks to form a non-columnar shape on a football field when they formed a Block P in 1907.

The Purdue Military Band forming a block P in 1922. (1923 Debris, Purdue University yearbook)

While marching bands involve large numbers of students performing on the field, schools tend to have only one mascot. (Nebraska, for some reason, has two.) The word "mascot" entered the English language in the 1880s due to a popular opera, *La Mascotte*, that concerned a farm girl whose presence brought bountiful crops to her farmer so long as the girl remained a virgin. It is unclear how long the farmer enjoyed bountiful crops, but we know the term "mascot" quickly came to describe a person or animal that brings good fortune.

Campus dogs were common early college mascots. Yale's Handsome Dan, a bulldog that appeared at games as early as 1890 was the first college mascot. Later Yale mascots included dogs of other breeds, but Yale ultimately chose Bulldogs as their team nickname, and all subsequent mascots have been bulldogs named Handsome Dan.

Navy began using a goat as its mascot in 1893. Unfortunately, the night before the 1912 Army-Navy game, Navy's goat died. Despite the tragedy, Navy went on to win the game. This led to a debate before the 1913 game on the advisability of sacrificing their new goat to ensure victory. Alas, the goat survived the day, and Navy lost the game, but the loss might have resulted from a college football first, the appearance of a costumed mascot on the Army sideline.

Army's costumed mule appeared at the Polo Grounds during their 1913 win over Navy. (George Grantham Bain Collection, Library of Congress)

Before going further, this is worth mentioning that mascots and nicknames often differ, and either one can precede the other. Both are symbolic representations of a team or school, but mascots are the physical embodiment of the symbol, while nicknames are just nicknames. Handsome Dan, the mascot, preceded the Bulldog nickname at Yale. The opposite occurred during the late 1800s when newspaper editors created short, snappy nicknames to describe teams in headlines, during which time the teams representing the Western University of Pennsylvania earned the unattractive nickname, the WUPs.

Pittsburgh's Golden Panther mascot on the sideline in 1922. (University of Pittsburgh Historic Photographs, Archives & Special Collections, University of Pittsburgh Library System)

When the school changed its name to the University of Pittsburgh in 1910, the students and alumni discarded the WUPs moniker, opting to be known as the Golden Panthers. Despite the new name, the panther lacked a physical manifestation until 1922 when "Roc," as Pitt's panther mascot is known, became the second or third costumed mascot to patrol college sidelines. There is some doubt about Roc being the second or third costumed mascot because a student wearing an African lion costume roamed the sidelines at Penn State the same season.

The fourth costumed mascot was Chief Illinek, who first performed his war dance during halftime of Illinois' 1926 game with Penn. Times were different then, but one must acknowledge there is nothing that honors a dispossessed Native American people quite like a white guy performing a fake war dance while dressed in the religious garb of a tribe different than the one he supposedly honors. Best as we can tell, Duke's Blue Devil was the fifth costumed mascot, and as his picture shows, his costume was every bit as sad looking as Pitt's panther.

Duke's Blue Devil, c. 1929-1930. (Duke University Archives)

The menagerie of costumed mascots remained limited until after WWII, when a few more came along, after which their adoption occurred at a slow, but steady, pace until they are now nearly universal.

Elizabeth Morrow's senior portrait. (University Archives, Spencer Research Library, University of Kansas Libraries)

Costumed mascots first appeared on the field in 1913, but things got even nuttier the following year when a woman cheerleader yelled for the first time. Ironically, the integration of cheerleading resulted from a Northwestern decision to segregate the sexes. It seems that Northwestern chose to seat men and women students separately at football games beginning in 1912. Kansas followed suit, thinking the men would be less distracted during games and cheer harder for their fellow students on the field. This left the Kansas women's section without a cheerleader, so they elected Elizabeth Morrow as their yeller in preparation for their 1914 rivalry game with Missouri. Morrow's performance at a women's rally several days before the game led to an invitation to perform at the men's rally a two days later and to join the male cheerleaders on the field for the big game.

Tulane was the next major college cheer team to include women, thanks to Rosa Hart's appearance along the sidelines in 1919. Unlike Elizabeth Morrow's tenure at Kansas, Rosa Hart's role at Tulane was sufficiently impressive that there are multiple images of Rosa performing along the sidelines. Each image shows her wearing an all-white outfit, like the male cheerleaders, along with some form of Tulane decoration. Women became part of many cheerleading squads in the 1930s and took on a more significant role on college campuses during WWII when there were fewer men on campus. After that, cheerleading became viewed as a predominantly female activity.

While cheerleading remains widespread, a college tradition that has mostly fallen by the wayside is the card stunt. Ironically, the first card stunts did not involve cards at all. Instead, a Stanford student named Thomas Jewell distributed white muslin to fellow students who tossed the muslin over their heads and shoulders to form a large "S" in Berkeley's stadium during the 1904 Big Game.

Rosa Hart of Tulane's coed cheerleading squad. (1920 Jambalaya, Tulane University yearbook)

Cal students improved the process in 1910 by using cards rather than cloth for their stunts, which allows Cal to lay claim to being the first to execute a card stunt. Although spreadsheets and computers make it easier to design card stunts nowadays, such stunts require a level of commitment to tradition lacking at most colleges. The schools whose student sections still execute card stunts and the year they began doing so include Illinois (1910), Cal (1910), USC (1922), UCLA (1922), and Ohio State (1938).

An imaginary scene shows 1905 team captains superimposed on a background from the 1904 Big Game when Stanford fans formed an S. (Postcard, Unknown Publisher, Personal Collection)

While card stunts have largely disappeared from college life, a once-popular activity that has gone extinct is the serpentine or snake dance. Football-fan serpentines once wound their way through town on the opening night of the football season, circled homecoming bonfires, and led teams from the train station back to campus upon returning from road victories. Primarily a West Coast tradition, it was known in the Midwest as well since Louis Elbel, the composer of Michigan's *The Victors* fight song, claimed to have danced in a serpentine following Michigan's victory over Chicago, the game that inspired him to write that dreadful tune. Serpentines also made frequent appearances on the field as they entertained fans at halftime or erupted on the field following big victories.

Washington State fans serpentine their way to form a W following a 1915 shutout of Oregon. (Art Oberg, Postcard, Personal Collection)

In-stadium serpentines died off in the 1920s, likely due to fans having less access to the field in the stadiums built that decade. They remained part of college homecoming eve activities into the 1930s and were still part of West Coast high school celebrations in the 1940s before slithering into the mists of time.

A tradition involving fans celebrating on the field that remains common is the tearing down of the goal posts after big wins. The first known instance of goal posts torn down in celebration came when Idaho bested Washington State 16-0 in 1912, which, given Idaho's nickname, the Vandals, seems appropriate. More amusing was the first known instance of a teardown coming at the hand of the losing team's fans. That occurred in 1914 when Parsons High School in Kansas lost to Chanute, 81-6. So disgusted were Parsons fans with the team's performance that they tore down their own goal posts and did not field another football team for six years.

Idaho fans tear down the goal posts following their defeat of Washington State in Pullman in 1912. (Postcard, Burns, Personal Collection)

Another football tradition is the playing of *The Star-Spangled Banner* before the kickoff. Despite being written in 1814, the anthem was seldom played outside of military ceremonies and selected concerts before WWI. That changed when the anthem sounded before each of the six World Series games in 1917, before leaking over to football. The first known instances of *The Star-Spangled Banner* playing before football games were the Wisconsin-Minnesota and Oregon-Mare Island Marines games on November 3, 1917.

After WWI, the anthem fell back into relative disuse and was heard only when military or school bands were in attendance. By WWII, advances in stadium sound systems enabled solo artists or recordings of the anthem to replace the live bands, allowing the anthem to become a standard element of sporting events across the country.

Of course, some football traditions originate from commercial interests, particularly opportunities for advertising and the media. One of America's lesser-known aviation pioneers was Thomas Scott Baldwin. He became the first successful American parachutist, when he left the safety of a balloon on January 30, 1885, and lived to tell the tale. Baldwin was the first to fly an airplane over the Mississippi River and remained an aviation pioneer throughout his life, which ended in 1923 while leading the lighter-than-air efforts for the Goodyear Tire and Rubber Company.

We do not know whether Baldwin ever flew over a football game, but the first known flight of a heavier-than-air craft at a football game came on November

11, 1911, when Oscar Brindley circled above the Harvard-Princeton game. That may not seem like a big deal, but the entire U.S. military had one aeroplane and three balloons at the time. Flying was new, which allowed Brindley's passenger, James H. Hare of *Collier's Weekly,* to take the first aerial photograph of a football game.

Collier's Weekly *published James H. Hare's photograph of the Harvard-Princeton contest two weeks after the game.* (Collier's Weekly, *November 18, 1911.)*

Following WWI, blimps, dirigibles, balloons, and similar craft outperformed airplanes for some tasks, leading to significant money being poured into researching and developing lighter-than-air machines. The lighter-than-air machines captured the public's attention everywhere they flew and became popular in the promotions and advertising world. Blimps gained their first connection to football in 1919 when the football team from the *U.S.S. Nevada* went on a recruiting tour accompanied by a Navy blimp. The connection to college football came in 1929 when the *Defender,* a Goodyear-Zeppelin blimp, appeared over the Oregon-Florida game for the opening of Madison Square Garden Stadium in Miami. Notably, when they dropped the game ball from the blimp they slowed its descent with a parachute since previous experience showed footballs dropped without parachutes burst upon hitting the ground.

The TC-13 blimp flies past Cleveland Stadium in 1933. (Goodyear Records, The University of Akron Archives)

Though Goodyear's blimps became technological anachronisms, the old school technology provided a steady aerial platform for new school technology when viewers first saw television images shot from a blimp during the 1955 Rose Bowl parade.

The mention of the Rose Bowl naturally leads to the issue of postseason play. The first postseason games in sunny locations came via a barnstorming tour by a team of former Yale players over the Christmas and New Year's holidays as 1896 transitioned to 1897. George Foster Sanford, later known for coaching Columbia and Rutgers, captained the Yale Consolidated team on a tour that defeated club teams in Nashville, Jackson, and New Orleans before crowds totaling more than 10,000. More important than the games themselves, the crowds and newspaper coverage garnered by the tour indicated there was an appetite for similar games.

The first true bowl game came five years later in Pasadena, a town whose name most Americans would not recognize had its fine citizens not scheduled a football game as part of the 1902 Tournament of Roses celebration. The Tournament of Roses attempted to continue the series following the 1902 game, but neither Stanford nor Cal was up to playing Wisconsin, the Eastern invitee, in 1903. Stanford and Cal's decision to drop football after the 1906 season put a further kibosh on the postseason game.

The Rose Bowl restarted in 1916 in part because teams in the Northwest began playing solid football. Washington State played in the 1916 game, Oregon played in 1917 and 1920 Rose Bowls, while teams from military training camps played in the 1918 and 1919 games. By the early 1920s, the California Wonder Teams were off and running, and the Rose Bowl became an institution that justified the building of Rose Bowl Stadium, which hosted its first Rose Bowl in 1923.

The first bowl game to successfully follow the Rose Bowl was the East-West Shrine game in San Francisco. Dreamed up by a few local Shriners to raise money for their children's hospital, the game showcased the top stars of the East and West. The 1925 game included players from recent classes, not just current college seniors, including the East's player-coach, Bill Ingram, a 1919 Naval Academy grad who was the head coach at Indiana at the time.

Lacking the slate of bowl games we have today, some schools scheduled independent games for a bit of holiday fun. Pitt's contest at Stanford following the 1922 season (during Pop Warner's transition) and Penn's trips to play Cal on New Year's Day 1925 and New Year's Eve 1927 were examples.

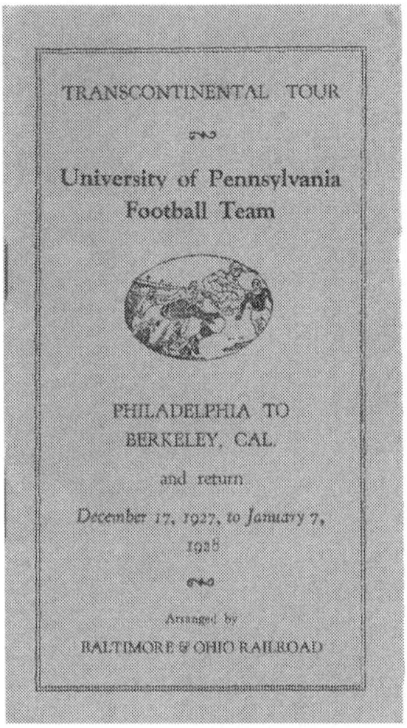

Itinerary for Penn's trip to play Cal in San Francisco on New Year's Eve 1927. After the game, Penn traveled to Pasadena for the January 2, 1928 Rose Bowl. (Personal Collection)

Various cities held games between conference all-stars or barnstorming NFL teams in the 1920s and early 1930s, but it was not until the mid-1930s that other longstanding bowls got their starts. Like the Rose Bowl, the Orange, Sugar, Cotton, and Sun Bowls began as festivals to promote tourism to their regions, but those were few and far between. Even as late as 1960, there were only eight bowl games, including the five already mentioned. It would not be until the rise of cable television that the number of bowl games expanded dramatically.

The evolution of the bowl system connects with football's naming of its national champion. Over its history, college football has determined its top-ranked or national championship team using four methods: the opinion of individual writers, mathematical formulas, polls, and playoff systems. Like All America teams, individual sportswriters or other football authorities named the national champions in the early days. Caspar Whitney, who named the first All America team, was the first to provide an end-of-season team ranking when he identified the country's top twenty-eight teams following the 1902 season. He followed that by naming the top 31 teams for 1903. Like others of his day, Whitney may have been a tad parochial when he included Phillips Exeter and Andover, Eastern prep schools, on the list of top college teams.

The second method, the use of mathematical systems, ranked teams based on their won/loss records, schedule strength, and the like. The value of these systems was their objectivity, but they were only as good as their underlying calculations. The first such systems arrived in 1925 through the work of Frank C. Dickinson, an economics professor at Illinois. Dickinson devised his system in response to the annual arguments over the naming of conference champions. Many conferences did not play round-robin schedules, which led to a desire to rank conferences teams despite the unbalanced schedules. The Dickinson System ranked conference teams based on their win percentage and then awarded points for winning, losing or tying games teams in the top or bottom half of the ranking. A Chicago clothing manufacturer, Jack Rissman, encouraged Dickinson to apply the system nationally and upped the ante by sponsoring the Rissman Trophy, later called the Knute Rockne Intercollegiate Memorial Trophy, which they awarded to conference and national champions during the 1920s and 1930s. Some viewed the Dickinson System as determining de facto national championship during its time, but it also produced nonsensical results that spurred others to seek alternatives.

An alternative emerged in 1934 when a poll of sportswriters identified the national champion. The poll came under criticism when it became clear that all the voters were personal friends of the person running the poll. The Associated Press switched formats in 1936 by having sports editors from across the country participate. The United Press International poll arrived in 1950 using a national panel of coaches to cast their ballots.

MANAGEMENT AND CONTROL

At the beginning of the middle era, the top football schools frequently played teams we would view as overwhelming mismatches today. The 1906 season saw Harvard play Bates, Bowdoin, and Williams; Texas faced the 26th Infantry, Haskell, and Daniel Baker; while the University of Washington battled the *U.S.S. Philadelphia*, Seattle High School, and Whitworth (twice). Such games were scheduled, in part, because many of the big state schools were simply not that big and had more in common with small colleges than they do today. In the 1910s, less than twenty percent of the school-age population graduated from high school, and less than ten percent of high school graduates attended college. The U.S. had only eight colleges and universities with enrollments over 5,000 students: Cal, Columbia, Cornell, Illinois, Michigan, Ohio State, Penn, and Wisconsin. Penn was the largest with just over 8,000 students. Washington State had less than 1,800 students when it won the 1916 Rose Bowl, and Oregon's enrollment was less than 800 students when it won the 1917 Rose Bowl.

Beyond being similar in size, large and small schools were more similar in the level of recruiting, and inducements offered to athletes. Under-the-table recruiting and subsidizing of athletes occurred among the teams competing at the highest level, but even those teams did not have full rosters of recruited, subsidized players. Most college football players simply showed up on campus and tried out for the team.

During the twenties and thirties, however, schools increasingly commercialized their football programs. Game attendance and booster interest led to subsidies for tuition, room and board, and other fees through networks of alumni or local business owners, all while school officials professed their belief in the amateur model. The subsidies evolved from being offered only to select players to being the norm for players at schools playing big-time football. Coaches at many schools coordinated with their alumni networks but were not directly involved in recruiting.

Newspaper exposes, and the Carnegie Foundation Report of 1929 documented the widespread nature of these subsidies, but they were not openly acknowledged until 1935 when the Southeastern Conference voted to end the hypocrisy and offer athletic scholarships in an above-board manner. The NCAA membership opposed the SEC's stance and passed a resolution against their compromising the amateur standard. The crux of the conflict was that the SEC schools did not philosophically oppose athletic scholarships and believed in administering them openly.

While the SEC headed down one philosophical path, Robert M. Hutchins, the president of the University of Chicago, took the other. Hutchins viewed big-time football as inconsistent with his school's academic mission and, after becoming Chicago's president in 1929, began squeezing the football program of resources and players. The team became progressively weaker until a program that had once been among the nation's best was no longer competitive in the Big Ten. Following the 1939 season, Hutchins convinced the school's Board of Trustees to drop football altogether. It was an unfathomable step, but they made a decision that no other institution with Chicago's history of gridiron success has ever made.

Some schools followed Chicago's philosophical lead by deemphasizing, but not dropping, football. In late 1945, the presidents of eight Eastern schools met and agreed to reduce their commitment to big-time athletics. (Those eight schools formed the Ivy League in 1954.) The Ivies continued fielding nationally relevant teams for a short time, but they fell several notches as they stepped away from the athletic arms race.

Continued concern over athletic scholarships and a desire to ensure that schools provided comparable benefits led to the NCAA formulating the Sanity Code in 1949. The Sanity Code had five provisions:

- Athletic scholarships could not cover more than the cost of tuition and fees plus one meal per day during the season.
- Scholarship aid was to be based on financial need,
- All assistance to athletes should come from the institution.
- Pay for jobs had to be consistent with the services rendered.
- Students in the top twenty-five percent of their class who maintained a B average could receive additional aid.

The Sanity Code was more restrictive than the SEC's scholarship plan in that it did not allow assistance for books, room and board, and restricted assistance to the student's financial need. Despite many schools knowingly violating its provisions, the 1949 NCAA convention approved the Sanity Code with little opposition.

The hypocrisy behind the vote might have continued had it not been for seven schools that publicly acknowledged they did not comply with the Sanity Code and did not intend to do so. The Seven Sinners -Virginia, VMI, Villanova, Maryland, Boston College, The Citadel, and Virginia Tech- were not rogue schools. They simply were unwilling to do one thing and say another. Their admission led to a 1950 convention vote to expel them from the NCAA. While the majority voted to expel the Seven Sinners, the vote fell short of the two-thirds majority needed for the resolution to pass. The failure to expel the Seven Sinners left the Sanity Code toothless, and it was voted out of the NCAA bylaws the following year. By doing so, the nation's schools effectively acknowledged that competing at a national level in football required a financial commitment approaching or exceeding that set by the SEC.

Beyond those dropping or deemphasizing football for philosophical reasons, others did so for financial concerns. The cost to field a scholarship football team increased with the move to two-platoon football in the second half of the 1940s. Whereas varsity rosters in the 1920s and 1930s had 25 to 35 players, two-platoon teams carried 50 to 60 players or more. As the expenses rose, some schools also faced reduced attendance due to competition from nearby NFL or AAFC teams, challenges restarting football after WWII, and the impact of televised football games. A number of schools dropped or deemphasized football for financial reasons. Many were urban, Catholic universities. Catholic University, Duquesne, Fordham, Georgetown, Santa Clara, and St. Mary's each played in the Cotton, Orange, or Sugar Bowls in the 1930s or 1940s, but dropped or deemphasized football between 1949 and 1954. Other schools that left big-time football during the period included Bradley, Case, Loyola Marymount, NYU, San Francisco, St. Louis, and Washington & Lee.

Marquette and Detroit lasted until the 1960s before making the same decision. Most of these schools continued offering athletic scholarships in basketball, so dropping football was not philosophical; it was a financial decision.

To forestall schools dropping football, the NCAA eliminated two-platoon football for the 1953 season, but it was too little too late. Those that pursued the high-level football path pushed for a 1957 NCAA resolution approving full scholarships. The same resolution limited schools to paying for one official visit per recruit, the signing of Letters of Intent by athletes, and the prohibition of contacts or funding by boosters and alumni. The core of these rules remains in place today.

Besides scholarships and expenses, other disagreements arose on eligibility issues, one of which was redshirting. The first reference to "redshirts" dates to 1917 and the red jerseys worn by Cornell's scrub or scout team. Southern schools often referred to their scrub teams as "bohunks" rather than redshirts, so redshirting was referred to as bohunking in the South into the late 1950s.

The first player known to have taken a redshirt year was Warren Alfson of Nebraska. Alfson farmed for three years after high school before enrolling at Nebraska in 1936. After playing on the freshman team, Alfson was a backup guard as a sophomore, and, not having played in a game by mid-season, asked the coaches not to play him the remainder of the year. By spending the rest of the season with the redshirts, Alfson retained three years of eligibility and went on to become a three-year starter and a senior All America on Nebraska's 1941 Rose Bowl team. Whether word of Alfson's approach became known to other coaches or they figured out the process independently, stashing players on the redshirt team became common.

The Big Ten, the Ivies, and selected other schools banned redshirting in the 1950s because it placed athletic goals ahead of the academic. A 1961 compromise led to an NCAA rule requiring redshirt players to complete their eligibility within five years of enrolling in a post-high school institution. (Previously, there was no limit on the number of redshirt seasons an athlete could take.) Some conferences, like the Big Ten, still did not allow redshirting and only opened that door in 1973.

The most significant eligibility barrier to shift during the middle era concerned racial segregation. Although the number of black football players at major colleges remained limited, numerous barriers were broken in college football and the broader sports world that encouraged more dramatic change in the modern era. While Fritz Pollard of Brown earned All America status in 1916 -as did Paul Robeson at Rutgers in 1918, and Brice Taylor of USC in 1925- only thirty-eight African Americans played major college football during the late 1930s.

The Missouri Valley Intercollegiate Athletic Association (MVIAA) and its offshoots illustrate how football's segregation policies worked and changed over time. Formed in 1907, its founding members included Iowa, Iowa State, Kansas, Missouri, Nebraska, and Washington University in St. Louis. Iowa left after one year, and other schools came and went, including the addition of Kansas State in 1913, Oklahoma in 1919, and Oklahoma State in 1925. From early only, Missouri Valley members followed a gentlemen's agreement that black athletes would not compete with whites in sports in which players came into physical contact with one another. A later policy allowed black players to participate in conference games that did not involve Missouri, Oklahoma, and Oklahoma State.

The Missouri Valley Conference broke apart in 1928. Most of the original members formed the Big Six (later the Big Seven and Big Eight) with the remainder retaining the Missouri Valley name and playing football at a competitive level below the Big Six. The Big Six followed a stricter version of the gentlemen's agreement in that only Iowa State had the occasional black athlete, but they were not allowed to play in games in the states of Missouri and Oklahoma.

Change was in the offing, however. The 1939 College All-Star game in Chicago invited black players to participate for the first time, even though black players could not yet play in the NFL. A month later, UCLA set a new standard by fielding a team with five black players, including starters Kenny Washington, Jackie Robinson, and Woody Strode in the backfield, and Ray Bartlett at end. Robinson later broke the color barrier in major league baseball. A few months earlier, the Los Angeles Rams purchased Kenny Washington's contract from the Hollywood Bears of the Pacific Coast Professional Football League, making Washington the first black athlete signed by an NFL team in thirteen years. Another bright light shined when SMU's all-white football team voted to play Penn State in the 1948 Cotton Bowl, despite Penn State having several black athletes on their roster.

While segregationist practices eased in some instances, the advocates of segregation dug in their heels in others. The Big Seven formalized their gentlemen's agreement in 1946 by barring black athletes in all sports. Despite the agreement, Kansas State announced they would play black athletes in all conference games, though they later pulled back and agreed their black athletes, once again, would not play in contests in Missouri and Oklahoma. This arrangement persisted until a 1950 court decision required the University of Oklahoma to open its doors to black students. With the Jim Crow laws declared illegal, the conference removed the discriminatory bylaw from its books. But old habits die hard, and it would not be until 1956 that Oklahoma and Colorado allowed black players on their rosters. Missouri waited until 1958.

The Missouri Valley Conference followed a path similar to the Big Seven due to its having Oklahoma State and Tulsa as members. The conference voted in December 1947 to end racially discriminatory practices by September 1950. All went to plan until Drake traveled to Stillwater for a mid-October game in 1951. Drake's star player, Johnny Bright, an African American who entered the game leading the nation in rushing and total offense, had played in Stillwater in 1949 without incident. No one expected trouble despite Bright spending Friday night at the home of a black preacher because he was not allowed at the team hotel.

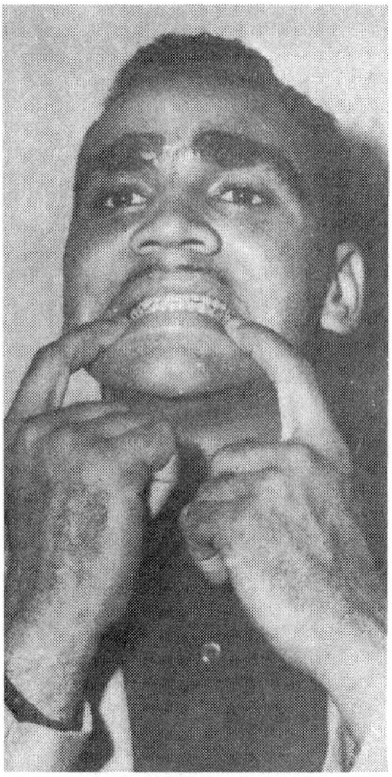

Johnny Bright, after the assault, showing the wires that kept his broken jaw shut. (1952 Quax, Drake University yearbook, Drake University Archives & Special Collections)

Bright was the subject of two questionable hits during Drake's first offensive series. After Drake regained possession, Bright handed the ball off and watched his teammate run around left end. As Bright stood in the backfield, an Oklahoma State player, Wilbanks Smith, hit Bright in the face with a combined punch and forearm shiver, breaking Bright's jaw. Captured in a Pulitzer Prize-winning series of photographs, the brutal incident earned nationwide scorn. Nevertheless, the conference concluded it did not have the power to punish the Oklahoma State player or team. Drake and Bradley left the Missouri Valley Conference in protest, and Oklahoma State did not apologize for the incident until 2005.

The rest of the 1950s saw both promising and discouraging incidents in college football. An encouraging event came in the lead up to the 1956 Sugar Bowl when Georgia Tech's team voted to play Pitt, knowing Pitt had a black player. Following the vote, Georgia's governor tried to stop Georgia Tech from playing Pitt, but his attempt failed, and Bob Grier became the first African American to play in the Sugar Bowl. Shortly after that, Louisiana passed a law banning athletic contests in which whites and blacks competed against one another, causing Villanova to cancel its 1956 game at LSU. The cancellation allowed LSU's football team to maintain its streak of not playing a team from outside the South since 1942, a streak that lasted until 1971. The NFL, whose only team south of Washington, D. C. was the Los Angeles Rams, was somewhat more willing to accept black players. In 1959, twelve percent of the league's players were black.

While the college football world began changing in the 1950s due to broader social forces, it also shifted due to new technologies that broadened and redefined fandom. The emergence of commercial radio in the 1920s and television in the 1950s altered the consumption of sports and generated new sources of money to support teams.

For both technical and organizational reasons, radio and television began with local offerings before shifting to a national orientation. The first commercial radio broadcasts were Pitt games in 1921, and the technology limited the broadcast to the local area. The radio technology quickly improved, as did the organization of networks like NBC Blue, which broadcast the 1927 Rose Bowl over fifty stations, laying claim to be the first coast-to-coast broadcast in U.S. history.

Colleges did not make money from the early broadcasts because radio stations operated without advertising. The business model changed within a few years as advertisers began sponsoring shows. Since only a limited number of companies could afford full sponsorships, radio stations began selling thirty- and sixty-second commercial slots rather than full shows. The downside to broadcasting games was that schools saw paid attendance drop in the early 1930s. Though these drops likely resulted from the economic conditions of the Great Depression, some conferences banned radio broadcasts for a year or two before allowing them again when paid attendance bounced back.

The 1930s also saw the emergence of television. Television stations and sales initially centered in Eastern cities, resulting in the first televised football game broadcast being the 1939 Fordham-Waynesburg game. Philadelphia's status as one of the first cities with television stations meant that Philco's Philadelphia station broadcasted every Penn home game from 1940 to 1949. Like other schools, Penn negotiated their broadcast rights individually and showed their games locally. The growth of television networks after WWII, brought another drop in paid attendance, so the alarm bells sounded, and the Big Ten, among others, banned televised broadcasts of their games for the 1950 season.

During the negotiations for the 1951 season, Penn and Notre Dame signed lucrative deals to televise their games to broader audiences, resulting in two reactions. First, Penn and Notre Dame's competitors told them they would be dropped from future schedules if they did not cancel their television contracts. Second, the NCAA membership voted for the NCAA to negotiate the television contracts and to limit the number of televised games. Ultimately, Penn and Notre Dame submitted and agreed to the NCAA plan.

It was a landmark moment for the NCAA. The NCAA television plan meant schools relinquished their rights to negotiate television contracts individually or as conferences. This ceding of power marked the beginning of the NCAA's transformation from an advisory organization to a powerful enforcement agency. For better or worse, the 1951 decision established the direction for the NCAA's television policies until they were ruled to violate antitrust provision in 1984.

The NCAA used the 1951 season to experiment with a mix of national and regional broadcasts, finding that regional broadcasts depressed paid attendance for games within the televised game's region more than nationally broadcast games. To minimize the impact on paid attendance, the NCAA moved forward with a schedule emphasizing national games of the week and limiting each school to one televised home game per season.

NBC, which held the NCAA television contract to broadcast one game per year in the early 1950s, lost the contract to ABC for the 1954 season. NBC then struck a deal with the forerunner of the CFL to show one game each week. A similar situation occurred on Sundays because NFL teams negotiated their television contracts individually, with most agreeing to deals with the DuMont network. Unfortunately for the NFL, DuMont had only eighteen affiliates in 1954, while NBC had 120 stations, so American television viewers had greater access to Canadian football during the mid-1950s than they did American football.

While American football competed with Canadian football for air time in the 1950s, the real battle for supremacy occurred between college football and the NFL. Professional football began in the 1890s, but was limited to a blue-collar audience and players in industrial towns. Most played their games on Sunday because that was the only day of the week most players and fans did not work in the factories. Sundays also allowed them to avoid competing with the colleges.

The first several years after WWI saw the rise of professional teams with varying budgets, talent levels, and business ethics. A subset of those teams formed the American Professional Football Association in 1920, renamed the National Football League in 1922. Most early NFL teams went belly-up, but a few survived, and others took the place of those that foundered. Despite the tenuous position of professional football in the early 1920s, it caused heartburn for the college football world. The American Football Coaches Association (AFCA) was founded in 1921 and voted in its first meeting to bar from college football those who played professionally and game officials who worked professional football games. Several conferences followed suit.

The college and NFL relationship took another hit when Illinois star, Red Grange, dropped out of school and played for the Chicago Bears one week after his final college game as a senior. He then went on a barnstorming tour that brought tremendous publicity to the NFL and a princely sum to Grange.

During the AFCA meeting that occurred in the wake of Grange's signing, the

AFCA barred from its group anyone associated with professional football. The NFL owners tried to make amends by agreeing they would not sign players until their class graduated, but the relationship remained tense. Nevertheless, individual AFCA members ignored the ban, including active college coaches who played pro football on Sundays. For example, the Brooklyn Horsemen players included two former members of Notre Dame's Four Horseman. Elmer Layden was the head coach at Columbia, and Harry Stuhldreher was the head coach at Villanova. The AFCA ban quickly fell apart, and while the relationship between the NFL and colleges improved, it remained salty for decades. During the 1960s, the NCAA did not allow college game telecasts to include commercials promoting NFL games and barred commentators from mentioning the performance of former collegians in the pros. It was as if the NCAA wished the NFL did not exist.

FOOTBALL BECAME football as we know it during the middle era, shifting from an archaic game to one easily recognizable to modern eyes. The same is true of the broader stadium experience. With few exceptions, major college games at the beginning of the era took place in simple stadiums before less than 5,000 fans. There were no lights, loudspeakers, mascots, or female cheerleaders, but all were present by the end of the era in stadiums seating tens of thousands with some approaching one hundred thousand.

As football entered the 1960s, further change was in the offing due to four key trends. First, the players began to reflect the greater integration occurring in society in general. If not in person, then on television, fans increasingly saw African Americans playing side by side with white teammates. The success and grace of many of these pioneers opened the door for others during the modern era.

Second, the game changed rapidly due to the influence of two-platoon football. Full-time and larger coaching staffs pushed the game to become increasingly specialized and sophisticated. Rosters grew in size, allowing teams to use players whose skill sets suited only one side of the ball. The quarterback position, in particular, could be filled by superior passers who might have been left off the field in the past for their defensive liabilities. The specialization of the quarterback, along with conceptual changes in play design, would open up the game more than had ever been the case.

Third, the rise of massive stadiums led to increased ticket revenues, which provided the funds to pay for additional coaches or to subsidize other sports at the college level. At the professional level, coaching staffs grew, and player salaries increased to the point that few athletes turned down the opportunity to play professional football as many had in the past.

Finally, the end of the middle era saw revenues begin to flow from television rights, a medium that provided virtual access to games at little or no direct cost to tens of millions of viewers. The revenues generated from media rights skyrocketed in the modern era and continue upwards. Media rights fees that once seemed astronomical appear quite earthly several decades later. For example, the rights fees for the 2012 Rose Bowl alone were equal to that of the entire 1984 college football regular season in constant dollars. The growth of those monies and their impact on the game are among the primary discussion points concerning football's modern era.

PART III

TELEVISION BECOMES KING: 1960 TO 2018

13

TELEVISION BECOMES KING (1960-2018)

Whereas ticket revenue drove the economics of football during the first two eras, money from media rights drove football in the modern era. The increase in media money has dramatically increased salaries and modified the venues in which teams train and play, all for the price of a few tradeoffs. Among the tradeoffs has been an increase in the number of regular season, playoff, and bowl games, and the television networks increasingly determining who plays whom and whether games begin morning, noon, or night.

The dawn of football's modern era in 1960 went unrecognized at the time. Unlike in 1906, there were no notable rule changes, dramatic shifts in play, or significant events outside the football world. Instead, football's new path began in March 1960 when the NCAA signed a television contract with ABC, then the least successful of the three major networks. That contract set off a chain of events that made television and related media the primary force shaping football over the last sixty years.

TELEVISION AND TEAM REVENUES

Before the NCAA negotiated a collective television contract in 1951, the NCAA's role had been limited to establishing game rules via volunteer committees of athletic officials from member schools, the coordination of national championships in select sports, and the administration of an annual convention in which member institutions voted on policies. The NCAA did not have any full-time employees; the Big Ten office in Chicago handled the NCAA's day-to-day work on a part-time basis. The NCAA's membership established policies through a one member-one vote process that gave the smallest private college the same voting power as the largest state school. That approach ended over the coming decades as the needs of small and large schools increasingly diverged.

The 1950s and 1960s saw enrollments swell at state universities. During the same period, most research-oriented private universities turned their backs on big-time athletics, and the nation's liberal arts colleges did not grow at a rate to sustain nationally-competitive athletic programs. Despite the widely varying types of schools and their commitment to athletics, the NCAA sponsored only one championship tournament per sport, so the less athletically-competitive schools had little opportunity to succeed in those championships. These differences resulted in the NCAA splitting into the University and College Divisions in 1956. Schools chose which division to compete in; school size and the presence or absence of athletic scholarships were not factors in the sorting process.

ABC won the contract for the 1960 season by tripling the amount NBC paid in 1959, all to broadcast one college game nationally on eight weekends and Thanksgiving, as well as three regional games on four other weekends. The number of televised football games was exceedingly low through today's eyes. Take the last weekend of October in 1960 as an example. The only football games televised that Saturday were the Michigan-Ohio State contest and a CFL game. Sunday was similar in that fans could watch an early afternoon NFL game followed by a late afternoon contest from the new American Football League (AFL). Some communities had highlight shows on Sunday morning covering the previous day's college games, but that was the extent of football coverage. Thus, fans had access to only three live American football games the entire weekend; they also lacked the technology to record games or access them on demand.

All the televised games involved University Division teams, with some appearing more than once. Twenty-seven different teams played in the twenty-one televised games that season. Big Ten teams appeared twelve times, the Pac-8 took seven slots, and the service academies earned six. The remaining conferences and the independents split the other seventeen appearances. The low number of televised games contributed to the relatively small fees collected by the NCAA. ABC paid $6.25 million for the television rights in 1960, or the equivalent of $53 million in 2019 dollars. By comparison, each school receiving a full share of the Big Ten Conference media rights fees in 2018 received $51.1 million across all sports. Thus, the money for the conference media rights paid to one Big Ten school in 2018 nearly equals the value in constant dollars of the NCAA's national football contract in 1960. The difference in relative fees is substantial, but the more fascinating story concerns the battles that ensued and the changes those battles brought to football.

The NCAA had national television contracts in the 1950s, while NFL teams negotiated their media contracts individually. A 1953 court ruling allowed the NFL to protect game attendance by blacking out television coverage within 75 miles of NFL home games; a ruling challenged in 1957 prior to settling out of court. Nevertheless, the incident increased the NFL's efforts to gain protection from antitrust laws. With antitrust legislation under discussion, the AFL announced in 1960 their intention to maximize their television coverage by playing games on Wednesday, Friday, and Saturday nights, in addition to regular Sunday afternoon games. Unease voiced by the colleges led the AFL to play only Sunday games, but the AFL also took the path of negotiating a league-wide contract with revenues sharing.

After Pete Rozelle became the NFL commissioner, the NFL shifted to a similar revenue-sharing contract for the 1961 season, until the courts rejected the agreement. That court ruling sped Congressional action, and the *Sports Broadcasting Act of 1961* passed, which exempted professional sports leagues from certain aspects of antitrust legislation. The act protected high schools and the colleges from the professional leagues by prohibiting the NFL and AFL from broadcasting games on Fridays and Saturdays between the second Friday in September and the second Saturday in December. The later merger of the NFL and AFL created a Sunday colossus that negotiated unified contracts and expertly marketed their product.

The NCAA, on the other hand, spent significant effort on internal battles that led to changes in its governance and financial models. The NCAA television contracts of the 1960s, which were voted on by schools large and small, added requirements to include several College Division games each year among the regional broadcasts. The networks complied with the rule, but maximized viewership by showing the less-popular College Division games in a handful of markets while showing the University Division games to the rest of the nation. The University Division teams viewed this as a Robin Hood approach that stole from the rich to pay the poor. They were equally upset that University Division schools that did not field football teams continued to vote on football-related legislation, including football's television contract.

The combination of issues led to the 1973 stratification of the NCAA into Divisions I, II, and III based on the resources devoted to each schools' athletic program. Broadly, Division III schools did not offer athletic scholarships beyond demonstrated financial need, D-II schools offered a limited number of athletic scholarships per sport, while Division I schools could offer the highest number of athletic scholarships per sport. The governance model also changed in that the members of each division voted only on legislation affecting their division, and the Division I schools that did not compete in football lost the ability to vote on football-related legislation.

The next major battle in the organization of college football came in 1978 with the creation of Division I-AA, a football-only designation. Unable to get the votes to split DI-A and DI-AA as the big schools desired, its initial implementation included only 38 DI-AA schools, most of whom had moved up from D-II. A second reorganization in 1982 established more stringent criteria for schools to remain in DI-A, resulting in DI-A having 96 members and DI-AA having 93 schools.

Although the creation of DI-AA, now referred to as the Football Championship Subdivision (FCS), relegated schools to a lower rung on the ladder, the change largely formalized the reality that those schools did not play at the highest level of college football. That is not to say that DI-AA teams could not beat DI-A teams any given Saturday. They could have, did, and still do, but those schools did not attract the in-stadium crowds or regional and national television audiences on par with the big boys.

The 1982 realignment better differentiated the levels of play within D-I football but left significant issues unresolved. Foremost among them were the voting influence of the Ivies and similar schools, the Robin Hood policies that guaranteed occasional television appearances by the football have-nots, as well as the NCAA's using football television money to support unrelated programs. These issues led to the formation of the College Football Association (CFA), which included members of the ACC, Big Eight, SEC, Southwest Conference, and major independents. In effect, the CFA included all the big boys other than the Big Ten and Pac-10. The CFA's primary goal was to negotiate a television contract for football separate from the NCAA.

After the Supreme Court ruled in 1984 that the NCAA could not stop schools from negotiating television contracts independently, the CFA negotiated an agreement with ABC, while the Big Ten and Pac-10 signed with CBS. Ironically, by negotiating one national contract, the NCAA had succeeded in pitting one network against the others to obtain the maximum price. With two contracts under negotiation in 1984 and only two networks bidding for those contracts (NBC declined to bid), the combined value of the two contracts proved to be only forty percent of the most recent NCAA agreement. It would take eight years for the fees to return to the pre-CFA level. Fans, on the other hand, benefited immediately by having two networks televising games, both of which expanded the number of games shown. The number of televised games tripled or quadrupled, more major conference teams gained air time, while the less popular conferences received little or no television coverage.

ABC returned to near-monopoly status in 1991 when they signed contracts with both the CFA and Big Ten/Pac-10 partnership with the plan to have multiple regional broadcasts each week. The exception was Notre Dame, which had not formally committed to the CFA arrangement during the negotiations process because they were not interested in ABC's regional coverage plan. Holding free agent status, Notre Dame signed a separate deal with NBC that provided the national exposure they desired.

The CFA also helped move college football toward determining its champion on the field rather than through polls. For more than a century, the highest level of college football named its national champion based on the opinion of one group or another, and those opinions often disagreed, leaving us with split national championships. Beyond that, the polls named those mythical national champions after the regular season until the Associated Press named its champion following the bowl season in 1968, and the United Press International did so in 1973.

After the 1990 and 1991 seasons ended with split national champions, the CFA and a handful of bowls created the Bowl Coalition, which paired the two highest-rated Bowl Coalition teams at the end of the regular season in a bowl game. The process paired the #1 and #2 teams in two of the Coalition's three years, but left an undefeated team out of one title game, and the Coalition never included the Big Ten and Pac-10 teams.

The demise of the Southwest Conference and Big Eight led to the creation of the Bowl Alliance in 1995, which had aims and issues similar to that of the CFA. The Bowl Alliance was succeeded in 1998 by the Bowl Championship Series (BCS), which ran from 1998 to 2013. The BCS solved several of its predecessors' problems by including the Big Ten, Pac-10, and the Rose Bowl, along with adding opportunities for non-Power 5 conference teams to participate. The BCS was an improvement, but its selection of two teams for the championship game left a constant concern that it might omit a third or fourth deserving candidate.

The desire to have the national title determined via a championship tournament became a reality with the College Football Playoff National Championship in 2014. By expanding to a four-team playoff, it became less likely a deserving team would be left out. Better yet, it produced a financial windfall. The twelve-year deal included the three-game championship series, four associated bowls, and rights to the announcement show, all for a price tag totaling $5.64 billion or $470 million per year.

TELEVISION'S BROADER IMPACT

The changes in the NCAA's governance were driven by the pursuit of television money and a desire to reduce the number of schools sharing those monies. The pursuit of television monies changed other elements of the game as well, including the number of games played per year, the number of bowl games, and conference sizes and membership.

Before television, the primary means of increasing football revenues were to play more games before larger crowds. During football's early era, the number of regular-season games varied widely from team to team and from year to year. It was not unusual for teams to play twelve to fifteen games in a year, sometimes playing several in a week. Chicago managed to play twenty-two games during the 1896 season, including four games during a holiday trip to the West Coast. After the crisis of 1905, Big Ten members limited themselves to five games per year before upping that number a few years later. The Big Ten allowed only eight games per year in the 1930s, expanding to ten per year during WWII, provided that two of the games were against teams from military training camps. SEC teams, on the other hand, commonly played eleven regular-season games per year starting in the second half of the 1930s, but that ended when the NCAA capped the regular season at ten games in 1955.

Capping the number of games at ten put financial pressure on less competitive conferences that tried to keep pace with the high number of scholarships awarded in some conferences in the 1960s and early 1970s. In 1970, the Western Athletic Conference proposed the addition of an eleventh game, and the change went into effect the same year. Similar financial pressure led to the approval of a twelfth game in 2005. The extra games increased ticket, concessions, and other direct revenues, while also increasing the number of games available for television.

The growth of bowl games has accompanied the expansion of regular-season games and is matched by a shift in the financial models for bowls. The 1960 season ended with eight major college bowl games compared to the thirty-nine that followed the 2018 season. One reason there were fewer bowl games back in the day was that some schools and conferences prohibited bowl participation. The restrictions were based on the dual desire to limit the commercialization of college football and to limit football's impact on the academic work of team members at the end of the semester. Notre Dame did not participate in bowl games from 1926 through 1969. Similarly, the Big Ten did not allow bowl participation until 1948, after which it sent its champion to the Rose Bowl, where it met the Pac-8 champ, also that conference's sole bowl representative. The Big Ten and Pac-8 changed course before the 1975 season when they allowed additional teams to play in bowl games.

Major College Bowl Games

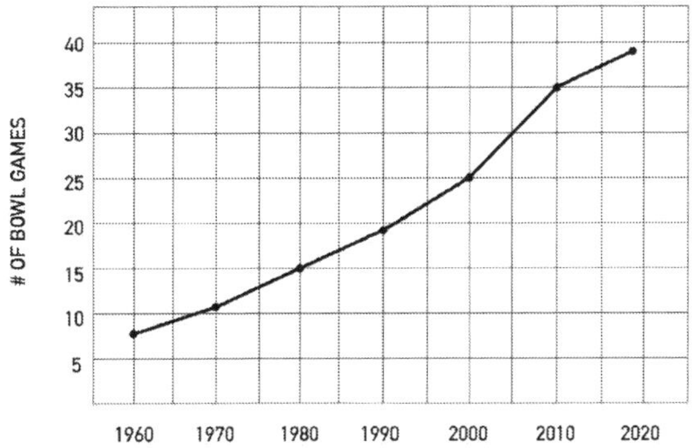

The number of bowl games has risen dramatically from 8 following the 1960 season to 39 following the 2018 season. (Data source: sports-reference.com)

Television money drives today's bowl games. During the 2018 bowl season, ESPN or its sibling networks televised thirty-five bowl games. Of those thirty-five games, fifteen were owned and operated by ESPN, and three by NFL teams. Other television networks owned and operated five other bowl games, making nearly sixty percent of all college bowl games made-for-TV events. That situation is not inherently good or bad, but it makes clear that most bowl games exist to provide content for television networks or to fill otherwise underutilized stadiums.

Television money increasingly drives who plays whom. In 1960, the NCAA's University Division had 121 football teams; 80 of which play at the FBS level today. The 41 that no longer play FBS football includes a few that dropped football, but most now play at lower levels. University Division football in 1960 included 12 conferences and 27 independents. Today, only the ACC, the Big Ten, and the SEC remain in substantially the same form, and even those have added new members. The Big Eight was reshaped in the 1990s and became the Big 12, while the AAUW became the Pac-8 after returning to a form similar to its Pacific Coast Conference days. It then expanded to become the Pac-10 and Pac-12.

Other University Division conferences in 1960 included the Border (Arizona and Arizona State were members), Middle Atlantic (Rutgers and Temple), the Missouri Valley, the Skyline, and the Southern (which included West Virginia). Each of those conferences disappeared or dropped a level, while new FBS conferences came into being. The combination of those moves means that only twenty-seven of eighty schools that played University Division football in 1960 are in the same conference today, and Notre Dame is the only 1960 independent that has remained so throughout the modern era.

Teams switched conferences for a variety of cultural, financial, and competitiveness reasons. Tulane's departure from the SEC in 1965 and South Carolina exiting the ACC in 1971 reflected local circumstances rather than broader trends, but the conference switching since the early 1990s has been largely driven by television money.

Take the Southwest Conference, which was on its death bed in the early 1990s, weakened by poor on-the-field performance, low football attendance at half its member schools, and a captive television audience limited to the states of Texas and Arkansas. When Arkansas, the only non-Texas school, announced its plans to leave for the SEC in 1990, the conference began falling apart, playing its last season in 1995. Half the remaining teams left for the Big 12, while others moved to the WAC and Conference USA.

The driver of conference expansion in the 1990s was the desire to play and televise conference championship games in football. Having added Arkansas and South Carolina in 1991, the twelve-team SEC initiated their conference championship game. Television networks were eager to broadcast the game and paid dearly for doing so.

A second driver of conference expansion was the introduction of conference-specific cable networks. Seeking schools in states with large populations and high numbers of cable subscribers, the Big Ten added Rutgers and Maryland. Since 2011, twelve schools have switched allegiances, and each Power 5 conference added two or more members.

While those changes may seem tumultuous to fans of Power 5 schools, it pales in comparison to what transpired among Group of 5 conferences (i.e., American Athletic Conference, Conference USA, the MAC, the Mountain West, the Sun Belt). Between 1960 and 2018, major college football has seen 231 changes in conference affiliation (an average of nearly four per year), and 199 or 86 percent of those changes have involved schools in the Group of 5 conferences or their equivalent at the time. Though it has returned to Power 5 status, the obstacle course TCU ran is instructive. TCU was a member of the Southwest Conference from 1923 until the conference disbanded after the 1995 season. It was among the three former Southwestern Conference teams that shifted to the Western Athletic Conference (WAC), remaining there until 2001 when it moved to Conference USA. That lasted four years before ascending to the Mountain West and then accepting an invitation to the Big 12 in 2012. That is a lot of hopping around, even for Horned Frogs.

SINCE PEOPLE first paid to watch intercollegiate athletic competitions, football has been the budgetary cash cow, subsidizing other sports and athletic departments overall. Football ticket revenues were the primary source of athletic department revenues until well into the modern era when funding sources became more diverse. Although total television revenues in 1960 were meager compared to today, they comprised about ten percent of a college athletic department's annual budget, and the pursuit of those incremental revenues became a significant force shaping college athletics.

The NCAA was still a small organization in 1960 that used a portion of the football television revenues for its operations while pursuing a share-the-wealth policy obligating the television networks to include lesser football programs among their broadcasts. Many of the most successful football programs objected to the share-the-wealth approach leading to power struggles that resulted in the restructuring of the NCAA into tiers based on competition level and popularity. The outcome of the power struggle was to remove the NCAA from its role in negotiating the television contract for football, allowing the top football schools to keep the television monies for themselves or, at least, to share within their conferences. In turn, with access to television monies largely determined by conference, membership in a Power 5 conference became essential to the financial health of athletic departments seeking to compete at the highest level. (Notre Dame is the exception.) This led to the demise of several conferences and altered the composition of those that remain.

Beyond changes in the conference structures and professional leagues, television and other monies have had a significant impact on the game itself. Money allowed for the expansion of coaching staffs, paid salaries that allowed professional players to train year-round, while also leading to instant replay, television timeouts, and *Monday Night Football.* The remaining chapters describe these and other innovations of the modern era.

14

THE BALL, THE FIELD, AND STADIUMS (1960-2018)

While there were changes to the ball, field, and stadiums during the modern era that directly impacted play on the field, most were aesthetic, addressed the creature comforts of players, or enhanced the fan experience and the generation of revenue. The growth of artificial turf as the primary playing surface upon which major college and pro football is played has been the biggest change in the playing field during the modern era, but its impact on the game has not been substantial compared to other factors. More substantive from a fan experience standpoint, has been the building and renovation of stadiums with luxury and other differential seating patterns, dramatic enhancements in scoreboards and video displays, and, of course, the rise of domes.

THE BALL

The dimensions of the football have remained largely consistent since the ball was made slimmer in 1934. Compared to the 1934 ball, the ball can now be within tolerance while being one-quarter-inch shorter along the length and between one quarter and one-half-inch narrower at the midsection.

The most significant change to the football in the modern era has been the addition of the striping to enhance the ball's visibility for night games. The National Federation of State High School Athletic Associations required a tan ball with two white stripes beginning in 1953, while continuing to allow the use of white or yellow footballs for night games. The NFL dropped the white ball for night games in 1956, substituting a tan ball with white stripes encircling the ball a few inches from either end. Quarterback complaints about the slippery stripes led the NFL to eliminate the stripes from the panel on which right-handed quarterbacks' thumbs rested. The NFL made comparable adjustments for left-handed quarterbacks before the league eliminated the striped ball in 1976. By that time, stadium lighting conditions had improved to the point that stripes were no longer necessary.

The NCAA, meanwhile, permitted the striped ball in 1965 and made it mandatory in 1975, at which point the white stripes were painted only on the two panels adjacent to the laces (the two top panels). The quality of stadium lighting has made striping unnecessary at the college level as well, but the striping remains because it provides a simple means to differentiate the college game from the pros.

Finally, it is worth noting that our gridiron colleagues north of the border use striped footballs at both the college and professional levels. Their stripes encircle the ball, so one is left to assume that Canadian thumbs do not slip as easily as American thumbs, despite most CFL quarterbacks being American imports.

THE FIELD

The football field's dimension and markings have seen few functional changes in the modern era. The most notable changes have narrowed the distance between the hash marks. The NFL hash marks went from twenty yards apart to 18 1/2 feet apart in 1972 so the hash marks aligned with the goal post uprights. The college hash marks shifted from 53 1/3 feet apart (one-third the width of the field) to 40 feet apart in 1993. Both changes aided offenses by reducing the impact of the short side of the field on play calling.

While there have been few functional changes to the field markings in the modern era, aesthetic changes to the football field are more common. The first notable change came in 1966 when Lamar Hunt, the owner of the Kansas City Chiefs, asked George Toma, the groundskeeper at Kansas City's Municipal Stadium, to make the Chiefs' field more vibrant. Toma responded with the first midfield decoration, a white circle with a red KC logo. He later painted the field numbers alternately gold and white with red outlines. Impressed by his efforts, the NFL asked Toma to apply his craft for the upcoming NFL Championship game in the Cotton Bowl and the AFL-NFL World Championship game, now referred to as Super Bowl I, at the Los Angeles Coliseum. For the NFL Championship game, Toma placed the NFL shield at the 50-yard line, Cowboys and Packers logos elsewhere on the field, and, for the first time, surrounded the field with a white border. Toma also designed a midfield crown logo for Super Bowl I (sometimes derided as the Burger King logo) and used the white border again.

The Super Bowl I halftime show occurred on a field with a midfield logo, and red and blue Lockney Lines marked within the white border. (JImberg13, WikiMedia Commons)

The white borders surrounding the field affected the outer Lockney Lines. Initially, the outer Lockney Lines were painted outside the sidelines rather than inside as they are today. Toma solved the problem for Super Bowl I by painting the outer Lockney Lines in red and blue to stand out from the white border. When the NFL recommended that all clubs place a white border around the football field for the 1968 season, many teams shifted the outer Lockney lines inside the sidelines where they remain today. The NCAA allows but does not require a white border around the field, but their 1986 recommendation to paint the area between the sidelines and coaches boxes forced teams to move the Lockney Lines inside the sideline as well.

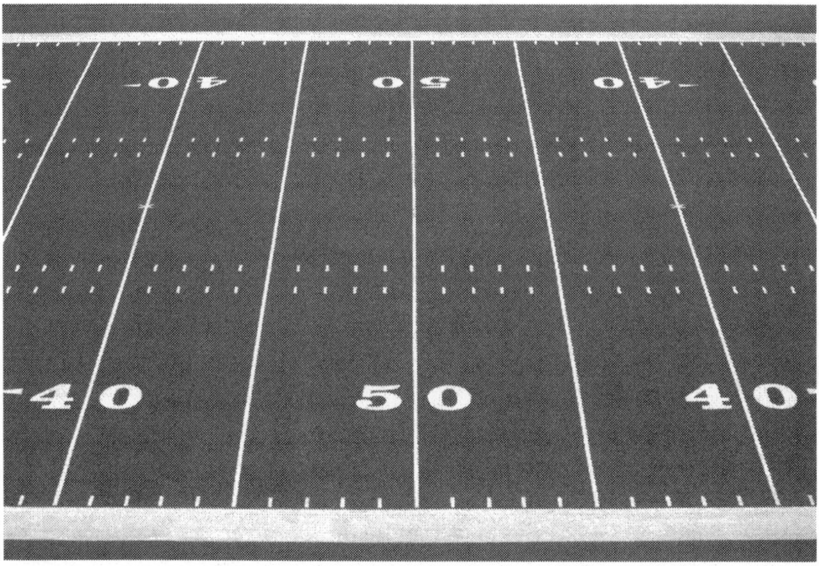

A football field with the outer Lockney Lines inside the white border surrounding the field. (Danny E. Hooks, Shutterstock)

In addition to these decorative changes, functional changes occurred in the areas surrounding the field, foremost of which were markings designating the team area behind the sidelines. Football fields did not require designated team areas when everyone on the sideline had to sit or kneel, but conditions changed with the liberalization of the coaching from the sideline rules. The NCAA first defined the team areas in 1957 as a marked area two feet behind the sideline between the 35-yard lines. Setting the team area two yards behind the sideline was meant to give the linesmen and chain gang room to roam along the sideline, but the space proved inadequate, so the team area was pushed back four additional feet in 1973. It expanded from the 35- to the 30-yard lines in 1978 and changed again in 1979 when they created a coaches box two yards from the sideline and a players area four yards from the sideline. The rule makers extended the team area to the 25-yard lines in 1983 before settling in for a long winter's nap.

The team area and coaches box became off-limits to media personnel in 1984. Sideline reporters can no longer interact with those inside the team box during games, so they are limited to breathlessly updating television viewers with what they overheard or observed along the sidelines. The rules still allow them to ask inane questions as coaches move to or from the locker room at halftime.

While George Toma and other groundskeepers kept busy devising new ways to paint their football fields, others were changing the composition of the field itself. It all started when the Houston Astrodome opened for the 1965 baseball season. Outfielders lost track of fly balls in the glare produced by the stadium's clear Lucite ceiling, so they addressed the problem by painting the Lucite panels. Doing so created a second problem: the painted panels did not allow sufficient sunlight for grass to grow, so an alternative field cover was needed.

The Astrodome was not the first indoor facility in the sporting world that needed artificial turf. Indoor games were played in the Chicago Coliseum in 1896 with clay substituting for grass. and the 1932 NFL championship game at Chicago Stadium used a mixture of dirt and tanbark (a byproduct of the tanning process). Unfortunately, the old-time solutions were inadequate when Houston had a problem, so they turned to Monsanto and its Chem-Grass product, invented two years earlier through a research and development effort to develop playing surfaces for urban youth.

ChemGrass covered the infield and sidelines by the beginning of the Astros' 1966 seasons, and, after performing adequately there, they installed it in the outfield partway through the season. As a result, ChemGrass covered the entire field for the University of Houston's football games that fall. Renamed AstroTurf in 1966, the former Chemgrass product had many first-generation problems. It had minimal padding, caused burns when exposed skin slid across its surface, and provided so much traction that it led to knee injuries, turf toe, and other injuries. Despite those issues, Indiana State installed Astro-Turf in 1967, four other college stadiums added it in 1968, and artificial turf began its slow progression towards dominance over grass.

Workers installing artificial turf at the Astrodome in preparation for a football game (Jet Lowe, Library of Congress)

The second generation of artificial turf arrived in the early 1980s and had longer fibers composed of new materials, sand in-fill, and generally performed more like natural grass. The third generation entered the U.S. market in the late 1990s with more grass-like fibers and sand and rubber pellets in-fill. The number of artificial turf installations soared and now includes 17 of 31 NFL stadiums and 87 of 130 FBS stadiums, along with two hybrid turf installations. The most troubling aspect of the latest generation of artificial turf has been the decision to manufacture it in any color under the sun. More accurately, the problem is the lack of judgment shown by those who have approved the blue, purple, and red football fields that soil perfectly good stadiums across the land.

Of course, there is nothing wrong with a little innovation when it serves a purpose, and we see that in the changes made to the goal posts during the modern era. As covered previously, college goal posts moved to the back of the end zone in 1927. The NFL did the same because they used the college rule book at the time. When the NFL created a separate rule book in 1933, they moved the goal posts back to the goal line where they remained until 1974 when the high number of field goals made by soccer-style kickers caused them to push the goal posts back to the end line. Canadian football, on the other hand, placed the uprights over the goal line from the beginning, and they remain there today.

Other changes to goal posts in the modern era are the distance between and height of the uprights, and the structural design of the posts. The distance between the uprights was set at 18 feet 6 inches in 1876 and remained as such until 1959 when the colleges sought to stimulate scoring by increasing the distance to 24 feet (23 feet 4 inches on the inside measurement). Interestingly, the rules committee initially approved a plan setting the uprights 26 feet apart but reduced it to 24 feet upon learning that most goal posts were constructed of wood, and the longest standard two-by-fours produced by lumber mills were 24 feet long.

Not much else happened with goal posts until a 1965 playoff game between the Green Bay Packers and the Baltimore Colts when Green Bay's Don Chandler made a field goal with 1:58 remaining to send the game into overtime. At the time, a single official judged NFL field goal by standing on the end line halfway between the uprights. Standing in that spot, Jim Tunney, the back judge for the playoff game, ruled that Chandler's kick flew over the upright, while the Colts believed the ball passed wide of the upright. The controversy led to a change in officiating practice so that officials stood beneath each of the two uprights moving forward. A change in the goal posts themselves was also forthcoming.

During the same season, a CFL game ended when one team's defensive linemen braced themselves against the goal posts during a goal line stand and prevented their opponent from scoring. The game's outcome caused Joel Rottman, a magazine and newspaper distributor, to lose a one-dollar bet, and he complained about the loss during a lunch meeting with his friend, Jim Trimble, the recently fired head coach of the Montreal Alouettes. While playing with his fork during the lunch, the idea struck Rottman that the fork represented a potential new design for goal posts. Rottman and Trimble then formed a company to design and build the "Tele-Goal" system. The Tele-Goal had one post anchored two yards behind the goal line, which goosenecked forward, so the crossbar and uprights hung above the goal line. (Functionally, the Tele-Goal is similar to the safety goal post of 1900, but has one post rather than two.) Their first installation came at Montreal's Autostade for use by the Montreal Bears of the Continental Football League. Rottman convinced his alma mater, the University of Miami, to install a set in the Orange Bowl for the 1966 season, while Trimble, a former head coach of the Philadelphia Eagles, lobbied Pete Rozelle and the NFL owners to approve the Tele-Goal for the 1967 season. Thinking the new goal post design might address the 1965 playoff game problem, the NFL approved the Tele-Goal as long it was redesigned such that its uprights rose twenty feet high rather than the then-standard ten feet. Rottman and Trimble agreed to the change, and the Tele-Goal became the NFL standard for the 1967 season. The NCAA mandated twenty-foot uprights in 1985.

The decision to switch to the Tele-Goal affected one of football's iconic plays during the 1967 Championship Game, commonly known as the Ice Bowl. In the game's closing seconds, Bart Starr executed a quarterback sneak behind the block of right guard, Jerry Kramer. Had the NFL not switched to the Tele-Goal that year, the play would have occurred virtually on top of the left goal post and potentially caused the Packers to change their play call. Thankfully, the Tele-Goal was in place, the play was successful, and the Cowboys lost. All was right with the world.

Bart Starr sneaks behind Jerry Kramer in the 1967 NFL Championship Game. Note where the left goal post would have been had the NFL not changed the goal post design. (Associated Press Photo)

The increased accuracy of soccer-style kickers resulted in the number and distance of field goals swinging in favor of the offense, so the college uprights returned to their 18 feet 6 inches of separation in 1991.

Regardless of the goal post location and design, kicked extra points and field goals flew into the crowd for years, after which the fans tossed the ball back onto the field. Tossing the ball back onto the field was particularly helpful behavior in the days when teams used a single ball the entire game. In the late 1930s, NFL teams began allowing fans to keep balls that entered the stands. That policy had a notable impact on the 1940 NFL Championship Game when the Chicago Bears beat the Washington Redskins 73-0. Late in the game, the Bears had kicked eleven of their twelve balls into the stands, so the

Bears attempted passes on their last two point-after-attempts to ensure they could finish the game.

A downside of allowing fans to keep balls that sailed into the stands were the injuries suffered by fans wrestling for the ball, leading some fans to sue the relevant stadium owners over the injuries they sustained. To avoid this situation, the folks managing Wisconsin's Camp Randall installed netting behind their goal posts in 1959 to prevent balls from entering the stands. The nets gained widespread use in the late 1960s and early 1970s, so life as a goal post net supplier was good, but boring until NFL Special Event chief, Jim Steeg, bought a Wilson tennis racquet emblazoned with Wilson's logo on the strings. The Wilson logo led Steeg to pursue the placing of the NFL shield on goal post nets, and his idea became a reality for the first time at the 2002 Pro Bowl.

In turn, a marketing agency took that idea and worked with Allstate Insurance to develop a similar concept for college football stadiums. The Allstate Good Hands® goal post net made its television debut on September 1, 2005, when Temple visited Arizona State. Its national, prime-time debut came a few days later during a Miami-Florida State game. Allstate has since patented various elements of goal post net systems, and their nets rise behind the goal posts in more than eighty FBS college football stadiums.

The Allstate Insurance Good Hands® Field Goal Net has a highly visible presence, including at the 2019 Sugar Bowl game. (Kelly L. Cox, Courtesy of Allstate Insurance)

Two other changes to the end zone area are worth noting. The first came in 1966 when pylons were first allowed to replace flags at the four corners of the end zone. The second change harkens back to a 1939 rule requiring teams to put the ball in play within 30 seconds of the officials spotting the ball. That rule led to a desire among quarterbacks to have a means of tracking the time left on the play clock. Jimmy Phelan, coach of the Los Angeles Dons in 1948, argued for a play clock near the field, but Phelan's suggestion was not acted on until the NFL adopted the 30-second play clock in 1976. The NCAA allowed schools or conferences to choose whether to use 25-second clocks on the field in 1979, with the Big Eight being the first to do so.

THE STADIUMS

Starting with Harvard Stadium, the football stadiums built in the early and middle eras had architectural flourishes that testified to each school's greatness but had few of the amenities expected in the modern stadium. Early stadiums were utilitarian and relatively inexpensive to build as a result. A study that analyzed the construction costs of professional baseball and football stadiums showed stadiums built in the last decade of the twentieth century cost twenty-seven times more (in constant dollars) than those built in the first two decades of the century. The cost trends affecting professional stadiums were mirrored at the college level because many of the features that drove increased costs were incorporated into college football stadiums as well. As one example, it is no longer acceptable for the superstructure under the grandstands to be exposed for all to see; schools must hide the girders with brickwork or other attractive finishes. Similarly, the grounds surrounding stadiums are now terraced and landscaped as expectations have risen across the board.

A key difference between professional and college football stadiums has been the fact that college stadiums are generally expanded, renovated, or rebuilt on the same site, while professional stadiums rise from scratch in new locations. College football stadiums with concrete stands on one side of the field became stadiums with concrete stands on both sides, the stands became taller or double-decked, and the end zones are enclosed. More recently, the addition of luxury seating moved high-status fans farther away from the field and closer to their televisions.

An extreme example of such a change came when Syracuse replaced venerable Archbold Stadium with the Carrier Dome. Named for a gift from the Carrier Corporation, which was itself named for Willis Carrier, the developer of the first modern air conditioner in 1902. Old Willis' air conditioning revolutionized where we live, how we build our workplaces and homes, and our sports stadiums or, at least, those games played indoors. Modern domed or covered stadiums simply would not exist if not for air conditioning.

Houston was the ideal spot for the first domed stadium due to its humidity and being home to NASA, which aimed to send a few Houstonians from one inhospitable location to another. It was the first Southern city with a major league baseball team, and its heat, humidity, and potential for rain called for something new, like an indoor stadium. The Harris County Domed Stadium, aka the Astrodome, opened in 1965. Despite the previously-discussed problems with its turf, the Astrodome was the trendsetter for the seventy-two domes and retractable-roof stadiums built in the U.S. and Canada since then. Like the food served at chain restaurants, the atmosphere in domes leans heavily to the boring side, but they provide a reliable experience for each game.

Despite its shortcomings, the Astrodome had a seminal influence on stadium designs. Although the Romans had the equivalent of luxury seating in their stadiums, such frills were not part of American stadiums until the Astrodome reintroduced the differentiated in-stadium experience based on your seat location. Located near the top of the stadium, the Astrodome's Skyboxes sat 24 to 30 people apiece with lavishly-appointed private suites behind the seating section. After appearing at the Astrodome, luxury boxes or suites became standard elements of new or renovated stadiums.

The first luxury seating in a college football stadium was the President's Champions Club at Georgia's Samford Stadium in 1967. Like others that followed, the club offered increased space, higher-quality food and drink, and social benefits beyond the standard stadium seat. The various suite and club designs drove many stadium renovations over the last several decades, and, as of 2015, only five college-controlled FBS stadiums were without some form of luxury seating.

The Astrodome's SkyBoxes came with broader menus. Slowly but surely, the recognition that all fans -not just the wealthy- might enjoy more diverse food selections came to the nation's vendors, and we have another Texan to thank for that by kickstarting the stadium nacho. Nachos date to the mid-1940s in Mexico before crossing the border and becoming available in Mexican restaurants in the States. Restaurants prepared nachos by heating each serving individually, a time-consuming process unsuitable for concession stands. Given Texas' history of pumping viscous fluids, it was only natural that concessionaire Frank Liberto realized he could eliminate the production bottleneck by warming cans of cheese so the resulting liquid could be ladled or pumped onto tortilla chips. The new gooey nachos premiered at baseball's Arlington Stadium in 1976 and transferred over to the Cowboy's Texas Stadium in 1978, where Howard Cosell filled broadcast dead time by praising the wonderful treat. Interest in nachos soon bubbled over and spurred the menu expansion of the 1980s and beyond.

Frank Liberto introduced the stadium nacho in 1976 that jumpstarted the move toward more diverse concession offerings. (Courtesy of Ricos Products Company)

The Astrodome's final contribution to the evolution of football stadiums was its pioneering scoreboard. Iowa was on the cutting edge of college stadiums in 1967 when it installed scoreboards 50 feet wide and 18 feet tall at either end of their stadium. Still, neither approached the exploding monster installed at the Astrodome two years earlier. The Astrodome's scoreboard was 474 feet long, could display messages and cartoons with its 50,000 incandescent light bulbs, all while synchronizing the display with sound effects.

The Astrodome scoreboard displays a cartoon cowboy and his six-shooters. (Carlos Rosales, AP Photo/Houston Chronicle, R32327)

The next major innovation in scoreboards came in 1980 when the Los Angeles Dodgers added a color video board comprised of a series of cathode ray tubes to show replays and other content. At 20 feet high and 28 feet wide, it was supplanted in 1987 by the 24 by 32 feet Sony Jumbotrons that appeared at Candlestick Park in San Francisco and Riverfront Stadium in Cincinnati. Just two years later, the Rogers Centre in Toronto installed a Jumbotron measuring 35 feet tall and 115 feet wide.

Scoreboards were revolutionized once again in 1997 when the first outdoor scoreboard using LED technology appeared at Baltimore's M&T Bank Stadium. Besides providing a more flexible scoreboard layout, LED technology made greater use of the color spectrum, making images sharper than those of their predecessors. Since Baltimore's installation, the race for more massive and highly-pixelated scoreboards has only become more intense. The Jacksonville Jaguars recently added two LED scoreboards that are 60 feet high and 362 feet long, while the oval Halo Display at Mercedes-Benz Stadium in Atlanta is 58 feet high and 1,075 feet long and, if nothing else, challenges our assumptions about the physical layout of scoreboards.

The final element in the evolution of stadiums during the modern era are the locker rooms that benefit players and coaches rather than fans. The gymnasiums of ancient Greece had designated areas for athletes to change their clothes, oil their bodies, and scrape themselves clean following their athletic activities. The modern incarnation of such areas, the locker room, gained its name from commercial and military storage facilities that divided their space into compartments or lockers. The term transferred over to Victorian Era athletic and golf clubs where members stored their equipment and changed into their athletic gear.

Early football stadiums did not always have locker rooms, mainly because those facilities were often available in nearby gymnasia. Those that existed had benches, lockers, shower rooms, and some level of training or medical equipment, but not much else.

This NFL locker room in 1969 was spacious, but lacked the luxurious fittings available today. (Photo by Warren K. Leffler, Library of Congress)

Locker rooms remained spartan until the late 1970s when newly-built stadiums incorporated expanded locker and training facilities. As free agency became part of the NFL, locker rooms were made more comfortable, luxurious, and spacious in an attempt to lure and retain players. A similar mechanism operates in college football with schools building palatial "sports performance centers" as recruiting tools to attract amateur athletes to their school.

FOOTBALL ENTERED the modern era as a game played on grass fields, though some multi-purpose stadiums had baseball infields as well. Since then, several generations of artificial turf have replaced grass at many locations. Besides bringing economic benefits and allowing an intensity of use that grass fields cannot support, artificial turf eliminates much of the unpredictability of games played on wet, muddy fields. Players do not slip, they retain their grip on the ball, and balls bounce cleanly on artificial turf. Play remains predictable, which has many benefits, but an element of chance and surprise that exists on grass fields has been lost along the way.

Similar points apply to domed stadiums and luxury boxes. Watching the game in an enclosed environment certainly makes games more comfortable. Neither rain, nor snow, nor gloom of night stays those mighty spectators from the swift consumption of their appointed round of beers, but such conditions mean that few tales will be told in the future of steadfast fans suffering through cold or rain with friends. For good or ill, stadiums have become showplaces that bring some of the comforts of home to the communal experience.

15

PLAY AND TECHNIQUE (1960-2018)

From football's beginnings, its rule makers sought to balance offense and defense as well as the kicking, rushing, and passing games. They did not seek balance in the sense that each was equal, only that they were in proportion to the preferences of the time. The preferences of the modern era leaned toward the forward pass as it became the predominant method of moving the ball. The average college offense gained fifty-three percent more yards per game in 2017 than in 1960, moving from 263 yards per game to 403. Over that time, rushing yards increased slightly from 169 to 174 per game while passing yards more than doubled from 94 to 229 per game. Offenses accomplished these feats by rushing six fewer times per game (45 to 39) and passing fifteen more times per game (16 attempts to 31).

Although the emergence of the passing game is the most visible change in offensive football in the modern era, changes in the run game and its blocking schemes have been notable as well. Although rushing yards per game have not changed dramatically, one must wonder how ineffective rushing attacks might be today had several key innovations not come along.

RUNNING

College offenses entered the modern era running the Wing T, Pro T, and a mishmash of other offenses. Most were run-oriented, putting little stress on defensive backfields. College football's run orientation intensified when option football exploded on the scene in the 1960s, dominated college football in the 1970s, and tailed off before reemerging in a new form to challenge defenses as dramatically as any offensive scheme to date. Before addressing option offenses, however, we need to address the old "sucker shift" and its impact on offensive line movement, or the lack of the same.

Trickery has long been part of football, but one generation's clever trick is another generation's unsportsmanlike conduct, and the sucker shift exemplifies such a change. Though largely forgotten today, during football's first 100 years, any or all offensive players could shift before the snap provided ten of them paused for one second before the ball was snapped. Even offensive linemen could move or shift after getting into a three- or four-point stance.

The false start penalty premiered in 1946 to keep teams from executing shifts that simulated plays (e.g., fullbacks spinning pre-snap as they might during the spinning handoffs of the time), but that did not stop sucker shifts or pre-snap movements from confusing defenses or drawing them offside. Forest Evashevski's Iowa teams of the 1950s used a particularly tricky sucker shift after aligning in a Wing T formation with wide offensive line splits. On signal, the offensive line rose out their three-point stances, moved laterally to converge into tight splits, while the four backfield players shifted into a Single Wing formation. Film from the time shows instances in which Iowa's shift caused the eight defenders in the box to jump, resulting in a defensive penalty. Sucker shifts were made illegal in 1968 under the rationale that the defensive players who were drawn offside were sometimes unable to return to a proper (safe) position before the offense snapped the ball. Most important, the new rule change made it illegal for offensive linemen to shift after placing a hand on the ground.

Soon after that, some offensive tackles began using two-point stances rather than three-point stances in an attempt to pass block speedy defensive ends. They also aligned further back from the line of scrimmage, which got out of hand, so the NFL added a 1977 rule specifying where offensive linemen had to align relative to the line of scrimmage or center.

While the NFL continued developing the passing game in the 1960s and 1970s, college football detoured and followed the option football path. The "double" option of the Split T was almost 25 years old when Bill Yeoman and his Houston team were practicing for their game with Penn State in 1964. The offense struggled that practice to block the defensive tackle on a halfback dive play, so a frustrated Yeoman told his offensive tackle to leave the defensive tackle unblocked. When the team reran the play, the unblocked defensive tackle penetrated the line, took himself out of the play, letting the dive back run downfield untouched. After rerunning the play with similar results, Yeoman recognized the play's potential and spent the offseason developing the inside veer, football's first "triple" option.

Against the 5-2 defense that was prevalent at the time, the inside veer used wide splits to spread the defense while leaving the playside defensive tackle and end unblocked. The quarterback ran parallel to the line of scrimmage, reading the unblocked defenders to determine whether to give the ball to the dive back, keep the ball and turn upfield, or pitch it to the sweeping back.

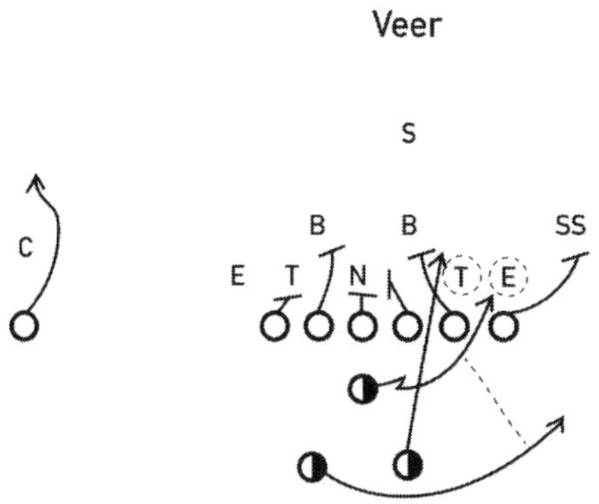

The Inside Veer aligned the backs behind the guards. The QB reads the defensive tackle for the dive and the defensive end for the pitch.

Whereas the Split T quarterback, who read only the defensive end, pitched the ball to the sweeping halfback using an underhand toss, the Veer quarterback used the thumb-under flick, prorating the wrist to lateral the ball. This became the standard technique for all down-the-line option quarterbacks, though a few coaches advocated for the basketball pass approach.

The second triple option attack of the 1960s was the Wishbone, which Texas debuted against Houston in 1968. Designed over the summer by assistant coach Emory Bellard, the Wishbone had elements of the Split T, the Veer, and other elements originating from somewhere in Bellard's fertile mind.

Wishbone Lead Option

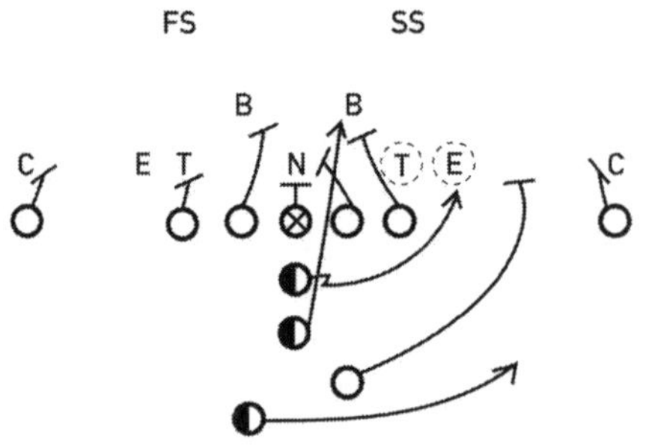

The Wishbone's Lead Option had the QB read the defensive tackle for the dive and the defensive end for the pitch.

The Wishbone's name derives from its distinctive backfield alignment, with the fullback directly behind the quarterback and two halfbacks behind and to the sides of the fullback. The Wishbone's core play, the lead option, resembles the Split T option play with a key difference being that the Split T quarterback reads only the defensive end. In contrast, the Wishbone quarterback reads the defensive tackle and the defensive end (assuming a 5-2 defense). Also, the Wishbone uses the fullback for the dive rather than the playside halfback as in the Split T, allowing the more powerful fullback to hit the hole faster. The Wishbone quickly dominated college football with teams running the Bone winning seven national championships from 1969 to 1979.

The Veer and Wishbone were innovative but did not help teams running more conventional offenses that used man or rule blocking. Man blocking requires the offensive player to block a particular defensive player regardless of the defender's post-snap movements. Rule blocking takes a different approach by giving blockers a series of if-then rules that specify who and how they should block. For example, the right offensive guard might have a sequence of rules such as "In," "On," and "Over." The "In" rule tells the guard to block anyone on the line of scrimmage to his inside gap. If no one is in that gap, he switches to the "On" rule and blocks the man aligned on him. If neither the "In" nor "On" rules apply, the "Over" rule tells the guard to block the first linebacker aligned over him or to his inside. The beauty of rule blocking is that it works regardless of the defensive alignment, but becomes complicated as the number of plays and blocking schemes increase.

Unlike man and rule blocking, area blocking makes blockers responsible for lanes rather than individual defenders. Originally, area blocking was used only with pairs of offensive linemen. Bear Bryant used area blocking at

Kentucky in 1951, as did Jim Tatum with Maryland in 1953. Vince Lombardi relied on man blocking rules, but used area or "do-dad" blocking when traditional man blocking rules were problematic. Zone blocking is area blocking on steroids. Instead of pairs of offensive linemen executing area blocks to solve local problems, the entire offensive line applies the area blocking philosophy. Thus, the Green Bay Power Sweep that used man blocking rules gives way to the outside zone play that has the playside offensive linemen step laterally before moving upfield to engage the defenders. Once engaged, the offensive linemen move the defenders somewhere, anywhere, often using the defensive players' momentum against them by driving the defenders further than they want to go in a given direction. The backside offensive lineman typically cut block the backside defenders.

Zone Blocking

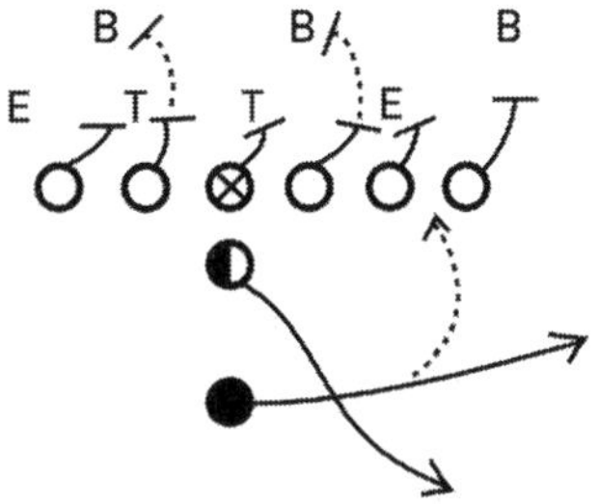

Combinations of offensive linemen target areas, double teaming or releasing to block the defender that appears in their lane.

Zone blocking changes the running back's responsibility as well. Whereas man blocking plays require the running back to run through a predefined hole, zone blocking plays do not. The running back still has specific reads, but the play relies heavily on the running back's ability to find holes that emerge when defensive players over pursue or pursue at different speeds than their teammates. Cutbacks are critical to zone plays, making the offensive line's backside blocking as crucial as its frontside blocking.

Zone blocking gained popularity during the 1980s, but a turning point for the scheme came when Alex Gibbs, a longtime college and professional offensive line coach joined the Denver Broncos in 1995. The Broncos built their offense around zone blocking and proved highly successful. The Bronco's success led more teams to adopt zone blocking, though a significant variation on zone blocking soon emerged.

Several football bloodlines merged on the campus of Glenville State during the 1994 season when the Pioneers, coached by Rich Rodriguez, ran the Run and Shoot offense, complemented by zone running plays. During practice one day, the offense aligned in a single back shotgun formation intent on running an inside zone play with the running back crossing in front of the quarterback to take the handoff. As can happen, the quarterback bobbled the snap and was unable to hand the ball to the running back. The quarterback, seeing the backside defensive end pinch inside to pursue the running back, kept the ball and ran it backside in the area just abandoned by the defensive end. Like Bill Yeoman in 1964, it was a Eureka moment for Rodriguez who recognized that the backside pursuit that threatened the inside zone run provided an opportunity for the quarterback to keep the ball and run away from the pursuit. Rodriguez turned the mistake into an option play now known as the zone read or read option. If the defensive end stayed home, the quarterback gave the ball to the running back. If the defender pursued the running back, the quarterback kept the ball and ran through the spot abandoned by the defensive end.

Zone Read

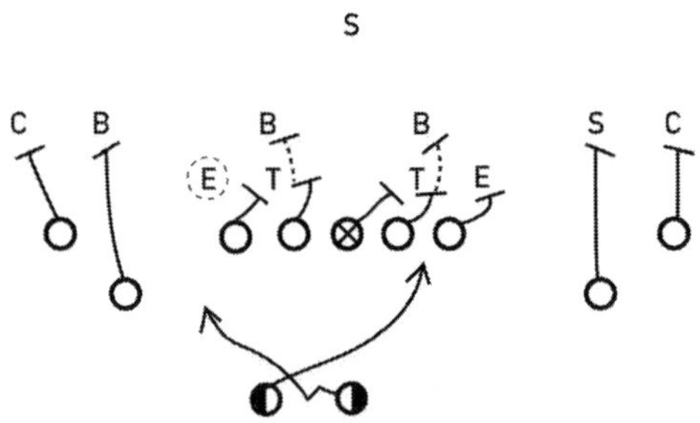

The zone read is generally run from a spread formation and is based on a backside read rather than the frontside read of previous option plays.

Unlike all previous option plays in which the quarterback reads frontside defenders and is himself a frontside run threat, the zone read uses a backside read, and the quarterback is a run threat to the backside. Even better, the zone read allows the quarterback to make the read five yards behind the line of scrimmage where he is in a more favorable position to pass the ball than Veer and Wishbone quarterbacks who made their reads while running parallel to and immediately behind the line of scrimmage. Pairing frontside and backside running threats with the passing options available in four-receiver sets results in a powerful combination that is difficult to defend.

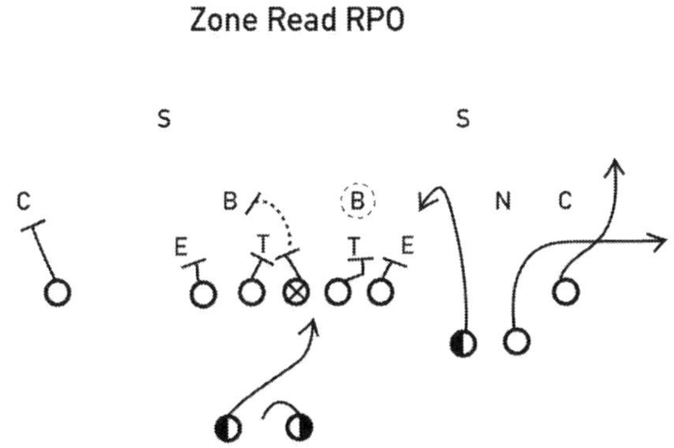

On this RPO, the QB reads the strong side linebacker. If the backer drops into coverage, the QB gives to the running back. If the backer steps up for the running back, the QB passes to the Y.

The zone read threat is extended by the development of Run Pass Option (RPO) plays, sometimes called package plays, that stack a run-pass read atop the zone read. An example RPO might have the quarterback read a linebacker pre- or post-snap to determine whether to run or pass the ball. Once determined, the quarterback executes the zone read play or passes the ball based on the linebacker's initial position or post-snap reaction. An interesting twist on RPOs is that if a team called an RPO every play of the game and correctly made each read, the defense would determine the offense' run-pass mix, not the offense.

PASSING

It is too early in the development of the zone read RPO to project its ultimate impact on football. What is clear, however, is that the concepts that underlie its passing components owe a debt to more conventional passing offenses that developed during the modern era, all of which were shaped by Sid Gillman. Gillman, the only coach named to both the college and pro football halls of fame, played at Ohio State before assisting at several schools. He was head coach at Miami, Cincinnati, the NFL's Los Angeles Rams, and then, most famously, the AFL's Los Angeles and San Diego Chargers from 1960 to 1969, where he won five division and one league title.

Before Gillman, receivers relied largely on their speed and cutting ability, with quarterbacks throwing the ball only after their receivers became open. Among Gillman's innovation was to standardize the depth and cuts of pass routes, making each route and its timing predictable. He also synched the timing of the routes to the quarterback's three-, five-, or seven-step dropback so quarterbacks could throw to a spot and have the ball arrive the moment

Sid Gillman (right) instructing Paul Dietzel, his center at Miami, and a key member of the Gillman coaching tree. (Image courtesy of the Walter Havighurst Special Collections and University Archives, Miami University Libraries, Oxford OH)

the receiver became open. Everyone uses timing routes today, but everyone who does so copies Gillman.

A second Gillman innovation was to combine routes that spread defenses horizontally and vertically. The ideal set of patterns would include a route in each of Gillman's five horizontal areas of the field: the two wide areas outside the field numbers, the two number areas (between the numbers and the hash marks), and the area in the middle of the field between the hash marks. Combinations of short, intermediate, and deep routes also stretched defenses in the vertical dimension.

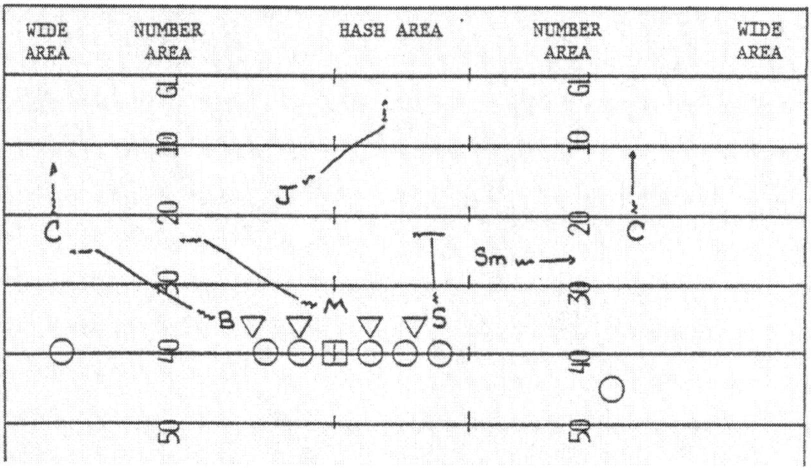

Gillman's Field Balance and Distribution Chart shows the field divided into five horizontal zones. (Courtesy of the Walter Havighurst Special Collections and University Archives, Miami University Libraries, Oxford OH)

Gillman's third innovation was his use of passing trees. Passing trees existed before Gillman, but he used passing trees to simplify and speed up his play calling. Gillman gave each route on the passing tree a number and designated plays using a three-digit number for his X, Y, and Z receivers (i.e., split end, tight end, and flanker). Routes run to the outside had even numbers, those run to the inside had odd numbers, and all could be supplemented by memorized or named routes.

Beyond his own success, Gillman's influence results from the use of his ideas by those in his coaching tree. While an assistant at West Point, he regularly talked shop with a New Jersey high school coach. When Gillman left West Point, he recommended that high school coach, Vince Lombardi, as his replacement and the rest is football history. Gillman's assistants at Miami of Ohio included Bo Schembechler, Paul Dietzel, Bill Arnsparger, John Pont, and Ara Parseghian. His assistants with the Chargers included Al Davis, Chuck Noll, George Allen, Dick Vermeil, Bum Phillips, and others who took elements of Gillman's thinking and incorporated them into their offenses.

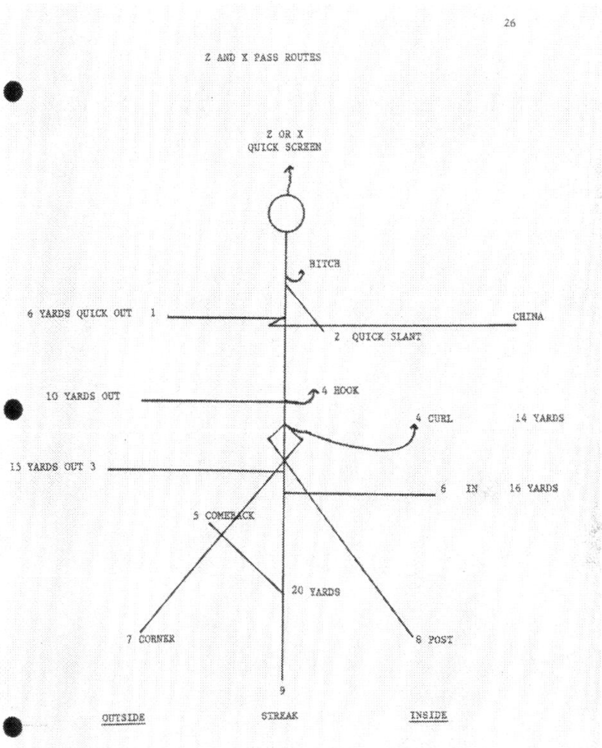

A playbook page showing Gillman's passing tree for the X and Z. The Y has a separate tree. (Courtesy of the Walter Havighurst Special Collections and University Archives, Miami University Libraries, Oxford OH)

Bill Walsh caught the Gillman bug while assisting Al Davis with the Raiders.

Gillman's philosophy of horizontally spreading the field influenced Walsh when he assisted the Cincinnati Bengals in the late 1960s and early 1970s. In 1970, the Bengals planned to use a vertical passing attack until their strong-armed quarterback, Greg Cook, was injured, and Virgil Carter took his place. Carter was smart and accurate but had less arm strength than his predecessor, so Walsh altered the offense to emphasize the short passing game and routes with potential for yards after the catch, an approach that evolved into the West Coast Offense.

Gillman was also an early advocate of option routes. Just as the Veer, Wishbone, and Zone Read offenses require the quarterback to make give-keep decisions by reading unblocked defenders, option routes extend that thinking to the passing game. There are many option route variations, but all have receivers modify their routes on-the-fly based on the defense's coverage, rather than running pre-determined routes. Bill Peterson, the Florida State coach, applied similar thinking when he created the "hot receiver" concept to deal with blitzing defenses in 1964.

The adage that there is nothing new in football is itself borrowed from the Book of Ecclesiastes, which reinforces the fact that many innovations come from reshaping the ideas of others. Among football formations, the spread formation provides an excellent example of the reshaping process at work. John Heisman used a spread formation at Georgia Tech in 1915. Adapting the traditional T formation, Heisman had his seven linemen, and three backs align five yards apart from one another to space out the defenders so he could run the ball. Today's spread more closely resembles the short punt formation, which featured a direct snap to the tailback and was the top passing formation of the 1930s. However, the short punt formation had its ends within a few yards of the tackles, and the backs were inside the ends, so it did not spread defenses horizontally based on alignment.

Gus Henderson, whose leadership brought USC to national prominence and a victory in the 1923 Rose Bowl, developed a passing-oriented spread formation at Tulsa in the 1920s and 1930s, before using it with the Los Angeles Bulldogs and Detroit Lions. His spread formation had two receivers set fifteen yards wide of the interior linemen, a slot, and a halfback. However, it retained the deep halfback and blocking quarterback of the Single Wing, so it remained archaic in some elements.

More critical to the development of the spread and bringing the passing game to football was Dutch Meyer at TCU. Meyer was the baseball coach at TCU and, after being promoted to head football coach as well, named one of his baseball recruits -Slingin' Sammy Baugh- the starting quarterback. TCU often aligned in an empty set (i.e., no running backs) with the ends spread wide and the backs slotted between the ends and the tackles.

After Meyer retired following the 1952 season, the spread took a hiatus until Red Hickey's San Francisco 49ers started using it halfway through the 1960 season when Y. A. Tittle and John Brodie split time at quarterback. Hickey resigned during the 1963 season and was a scout for the Dallas Cowboys in 1975 when Tom Landry revived the formation with Roger Staubach running it on third down and in two-minute drills. Though the Cowboys lost to the Steelers in the Super Bowl that season, the formation proved versatile, and the single-back spread, or "11" personnel came into widespread use in the NFL.

Landry's switching to the spread on third downs contributed to the increased use of personnel groupings. Some teams used code name designations (e.g., the 1985 Cincinnati Bengals' "Bear" package), but most used two-digit designations such as "21" or "12" in which the first digit indicated the number of running backs in the grouping and the second digit indicated the number of tight ends.

Defenses followed suit when running nickel, dime, or other packages to match the offensive formations. This led to cat-and-mouse games in which offenses tried to minimize the ability of defenses to substitute players in response to offensive groupings and defensive players feigning injuries in response. The NFL added a rule in 1989 to ensure defenses had sufficient time to match offensive substitutions. The NCAA added a comparable rule in 2005.

Beyond the strategic innovations in the passing game, the liberalization of blocking rules provided a dramatic aid to the passing game as well. Until 1977, the rules required blockers to keep their hands on their chests while blocking, though blockers had more freedom in actual play. The standard pass blocking technique for offensive lineman was to punch and drop, striking upwards with both fists into the defender's chest before dropping back a step and repeating the sequence until the whistle. A 1977 rule change allowed blockers to extend their arms halfway, followed in 1980 with the ability to fully extend the arms while keeping the fists closed. (The arms could be extended only in retreat, not when moving forward.) The 1981 rules allowed blockers to open their hands while blocking behind the line of scrimmage, and finally, a 1985 rule change allowed blockers to extend their arms anywhere on the field. The rule changes and adjustments in techniques dramatically enhanced pass protection, contributing to 1982 being the first season in which college teams passed for more yards than they ran the ball. The same year NFL teams attempted more passes than runs for the first time.

KICKING

Two elements of the kicking game disappeared during the middle era. One was the virtual elimination of conventional-style kickers from football. The other resulted from a 1967 rule change that eliminated the return kick, a seldom-used and little-recognized holdover from football's rugby days. A return kick occurred when a player took possession of the ball on a kickoff, punt, fumble recovery, or interception, and immediately punted the ball back to the team that had lost possession. Although the idea of kicking the ball back to the opponent seems bizarre today, the return kick fit the field position game played before the 1940s when teams averaged less than fourteen points per game. Return kicks also saw use against teams that did not keep a safety or two back after kicking or punting. Back in the day, those safety men not only were the last line of defense, but they returned the ball following a return kick.

The return kick receives mention in the NCAA rule book today only as an example of an illegal kick, but return kicks are alive and well north of the border, largely due to the single or rouge. Canadian football rules award one point to the kicking team when a kickoff, missed field goal, or punt enters the end zone and is not run or return kicked out of the end zone by the receiving team. Depending on one's perspective, Canadian games periodically descend to the infamy or rise to the glory of a series of return kicks as the teams punt the ball back and forth to score a point or avoid the same.

Paul Douglas while playing for Illinois. (1950 Illio, University of Illinois yearbook, Illini Media)

While the return kick had seen little use for decades at the time it was eliminated from American football, the transition from conventional- to soccer-style kicking led to their increased specialization and an expansion of the kicker's role. Specialist kickers were few and far between until liberalized substitution rules came along. Until then, it seldom made sense to insert a kicker into the game unless they could perform adequately on offense and defense. Specialist kickers might find spots on larger college rosters and get the opportunity to kick near the end of a quarter, but that was not the case on the smaller pro rosters. NFL rosters were limited to 16 players in the 1920s, growing to 33 by the late 1950s, so kickers had to make pro rosters as position players first. The combination of position players handling the kicking duties and almost all of them using the conventional kicking style contributed to kicking being much less effective than today.

Although Pete Gogolak receives credit for popularizing soccer-style kicking in the 1960s, soccer-style kickers were around before he laced his boots. Most early soccer-style kickers had soccer backgrounds and were functional position players as well. One such player was Paul Douglas, a defensive back at Illinois from 1948 to 1950. Though not foreign-born, Douglas grew up in St. Louis, then one of the few soccer hotbeds in the U.S., and learned to kick soccer style. After graduating from Illinois, Douglas spent two years in the Air Force and was signed by the New York Giants upon his return.

Douglas was a highly touted signee and considered a possible starter. He handled kickoff duties during several exhibition games and intercepted a George Blanda pass while on defense, but did not make the final roster and never played in a regular-season NFL game.

Another early soccer-style kicker was Jim Fraser, an offensive guard-linebacker at Wisconsin whose Scottish immigrant parents taught him to kick soccer-style, leading him to kickoff like a Scotsman for the Badgers during the 1957 and 1958 seasons. Fraser spent 1959 with the Hamilton Tiger-Cats of the CFL and signed with the San Diego Chargers in 1960, but was drafted into the Army and spent two years as a paratrooper. Upon his discharge, Fraser signed with the Denver Broncos, where he played linebacker and led the AFL in punting average in 1962, 1963, and 1964. Twice during the 1962 season, Fraser kicked extra points for the Broncos because their regular kicker, Gene Mingo, was unavailable. (On one of those occasions, Mingo, the starting halfback, scored on an 82-yard run and needed a rest.) Since Fraser kicked those extra points soccer-style in 1962 (two years before Pete Gogolak entered the AFL), he was the first person to kick soccer-style in a regular season, professional football game in the U.S.

Pete Gogolak of Cornell kicking during the 1963 season. (1964 Cornellian, Division of Rare and Manuscript Collections, Cornell University Library)

Although Douglas and Fraser preceded Gogolak, the impetus to switch kicking styles came from the new substitution rules and the national attention Pete Gogolak received while booting the oval for Cornell from 1961 to 1963, the AFL's Buffalo Bills in 1964 and 1965, and the NFL's New York Giants from 1966 to 1974. Gogolak's brother, Charlie, followed him, as did a host of foreign- and native-born soccer-style kickers that dominated the position by the mid-1980s.

With soccer-style kickers booting the ball farther than their conventional friends, fewer kickoffs were returned. The kickoff was moved back to the 35-yard line in 1986 and to the 30-yard line in 2007. Although kickoffs can be among football's most exciting plays, they are also among the most dangerous. In an attempt to reduce the number of returns, a 2018 rule allowed the receiving team to fair catch the kickoff and take the ball on their 35-yard line.

Soccer-style kickers also dramatically affected the number of field goals attempted and made. The NCAA first tracked statistics in 1937, a year in which there were only 47 field goals made in all of major college football. Between 1938 and 1957, major college teams never kicked more than 83 field goals in a year, typically notching 40 to 60 made field goals. The number of field goals increased in the late 1950s due to the widening of the college uprights and substitution rules allowed specialist snappers, holders, and kickers to enter the game. And changes in kicking techniques increased the accuracy and distance of attempted field goals.

The combination of these factors resulted in the average number of field goals made per game increasing from 0.09 in 1958 to 1.13 in 1987 (more than a twelve-fold increase). Similarly, the PAT conversion rate rose from 68.6 percent in 1959 to 94.9 percent in 1987. Believing things had gone too far, the NCAA banned the use of tees for field goals and extra points in 1988, resulting in a slight reduction in field goals made per game. Moving the hash marks 6 feet 8 inches closer to the center of the field in 1993 made field goals easier once again. By 2017, major college teams averaged 1.08 field goals per game and completed 96.6 percent of their kicked PATs.

Regardless of the kicking style, the kicker's job is to send the ball through the uprights on each field goal or extra point attempt. The opposing team's job is to block the kick or, short of that, find a means of distracting the kicker. A favorite method among today's coaches is to "freeze" or "ice" the kicker. The term "icing the kicker" first appeared in the mid- to late-1980s, but the first identified instance of an opposing team calling a timeout before a late kick attempt came when Duffy Daugherty and Michigan State did so versus Iowa in 1969. As it turned out, Iowa's Al Scheutte made the extra point attempt with 1:25 left in the game, and the Hawkeyes hung on for a 19-18 victory.

The tactic was taken to its logical conclusion after a 2004 NFL rule change allowed coaches to call timeouts from the sideline. (Previously, only players on the field could call a timeout). The Denver Broncos coach, Mike Shanahan, leveraged the new rule in 2007 by calling a timeout a split second before the kicking team snapped the football. The Oakland Raiders' Sebastian Janikowski famously made the disallowed attempt and then missed the attempt that counted.

Just as the rule makers gave kickers as assist in 1958 by widening the uprights, they gave punters a break in 1962. Before then, punts downed inside the receiving team's 10-yard line became touchbacks. Punts had to go out of bounds to pin an opponent inside the 10-yard line. The 1962 rule that gave receiving teams the ball at the spot it was downed substantially changed punting strategy.

The other big change in punting during the modern era has been the increased use of rugby-style punting. Although we think of rugby-style punting as something new, it is as old as the game of football itself and was quite common before 1920.

The rebirth of the rugby-style punt began in 1993 when Arizona's special teams coordinator, Rich Ellerson, used rugby-style approaches to increase the team's net punting average. Steve McLaughlin, his kicker-punter won the Lou Groza Award the following year. In 1995, Darren Bennett became the first punter to make the NFL after a career playing Australian Rules football. (Most Australian punters hone their skills playing "footy" or Australian rules football rather than rugby.) The Australians brought not only the punt-on-the-run technique but the more subtle change of dropping the ball vertically rather than horizontally and kicking the bottom third of the ball rather than the midsection. While the down under approach limits the punt's distance, the backspin helps keep punts from rolling into the end zone.

SCORING

College football's scoring rules changed seven times between 1876 and 1912. Another set of changes occurred in 1958 when teams received the option to earn two points by running or passing on the try after touchdown. The one-point safety arrived the same year.

The only change in scoring methods during the modern era came in 1988. Up to that point, the ball was whistled dead on extra point attempts once the defense blocked the kick, intercepted a pass, or recovered a fumble. As of 1988, blocked PAT attempts and intercepted passes can be advanced with the defense scoring two points by returning the ball to the opposite end zone. Finally, a 1990 rule allowed defensive players to advance recovered fumbles, giving defenses one more method of scoring.

Of course, the biggest change related to scoring came in football's handling of tie games. There had been attempts to limit the number of tie games over the years; returning the goals posts to the goal line (NFL) and adding the two-point conversion (NCAA) were among those attempts. Still, the lack of play-offs in college and professional football made tie-breaking processes unnecessary.

Such was not the case at other levels of football where playoffs existed and various tie-breaking procedures developed over the years. In the first part of the 1900s, the U.S. Navy sponsored football leagues with each ship fielding a team. On the East Coast, the league winners in the four major ports advanced to a playoff for the coast championship. It just so happened that the 1915 playoff game between the *U.S.S. Wyoming* and *U.S.S. South Carolina* ended in a tie and, lacking set procedures, league officials decided the teams should play a tiebreaker game the following day.

Service football provided another tiebreaker solution in 1918 when the Rose Bowl selection committee created a five-team tournament among the top West Coast service elevens to determine which team would face the Great Lakes Naval Training Station in the 1919 Rose Bowl. After one game ended in a tie, the Rose Bowl Committee used the comparative score approach to choose which team advanced. E. K. Hall, who followed Walter Camp as the secretary of the college football rules committee, suggested that committees break ties when post-season tournaments were held in 1931 to raise money for charity. Topping Hall's list of nine tie-breaking criteria for judges was the "Diversity and variety of strategy and method of attack," followed by giving "weight to the general excellence of team play as against starring of individuals."[40] Only his third criteria, total yardage gained in the game, relied on objective, game results rather than subjective assessments of the committee. Even that measure was problematic because college football did not yet have an agreed-upon system of tracking game statistics.

The impetus for developing better tie-breaking procedures came with the creation of state high school football championships. Initially, states broke ties using game statistics, awarding the game to the team that had most frequently penetrated their opponent's 5-, 10-, or 20-yard line or the team gaining the highest number of first downs. Other states gave each team the ball at the 50-yard line and awarded the game to the team that scored the most points or gained the most yardage.

The 1966 version of the Game of the Century between #1 Notre Dame and #2 Michigan State was among the greatest college football games to end in a tie. (Associated Press Photo)

Kansas used a version of the game statistics method when it introduced high school playoffs in 1969. Still, few were happy with the method, leading Brice Durbin, the Executive Director of the Kansas State High School Activities Association, to develop the "Kansas Rules." The Kansas Rules settled ties by giving each team the ball on the 10-yard line with four downs to score. Each team received an equal number of possessions until one outscored the other.

The NCAA adopted a version of the Kansas Rules in 1973 when national championship playoffs began in Divisions II and III. The first game to use the rule was an overtime loss by Carroll University to Buena Vista in the Division III playoffs in 1976. The original NCAA rules gave each team the ball on the 15-yard line and did not allow defensive scoring. Beginning in 1985, each team received the ball on the 25-yard line. At the major college level, the overtime rules were implemented for bowl games following the 1995 season and became a part of regular-season and bowl games starting in 1996.

DEFENSE

The defensive side of the ball has been underappreciated for much of football's history. Before two-platoon football, teams spent the bulk of their practice time on the offensive side of the game, offensive roles defined players' descriptions and numbering, and stardom primarily resulted from offensive and kicking skills. The game's statistics reflect the limited attention given to the defense. The most important element of defensive play is to tackle the ball carrier, yet the NCAA only began tracking solo and assisted tackles in 2000, sixty-three years after first tracking offensive statistics. College coaches dedicated numerous books to offensive systems (e.g., Don Faurot's *Football: Secrets of the "Split T" Formation)*, but period books covering defensive systems are hard to find. Similarly, books that cover football coaching more broadly such a Dana X. Bible's *Championship Football* or Bernie Bierman's *Winning Football* commonly devote four to five times as many chapters to offensive play as to defensive play. (This author is guilty of the same crime.)

Until late in the middle era, defensive strategy focused on sound alignment combined with effective individual play and techniques. Defenses did not attack and disrupt offenses; they reacted to them. Linebacker "red dogs" and movement by defensive linemen in the late 1940s and early 1950s marked the first consistent attempts by defenses to change the terms of the battle by pressuring the offense. That has changed, of course, and the primary story of defensive football during the modern era has been the movement toward aggressiveness and dictating terms to offenses.

Part and parcel with dictating terms is creating confusion on the offensive side. Defenses have long switched formations from game to game based on the opponent's offensive style and made situational adjustments from down to down, but whatever the call, they lined up in that formation and stayed there. That changed when Eddie Erdelatz, Navy's coach, introduced the Jitterbug Defense in 1957. Implemented at mid-season, the Jitterbug confused offenses by switching from one defense to another after the offense came to the line of scrimmage. On one play in their 1958 Cotton Bowl victory, Navy's defense aligned in a 53 defense, shifted to a 62 when the middle linebacker moved into a three-point stance on the line, before another linebacker took a two-point stance in the line to make it a 71 defense.

While the Jitterbug itself had a short life, the concept of disguising defenses has remained and morphed, particularly as part of defending the pass. This morphing coincided with the use of option routes in the passing game that require receivers to recognize defensive coverages on the fly and alter their patterns accordingly. Getting a team's receivers and quarterbacks on the same page against all potential coverages is difficult by itself, but defenses that disguised their coverage made that process more difficult. Bart Starr encapsulated the shift toward disguising defenses and coverages in 1966, saying:

> There is no single general rule for picking apart defenses. You just have to understand defenses and you have to be forever alert. Nowadays, they're doing things on defense that were unheard of a decade ago. They disguise their

> coverages and they don't advertise their reddogs and they match every audible you call with one of their own.[41]

Offensive players read defenses based on their positioning, stance, and where the defensive players are looking. They also monitor how defensive players react to offensive shifts and motion. Of course, if offenses understand those reads, so do defenses, and they counteract those clues by showing pre-snap looks that differ from their post-snap actions. This cat-and-mouse game is extended by defenses possessing players who not only can show multiple looks, but have the skills to execute them. The middle linebacker of the Tampa 2, who is capable of playing run defense and also dropping deep into coverage, is one example of the many hybrid defensive roles that emerged in recent decades.

Beyond the broad changes in defenses during the modern era have been several specific innovations that came into near-universal use. The development of pocket pass protection in the 1950s resulted in quarterbacks having more time to throw than in the past. That forced defenses had to find methods to confuse and pressure quarterbacks when blitzing linebackers proved insufficient, such as the St. Louis football Cardinals of the early 1960s blitzing their free safety, Larry Wilson. As originally conceived, St. Louis brought the free safety along with the three linebackers in an all-out effort to pressure the quarterback. It was a high-risk maneuver that depended on reaching the quarterback before he could get the ball to an open receiver.

Teams of the time paired blitzes with man coverage, so safety blitzes left defenses a man short in pass defense. This approach became riskier against the short passing game of the West Coast Offense that came on the scene in the early 1980s, so Dick Lebeau countered that challenge by using the zone blitz. As the New York Giants had done in the 1950s, Lebeau blitzed a safety or linebacker while dropping a defensive lineman into an underneath zone.

Another innovation during the modern era was the development of nickel and dime packages. The first nickel defense solved a particular problem, and, in that case, the problem was Mike Ditka. Ditka was drafted by the Chicago Bears in 1961 and immediately caused problems for defensive coaches, including the Philadelphia Eagles' defensive back coach, Jerry Williams. To cover Ditka in passing situations, Williams modified the Eagles' 43 defense by inserting a fifth defensive back in place of an outside linebacker.

George Allen copied the Eagles' adjustment and did the same while coining the term "nickel" defense. As coach of the Los Angeles Rams in 1966, Allen had the Fearsome Foursome, who could pressure quarterbacks without blitzing. That allowed him to defend passes from the nickel defense, which he extended by using the "dime" or 3-2-6 alignment by 1969. Nickel and dime defenses were further popularized by Don Shula and the Miami Dolphins in the 1970s and have since become commonplace throughout football.

Nickel and dime defenses became widespread because they proved effective at slowing down offenses, but defensive innovations that are too effective run the risk of being outlawed. Such was the case for the bump and run technique. The origins of the bump and run are a bit murky. Numerous players and coaches claim credit for its development, but the most convincing story places the bump and run's origins at the feet of a Naismith Memorial Basketball Hall of Fame inductee, K. C. Jones. Jones, along with Bill Russell, won NCAA basketball championships in 1955 and 1956 for the University of San Francisco, as well as the 1956 Olympic gold medal. Jones did not receive a guaranteed contract from the Boston Celtics when he left the Army in 1958, so he accepted an invitation to the Los Angeles Rams training camp after being drafted by then-general manager, Pete Rozelle.

Jack Faulkner, the Rams' defensive backfield coach, saw that Jones, rather than playing back from the line, lined up directly across from the receiver, much like he did when guarding an opponent on the basketball court. As the receiver headed downfield, Jones used his body to shield the receiver as the pass pattern developed. Jones was in the position to make the Rams' final roster, but he quit during the preseason to concentrate on basketball. Given his twelve NBA championships as a player, assistant coach, and head coach, leaving football was likely the right decision.

Still, Jack Faulkner appreciated Jones' approach and began teaching it to his players as an assistant with the AFL's Los Angeles Chargers. Faulkner's fellow assistant coaches, Chuck Noll and Al Davis, implemented the technique a few years down the road when they became head coaches. Faulkner became the Denver Broncos head coach in 1962 where the technique was taught to Willie Brown, who, after being traded to the Oakland Raiders, paired with Kent McLoughlan to execute the first full implementation of the bump and run.

In addition to helping cover the receiver, the technique disrupted the timing of routes even when receivers were able to escape the defensive backs' clutches. The bump and run became so effective that offenses had trouble moving the ball. As a result, the NFL changed its pass defense rules in 1983, so defenders could no longer hit an eligible receiver more than five yards from the line of scrimmage. (College football does not have this rule and allows defenders to contact the receiver anywhere on the field.)

NFL rules limiting contact with eligible receivers have contributed to the growth of the passing game since the mid-1980s, particularly the short passing game that relies on timing and receivers releasing quickly from the line of scrimmage.

THE TRANSITION from the Single Wing to the modern T that occurred in the 1940s and 1950s shifted the focus of offensive football from the triple threat tailback to the single threat quarterback. T formation quarterbacks were valued for their ability to throw the ball, not to run with it, and football implemented numerous rules to protect them while in the pocket. The quarterbacks in the Veer and Wishbone attacks of the 1960s and 1970s made reads while running parallel to the line of scrimmage, severely limiting the passing attacks in those offenses. Quarterbacks in the zone read offense that emerged in the 1990s made their reads five yards behind the line of scrimmage. Like Single Wing tailbacks, the challenge provided by dual-threat quarterbacks is substantial, but the limited number of players sufficiently adept at running and throwing at a level needed to execute modern offenses keeps coaches using and seeking alternative approaches.

Football witnessed a revolution in the art of kicking during the modern era. Whereas the innovations on the offensive side of the ball were largely schematic, the changes in the kicking game came through new techniques. Moreover, rather than rely on position players to handle kicking duties, the accuracy and distance achieved by specialist soccer-style kickers justified devoting roster spots to the sidewinders with similar moves occurring with specialist punters and long snappers.

Defensive play became more aggressive and strategic during the modern era. Safety, corner, and zone blitzes all emerged to pressure and confuse quarterbacks, but the most significant change in defensive tactics has been the move toward playing multiple defenses and coverages, all while disguising them from the offense. In the age of modern passing attacks, defensive disguises are only as effective as the defenders' ability to carry out their various assignments, leading to an increasing shift to hybrid players with the combination of speed and power to perform multiple roles on the field.

16

PLAYER EQUIPMENT (1960-2018)

Changes in the equipment used by players during the modern era was affected by advances in technology and materials sciences, modifications of football rules, and increasingly, by aesthetics and fashion. During the first decades of the modern era, many new technologies and materials used in football gear came from outside the sporting goods industry, while more recent innovations came from research and development initiatives targeting the sporting goods and leisure markets. Beyond the advances in equipment has been the development of formal standards and tests that helmets, in particular, must meet to be used on the field.

Today's athletes are not the first to be interested in looking good in their uniforms. The friction strips of the 1920s had functional value, but their arrangement was intended to be eye-pleasing. The emphasis on fashion has never been greater and reaches its apex in the many uniform combinations worn by the University of Oregon football team.

PADDING AND INJURY PREVENTION

Through football's history, players have consistently chosen to wear equipment that affords protection, while also minimizing the equipment worn. An apparent exception to that rule occurred during the 1970s and 1980s when players wore more and bigger pads than during any other period.

At the start of the modern era, the profile of shoulder pads was similar to those of previous decades. Shoulder pads typically rose only an inch or two above the shoulders and extended only slightly past the upper arm. Increased concerns about shoulder injuries led equipment manufacturers to increase the height and width of shoulder pads in the 1970s, reaching a point in the

1980s in which they looked like "treehouse(s) for the head."[42] Later research showed the bigger and taller shoulder pads did little to prevent shoulder injuries, so the trend reversed. Offensive linemen shifted to wearing rounded, low-profile shoulder pads that were harder for defensive linemen to grab, while skill position players sought smaller pads for increased freedom of movement. Some saw smaller shoulder pads as a fashion statement as well, believing the smaller pads made them appear faster and more athletic than the bulky pads of the past. In addition, enhancements in materials and design meant that smaller shoulder pads provided as much or more protection than their bulky predecessors. At the same time that shoulder pads became narrower and shorter, they crept further down the chest to add protection for the ribs. Supplemental back plates also came into play.

The same period saw an increase in the number of arm pads worn by many positions, particularly offensive linemen. Unable to extend their hands to block defenders, their techniques focused on punching and shivering the forearms into defensive players. Being the most intelligent position group in football, offensive linemen opted to wear pads to protect their arms. As blocking rules were liberalized in the late 1970s to mid-1980 and offensive players were allowed to extend their arms, the need for multiple arm pads disappeared.

Hall of Fame offensive guard, Gene Upshaw holds the game ball above his well-padded arms following Super Bowl XV in 1981. (Cliff Welch, Icon Sportswire)

Pads that protected the ribs have been around since at least the 1930s when homemade, and commercially available rib protectors came available. Early rib protectors used the same materials as the shoulder pads and hip pads of the time: leather or plastic over felt or foam rubber pads. While these offered some protection for healthy players, they were less effective for players already suffering from sore or broken ribs. The lack of effective rib protection became more problematic as quarterbacks increasingly threw from the pocket, leaving themselves vulnerable to being hit in the ribs.

Byron Donzis was among those who had a significant impact on rib pads, and the use of advanced materials in football pads more generally. Donzis came to Dan Pastorini's assistance when the Houston Oilers' quarterback suffered three broken ribs in a late-season game in 1978. While Pastorini was sitting in a hospital bed, two men, who were not authorized to be there, stepped into Pastorini's room. One was Donzis, who, wearing a padded vest, raised his arms over his head while the other man struck him in the ribs with a baseball bat. Donzis did not flinch, which rightly convinced Pastorini that a similar vest might serve him well.

Donzis' flak jacket was made of plastics capable of stopping a bullet and urethane foam that cushioned blows by distributing the forces across a broader surface. It provided enough protection that Pastorini played in a wildcard game several weeks later, leading the Houston Oilers to the AFC Championship game. With the help of a $190,000 grant from the NFL, Donzis designed other pads using similar materials, ultimately obtaining patents related to protective padding. Donzis' approach has since spread to a range of football, hockey, and other sporting goods equipment to prevent injuries, not just to protect those who have suffered injuries.

Bill Fralic, a two-time All American offensive tackle at Pitt, sporting a neck roll for his publicity shot. (University of Pittsburgh Historic Photographs, Archives & Special Collections, University of Pittsburgh Library System)

Another popular device that saw its usage rise and fall was the neck roll, which Wilson introduced in 1961. The neck roll acted as a cushion when a players' head was pushed back when striking with the face mask. Later, cowboy collars performed a similar function but were integrated into the shoulder pads. Regardless of their functional value, neck pads became a fashion statement, seemingly because they communicated that the player wearing a neck roll played aggressively enough to require one.

Neck rolls fell out of favor when tackling techniques changed, and players no longer planted their face masks in the ball carrier's sternum, obviating the need to cushion the back of the helmet and neck. Allowing offensive lineman to extend their arms when blocking has a similar effect. Finally, another reason for the demise of neck rolls was the lack of proof of their effectiveness.

The use of knee braces by football players originated with Mike Murphy, who is primarily known for working as the athletic trainer at Yale and Penn, and for coaching the 1904, 1908, and 1912 U.S. track and field Olympic teams. Murphy developed custom-made braces before cornering the market with standardized braces shortly after the turn of the century.

Like face masks and rib protectors, knee braces first came into use among the injured. That remained their primary use until USC became the first school to use them in preventive fashion in the late 1960s, with the Los Angeles Rams and Cleveland Browns being the first NFL teams to require their offensive linemen to wear them in the early 1970s.

Spalding had moved on from Mike Murphy's knee brace design by 1920, but they still sold his rub-in liniment. (1920 Spalding's Official Football Guide)

Today, knee braces are largely used to prevent injury among college offensive linemen and quarterbacks (on their lead leg). Most positions do not use knee braces for preventive purposes because the devices are uncomfortable, limit mobility, and smell bad after limited use, none of which seem to bother offensive linemen. Likewise, knee braces are more popular in the college game than the NFL because the collective bargaining agreement prevents NFL teams from forcing players to wear them. College players lack such leverage.

While knee injuries have negatively affected the careers of many football players, the most significant issue facing football today is player safety and, specifically, concerns about concussions and Chronic Traumatic

Encephalopathy (CTE). The plastic helmets with suspension or foam padding systems used in the 1950s and 1960s took a step forward when Riddell introduced air bladders in their Micro-Fit helmets in 1969. Using the same needle and hand pump that inflated footballs, the air bladders could be inflated or deflated to provide the maximum available protection for players at the time.

Concern about the link between injuries, equipment, and technique led to the formation of the National Operating Committee on Standards for Athletic Equipment (NOCSAE) in 1970. Charged with understanding the nature of head injuries and helping mitigate them, the NOCSAE sponsored studies to calibrate standards and test procedures for new, and equally important, reconditioned helmets. The tests identified many low-quality helmets and, combined with lawsuits against helmet manufacturers, led to the number of helmet manufacturers dropping from twenty-one to three by 1983.

The remaining manufacturers have shifted their attention to reducing the prevalence of concussions. After a study of NFL films showed that seventy percent of concussions resulted from blows to the side of the head, Riddell released the Revolution helmet in 2002 that features a plastic shell extending further down the jaw than other models. More recent developments by traditional manufacturers have included helmet shells with sections or components that disburse energy.

New helmet manufacturers have entered the market in recent years. Vicis, for example, created the highest-rated helmet models using a flexible outer shell that surrounds a columnar layer that contorts to reduce linear and rotational forces, all of which are intended to reduce concussions.

In addition to changes in helmet design have been similar modifications to the design and use of face masks. When the modern era dawned, players in a range of positions wore single bar face masks. That shifted in the 1960s to quarterbacks and kickers wearing single bars, while running backs and receivers used double-barred masks. Some linemen wore cages or double-bar masks with a third bar running vertically between the top of the double-bar mask and the helmet shell above the nose.

Missouri's quarterback, Gary Lane, wears a single-bar mask in 1964 while being pursued by Colorado players wearing double-bar and cage face masks. (Courtesy of the University of Missouri, MU Libraries.)

The Los Angeles Rams became the first NFL team to require players to wear face masks in 1954, but even after the NFL required all players to wear them, players could appeal to play without one. Almost every position player chose to wear a face mask, but numerous punters, kickers, and holders claimed the face masks interfered with their vision, so they did not wear them. Some position players who kicked, punted, or held on kicks swapped their masked helmet for an unmasked helmet when performing special teams duties.

The last NFL position player to go without a face mask was Tommy McDonald, a Split T halfback on the record-setting Oklahoma teams of the mid-1950s. McDonald was a flanker for five NFL teams from 1957 to 1968 and argued that he did not get hit in the face as a flanker. Several punters and kickers that played in the mid-1970s were the last NFL players to go without face masks.

The last college player to play without a face mask is entirely unclear, largely because the NCAA did not make face masks mandatory until 1993. John Adams, the Secretary of the NCAA Football Rules Committee at the time, was quoted in July 1993 as saying: "It seems there never was a rule for face masks. Everyone had worn them for years but nobody realized they weren't mandatory. Now, they will be."[42] A few months later, Adams told a different story: "We've known all along that the face mask rule wasn't on the books. You would never see a player a player without one, but we just finally got around to making it official."[43] Regardless, the NCAA's delay in instituting a rule requiring the use of face masks may be the best example of how football's rules often lag actual practice.

While face masks provided significant protection of the eyes, they did not prevent fingers or objects from periodically coming into contact with players' eyes. The first effective method to prevent the gouging of eyes was the development of eye shields, which came to football from hockey. The clear plastic eye shields used in industrial settings migrated to hockey in the mid-1970s. A player who had lost an eye playing junior hockey received the NHL's approval to use a helmet and eye shield in June 1975. The same month, a report to the Canadian Amateur Hockey Association concerning eye injuries led them to allow players to wear eye shields, with or without a physician's order. Eye shields became mandatory at the amateur level in Canadian hockey in 1981.

Following hockey's lead, eye shields entered the football world in 1982 or 1984, depending on who you believe. Joe Devlin of the Buffalo Bills is said to have worn an eye shield in a January 1982 playoff game against Cincinnati. More evidence indicates that Mark Mullaney, a defensive lineman for the Minneapolis Vikings, began wearing one early in the 1984 season after suffering an eye injury. Although part of the initial desire for visors was their ability to block the sun when tinted, the NFL banned tinted eye shields in 1998, and the NCAA followed suit in 2006.

At the other end of the body from the head are players' shoes and particularly their cleats. Football teams have long varied the length of cleats based on the playing field conditions. Some players wore long cleats in favorable conditions because the longer spikes dug further into the turf and increased their cutting ability. Unfortunately, the longer cleats can grip too well, leading to knee and ankle injuries. As the evidence mounted regarding long cleats, the medical community advised players to wear molded rubber cleats, and the national high school rules committee recommended their use in 1954. Molded cleats were worn by college players as well, particularly those who had already suffered knee injuries. Finally, the NCAA limited cleat length to 1/2 inch in 1970.

Although one might think that a rule limiting cleats to 1/2 inch would be difficult to evade, that assumption underestimates the ingenuity of football coaches when they have something stuck in their craw, particularly someone like Bo Schembechler. Schembechler's Michigan teams played in the 1976 Orange Bowl, and the 1977 and 1978 Rose Bowls. Unfortunately for Bo, Michigan lost each game, and Bo placed partial blame on the natural grass surfaces at the two bowls. Before the 1978 season, Schembechler ordered his equipment managers to insert washers between the soles of his players' shoes and their half-inch cleats. The NCAA rule required only that the cleats themselves not exceed one-half inch and said nothing about using washers, so Michigan's shoes were legal. It is impossible to know how much value

Michigan received from the washers, but at season's end, they lost the Rose Bowl for the third straight year, suffering the agony of da' cleat. The rule makers of 1979 addressed Bo's sneakiness by revising the rule to focus not on cleat length, but on limiting to one-half inch the distance from the sole of the shoe to the end of the cleat.

Beyond the protective properties of football equipment, other changes to equipment came out of the chemical industry's research laboratories. One such company, Du Pont, sought an alternative fiber for use in women's undergarments when they created *Lycra*. Generically known as *Spandex*, this miracle fiber was lighter, more durable, more easily dyed, and possessed three times the restraining power of the material it replaced. Even more, *Spandex* could be machine washed and dried. *Spandex* quickly found its way into many products, including football uniforms. Mixed with nylon and other fibers, Spandex allowed football pants and jerseys of the mid-1960s to be more form-fitting, which kept players' pads in place while lessening their opponents' ability to grab the fabric.

Uniform fabrics also featured wicking properties to draw moisture away from the body. The cotton shirt and shorts worn under football pads for the first half of the modern era absorbed up to twenty-five times their weight in water, so wicking fabrics came into use with undergarments. The fact that wicking fabrics also help with temperature regulation provided an additional reason these fabrics became widespread in the football world.

Despite the many advances in uniforms, a few developments went off the rails. The most bizarre idea of the modern era came from the World Football League in 1975. Based on the advice of a management consultant, William B. Finnernan, the league announced that its players would wear pants differing in color by position group. Offensive linemen would pop purple pants, running backs would wear green garb, and orange pants would brighten the legs of the receivers. Defensive players were to wear an equally ridiculous collection of colors while quarterbacks and kickers would wear white. Despite the cornucopia of colors conflicting with the team jersey and helmet colors, the WFL's rules committee agreed to test the colored pants during several exhibition games. Thankfully, the first of those games featured the Memphis Southmen who had signed Larry Csonka, Jim Kiick, and Paul Warfield away from the Miami Dolphins. The star signees refused to wear the colored pants, forcing the league to announce it would study the idea further before later canceling the colored pants plan altogether.

Another bad uniform idea was the tearaway football jerseys worn by teams in the 1960s and 1970s. Like songs that teenagers do not recognize as decades-old hits, tearaway jerseys have a long history. Although some attribute tearaway jerseys to Howard Jones of USC or Slip Madigan of St. Mary's, all signs point to Fritz Crisler originating the tearable wearables while coaching

Princeton. It seems that one of Crisler's Princeton backs was tackled when a Yale defender grabbed the back's jersey five yards short of the goal line. Crisler was not amused and ordered tearable jerseys for the following year's game. (Tearaway jerseys were made of easily-torn fabric, constructed with minimal stitching, or both.) Crisler later took his tearaway jerseys and goofy helmets to Ann Arbor, where Tom Harmon became famous for wearing tattered jerseys during his 1940 Heisman run.

Michigan's Tom Harmon with a torn jersey in an image autographed to his coach, Fritz Crisler. (Bentley Historical Library, University of Michigan)

Tearaway jerseys became commonplace and troublesome in the late 1940s and 1950s. The rules of the time required an official timeout whenever a player tore his jersey, which proved problematic at times. The 1956 Cotton Bowl, for one, had seventeen timeouts called due to one torn jersey or another. Enough was enough, and several weeks later, the rule was changed, so a torn jersey resulted in a timeout charged to the offending team, a stiff penalty that made tearaways less common.

Conditions changed with the liberalization of the substitution rules in the first half of the 1960s. The new rules allowed players with torn jerseys to be substituted, and the need for timeouts avoided, so tearaway jerseys became all the rage again. Texas wore them in 1968, the same year they introduced the Wishbone.

The beginning of the end of the tearaway jersey came when the NFL barred them in 1978, reasoning that shoulder pads that were not restrained by jerseys presented a danger to other players. Beyond that, tearaway jerseys simply were not consistent with an image-focused NFL that had detailed rules requiring players to keep their socks pulled up. The NCAA followed suit in 1982 and banned tearaway jerseys for both safety and cost reasons.

Good ideas sometimes emerge from bad ideas, and that was the case with substances used to improve the grip of running backs and ends. As far back as 1893, Yalies applied resin to their hands after learning Harvard planned to wear leather uniforms in The Game that year. The use of sticky or tacky substances to aid in catching goes back at least to the 1930s when Cecil Cushman, the longtime coach at the University of Redlands, developed "Stickum" for his ball handlers.

Stickum was seldom a problem until 1977 when Lester Hayes, a rookie cornerback with the Oakland Raiders, was introduced to the product by his teammate, Fred Biletnikoff. Hayes soon applied Stickum to his hands in such quantity that opposing players complained it affected their ability to snap, throw, and otherwise handle the ball. The excessive Stickum era ended when the NFL banned sticky and slippery substances altogether.

Fred Biletnikoff applies Stickum to his hands as blades of grass cling to the excess Stickum on his jersey and pants. (Cliff Welch, Icon Sportswire)

Looking for a different aid to help catch or handle the ball, players experimented with various types of gloves. Doug Flutie, played with glass cutter gloves in the CFL, while others used neoprene scuba diving gloves. Ultimately, the athletic apparel manufacturers introduced football gloves made of propriety materials and surfaces to help receivers catch balls they would be less likely to grab with their bare hands. Beyond their functional value, gloves are among the most highly stylized elements of football uniforms today and one that allows for some level of individual expression.

OTHER EQUIPMENT CHANGES

The addition of numbers on player jerseys, the move toward white road jerseys, and TV numbers are examples of middle era equipment changes that did not provide better protection or otherwise enhance player performance. A handful of similar changes occurred during the modern era.

The first was the addition of player names on the back of their jerseys. Adding player names on jerseys goes back at least as far back as 1916 when a Philadelphia high school added player names on their basketball uniforms. Santa Clara did the same in the 1930s, but the idea did not become popular until 1960 when the Chicago White Sox added player names on the back of their road jerseys. Capitalizing on the White Sox' idea, the American Football League owners did the same for their inaugural season in 1960, while NFL players remained nameless until 1970 when they gained approval during the reconciliation of AFL and NFL rule differences.

Defensive guard Bill Kirchiro awaits the Penn State offense during Maryland's first win over the Nittany Lions. (1962 Terrapin, University of Maryland yearbook)

Maryland became the first college football team where everybody knows your name when they added surnames in 1961. As with other changes in uniforms driven by television, names on the backs of jerseys primarily helped fans watching games on television identify who was who on the field.

There were several period changes in uniforms or equipment for which the person or team that developed the innovation does not receive appropriate credit. Take the case of the playbook wristbands (aka wrist coaches). Anyone who knows any football lore recognizes that Tom Matte of the Baltimore Colts wore the first playbook wristband in 1965. The 1965 season held much promise for the Baltimore Colts, and they fulfilled that promise until Johnny Unitas was injured in the third to last game of the season. Second-string quarterback Gary Cuozzo separated his shoulder in the next game, leaving the signal-calling duties to Tom Matte, a halfback who had played quarterback at Ohio State. Since Matte had not played quarterback in the NFL, his coach, Don Shula, provided Matte with a wristband listing key plays for Matte's use in the regular-season finale and upcoming playoff game.

While the NFL would have you believe Matte was the first player to wear a playbook wristband, at least two others preceded him. The first was LSU quarterback Jimmy Field, who, while playing both ways for Paul Dietzel against Florida in 1960, wore a wristband listing offensive and defensive plays. Well, he wore the wristband for part of the game because it mysteriously left his arm while at the bottom of a pile during the second quarter. Field and Dietzel notified the officials of the missing wristband, but it was nowhere to be found until it appeared on the Florida bench at halftime. The Florida coaches later claimed they did not use the information on the wristband and planned to return it to LSU. Whatever the truth may be regarding Florida's possessing the wristband, Field, a sophomore at the time, used the wristband for the rest of his LSU career.

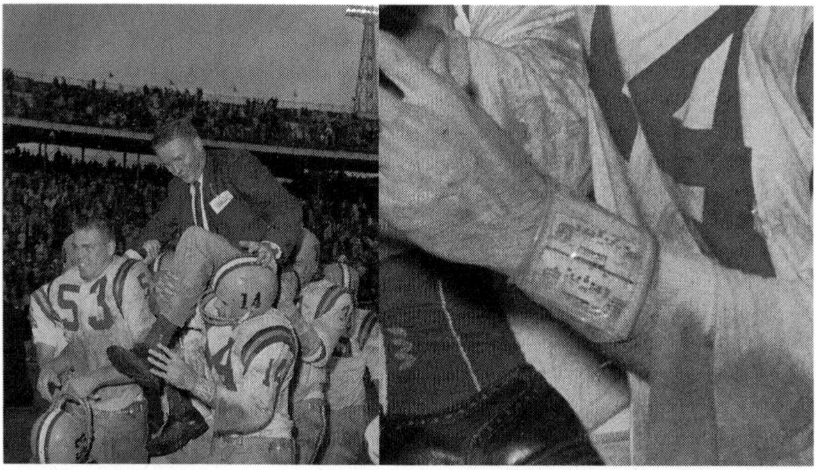

On the left, Jimmy Field (#14) helps carry LSU Paul Dietzel off the field following the 1962 Orange Bowl. The image on the right is a closeup of Field's wristband. (Harold Valentine, Associated Press Photo)

Kentucky also made us of playbook wristbands during the 1962 and 1963 seasons. Quarterback Jerry Woolum used one during the 1962 season, and both the quarterbacks and linebackers used them during the 1963 season.

While playbook wristbands originally served as reminders for quarterbacks or linebackers who called their own plays, their role changed once coaching from the sideline became legal. Ultimately, playbook wristbands transitioned into lists of numbers and associated plays so that coaches could signal in plays using only the associated number.

The second element of football gear with commonly misattributed origins are white shoes. Like the Ford Model T, football shoes came in one color, black, until Ted Collins, the owner of the NFL's Boston Yanks in 1946, told his running backs to wear white shoes so fans could more easily follow their movements on the field. Despite a spate of publicity following Collins' preseason announcement, it is unclear whether the Yanks' backs wore white shoes that year. White shoes were not heard from again until the 1962 Army-Navy game when Army was coached by newly-hired Paul Dietzel, who had a soft spot for goofy, inspirational tactics. Since Roger Staubach was the Navy quarterback that year, Army needed plenty of inspiration. Oddly, the first tactic Dietzel employed was to skip pre-game warmups and keep the Army team in the locker room until just before the playing of the national anthem. At that point, Army rushed onto the field wearing white shoes. Unfortunately, the cadets got off on the wrong foot, losing the game 34-14.

Army defenders wearing white jerseys and white shoes during the 1962 Army-Navy game. (1963 Lucky Bag, United States Naval Academy yearbook)

Two years later, Joe Namath was Alabama's black-shoe-wearing quarterback until he decided to cover his black shoes with white athletic tape for every game but one, during which he injured his knee. Viewing his taped shoes as a good luck charm, Namath taped his black shoes white when he moved to the NFL. Namath arrived at his locker before the fourth game of his rookie season to find the equipment manager had ordered Namath a pair of white shoes, so Namath wore white shoes without tape going forward. Joe Namath's shoe color choice changed football fashion forever and, by 1999, all but one NFL team wore white shoes. Black shoes made a comeback, and football shoes are now worn in a variety of team colors as well.

The final example of misattribution revolves around the award decals worn on players' helmets. No team is better known for plastering award decals on their helmets than Ohio State with their buckeye leaves. While Ohio State was not the first to bestow these awards, the correct answer remains up in the air. All indications are that the awards originated with Gene Stauber; the question is whether he first used them while assisting Pete Elliott at Nebraska or California. Elliott suggested in a 2007 interview that Stauber first employed them at Nebraska, but there is no other evidence to support that claim. Stauber was Nebraska's freshmen coach in 1956, the only year he and Elliott coached together in Lincoln, so it is unlikely that he created a varsity award for those making an interception.

Pete Elliott took the California job after the 1956 season, and Stauber tagged along. Still, it is not until the 1958 season that newspaper articles mention Stauber awarding gold stars to players who made interceptions. Stauber had served in Europe during WWII, working in a unit that wrote battle citations, and he wrote similar passages to accompany the football gold stars. One of his defensive backs in 1958 was Joe Kapp, who played quarterback on offense and won an NFL championship in 1969 doing the same. Kapp's citation for an interception during their Rose Bowl season read:

> For conspicuous excellence on pass defense Oct. 18, 1958, versus USC. Your alert interception of a crucial point-after-touchdown pass denied our opponents the opportunity to tie us and subsequently assured our victory. Our congratulations and best wishes for many more interceptions. Good Hunting![45]

The gold stars placed on Cal's blue helmets lack the contrast to appear in many period photographs but are apparent in some images from the 1959 season.

The ball carrier, Cal's Wayne Crow, with three stars on his helmet during Cal's 1959 game with USC. (1960 Blue and Gold, University of California yearbook)

Stars appeared on the helmets of the College of Wooster in 1959 and at Rutgers in 1960 before Utah began awarding white football decals for interceptions in 1962. The practice became more widespread, variously applying to offensive and defensive players. Ohio State did not apply buckeye leaves to their helmets until 1968, several years after Bo Schembechler used award decals with his Miami of Ohio team.

The final aspect of player equipment that warrants coverage is the extent to which team gear has become a marketing platform for sporting goods manufacturers. The sporting goods industry has been a pioneer in the product placement form of marketing. Professional athletes have long received free equipment or money to use one manufacturer's equipment over another, and star athletes received payment for the sale of baseball gloves, four irons, and footballs purportedly modeled after the equipment they used. Rockne, Heisman, Zuppke, and any number of other top coaches endorsed sporting goods brands as well.

Paying amateur athletes under the table to wear a particular brand during competition is a different story that began in Germany. Adidas and Puma, German athletic brands founded by the feuding Dassler brothers, fought bitterly over the track shoe market among amateur, international, and Olympic competitors. What started with providing free equipment and cash to a German sprinter in 1960 transitioned into the Battle of the Brands with widespread payments to athletes wearing branded shoes at the 1968 Summer Olympics. That, in turn, led to an explosive *Sports Illustrated* cover story in 1969.

Those inside the shoe industry did not need a *Sports Illustrated* article to know that college athletics provided a similar opportunity for product placement. Instead of paying individual players to wear their shoes, however, they paid the head coach. News of these deals was brought to the public's awareness in 1978 by a *Washington Post* article about seventeen college basketball coaches who received payments from Nike. The payments were not NCAA violations but marked the beginning of the now-standard process of apparel companies paying coaches, schools, and leagues to be the exclusive provider of uniforms and team apparel. Those deals now pay universities millions or tens of millions of dollars per year to supply those schools with uniforms and equipment, and to sell their associated team gear to the public.

All such deals hang on the assumption that the gear worn by the athletes, coaches, and others display the brand logos of the sponsoring companies. To avoid having the uniforms and other game equipment degenerate into moving billboards, the NCAA set standards for the location, type, and size of logos. They eliminated commercial logos from football fields in 1977 before loosening those standards for neutral-site and bowl game sponsors, and for entities that own stadium or field naming rights.

Regulations on the number and size of logos on player gear emerged after manufacturers plastered too many logos on their shoes. Some had logos on either side, the heal, and the elongated tongue that flipped over to cover the shoestrings. (Such was the style of the time.) The proliferation of logos led the NCAA to institute a limit of one logo per shoe and to limit the logo's size to 1.5-inch square. Since logos appeared on other parts of the uniforms, the NCAA revised the rule in 1999, so the manufacturers could place a single logo no larger than 2 1/4 inches on each item.

Pac-12 officials in Under Armour gear before Washington's 2019 Spring Game. (Joseph Weiser, Icon Sportswire)

A subplot in the product placement battle in college football involved Under Armour signing deals with conferences to supply the officials with game uniforms. Naturally, the Under Armour logo appears on the front and back of each shirt, and the officials' hats. The logo on referees' shirts appears on television each of the approximately twenty-two times per game the referee signals a penalty.

Another sidelight in the player-as-billboard phenomenon is the explosion in the number of jerseys and uniforms worn by teams. Teams that once had one uniform expanded their wardrobe to include road versions back in the 1950s, and that was as far as it went. Minor league baseball clubs occasionally sponsored "Old Timers" nights during which players wore throwback uniforms. The Triple-I League of Indiana, Illinois, and Iowa sponsored such an event in July 1952 with the players across the league wearing 1890s era uniforms. The Triple-I togs were followed in 1956 by the 1890s era uniforms worn by the Albuquerque Dukes and Amarillo Gold Sox in celebration of Albuquerque's 250th anniversary. Old-style uniforms returned to the attic until 1990 when the Chicago White Sox suited up in baggy style to celebrate the opening of their new stadium, and before you knew it, everyone was doing it. The NHL's Original Six wore throwback uniforms in 1991 to celebrate the league's 75th anniversary, and the NFL went that route in 1994 for its 75th anniversary.

Of course, no one does third jerseys or fourth jerseys or fifth jerseys better (or more) than Oregon. Sponsored by Nike since 1996, Oregon's game-to-game variations in uniform colors, helmet decorations, and other elements have little to do with functionality and everything to do with fashion, which generally means people either love them or hate them.

THREE PRIMARY FACTORS drove changes in player equipment during the modern era. First and foremost have been new forms of padding and equipment that better protect players against injury and enhance their comfort. Plastic helmets and face masks achieved universal adoption during this period and helped deliver a dramatic reduction in the number of acute head injuries. The focus of helmet design has since shifted to reducing concussions and the severity of subconcussive impacts. The other broad functional trend has been the use of lighter pads and materials that help dissipate heat to reduce heat-related complications among players.

Beyond the functional value of uniform and equipment changes, several have been geared toward player recognition. Adding player names on the backs of jerseys and recognizing player achievements with award decals emerged during the modern era. However, the football world remains divided between those who employ these recognition devices and those who do not.

The third factor in driving changes in player equipment during the modern era was the shift toward viewing team uniforms as fashion statements and merchandising opportunities. Starting with the product placement efforts of shoe companies in the early 1960s, college and professional athletes morphed into walking or running billboards for equipment and apparel brands. The NFL allows teams to modify their uniform once every five years. In contrast, while traditional uniforms hold an honored place in college football, the NCAA does not require consistency in uniforms. That has opened the door to the consistently inconsistent approach to uniforms pioneered by Oregon and partially adopted by other schools. As with the devices that recognize individual players, teams take different approaches to the uniform consistency issue, which contributes to another difference between college and professional football.

17

COACHES AND OFFICIALS (1960-2018)

With millions or tens of millions of dollars as risk based on a team's performance, today's football staffs leave no stone unturned, focusing on increasingly minute elements of the game. College and professional teams require more staff members to scout and solicit talent, coach those brought on board, and continuously evaluate team members via practice and game film. Players have become investments optimized through strength and conditioning programs, nutrition, and sports psychology, and, in the case of college players, their academic eligibility. Each of these elements came into play or expanded during the modern era, as did the facilities and staff needed to provide these services.

Similarly, the stakes have increased for the game's officials. At the highest level of the game, we ensure their accuracy through robust training and evaluation systems, increased numbers of officials on the field, in-game video review processes, and, most recently, by shifting from part-time to full-time officials. Each strategy attempts to minimize missed or incorrect calls that might influence the outcome of games.

COACHES AND COACHING

Two-platoon football allowed for player specialization such that players who excelled on one side of the ball, but not the other, could make an impact on the field. It helped players whose bodies and skills were best suited to one offensive or defensive position, particularly with quarterbacks. (How many pro-style quarterbacks in the NFL today could play defensive back effectively like their predecessors, particularly those over 40 years of age?) Along with player specialization has come the specialization and expansion of coaching staffs, including on-field coaches, strength and conditioning staff, quality control and analytical staff, nutritionists, and others. Each group plays a role in the large enterprises that compete in major college and professional football today.

The growth of two-platoon football contributed to the specialization and growth of coaching staffs. Conceiving of and teaching increasingly specialized and complex schemes to players required more coaches, as did the level of adjustments made for each week's opponents. The typical college staff had four or five coaches in the 1920s, including a head coach, backfield coach, line coach, end coach, and a freshmen coach. One assistant led the offense or defense, while the head coach oversaw the other unit. Even those staffs were not dedicated, however, since most assistants coached other sports or were part-time employees.

Staffs continued growing, and head coaches took on more non-football tasks in the 1960s, leading to the creation of the now-common Offensive and Defensive Coordinator roles. The trend toward larger staffs continued unabated until the NCAA limited teams to eight full-time coaches in 1976. (Numerous schools had to cut their staffs when the rule was enacted.) A ninth coach was allowed in 1983 and a tenth in 2018.

The growth of coaching staffs also impacted the role of coaches during games, particularly as substitution rules became more liberal. The easing of the college substitution rules in the early 1960s gave coaches the ability to illegally call plays by shuttling players in and out of the game. After coaching from the sideline became legal in 1967, Ohio State and others shifted to baseball-like, arm signals to send plays to their quarterbacks or defensive captains.

Similarly, the rules evolved on coaches' ability to confer with players during timeouts and between quarters. The 1967 rule change allowed one player to confer with the head coach during a timeout. The following year, the rule allowed one player to talk with either the head coach or an assistant. Selected state high school associations experimented with allowing all eleven players to confer with their coaches during the 1970s, and a nationwide rule went into effect at the high school level in 1982. The NCAA made a similar change in the early 1980s, though the NCAA's records are unclear as to which year the change occurred.

Dan Marino consults with head coach Jackie Sherrill and quarterbacks coach Joe Pendry in 1978. (University of Pittsburgh Historic Photographs, Archives & Special Collections, University of Pittsburgh Library System)

The transition to coaches calling plays came a bit later in the professional leagues. Pro quarterbacks were more knowledgeable, experienced, and had spent their college and pro careers calling plays, so they remained the primary play callers until the 1970s when the baseball-signal approach caught on in the NFL. Improvements in technology, and the NFL's reducing the time between plays from 45 to 40 seconds resulted in the NFL approving electronic headsets for quarterbacks in 1994. Defensive captains gained use of the helmet headsets in 2008.

The most recent means of signaling plays emerged among teams running no-huddle offenses. Given the need to quickly communicate formations and plays to ensure hurry-up offenses hurry, coaches began calling plays via signs with seemingly random images. Pioneered by Glen Elarbee, then a graduate assistant with Oklahoma State, the signs were used in the 2008 Holiday Bowl game against Oregon. Oregon's coach, Chip Kelly, adopted the approach and popularized it the following year

Oklahoma State using signs to signal plays during the 2008 season. (L. Scott Mann, Icon Sportswire)

While the use of signs along the sidelines is a decidedly analog approach to coaching, the coaching profession has long had a subset of coaches ready to apply the latest technologies to enhance their sideline operations. Northwestern's Glenn Thistlewaite used sideline telephones to communicate with assistant coaches in the press box in the 1920s, and Chuck Mather, the head coach at Ohio's Massillon High School, was the first to use closed-circuit television along the sideline to obtain a birds-eye view of the action. Mather must have found value in the closed-circuit process because he set up a similar system when he left Massillon to become the head coach at Kansas in 1954. The use of electronic systems took off in the early 1960s. Hayden Fry, then coaching SMU, used the Electrowriter, a fax-like machine that allowed coaches in the press box to draw and send images of opponents' formations to the sideline. However, concerns about the cost of the ever-changing electronic equipment and fear of creeping computerization led the Big Ten to ban closed-circuit televisions and similar equipment from the sideline in 1965. The NCAA did the same in 1967. The NFL has been more forgiving by allowing sideline use of Polaroid and similar printed images, before moving to tablets and other devices.

Although coaches have more responsibility today than they had in the past, the dramatic increase in their compensation levels is not a function of changes in their role. Instead, television and other monies have increased the resources at the college and pro levels, and the willingness of organizations to up the salary ante to avoid failure.

Although a few superstar coaches made significant money at the beginning of the modern era, most head coaches earned salaries comparable to a corporate middle manager. Coaches supplemented their earnings from television shows, endorsements, and sweetheart automobile and real estate deals, but their overall financial packages did not approach those of today.

Hot, young coaches today sign contracts worth more than $5 million per year. By contrast, Ara Parseghian took Northwestern from a winless program to the #2 ranking before Notre Dame hired him as its head coach in December 1963. The hottest young coach at the time, Parseghian took the Notre Dame job for $20,000 per year ($165,000 in 2019 dollars). Despite Parseghian having one year left on his Northwestern contract when he moved to Notre Dame, Northwestern did not enforce the remaining year of the contract, a practice that changed in the 1970s.

The sequence of events that sent football down the contract buyout path started when Jim Sweeney resigned as Washington State's head coach following the 1975 season. Although Sweeney had success before and after Washington State, he had little in Pullman. Ray Nagel, the Cougars Athletic Director, then replaced Sweeney with Jackie Sherrill, an up-and-coming assistant coach from Pitt. Sherrill went 3-8 with the Cougars in 1976 before returning to Pitt for the head job.

By then, Ray Nagel had resigned as the AD, and Sam Jankovich took over. Jankovich quickly inked Warren Powers, a Nebraska assistant, to a multi-year contract, after which Powers led the Cougars to a 6-5 campaign in 1977, including a big win over the Cornhuskers. Following the 1977 season, Powers resigned to take over the Missouri program. Now looking at having a fourth head football coach in as many years, Jankovich enforced Power's contract, demanding Powers pay Washington State $55,000 plus interest. It was a sizable penalty for 1977 because Powers only made $32,000 per year as WSU's coach ($135,000 in 2019 dollars) and received only $3,000 more per year to move to Missouri. Over the next several years, Powers paid almost all the penalty out of his own pocket, setting the stage for the enforcement of buyout clauses when future coaches skipped town.

Football coach salaries have since skyrocketed. The 2018 football season opened with twenty-four football coaches making annual salaries of more than $4 million, forty-four making $3 million or more, sixty making $2 million or more, and eighty-two making $1 million or more per year. Salaries for coaches in non-revenue sports have seen dramatic climbs as well.

. . .

PRACTICE AND PRACTICE EQUIPMENT

Many football practice activities employed today were in use in 1960, while some activities once considered sacred have largely disappeared. Tackling dummies and blocking sleds remain in common use at football practices nationwide, but the quintessential practice equipment used by lineman today are chutes. Chutes are simple frames that teach linemen to stay low when coming out of their stances. Those that get too high ding their heads against the chutes, suffering an injury that is more emotional than physical. The predecessor of the chute was the charging fence, which was in use by at least 1912.

The charging fence, akin to a limbo bar, was a training innovation for its day. (Popular Mechanics, December 1912)

It is not entirely clear which coach or school developed chutes. One source says they originated with Bear Bryant's staff at Texas A&M (1954 to 1957) and were called "cattle gaps" or at Alabama after Bryant moved there in 1958. We know chutes were used by Milt Bruhn, Wisconsin's coach in 1956, though he indicated he borrowed the idea from Bud Wilkinson, Bruhn's college teammate. Earlier still is a 1953 image showing a Kansas player using a chute or "pipe trellis" as it was called at the time. Chutes gained popularity in the mid-1960s and saw widespread use, so teams are now more likely to have chutes on the practice field than the old seven-man sled.

Wisconsin head coach Milt Bruhn demonstrates the team's new chutes prior to the 1956 season. (Olson, Clarence E., Capital Times, *August 21, 1956.)*

The most important change in football practice during the modern era has been the reduction in the level and intensity of contact. From the beginning of football, team captains and coaches understood the obvious: the likelihood of injuries increases with the amount of full contact. To limit injuries, coaches developed tackling dummies, blocking sleds, and other equipment to reduce the frequency of players hitting one another. Coaches also adopted "tag" (now called "thud") techniques to simulate game conditions while keeping blockers and tacklers on their feet. At least as far back as the 1910s, coaches limited contact in practice following hard-fought games, a spurt of injuries, and on the day or two leading up to games, but few went as far as Bob Folwell, who employed limited in-season contact as his standard approach at Lafayette, Washington & Jefferson, and Penn. Had Folwell not died in 1928 at age 42, his status as a top coach might have led others to adopt his thinking.

The seeds of change in rethinking the level of contact in practice came from several formal studies that examined football injuries and training practices. Blyth and Mueller's study of North Carolina high schools between 1969 and 1972 examined injury rates based on school size, player age, equipment, coaches' profiles, and practice activities. They found that just over half of football injuries occurred in practice; scrimmaging and live tackling drills accounted for the highest percentage of those injuries. Selected schools agreed to limit scrimmaging and other contact drills during the third and fourth years of the study. Those schools saw their injury rates drop by fourteen percent. The reduced-contact schools also improved their records during years three and four, countering the argument that teams needed to hit regularly in practice to win. Despite the findings, the study results had limited short-term impact in the football world.

Among the first to reduce the level of hitting in practice were NFL coaches whose players were long past learning the game's fundamentals. George Seifert, the San Francisco 49ers head coach from 1989 to 1996, limited both preseason and regular season contact. Seifert viewed limited contact in practice as a means of keeping players healthy and fresh throughout the long NFL season. His two Super Bowl wins while head coach of the 49ers helped convince other NFL coaches of the wisdom of his approach.

The NCAA's approach was to reduce the number of spring practices from twenty to fifteen in 1990, only ten of which could include contact. Similarly, the NCAA limited two-a-days to an every other day basis in 2003.

Before 2005, the driver of limiting contact in practice was the general desire to limit injuries, but that changed with the first published evidence of CTE in former football players. The conversation shifted again in 2009 with the linking of CTE to repetitive, subconcussive hits, not just concussions. Coaches at all levels looked for ways to reduce hitting in practice, largely by reducing the number of practices in which players hit one another. That line of thinking was taken to its logical conclusion in 2010 when Dartmouth coach, Buddy Teevens, eliminated tackling in practice, a stance later adopted by the Ivy League as a whole during the regular season.

Teevens was not alone. The NFL and NFLPA agreed in 2011 to limit contact during the preseason and to hold only fourteen padded practices during the regular season. A 2014 NCAA recommendation called for contact no more than two practices per week during the season, four times per week during preseason, and in no more than eight of fifteen spring practices. Various state high school athletic associations have adopted more stringent standards than the NCAA's, as has the CFL, which, in 2017, eliminated all practice contact during the regular season.

In addition to limiting the amount of contact that occurs during football practice at many levels, teams have also moved toward rugby-style tackling techniques and established controlled contact procedures in full-speed drills to eliminate players "lighting up" teammates in practice.

CONDITIONING AND DIET

Knowledge of athletic conditioning and nutrition developed over the first ninety years of football, but much of that knowledge was pre-scientific, based primarily on the scattered observations of practitioners. Some practitioners were more observant or insightful than others, but little of the rationale for coaching and training practices came from the controlled study of athletes, particularly elite athletes. That changed in the modern era as sports medicine and sports science advanced our understanding of the human body. These advances have generally made sports safer, though some elements, such as the use of anabolic steroids, had the opposite effect.

While studies conducted as far back as the 1930s showed that high school football players were often injured during the first two weeks of football practice, that knowledge did not result in a push for earlier, more consistent training. Instead, it led to rules banning pads for the first several days of camp, in an attempt to acclimate athletes to the physical demands of the game. The real problem, of course, was that many athletes at all competitive levels arrived at the first practice of the season unprepared for the rigors of football and several days of training were not sufficient to change that.

This attitude began to change in the latter half of the 1950s when American track and field coaches saw that Russian and other European athletes trained year-round and followed more difficult regimens than was typical here. The situation led to increased calls for American Olympic athletes to participate in year-round conditioning programs. As the American medical and scientific communities became more involved in sports, they found that injuries were more common among athletes put through crash conditioning courses rather than gradual conditioning processes.

By the mid-1960s, the American College of Sports Medicine, the American Medical Association, and others recommended year-round training programs for athletes. The adoption of such programs in the football world was spotty. Some coaches emphasized offseason conditioning; others paid little attention. Kentucky deemed its offseason program sufficiently important that they made the program mandatory, and their football coaches directly oversaw the process. Both steps violated NCAA rules, resulting in Kentucky receiving a one-year probation penalty in 1964. Even those schools that embraced offseason conditioning programs did not push their athletes to the level that is typical today. For example, a University of Arizona football conditioning program of that era consisted of 30-minute workouts five days per week that included six 40-yard dashes, a half-mile run, and sets of pushups and sit-ups. That was it.

Even NFL teams did not embrace consistent offseason workouts. The Green Bay Packers, who dominated the NFL in the 1960s, did not have an offseason workout routine until Vince Lombardi resigned. His former assistant and the new head coach, Phil Bengston, instituted an offseason conditioning program for the 1969 season, but did not introduce the program to the team until April. Similarly, few teams embraced weight training during much of the 1960s.

Among the more important advances in football's offseason conditioning regimens has been the growth of weight training. Weight training had little support in the football community due to the widely-held belief that lifters became muscle-bound. Many others believed athletes had a natural level of strength that could not be improved, which made lifting a futile attempt to remedy a natural deficiency.

Interest in weight training as a means to improve football performance was sparked when Alvin Roy, the owner of a Baton Rouge gym, convinced Istrouma High School to allow him to train their football team following their disappointing 1954 season. Istrouma won the state football championship after their first year of weight training. The fact that Billy Cannon, the future Heisman Trophy winner, played for Istrouma did little to reduce the perceived contribution of weight training to the team's success.

Alvin Roy followed Billy Cannon to LSU. Just as Istrouma High had tremendous success in their first season after weight training, the Tigers won the 1958 national title following their first year of lifting as well. In 1963, Sid Gillman and the San Diego Chargers hired Alvin Roy as the first strength and conditioning coach in professional football, a move that was fodder for jokes among newspaper columnists of the day. The Chargers used a combination of isometric and free weight training, along with the steroid, Dianabol, and, like Istrouma and LSU, they won a championship in their first year of weight training.

Boyd Epley spotting Husker defensive lineman Mike Fultz during a 1975 training session. (Reprinted with permission from The Omaha News-Herald)

Various college teams used isometrics and free weight training in the 1960s, but Nebraska became the first college team to hire a full-time strength coach when they added Boyd Epley in 1969. Epley started the program by ordering a set of free weights for their 416 square foot facility. Nebraska's success on the field sold college programs on the benefits of weight training, and the lives of football players have never been the same.

Year-round conditioning and weight training, improved nutrition, and the specialization of players have contributed to substantial increases in the size of today's college and professional football players. During the 1920s and 1930s, players were relatively similar in height and weight across positions, and few NFL players exceeded 260 pounds. In 1960, no NFL player weighed 300 pounds. Now, of course, every NFL roster and most

FBS rosters have numerous players, particularly offensive linemen, exceeding that mark.

The modern era also saw a dramatic turnaround in water discipline or limiting players' access to water during practice and games. Water discipline was standard practice in the early 1960s and became more problematic with the increased padding worn by players. The padding of the era was not designed to dissipate heat or wick sweat, leading to innumerable cases of heat prostration in football practices and games. Such issues led a research team at the Florida College of Medicine to investigate preventive measures.

Florida's coach, Ray Graves, was an open-minded man who had himself suffered through water-deprived practices as a player at Tennessee, but Graves was cautious as well. He allowed the researchers to work only with the freshman team. (Even then, he forbade them from including a star quarterback recruit in the research.) The research team spent the 1965 season monitoring ten team members and collecting their sweat to determine its makeup. They discovered that players lost up to fifteen pounds of sweat per game, leading them to formulate drinks to replenish the minerals lost in all that sweat. Early formulations tasted terrible but improved over time.

The new product, called Gatorade, was made available to the entire Florida team during the 1966 season when the team achieved a 9-2 record, including several comeback wins. The drink received credit for helping the Gators maintain a higher level of play than their opponents during the fourth quarter of games. It also made Steve Spurrier the first Gatorade-drinking Heisman Trophy winner following the season.

Gatorade quickly became the dominant brand in the product category it created and retains that position today. First commercialized by Stokely Van Camp in 1969, it retailed as a powder and in liquid form in cans similar to those in which Van Camp sold its pork and beans. Glass bottles soon followed, and the ubiquitous plastic bottles came along in 1989. Gatorade's commercial success and the awareness it brought to proper hydration were primary contributors to water discipline disappearing from football fields during the modern era.

Florida assistant coach Ed Kensler talks with his quarterback, Steve Spurrier, who drinks Gatorade from the milk carton-style containers used during the 1966 season. (University Archives, Special and Area Studies Collections, George A. Smathers Libraries, University of Florida, Gainesville, Florida.)

Gatorade was a smart product supported by brilliant marketing that also benefited from luck. The product became an NFL sponsor in 1968 and the official drink of the NFL in 1983, so Gatorade's orange jugs and green cups popped up on every NFL (and most college) sidelines. Television broadcasts of games regularly showed players using the product, lending further credibility to the brand.

Besides being the first sports drink, Gatorade's luck and its secondary relevance to this book came in 1986 during the run-up to the New York Giants winning Super Bowl XXI. Some claim the Chicago Bears introduced the Gatorade Dump (now the Gatorade Shower) to Mike Ditka in 1985, a claim for which NFL Films' Steve Sabol found no evidence. More accurately, the first Gatorade Dump fell on Bill Parcells' head near the end of the October 27, 1985 victory over the New Orleans Saints. Parcells, whose job was in jeopardy at the time, spent the week leading up to the Giants-Saints game challenging the manhood of his nose tackle, Jim Burt. As the clock wound down on the Giants' victory, Burt poured a jug of Gatorade on Parcells in celebration of the impending victory, and to acknowledge his having met Parcells' challenge. Since then, teams have poured positive on their coaches in celebration of impending victories.

As teams took steps to increase the athletic performance of their players, they also put greater focus on the performance levels of the raw material they recruited and drafted. The NFL draft began in 1936 as a means of spreading football talent across the league, but the draft only performed its function when teams drafted wisely. During the early draft years, many teams did little scouting of college prospects, basing their picks on word of mouth or, in some cases, lists of players in *Street & Smith's* or similar publications. Teams had so little information on prospects that the Washington Redskins used their first-round pick in the 1946 draft to select UCLA running back Cal Rossi, despite Rossi being a junior with another year of college eligibility. The Redskins forfeited that pick and selected Rossi in the first round of the 1947 draft as well, only to watch Rossi enlist in the Navy and never play a down of professional football.

Teams slowly built scouting staffs to identify and evaluate college talent, with some teams being more systematic than others. Among the highly organized was the Cleveland Browns, led by Paul Brown and assisted by Weeb Ewbank. Ewbank left the Browns to take over the Baltimore Colts in 1954, which resulted in the Colts joining the Browns as the pioneers in using the 40-yard dash as the primary measure of speed when scouting college players.

Paul Brown chose the 40-yard dash as his preferred measure of football speed because it matched the distance of a typical punt. Although one can argue whether forty yards is the ideal measure, it provided a consistent metric regardless of a player's region, position, or experience. Over time, the forty became one of many measures teams used as the talent acquisition process became more organized in college and professional football.

Paul Brown's 1952 Bowman football card while the coach of the Cleveland Browns. Presumably, he is holding a stopwatch. (Wikipedia Commons)

To save money on scouting, the Lions, Eagles, Steelers Talent Organization (LESTO) formed in 1964 so the "combined" teams could share resources and information. Several other scouting services followed, and the combinations have remained a central part of the NFL universe. Today, combination or combine scouts focus on players with one year of college eligibility remaining, winnowing the list of candidates to those with NFL potential. Team scouts evaluate players during their final year of college competition. Further efficiencies in scouting came in 1982 when one scouting service invited prospects to a National Invitation Camp for testing and evaluation by member teams. Rival scouting services developed similar camps before they consolidated in 1985, giving birth to The Combine.

The subculture of draftniks and combine junkies emerged after the creation of sports-oriented television networks. ESPN hit the air or, more accurately, the cables in 1979, with its NFL draft show premiering the next year. The creation of the NFL Network in 2003 brought coverage of the combine to the nation's screens as well.

A similar phenomenon, the rise of recruitniks, occurred in the college football world with the development of recruiting sites and discussion boards in the early 2000s. These sites allowed fans of schools to learn which high school players received scholarship offers from which schools, the ratings of those recruits, and the ability to view highlight films of those athletes.

A more problematic aspect of enhancing athletic performance came into play in the 1960s in the form of various drugs. Although athletes have used performance-enhancing drugs since the Ancient Greeks, their modern incarnation arose in Europe in the 1950s with the use of amphetamines among cyclists and steroids by weightlifters. Steroids moved from weightlifting to football with the hiring of Alvin Roy by the San Diego Chargers in 1963. Various painkillers came into regular use as well. Testimony by former players suggested the San Diego Chargers received more than 10,000 doses of prescription drugs of different types between 1966 and 1969. Drugs were commonly administered by other NFL teams to enhance player performance or to mask injuries and allow players to perform. The use of street and recreational drugs are also problematic due to the legal and league image issues they raise. The NFL and the NFL Players Association (NFLPA) agreed through collective bargaining to allow drug testing during the preseason and for reasonable cause beginning in 1983.

The NCAA's first foray into drug legislation was to ban the administration of non-therapeutic or non-healing drugs. The NCAA instituted a drug-testing program in 1986 for anabolic steroids, stimulants, and diuretics, as well as street drugs. The NCAA's plan applied at all levels and sports, and tested selected competitors before national championship events and football bowl games. Those testing positive were not allowed to compete in the national competition.

OFFICIALS

Football officials entered the modern era as the unquestioned authorities and controllers of the game during play. Referees made the final decision on all calls and rules interpretations. However, the changing passing game challenged the four and five-person officiating crews of the early 1960s. With the ball thrown more often and farther downfield, the officiating crews adjusted to keep pace with the game.

Officiating crews began taking on their modern form in 1894 when the roles of the referee, umpire, and linesman were distinguished. The introduction of the forward pass led to the addition of the field judge to monitor the downfield passing game in 1908. The continued expansion of the passing game after WWII brought the addition of the NFL's back judge in 1947. Some college conferences also experimented with the back judge, and the NCAA made them optional in 1955. (College officiating crews varied in size then and now based on the budgets available at each competitive level.)

The NFL added the line judge in 1965 to monitor line play, judge forward passes versus laterals, and confirm whether forward passes occurred from behind the line of scrimmage. The addition of the line judge freed the referee to concentrate on the all-valuable quarterback and assess late hits and the like. College football added line judges in 1972.

Concerns about tight ends and other receivers being held and interfered with fifteen to twenty yards downfield led to the NFL's 1978 addition of the side judge, positioned with the field and back judges in the defensive backfield. The NCAA followed suit in 1983 and has since one-upped the NFL by adding an eighth official, the center judge, positioned behind and to the left of the offensive formation to assist the referee in monitoring line play.

Alignment of Officials

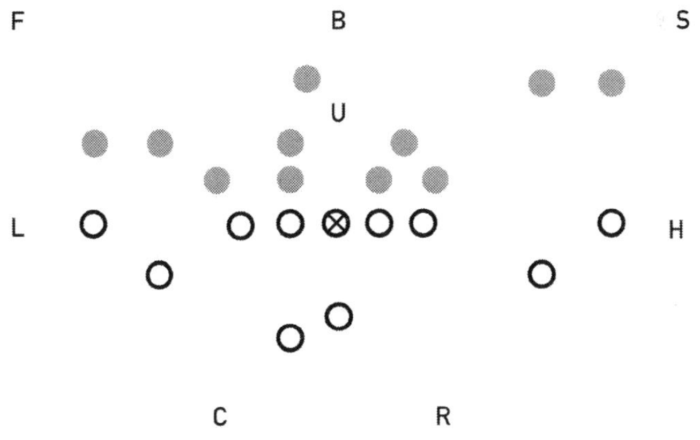

The alignment of each official in an eight-person crew: center judge (C), referee (R), line judge (L), head linesman (H), umpire (U), field judge (F), back judge (B), and side judge (S).

Other notable changes in officiating crews included the NFL's repositioning of the umpire. Until 2010, the NFL umpire stood behind the linebackers, where they sometimes interfered with play, so the umpire relocated to the offensive backfield. Finally, with the advent of female officials in the NFL, the league swapped the Head Linesman label for the gender-neutral Down Judge.

To increase the consistency of the officiating, college football adapted the composition of crews as well. College football entered the modern era with some conferences or regional organizations scheduling crews that worked together every week. Others used unique combinations each game. The crew makeup also was jumbled for some nonconference games. Less competitive visiting teams had to accept contracts calling for officials assigned by the home team's conference. Games between evenly-matched nonconference opponents, however, used split officiating crews or crews from a third conference. (The fact that teams insisted on split officiating crews showed there were concerns about impartiality or, at least, consistency of officiating from conference to conference.) Split officiating crews were justified by their reduced travel costs (which were borne by the home team) since half the officials lived in-region. The downside of split crews was their lack of familiarity with one another, inconsistency in officiating mechanics from region to region, and, in some cases, a lack of trust among the officials across conferences.

In the end, all it took to eliminate split crews was a year with multiple disputed calls, and that year was 1990. The year began with a controversial holding call by a Pac-10 official against Michigan on an otherwise successful fourth-quarter fake punt in the Rose Bowl. Later that year, Colorado's infamous fifth down play versus Missouri helped Colorado earn a national championship in one poll. Split officiating crews disappeared from the college football world in 1991.

Officiating crews have handled sixty-minute games since 1912, but the elapsed time to complete games continued to lengthen. From the opening kickoff to the final gun, major college football games averaged two hours and twenty minutes in 1969. (Those games were even longer than in 1968 because it was the first year the clock stopped after each first down.) By 2017, the average game length increased by an hour. Many factors contribute to their increased length. Foremost was the time devoted to commercial breaks. College football's television contract for 1969 allowed eighteen minutes of commercial time per game, whereas a typical game today includes more than fifty minutes of commercials. As important, only one college football game per week was televised in 1969, so the eighteen minutes of commercials applied to relatively few games. Today, the majority of games are televised or streamed, meaning that allotted television commercials increase the length of a far higher proportion of games each week.

It may be surprising to some that the increased prevalence of the passing game has had minimal impact on game length, despite the game clock stopping on incomplete passes. While the average number of passes thrown per team per game rose from 25.5 to 31.1 between 1969 and 2017, the number of completions increased at a faster rate (from 12.0 to 18.4) with the result that teams average only one more incompletion per game. Thus, only two more clock stoppages per game result from the increased use of the pass.

The NCAA took several steps to shorten games in 2007, including:

- Reducing the number of touchbacks by lowering the height of kicking tees from two inches to one inch
- Starting the clock when the ball is kicked rather than touched by the return man, and
- Starting the clock upon spotting the ball following a change of possession rather than at the offense's first snap.

The combination helped reduce the average game length by fourteen minutes, but the reduced game length also resulted in thirteen fewer plays and five fewer points scored per game. The loss of plays and points led to protests by coaches and fans, so they reversed the latter two rules the following year. The NCAA also followed the NFL's lead in 2008 by using a forty-second play clock that starts at the end of the previous play rather than a twenty-five-second clock that starts when the ball is spotted. Since then, no substantive rule changes have been targeted at reducing the length of games despite time being committed to overtime periods and video reviews.

A clock management change during the modern era was the 1982 elimination of the penalty against quarterbacks throwing the ball out of bounds to stop the clock. Better yet, a 1990 rule allowed quarterbacks to stop the clock by spiking the ball.

The popularization of referees' penalty signals in the late 1920s helped everyone in the stadium and listening by radio better understand game events. The same is now true of the microphones used by referees to announce the nature of penalties. First used in a Thanksgiving Day game between the St. Louis Cardinals and Buffalo Bills in 1975, the technology went into full-time use in 1976. With the cameras aimed at the officials and microphones capturing their voices, the change had the unexpected impact of making minor celebrities of some referees (or their biceps, in the case of Ed Hochuli). NFL referees' use of microphones quickly transferred over to college football with the noticeable difference being that the names of college players charged with penalties were not announced to the crowd until 2004.

Despite the march of technology, referees continue gesticulating the signals we all know and love.

A referee watching the video monitor during a play review at Ohio State in 2017. (Scott W. Grau, Icon Sportswire)

A more substantive intervention of technology in the game was the NFL's limited use of instant replay by off-the-field officials in 1986. Though limited in the scope of plays subject to review, instant replay enhanced the accuracy of calls beyond that which might have occurred by increasing the number of officials. The NFL eliminated instant replay for the 1992 season after a study showed that ten percent of overturned calls were incorrectly changed. After further review and system enhancements, the NFL gave instant replay a second look in 1999. That time the referee on the field made the final decision on the reviewed play.

The NCAA allowed the Big Ten to experiment with instant replay in 1991 but opted not to institute the technology due to concerns that instant replays would lengthen games. The fact that many college games were not broadcast by television crews using large numbers of cameras was also problematic. Instant replay made a return appearance in the Big Ten in 2004, saw duty in eight other conferences in 2005, and was adopted by the NCAA as a whole in 2006.

Like other actors in the game of football, the game officials have benefited economically due to the sport's popularity. At the beginning of the middle era, game officials were hired by each institution rather than through conference-wide systems. To avoid bidding wars for officials, the football rules committee recommended a sliding pay scale for officials: $100 per Class A game, $75 per Class B game, $50 per Class C game, and $25 per Class D game. While it is unclear which schools belonged to each class, we know the big Eastern games were Class A since those officials earned $100 per game, the equivalent of almost $2,800 today. Most officials did not make anywhere near that much since the Big Ten announced in 1917 that their officials would earn $25 per game or just short of $500 today.

Major college officials made $100 per game by the mid-1930s and were still in that range in 1955 when the Big Ten upped the ante to $100 to $125 per game ($950 to $1,175 today). In addition, they received medical and death benefits while traveling to and from games, though it is unclear whether vision benefits were part of the package. Although officials' pay increased during the modern era, substantial increases have been limited to NFL officials

TELEVISION and other revenues dramatically changed the compensation levels of football coaches at the college and professional levels while also providing the funding for larger coaching and support staffs. The latter enabled greater specialization on and off the field, which now takes advantage of tremendous advances in weight training, sports science, and nutrition that have reshaped football players, resulting in players who are bigger, faster, and stronger than earlier generations.

Officiating crews also grew in size during the modern era as the passing game spread players vertically and horizontally. Each new crew member eased the burden, but could not eliminate all errors in judgment. Instant replay can now overturn the judgment of officials on the field, but the officiating crew as a whole retains full authority to control the game.

18

OFF THE FIELD (1960-2018)

Football witnessed dramatic off-the-field changes during the modern era, and the most dramatic of those was the explosion of television and related services. College and professional football started the era with one or two games per week televised in a given market before reaching the point at which virtually every game was available through one technology or another. In addition to more games being televised, the technologies employed have dramatically improved the viewer experience to the point that it competes favorably with the in-stadium experience. Such is the case despite dramatic enhancements in the fan-friendliness of stadiums and the movement toward the crowd becoming an active participant in the games themselves.

These changes in football have not occurred in isolation from broader social trends. Football's position within American culture provided it the opportunity to both lead and reflect changes in racial attitudes. Football and sports, in general, were among the first elements of society to open its doors to African Americans, and the game has since become dominated by African American players at the major college and professional levels.

TELEVISION

Chapter 13 covered the financial impact of television on the game of football, particularly how the composition of leagues and conferences, game schedules, and the like changed in the pursuit of television money. The modern era also saw substantial changes in television technologies and other aspects of game coverage. Like the game itself, television coverage evolved through a series of failed attempts and successful innovations.

The television revolution began when the NCAA signed a national contract with ABC in 1960, which resulted in ABC hiring a little-known producer from NBC, Roone Arledge. Arledge proved to be the most important innovator in the history of sports broadcasting. Techniques introduced under his watch included slow-motion, sideline sound booms, crowd shots, and in-depth player profiles. Arledge also introduced fans to prime time sports with his revolutionary coverage of the 1968 Summer Olympics and *Monday Night Football.* By revolutionizing television coverage of football and other sports, Arledge changed how the game was consumed and perceived by millions of fans.

Among changes in television coverage driven by Arledge was the evolution of the announcers. The announcers of the first televised football games took their cues from radio. Whereas radio announcers described the events on the field to an audience that could not see the game, it became the television announcer's job to supplement the action seen on the small screens. Early television broadcasts of football followed radio broadcasting's pattern of using two professional broadcasters, one handling play-by-play and the other providing color commentary. By the mid-1950s, however, the football color commentator role was taken over by former players or coaches who could interpret the action on the field, a model that remains in place today.

After revising the play-by-play and color model, there were few changes in the announcing of games until *Monday Night Football* debuted in 1970. In addition to broadcasting games in prime time, *Monday Night Football* introduced the three-person announcing crew. More important, while fans had long developed connections with radio and television announcers, *Monday Night Footbal*l was the first to position the announcing team and its chemistry as central to the show's entertainment value. Color announcers traditionally complemented the play-by-play man, and the conflicts between Don Meredith and Howard Cosell often subordinated Keith Jackson's play-by-play work. Their interplay helped redefine the nature of sports announcing with the interactions of the announcers fueling interest in *Monday Night Football* and, later, in-studio and analyst shows.

Stepping back a few decades, the Dumont Network dominated NFL broadcasting in the first half of the 1950s, but when the DuMont Network folded in 1956, eleven of the twelve NFL teams contracted with CBS. The next year, CBS introduced the first pre-game show, a 15-minute segment hosted by Bud Palmer, a former Princeton and New York Knicks player. Palmer was replaced by Johnny Lujack, the former Notre Dame star, for the 1958 and 1959 seasons before Lujack gave way to Chris Schenkel. Any number of variations on the pre-game show has paraded before television audiences since then, but the most significant innovation in pre-game shows was ESPN's *College GameDay's* transition from a studio show to one shot on location. Launched as a one-hour studio show in 1987, *College GameDay* went on site for the first time when #2 Florida State traveled to #1 Notre Dame in November 1993. Being on-site for a highly-anticipated game with a live audience proved attractive to fans at the location and in the television audience. *GameDay* has since become an institution. Being selected to host or play in a game featured on *College GameDay* means the game or site matters. *College GameDay's* appearances at less-heralded campuses also bring attention to the fact that something special happens there.

Halftime shows on television are a different story. Like radio broadcasts, the halftime shows of early television included interviews, the scores of other games, and marching bands. Well into the 1970s, the marching bands performing in the stadium received substantial air time as if the networks were recreating the in-stadium experience. College marching bands provided the main halftime show at seven of the first nine Super Bowls, followed by fifteen years of *Up With People* or pop stars performing with college bands.

Still, the primary reason halftime shows did not feature video highlights of other games was that only one or two college games were broadcast each Saturday, so the networks did not have cameras at other games to capture highlights. Moreover, the technologies of the 1940s and 1950s did not allow the recording of television shows, including football games. There was simply too much data to transmit, store, and create highlight clips. By the time the number of televised games expanded in the second half of the 1980s, the state of technology had improved to make game highlights available, and the central studio show with extensive highlights blossomed.

Besides the advances needed to show highlights of other games, the desire to replay action during games drove innovation in the television community. George Retzlaff, a producer for CBC's *Hockey Night in Canada*, used a "wet film" process in 1955 to record and replay goals within thirty seconds, but his approach did not catch on. At the beginning of the 1960s, the technology to record games electronically emerged, without the tools to quickly access specific segments of footage, delaying the replays shown during a broadcast by several minutes. That technical problem was solved by CBS Sports Director Tony Verna, setting the stage for "instant" replay.

Verna first used his "instant replay" technology when broadcasting the 1963 Army-Navy game, a game postponed by one week due to the assassination of John F. Kennedy on November 22. Army-Navy was among the top games of the year. Second-ranked Navy, was led by Heisman Trophy-winning quarterback Roger Staubach, an excellent scrambler, and Verna saw instant replay as a means of highlighting Staubach's skills. Technical glitches during the broadcast prevented Verna from using instant replay to show any of Staubach's runs. Instead, the first and only use of instant replay that game was a one-yard, touchdown run by Army quarterback, Rollie Stichweh. Since it was the first use of instant replay on television, Chris Schenkel had to inform viewers that Army had not scored a second touchdown; CBS was simply replaying the touchdown play for its viewers.

Rollie Stichweh's fourth-quarter touchdown in the 1963 Army-Navy game was reprised by the first use of instant replay. (U.S. Army Signal Corps, United States Military Academy)

Instant replay revolutionized sports broadcasting by changing how games were viewed and analyzed. Great plays and close calls were seen not once, but twice or three times, giving viewers insight into the game that was not available to those in attendance. (In-stadium video scoreboards were nearly two decades in the future.)

The networks also advanced the quality of broadcasts generally, and the use of instant replay specifically, by increasing the number of cameras used per game. The first NFL game telecast in 1939 used two cameras. Most regular-season games used five cameras throughout the 1960s. When Roone Arledge introduced *Monday Night Football* in 1970, he sought to make the game more spectacular while personalizing the game and educating fans, particularly women. *Monday Night Football* used pre-recorded profiles of star players, now a common technique, and dedicated four cameras solely for color commentary. The increased number of cameras allowed for closeup shots of players on the sidelines and increased the likelihood of capturing critical game action, making it available for explanation. He dedicated another camera to superimposing graphics on the screen, which saw expanded use on *Monday Night Football*.

While Roone Arledge understood the value of showing the game from additional angles, Garrett Brown provided entirely new views of the game through two inventions, one a novelty and the other revolutionary. Brown invented the *SkyCam*, which provided its first overhead views during two NFL exhibition games in 1984. The NFL chose not to adopt the *SkyCam* that season due to reliability issues, but it saw use in the 1984 Army-Navy game and the 1985 Orange Bowl before being dropped from use in football due to its expense. The *SkyCam* appeared over football fields again in 2001 as a tool to make the XFL appear innovative and edgy. Its use with the XFL convinced the NFL of the camera's value, and it came into use at NFL games the following year.

While the *SkyCam* did not revolutionize television broadcasting, an earlier Brown invention, the *Steadicam*, had a more significant impact. A long-standing challenge for filmmakers and broadcasters was that shots taken from moving cameras produced bouncy images unless the cameras were positioned on trucks or dollies rolling on preconfigured tracks.

Since the tracks were not an option on or around football fields, telecasts used fixed cameras positioned high in the stands and or on trucks positioned behind the bench. To allow fluid camera movements without the resulting jerkiness, Brown mounted stabilizers on vests and camera operators attached their cameras to the stabilizers, which allowed them to move in and out of the action while producing steady shots. The *Steadicam* contributed to the 1976 movie *Bound for Glory*, which earned the Oscar for cinematography. Most people first saw the *Steadicam's* output watching Dustin Hoffman run through New York City in *Marathon Man* and Sylvester Stallone running up the steps of the Philadelphia Museum of Art in *Rocky*. Brown received an Engineering Oscar two years later for the *Steadicam*.

The Cowboy's Dez Bryant shows off to the Steadicam operator following a touchdown catch in 2016. (Andrew Dieb, Icon Sportswire)

The *Steadicam* had immediate application for football, enhancing the value of cameras along the sidelines and behind the end zones. The *Steadicam* allowed shots from eye level or lower, enabled the operator to move in or out of the action, or to precede or follow a player walking on the field. Largely due to the *Steadicam,* Brown received a Lifetime Achievement Award as part of the Engineering Emmys in 2015.

Another series of enhancements that changed the viewing experience was the improvement in on-screen graphics. On-screen graphics saw little use in early television for several reasons. First, early television screens were not sharp and were fuzzier near the edges of the screen, the best spot for informational graphics. Second, television graphics of the time had to be produced and the physical rolls hand-cranked before cameras, which made graphics production expensive and slow. The process was fine for the ending credits but not the down, distance, and score of a football game. Although improvements came in that process, on-screen graphics remained primitive until the late 1960s when computer-generated versions arrived.

Television and computer technology continued advancing, but the next innovation in graphics came from a change in business requirements, rather than technology. Into the mid-1990s, the networks had not yet used continuously-displayed graphics. As the 1994 World Cup approached, however, ABC and

ESPN needed a method to capture advertising revenue from a sport that did not have the frequent stoppages of play typical of football, baseball, and basketball. Their solution was to continuously display the game's score in a header graphic that included a sponsor's logo.

David Hill, who moved from Sky Sports in Britain to America's Fox Sports the same year, had long been frustrated by European networks' failure to display the match score during soccer games. Once in the U.S., he applied ABC's World Cup approach via the "FoxBox" on NFL broadcasts, a continuously-displayed graphical bug showing essential game information.

After the FoxBox, each network designed and revised its version of continuously-displayed graphics. Arguments over the best style, content, and location (top, bottom, or corner) of those graphics are ongoing, but the next most valuable football graphic to date has been the "1st and Ten" line drawn at the yard to gain. Introduced during a Sunday night Baltimore Colts-Cincinnati Bengals game in 1998, it is an elegantly simple tool that enhances the viewer experience. Like other successful technologies, it has been universally copied and now is a standard part of televised football games.

The announcers, camera operators, and technology required to televise a game cost money, and the primary method of funding broadcasts are commercials. Despite television contracts allowing far fewer commercials per game than today, the networks of the 1950s had difficulty squeezing in the allotted number of ads. The norm and rules allowed them to show ads that extended a natural break in the action (e.g., following an extra point), but not create a break in the action (e.g., following a punt). That changed in 1958 when the NFL first permitted referees to call a "television timeout" during the first and third quarters of games when a timeout had not occurred during the first ten minutes of play. (Imagine watching ten minutes of elapsed play in an NFL game today without seeing a commercial.) The television timeouts that interrupted the flow of the game seemed jarring at the time, causing sportswriter, Red Smith, to express his thoughts:

> By my own naïve standards, I profess to see a vast difference between permitting sponsorship of a sporting event and catering to the convenience of the sponsors. If breweries can stop the game then what comes next?
>
> Will they tell the Colts to draft a halfback from Colorado? Will they ask Paul Brown to hold the score down so the audience doesn't get restless? ....
>
> All kidding aside, I think someone ought to speak up for the principle that sponsors should take games as they come, and not manipulate them for their own convenience.[46]

We all know how that turned out. Today's viewer may not like the commercials that upset Red Smith, but grudgingly accept them as part of the price paid to watch games on television.

GAME ATMOSPHERE

While stadium crowds have long cheered and jeered players, coaches, and officials, the limits on acceptable crowd behavior were stricter in the past than today. The booing of game officials in 1946 led the Pacific Coast Conference, the forerunner of today's Pac-12, to empower referees to penalize teams whose supporters booed officials' calls or mockingly counted their strides as they stepped off penalties. Taking a similar stick approach, Wisconsin's Athletic Board permitted their administrators to forfeit games if the home crowd's behavior proved troublesome, while the SEC sportswriters took the carrot approach in 1958 by creating a sportsmanship award for the school whose football and basketball crowds were best-behaved.

Some stadiums and crowds had a presence that others lacked, but the idea that particular football stadiums and crowds were intimidating was simply not part of the thinking. That outlook changed in the modern era as crowds became rowdier, noisier, and began to see themselves as having the potential, the right, and the duty to influence the outcome of games through their boisterousness.

It is difficult to compare the noisiness of football crowds over time, but the first rule to limit crowd noise arrived in 1975. It seems that in the late 1930s or early 1940s, fans of Mississippi State applied the old reverse psychology and embraced the cowbell as a symbol of their fandom. Over the years, Mississippi State fans made greater use of their cowbells until Auburn complained their players could not hear their quarterback's signals during their visit to Starkville in 1974. The following spring, the SEC presidents voted to ban artificial noisemakers, and, despite some protests, it became all quiet on the Southern front.

Fans in other locations used their voices rather than cowbells to interrupt the visiting teams' signals, leading to a 1978 rule allowing referees to issue two warnings per play to the home team before charging a timeout if the noise did not subside. Home teams lacking a timeout were assessed a five-yard penalty. The rule was changed in 1981 to give teams only two warnings per game, and that version remained in place through the 2005 season. The NFL adopted a similar set of rules in 1989 but enforced them spottily. The need for noise level penalties largely disappeared as offenses adapted by using silent counts, leading to the penalties dropping from the books. Nevertheless, the SEC rule against artificial noisemakers remains in effect.

The second aspect of fan behavior emerging in the modern era was The Wave, known outside the U.S. and Canada as "The Mexican Wave" because most of the world gained exposure to it during the 1986 World Cup played in Mexico.

The wave did not originate in Mexico, but in Oakland-Alameda County Coliseum during a New York Yankees-Oakland Athletics playoff game in 1981. "Krazy" George Henderson, a professional cheerleader, had previously led crowds in wave-like activities, but the playoff game was the first time a full-blown wave occurred. Fans of Washington Husky football picked it up two weeks later, and the tide rolled on from there. The repertoire of Wavemakers has expanded and now includes versions that circle stadiums in slow motion, reverse themselves, or split apart before crashing into one another.

Among the more tribal changes in fan behavior during the modern era has been the trend of fans dutifully wearing team colors and gear to games. Wearing team colors, mainly clothing with team logos and slogans, is now the norm, but it was not always so. Back in the day, it was enough to wear a pin or ribbon with your school colors or a slogan. Men attended games in suits and wore fedoras. Women wore dresses and liked it. (They still do at many Southern schools.)

Queen Elizabeth II takes in the 1957 Maryland-North Carolina game amidst a crowd of men in jackets and ties, and women in dresses and hats. The woman at the bottom right unabashedly wore a mink stole to the game. (Warren K. Leffler, Library of Congress)

Fans did not wear team gear in the old days in part because more formal dress was the norm, but also because team apparel was not available to the general fan. Team gear was limited to practice gear such as white or gray cotton sweatshirts, sweatpants, and t-shirts with team names stenciled in spray paint. (Schools labeled these items to make athletes think twice before pilfering the items which, of course, had the opposite effect.) Here and there, team jerseys and other gear could be acquired through the sporting goods shops that supplied college and professional teams with their uniforms. The local stores ordered extra gear, added appropriate numbers and logos, and sold the goods to the public. These unlicensed sales occurred in such low volumes through the 1970s that few teams bothered enforcing their trademarks.

All that changed in the early 1980s with the growth of brands such as Nutmeg Mills and Starter. The newly-founded Collegiate Licensing Company brokered nonexclusive deals with brands to sell products comparable to those supplied to the teams. Team apparel proved popular with the public, particularly as everyday fashion became more casual. The rise of the fitness culture and the growing popularity of athletic casual clothing also contributed to the trend.

Following on the heels of fans wearing team colors to games is the phenomenon of fans universally wearing a team color. 'Colorouts' originated outside of football and outside the good ol' U.S.A. when Calgary Flames fans created the "C of Red" during the 1986 Stanley Cup playoff series with the Edmonton Oilers. Edmonton won the two previous Stanley Cups and was gunning for a third, causing Edmonton fans to wear hats to their home games as part of the "Hat Trick Fever" campaign. In response, Calgary fans wore red to their home games, particularly Calgary's red away sweaters, and a phenomenon was born. Whiteouts arrived when Calgary and Edmonton met in the playoffs the following year, with Edmonton fans wearing white to their home games.

Fan color coordination moved south in 2004 when Penn State managed the first marginally-successful whiteout in football for the Purdue game. Although the campaign worked, few noticed until Whiteout II, which occurred for a nationally televised night game with Ohio State in 2005. Penn State's game with Notre Dame in 2007 set another standard when the whiteout spread from the student section to the full stadium.

MANAGEMENT AND CONTROL

Before television revenues flooded college football, cost control was among the sport's top issues. Nine schools playing University Division football in 1960 have since dropped the sport, while fifty schools that did not field University Division teams in 1960 now participate at the FBS level. Among the schools dropping football, five were private: Marquette (1960), Detroit (1965), Tampa (1975), Villanova (1981, reinstated in 1984), and Pacific (1996). Four public institutions dropped football as well: Texas-Arlington (1982), Wichita State (1987), Cal State, Long Beach (1992), and Cal State, Fullerton (1993). Each school played a mid-major schedule at the time they dropped football, so none had an impact like the University of Chicago's dropping from the Big Ten.

Of the fifty schools that moved into college football's highest level during the modern era, seven did not exist in 1960, and eight did not have football teams until 2000 or after. Like others before them, most run their programs at significant deficits and aspire to the success achieved by Boise State or Central Florida. Some even hope for the success of Florida State, which became college football's greatest Cinderella story after restarting its football team in 1947 following four decades as an all-female university.

Although the cost of running major college football programs has increased during the modern era, there have been several efforts to reduce costs, including placing limits on the number of football scholarships per school. In 1970, the SEC allowed forty scholarships per year, the Big Eight forty-five, and the Southwest Conference fifty. To save money and increase competitiveness, the NCAA moved in 1973 to limit football scholarships to 30 per year and 105 overall. Thanks in part to financial pressures stemming from Title IX's passage, the limits were further reduced to 30 and 95 in 1975, to 30 and 92 in 1992, and to 25 and 85 in 1994. Besides lowering costs, the scholarship limits reduced the stockpiling of talent. Players who might have sat on a top team's bench instead took their talents to other schools, allowing a greater number of teams to compete at the top level.

Another cost-saving measure taken up by the NCAA affected player eligibility. For the bulk of football's history, schools or conferences set the eligibility rules. The NCAA had little involvement on these issues until its role expanded in the 1950s. Among the more controversial rules was the NCAA's three-year eligibility standard, often interpreted as barring freshmen from varsity competition. More accurately, the NCAA rule only limited participation in NCAA-sponsored championship competitions to three seasons. Freshmen could compete during the regular season if their school and conference allowed them to do so (many did not), but could only compete in NCAA championship competition in three of their four years on campus. (In sports for which NCAA championships acted as qualifiers for the Olympic Trials, the NCAA allowed freshmen to compete in the championship events during the Olympic years. Points earned by freshmen did not count toward team totals.)

Due to the expense related to their freshmen teams traveling across their geographically-dispersed conference, the Western Athletic Conference proposed making freshmen eligible in 1968. Surprisingly, the measure passed, and freshmen became eligible for NCAA postseason events in all sports other than football and basketball. Conferences such as the Big Ten, Pac-8, and ECAC continued to ban freshmen despite the NCAA rule change. Freshmen became eligible for football and basketball in the College Division in 1971 and all sports at the University Division level in 1972.

The most significant eligibility issue of the modern era has been the move away from segregated playing fields. At the beginning of the modern era, Southern blacks had two options for playing college football. They could obtain one of the limited spots for black players on integrated Northern or West Coast teams, or they could play at one of the historically black college or universities (HBCUs) in the South. Both became important paths into the NFL and AFL, but the AFL signed black players more aggressively than the NFL. The Kansas City Chiefs were among the most aggressive, employing a black scout proficient at identifying talent in the HBCUs. The success of Kansas City's approach was demonstrated by the Chiefs starting eight HCBU alumni when they defeated the Minnesota Vikings in Super Bowl IV. Other teams followed their lead.

At the college level, integration was the norm for Northern and Western teams in the 1960s, but black players still numbered in the low single-digits at most schools. Some schools became known for recruiting black players more aggressively and benefitted from doing so. Minnesota, under Marty Warmuth, was among the first schools to recruit multiple African American players in a recruiting class and was the first major college team with a black quarterback. Elsewhere in the Big Ten, Michigan State seized the torch under Duffy Daugherty. Daugherty, who was well-liked by Southern white coaches, was tipped off to promising Southern black players by coaches who could not recruit such players. Michigan State's Big Ten-winning 1965 and 1966 teams had eighteen and seventeen black players, respectively, and included four of the top eight players selected in the 1967 NFL draft. Michigan State's success pushed other Northern and Western teams further along the integration path. USC had seven black players on its 1967 national championship team and twenty-three on its 1972 national championship team. The 1969 national championship won by Texas was the last earned by an all-white team.

Michigan State's 1965 football team had 17 African Americans among the 39 players included in the team picture. (Michigan State University Archives and Historical Collections)

Segregation at Southern schools began collapsing under social, legal, and competitive pressures with schools in the border states integrating first and the Deep South schools integrating last. The SEC became integrated when Nate Northington played for Kentucky during the 1967 season. Alabama's loss to a slightly integrated Tennessee team in 1969 and to a somewhat more integrated USC team in 1970 increased the pressure for Alabama to integrate its football team. Ole Miss and LSU were the last major schools to integrate, waiting until 1972. Longer-term, recruiting players regardless of race has resulted in black players comprising 49.2 percent of FBS football players in 2018 and 69.7 percent of NFL players in 2016.

The opening of opportunities ultimately reached coaching staffs as well. The first black head coach at a predominantly white college or university was Don Hudson, who ran the program at Macalester from 1972 to 1975 before moving to his alma mater, Lincoln University. Willie Jeffries became the first black head coach at the major college level when he took over Wichita State in 1979 and was followed by Dennis Green at Northwestern in 1981. At the NFL level, Art Shell became the Oakland Raiders head coach partway through the 1989 season and remained in that capacity through the 1994 season. His appointment made him the first African American head coach in the modern NFL. (Fritz Pollard coached the Akron Pros and other teams in the 1920s.)

Concern about the limits on college players moving to professional football popped up several times during the modern era. The NFL banned the signing of college players before their class graduated in 1926, but the issue of signing players with remaining college eligibility cropped up again when the USFL challenged the NFL from 1983 to 1985. Although the USFL had its own rules against signing players early, they made an exception when the New Jersey Generals signed Herschel Walker following his Heisman Trophy-winning, junior season in 1982.

The following year, several players with remaining college eligibility sued the USFL for inclusion in their draft. One, Robert Boris, a punter from Arizona, won his suit, by which time he had already signed with and played for the Oklahoma Outlaws. Several days after the ruling, Marcus Dupree signed with the New Orleans Breakers for their 1984 spring season. Dupree was an interesting case. A freshmen sensation at Oklahoma in 1982, Dupree transferred to Southern Mississippi partway through the 1983 season, and the requirement that he sit one season meant he was ineligible for major college football until the 1985 season.

In 1987, several college players were exposed after signing with agents before their senior seasons, after which the NCAA declared the players ineligible. With the NCAA having declared the players ineligible, the NFL feared legal action if they did not grant these players access to their league, so they held a supplemental draft for players who were ineligible to play. (The NCAA was hard-pressed to complain about the NFL's actions since they were the ones that had declared the players ineligible in the first place.) Over the next several years, the NFL allowed players to submit for the draft if they graduated early, or experienced "hardship" circumstances. That process proved a mess, and in 1991, the NFL allowed any player to declare for the draft who was three years removed from high school.

The final significant issue of the modern era has been the issue of player safety. From 1931 to 1961, football averaged nearly 18 direct deaths per year, increasing to more than 25 per year from 1966 to 1972, before falling sharply. The annual count of deaths directly attributable to football has hit double digits only once since 1977. Although researchers cannot determine causal links, most believe the increase in deaths in the late 1960s resulted from players adopting unsafe blocking and tackling techniques. Specifically, the changeover to plastic helmets and the adoption of face masks offered higher levels of protection for players wearing helmets. Contemporary observers noted that improved helmets led players to use their heads as weapons when blocking and tackling, and coaching techniques encouraged the same. As Ohio State coach Woody Hayes described the preferred blocking technique:

> We teach our boys to spear and gore. We want them to plant that helmet right under a guy's chin. A boy who blocks with his head down gets hurt. I want them to stick that face mask right in the opponent's neck.[47]

While Hayes did not advocate spearing in today's use of the term, the point remains that one of the nation's leading college coaches instructed his players to lead with their face masks when tackling. He was not alone.

Helmet designs of the era exacerbated the effect of these techniques. In particular, the helmet shells of the 1960s and early 1970s extended further down the neck than they do today, and the hard plastic at the base of the helmet back lacked padding. The unfortunate effect was that a significant portion of football fatalities during the time came from helmets being forced back against the neck in guillotine fashion. Football fatalities fell dramatically after the late 1970s when rule changes made it illegal to initiate contact with the helmet when blocking or tackling. Moreover, rules changes that allowed offensive players to extend their arms while blocking resulted in new techniques that reduced the use of the helmet when blocking.

Of course, while the number of deaths resulting from acute injuries has dropped substantially, the concern has shifted to the game's connection to CTE. The research initially linked concussions to CTE, leading to rule changes such as the outlawing of helmet-to-helmet contact. More recently, the research focus has shifted, with scientists concluding that cumulative subconcussive hits are the main cause of CTE. The initial effect of these findings has been efforts to limit the nature and frequency of hitting during practice to reduce subconcussive hits. However, subconcussive hits are an inherent part of football as played today. Substantially reducing subconcussive hits will be difficult to achieve without making fundamental adjustments to the game.

TELEVISION CHANGED football due to the substantial increases in money paid for the broadcast rights. At the same time, the science of television broadcasting saw innovations ranging from technological advances in cameras, on-screen graphics, displays, data storage, and communication technologies, while the art of broadcasting changed with aesthetic and social forces. The combination made televised football more accessible and popular, which, in turn, made additional financial resources available to the teams and players involved in the game. However, these monies came at a price as the game increasingly answered to its television sponsors, while trying to satisfy the television audience.

Although more limited in number compared to previous eras, new traditions and behaviors affected the in-stadium fan experience during the modern era. Many new traditions involved the larger fan base becoming part of the show, as opposed to the limited number of cheerleaders and band members.

As in earlier eras, college football continued to wrestle with issues surrounding the role of football in the nation's colleges and universities, particularly issues of player eligibility and amateurism. The eligibility issue that saw the most dramatic change was the opening of the college game to African American players. Southern teams opened their rosters to black players during the 1960s and 1970s, while Northern and West Coast teams moved beyond de facto quotas during the same period. Parallel steps occurred in the professional game, albeit more quickly. Times have changed at the player level, and African American athletes now represent nearly half of all football players at the FBS level and well more than half of NFL players.

PART IV

EPILOGUE

EPILOGUE

The Rutgers and Princeton students facing one another on a November afternoon in 1869 could not have imagined how their game would evolve over the next 150 years. Playing only four years after the Civil War ended, they used a round ball and rules roughly similar to the Association or soccer game. The attendees at the first Intercollegiate Football Association meeting seven years later agreed to play a version of rugby rather than soccer, and away we went. They and their successors met over the next decade or two, tweaking the rules until their version of rugby became a new sport, gridiron football.

Visionary rule makers drove gridiron football's evolution at times, but most modifications arrived haphazardly, largely through individuals seeking competitive, safety, or financial advantages without connection to a grand plan. Some new ideas and equipment proved advantageous, gained broad acceptance, and became standard practice. Many changes were codified in the rules only after they saw widespread use. In some cases, individual adaptations proved excessive or unattractive, leading the powers-that-be to implement rules outlawing or stifling those adaptations.

Of course, some changes had greater impacts than others. Among the many thousands of changes that occurred over the last 150 years, eleven stand out for influencing the path football took to arrive at today's game. The eleven critical changes in football's history and the timing of their arrival include:

- 1880: Scrummage to scrimmage
- 1882: System of downs
- 1884: Blocking

- 1903: Seven offensive players on the line of scrimmage
- 1906: Forward pass
- 1932: Hash marks
- 1941: Option plays
- 1941: Unlimited substitutions
- 1950s: Plastic helmets and face masks
- 1960s: Television money
- 1960s: Racial integration

The first three changes occurred in the 1880s and were building blocks for sending football in a direction different from rugby. Transitioning from the scrummage to scrimmage and moving to the system of downs directed football toward controlled, episodic play rather than the free-flowing play of rugby or soccer. The structured plays and detailed planning that exists in football today would not have emerged without those rules. Still, the same period witnessed what is arguably the most consequential rule change in the history of football: the legalization of blocking. Legalized blocking permitted offensive players to attack defenders, dramatically increasing the number of collisions per play. Football inherited tackling from rugby, but the acceptance of blocking fundamentally altered the game, leading to the V formation, the flying wedge, momentum and mass plays, and other elements subsequently banished from football. While the rule makers succeeded in striking the most brutal forms of blocking from the game, the acceptance of blocking pushed players to pad their bodies and wear headgear, ultimately leading to all the protective equipment worn by players over the years.

Legalized blocking also led directly to the brutal game of the late 1890s and early 1900s. The 1903 rule requiring seven players on the line of scrimmage at the snap eliminated mass plays but did nothing to help offenses move the ball, so teams continued smashing into one another in tight formations. Had the game not accepted blocking, football might not have needed the forward pass to open up the game. Had blocking not been legalized, North America might have returned to playing rugby with the rest of the world rather than following its unique path. In short, without blocking, gridiron football might not have emerged as a distinct sport.

But it did, and it slowly transformed from a game that emphasized kicking and running to one in which the forward pass became dominant. That transition took time After easing many restrictions on the forward pass by 1912, another seventy years passed before college offenses threw for more yards than they ran.

The most significant change to football's playing field was the 1932 introduction of hash marks. Hash marks modified football by ensuring teams could run or pass to the left or the right regardless of where the previous play ended. Within a decade, that directional balance helped spur dropback passing by giving offenses the ability to stretch the field horizontally and vertically.

Following on the heels of the hash mark was the Split T offense, which introduced option football. A conceptual breakthrough, the option meant that offenses no longer needed to predetermine who carried the ball on a given play. Instead, the actions of the defense determined who received the ball. The option concept then transferred to the passing game with quarterbacks and receivers reading defenses to determine the route to run and where to throw the ball. Option football has reached its most advanced form with today's RPOs, with the reads determining whether to run or pass the ball, while defenses turn the tables by disguising their actions.

On the player equipment side, the most critical change during football's history has been the combination of hard plastic helmets and face masks that came into widespread use in the late 1950s. The combination led to blocking and tackling techniques that subjected players' heads to more frequent and forceful contact. A comparison of game films from before and after these helmets came into use shows today's game to be faster, more violent, and played with more reckless abandon. Advancements in helmet technology, revised techniques, and rule changes discourage aspects of those behaviors. Still, current CTE research indicates we need additional adjustments to enhance player safety.

The player specialization resulting from unlimited substitutions adds to the speed and violence of today's game. Unlimited substitution rules allowed players to focus only on offense, defense, or special teams, halving the number of plays per game and giving players more rest. Unlimited substitutions also mean players' skills better match their positions, and they receive enhanced coaching from expanded and focused coaching staffs. Professional football's retention of unlimited substitutions in the 1950s contributed to its developing a more open, sophisticated game that emphasized passing. Its more exciting style of play positioned professional football to take advantage of the growing appetite for televised sports programming in the early 1960s. The money that poured in allowed professional football to become truly professional as players and coaches focused on their craft year-round. Similar changes occurred in college football when its television money ballooned several decades later. The specialization movement coincided with coaches taking the game out of the players' hands, as evidenced by situational substitutions. An old school quarterback was simply incapable of swapping out the mix of backs and receivers from play to play that occurs in many offenses today.

The last significant change in the game was the opening of major college and professional football to black players. Despite some participation in the late

1880s, the predominantly white college and the professional teams barred or limited African American players until the 1960s. Football, and the sporting world in general, were both a cause and reflection of broader social changes that reduced those barriers, and innumerable impacts have resulted on and off the field.

Each of the eleven critical changes occurred or started during football's first one-hundred years. They have continued influencing the game in the last fifty years, with several having had their most significant impact in recent years. In the meantime, football continues to change and adapt to new circumstances as its practitioners innovate, seek competitive advantage, and adjust to the external environment.

Today, football faces the greatest threat to its existence since 1905. The challenge is insidious, stemming from the very nature of the game. Football is a collision sport, and the best available science tells us that CTE stems from the cumulative effect of its collisions. Football will need to change foundational elements of the sport to address the CTE challenge. Changes in the margin will be insufficient.

Given the need for fundamental change, we turn to ideas to make football safer and inform those thoughts using knowledge of the game's past. As it turns out, football's future lies in its past.

THE FUTURE OF FOOTBALL

Barring unanticipated improvements in helmet technology, the primary means of making football safer is to reduce the frequency and impact of football's fundamentals: blocking and tackling.

Identifying how to modify core elements of football is challenging, but recognizing the difference between direct and indirect approaches helps identify potential solutions. Direct rules prohibit dangerous behaviors or acts and penalize those who exhibit them. Outside of football, a 25 mile-per-hour speed limit on a city side street is an example of a direct rule. The rule targets the undesirable behavior itself, and those found to violate the rule suffer penalties. The indirect approach, on the other hand, attempts to reduce undesirable behavior by altering the conditions in which the behavior occurs. An indirect approach to slowing traffic is to place speed bumps on streets, so drivers traveling at excess speed suffer the unpleasant consequence of their behavior.

Examples of direct rules in football include those prohibiting clipping, face masking, crackback blocks, chop blocks, clotheslining, spearing, and targeting. Each forbids particular acts and penalizes teams whose players commit the offenses. Indirect rules in football encourage or discourage target behaviors by altering their surrounding parameters. Take momentum and mass plays, for example. Rather than penalizing those plays directly, the rules limit the number of players in motion and require seven offensive players on the line of scrimmage at the snap. Referees do not penalize momentum and mass plays; they penalize the conditions that enable momentum and mass plays.

To date, many attempts to make football safer have applied the direct approach and outlawed dangerous forms of tackling, leaving the game with few options to further restrict tackling short of moving to a two-hand touch or flag game. Placing additional restrictions on tackling will not solve football's collision problem. Instead, the game must focus on the source of most collisions in football and reduce the frequency and intensity of blocking. Doing so would follow the lead of earlier generations that implemented rules favoring a more open game.

One concern voiced about the open game approach is that it will lead to more high-speed collisions. We will need to monitor this concern, but research from today's game suggests a more open game will not lead to many more severe collisions. Broadly, available research shows running backs and quarterbacks receive the highest number of severe hits today. Offensive and defensive linemen are next, followed by linebackers, wide receivers, and defensive backs, indicating that the positions that play in comparatively open space have the fewest severe collisions. Running backs and quarterbacks operate in both tight and open space, and both suffer collisions because they carry the ball more than other positions. Adapting the rules to give them more space should be beneficial. Likewise, rules that encourage getting the ball to wide receivers more frequently and that reduce the severity and number of hits among offensive and defensive lines are critical.

Below are a handful of ideas to make football safer. The ideas least disruptive to the current game are listed first, but those are also the least likely to impact player safety significantly.

Neutral Zone and Stances. Whereas the American neutral zone is the length of the football, Canadian rules require the defense to align at least one yard from the ball. While the additional yard between the offensive and defensive linemen may not reduce the number of collisions, it reduces the intensity of contact among linemen and the level of helmet-to-helmet contact.

As others have argued, we should also eliminate three- and four-point stances that allow players to come off the ball with increased power and speed while also staying low. Like the expanded neutral zone, eliminating three- and four-point stances would reduce the number and intensity of helmet-to-helmet hits among down linemen. Combining an expanded neutral zone with the two-point stance requirements should be particularly useful in lowering helmet-to-helmet contact among interior linemen.

Isolation Blocking. While there are various forms of isolation blocks, all involve blocking patterns in which the offensive line leaves a particular defender unblocked. A fullback, H back, or other offensive player positioned behind the line of scrimmage then attacks the isolated defender, often resulting in a substantial collision.

Isolation blocks represent the last vestige of momentum plays in football. Given the severity of isolation blocks, we could make it illegal for players behind the line of scrimmage to block defenders located in the tackle box. Those located behind the line of scrimmage at the snap could execute retreat-style blocks commonly used in pass blocking.

Fifteen Yards Per First Down. The rule makers of 1906 doubled the number of yards needed to earn a first down, and their counterparts in 1912 gave teams four downs rather than three to gain those yards. Both changes took the indirect approach by encouraging teams to find new methods to move the ball. Requiring teams to gain fifteen or twenty yards to earn a first down would cause coaches to pass more often, and to create new plays and formations. Teams would immediately adjust their playcalling under the new rules, while more creative solutions involving formations and offensive design would arrive over the long term.

Player Spacing. Football first required offenses to have seven players on the line of scrimmage in 1903. Despite this longstanding requirement related to vertical positioning, football has never had rules concerning horizontal positioning. Offenses have the freedom to position players anywhere between the sidelines, but they universally place the center, two guards, and two tackles close to the ball. Power-oriented formations also position a fullback, one or more tight ends, or others close to the ball.

The problem with positioning offensive linemen and others close together is that proximity promotes collisions. We could encourage offenses to spread out by starting every play in the horizontal middle of the field and require at least three receivers to be on or outside the hash marks at the snap.

Beyond increasing the horizontal spread of eligible receivers, other rules could require or encourage more spacing between the offensive linemen. Traditionalists will oppose rules that increase the spread among offensive linemen because such rules will reduce the beloved *mano y mano* battles inherent in power football. Of course, that is precisely the point.

A Bigger Field and Reduced-Player Football. Some have argued that American football can reduce the number and intensity of collisions by adopting the Canadian field, which has a 55-yard line, is 15 yards wider, and has end zones 20 yards deep. In combination, the Canadian field has forty-three percent more surface area than the American field.

The notion that a larger playing field leads to a more open game has merit.

(We see this effect with the larger rinks in international hockey that promote a more open and speed-oriented game than in the NHL.) Walter Camp advocated for enlarging the football field in 1906, but Harvard Stadium's reinforced concrete stands were a key reason the idea did not move forward. The same situation exists at venerable Harvard Stadium today, and the tens of thousands of professional, college, high school, and other stadiums currently configured for the American football field compound the problem.

Widening the American football field is simply not practical, but we can increase the square footage per player by taking a different route. That is, we can leave the American field as is and reduce the number of players per side. There is nothing magical about football teams having eleven players per side; the number is arbitrary.

What would the reduced-player game look like? Many high schools with limited enrollments play six-, eight-, or nine-man football today. They generally play on smaller-than-regulation fields due to the desire to have their game mirror the spacing of eleven-man football. Playing with nine players per side on a regulation field would increase the square footage per player by twenty-two percent, resulting in a game that emphasizes speed, elusiveness, and athleticism while reducing, but not eliminating, the role of power.

The nine-player game could require teams to have five players on the line of scrimmage with the three interior positions being ineligible receivers. Eliminating two interior line positions would substantially reduce the number of collisions that result from blocking, assuming offenses continued along the conventional path. More likely, new schemes would develop that require quicker, more nimble linemen whose ability to shield rather than overpower defenders is critical. Similar changes could occur on the defensive side of the ball as well.

Eliminating Plastic Helmets and Face Masks. A common suggestion for making football safer calls for the elimination of plastic helmets and face masks. Proponents of this approach argue that removing face masks and using softer headgear would force players to modify their blocking and tackling techniques, resulting in a more rugby-like game. Such suggestions make little sense, and the reasons are quite simple. First, rugby has significant concussion and head injury problems of its own, so it does not provide as attractive an alternative as some might think. Second, football shifted toward helmets with hard shells to limit or eliminate skull fractures. Playing football with soft-shelled helmets will cause an increase in skull fractures unless the game is changed more radically than has been suggested here, such as by eliminating blocking. Similarly, football embraced face masks because they prevented broken noses, gashed cheeks, broken orbital bones, and significant orthodontic bills, which will return without face masks.

Proponents of eliminating today's helmets point to rugby as the guide to football's future. While there are more than twice as many tackles in a rugby match as in a football game, rugby does not allow blocking, so there are far fewer collisions. While we can work to limit football's collisions, those playing the game need protection when those collisions occur. Of course, football could eliminate blocking entirely, but we might as well play rugby if we take that step.

Whatever measures we implement, however, the history of football tells us that the wheels of change can be slow to turn. The football world can quickly comply with new rules, but it takes time to shift from compliance to integration of the new rules, and the delay will be longer the more fundamental the rule change. Rules that alter foundational elements of the game require new ways of thinking, and new ideas take time to gestate. It took the better part of a decade after legalizing the forward pass for most of the football world to recognize its potential. Merely changing the rule book to allow the forward pass was not sufficient to change the game.

Similarly, the 1941 rule allowing unlimited substitutions revolutionized football by allowing specialization, but it took nearly five full seasons before Fritz Crisler stumbled on the idea of platooning his offense and defense. Once introduced, platooning became mainstream in short order, yet several decades passed before situational substitutions were used outside the kicking game.

Beyond the required gestation period, the pace of change is slowed by stubbornness, by a refusal to part with old ways. Amos Alonzo Stagg advocated for eliminating kickoffs as a safety measure in 1910, yet it remains part of the game despite continued evidence of its danger. There have been several half-hearted attempts to reduce the number of kickoff returns in recent years, but the kickoff remains inherently dangerous. We should eliminate the kickoff, and the failure to do so encapsulates the challenge facing football. If we are unwilling to eliminate the kickoff, how can we expect to see foundational changes occur?

While one can argue the wisdom of the specific changes discussed above, the football community must recognize that change is needed to keep the game viable. Football's CTE problem goes to the core of the game, and that makes accepting change difficult. Still, football's rules, techniques, and schemes have evolved since the sport began, and change will continue in the future. The many thousands of past changes have produced the game that we know and love today. It will be difficult to accept the necessary changes to make football safer, but the game has successfully adapted over the last 150 years and will do so in the future.

APPENDIX I: 1876 INTERCOLLEGIATE FOOTBALL ASSOCIATION RULES

The following lists the rules established at the November 23, 1876 meeting of the Intercollegiate Football Association.

Rule 1: A drop kick, or drop, is made by letting the ball fall from the hands and kicking it the very instant is rises.

Rule 2: A place kick, or place, is made by kicking the ball after it has been placed in a nick made in the ground for the purpose of keeping it at rest.

Rule 3: A punt is made by letting the ball fall from the hands and kicking it before it hits the ground.

Rule 4: Each goal shall be composed of two upright posts exceeding 11 feet in height from the ground and placed 18 feet 6 inches apart, with a cross-bar 10 feet from the ground.

Rule 5: A goal may be obtained by kicking the ball from the field of play direct (i.e., without touching the ground or the dress of person of any player on either side) over the cross-bar of the opponents' goal. Whether it touch such cross-bar or the posts it is called a poster and is not a goal.

Rule 6: A goal may be obtained by any type of kick except a punt.

Rule 7: A match shall be decided by the majority of touchdowns; a goal shall be equal to four touchdowns; but in case of a tie a goal kicked from a touchdown shall take precedence over four touchdowns.

Rule 8: The ball is dead when it rests absolutely motionless on the ground.

Rule 9: A touchdown is when a player, putting his hand upon the ball on the ground in touch or in goal stops it so it remains dead or fairly so.

Rule 10: A tackle is made when the holder of the ball is held by one or more players of the opposite side.

Rule 11: A scrummage takes place when the holder of the ball, being in the field of play, puts it on the ground in front of him, and all who have closed around on the respective sides endeavor to push their opponents back, and by kicking the ball, to drive it in the direction of the opposite goal-line.

Rule 12: A player may take up the ball whenever it is rolling or bounding except in a scrummage.

Rule 13: It is not lawful to take up the ball when dead (except in order to bring it out after it has been touched down in touch or in goal) for any purpose whatsoever. Whenever the ball shall have been so unlawfully taken up it shall at once be brought back to where it was taken up and there put down.

Rule 14: In a scrummage it is not lawful for the man who has the ball to pick it up with the hand under any circumstance whatsoever.

Rule 15: It is lawful to any player who has the ball to run with it, and if he does so it is called a run. If a player runs with the ball and gets behind his opponents' goal-line and there touches it down, it is called a run in.

Rule 16: It is lawful to run in anywhere across the goal-line.

Rule 17: The goal-line is in goal and the touch-line in touch.

Rule 18: In the event of any player holding or running with the ball being tackled, and the ball fairly held, he must at once cry down, and there put it down.

Rule 19: A maul-in goal is when the holder of the ball is tackled inside the goal-line, or, being tackled immediately outside, is carried and pushed across it, and he, or the opposite side, or both, endeavor to touch the ball down. In all cases when so touched down, the ball shall belong to the side of the players of the side who first had possession of it before the maul commenced, unless the opposite side have gained complete possession of it.

Rule 20: In case of a maul-in goal, those players only who are touching the ball with their hands when it crosses the goal-line may continue the maul-in goal, and when a player has once removed his hold of the ball after it is inside the goal-line, he may not again join the maul, and if he attempts to do so, may be dragged out by the opposite side; but if a player when running in is tackled inside the goal-line, then only the player who first tackled him, or if two or more tackle simultaneously, they only may join in the maul.

Rule 21: Touch-in-goal. Immediately the ball, whether in the hands of a player (except for the purpose of a punt-out – see Rule 29) or not, goes into touch in goal, it is at once dead and out of the game, and must be brought out by Rules 41 and 42.

Rule 22: Every player is on side, but is put off side if he enters a scrummage from his opponents' side; or, being in a scrummage/scrimmage, gets in front of the ball, or when that ball has been kicked, touched, or is being run with by one of his own side behind him (i.e., between himself and his goal-line). No player can be off side in his own goal.

Rule 23: Every player when off side is out of the game and shall not touch the ball in any case whatsoever, either in or out of touch or goal, or in any way interrupt or obstruct any player, until his is again on side.

Rule 24: A player being off side is put on side when the ball has been kicked by, or has touched the dress or person of, any player of the opposite side, or when one of his own side has run in front of him, either with the ball or having kicked it when behind him.

Rule 25: When a player has the ball none of his opponents who at the time are off side may commence or attempt to tackle or otherwise interrupt such player.

Rule 26: Throwing back. It is lawful for any player who has the ball to throw it backward toward his own goal, or to pass it back to any player of his side who is at the time behind him, in accordance with the rules of on side.

Rule 27: Knocking on, i.e. deliberately hitting the ball with the hand, and throwing it forward, i.e., throwing the ball in the direction of the opponents' goal-line are not lawful. If the ball be either knocked on or thrown forward, the captain of the opposite side may (unless a fair catch has been made a provided by the next rule) require to have it brought back to the spot where it was knocked down or throw forward and there put it down.

Rule 28: A fair catch is a catch made direct from a kick or a throw forward, or a knock on by one of the opponents' side, or from a punt-out or punt-on (see Rules 29 and 30), provided the catcher makes a mark with his heel at the spot where he made the catch and no other of his side touch the ball. (see Rules 43 and 44.)

Rule 29: A punt-out is a punt made after a touchdown by a player from behind his opponent's goal, and from touch in goal if necessary, toward his own side, who must stand outside the goal-line and endeavor to make a fair catch or to get the ball and run in or drop a goal.

Rule 30: A punt on is a punt made in a manner similar to a punt-out, and from touch, if necessary, by a player who has made a fair catch from a punt-out or another punt-on.

Rule 31: Touch. If a ball goes into touch, the first player on his side who touches it down must bring it to the spot where it crossed the touch-line; or if a player when running with the ball cross of put any part of either foot across the touch-line, he must return with the ball to the spot where the line was so crossed and return with the ball to the spot where the line was so crossed and thence return into the field of play in one of the modes provided by the following rule.

Rule 32: He must then himself, or by one of his own side, either bound the ball into the field of play and then run with it, kick it, or throw it back to his own side; or throw it out at right angles to the touch-line; or walk it with it at right angles to the touch-line any distance not less than five nor more than fifteen yards, and there put it down, first declaring how far he intends to walk out.

Rule 33: If two or more players holding the ball are pushed into touch, the ball shall belong in touch to the players who first had hold of it in the field of play and has not released his hold of it.

Rule 34: If the ball, when thrown out of touch, be not thrown out at right angles to the touch-line, the captain of either side may at once claim to have it thrown out again.

Rule 35: A catch made when the ball is thrown out of touch is not a fair catch.

Rule 36: Kick-off is a place kick from the center of the field, and cannot count as a goal. The opposite side must stand at least ten yards in front of the ball until it has been kicked.

Rule 37: The ball shall be kicked off (i) at the commencement of the game (ii) after a goal has been obtained.

Rule 38: The sides shall change goals as often as and whenever a goal is obtained, unless it has otherwise been agreed by the captains before the commencement of the match.

Rule 39: The captains of the respective sides will toss up before the commencement of the match; the winner of the toss shall have the option of the choice of goals or of the kick-off

Rule 40: Whenever a goal has been obtained the side which lost the goal shall then kick off.

Rule 41: Kick-out is a drop kick by one of the players of the side which has had to touch the ball down in their own goal, or into whose touch in goal the ball has gone (Rule 21), and is the mode of bringing the ball again into play, and cannot count as a goal.

Rule 42: Kick-out must be a drop kick and from not more than twenty-five yards outside the kicker's goal; if the ball when kicked-out pitch in touch, it must be taken back and kicked out again. The kicker's side must be behind the ball when it is kicked.

Rule 43: A player who has made and claimed a fair catch shall therefore either take a drop kick or a punt or place the ball or a place kick.

Rule 44: After a fair catch has been made the opposite side may come up to the catcher's mark, and except in cases under Rule 30/50, the catcher's side retiring, the ball shall be kicked from such mark, or from a spot any distance behind it.

Rule 45: A player may touch the ball down in his own goal at any time.

Rule 46: A side having touched the ball down in their opponents' goal shall try at goal either by a place kick or a punt-out.

Rule 47: If a try at goal be made by a place kick, a player of the side which has touched the ball down shall bring it up to the goal-line (subject to Rule 48) in a straight line from, and opposite to, the spot where the ball was touched down, and there make a mark on the goal-line and thence walk straight out with it at right angles to the goal-line, to such distance as he thinks proper, and there place it for another of his side to kick. The kicker's side must be behind the ball when it is kicked and the opposite side must remain behind their goal-line until the ball has been placed on the ground. (See Rules 54 and 55.)

Rule 48: If the ball has been touched down between the goal-posts it may be brought out in a straight line from either of such posts.

Rule 49: If the try at goal be by a punt-out (see Rule 29) a player of the side which has touched the ball down shall bring it straight up to the goal-line opposite to the spot where it was touched down, and there make a mark on the goal-line, and then punt out from the touch-in-goal if necessary, or from any part behind the goal-line not near to the goal-post than such mark, beyond which it is not lawful for the opposite side (who must keep behind their goal-line) to pass until the ball has been kicked. (See Rules 54 and 55.)

Rule 50: If a fair catch be made from a punt-out or punt-on, the catcher may proceed either as provided by Rules 43 or 44, or he himself take a punt-on, in which case the mark made in making the fair catch shall be regarded (for the purpose of determining as well the position of the player who makes the punt-on as of the other players of both sides) as the mark made on the goal-line in the case of a punt-out.

Rule 51: A catch made in touch from a punt-out or a punt-on is not a fair catch; the ball must be then taken or thrown out of touch as provided by Rule 32. But if the catch be made in touch in goal the ball is at once dead and must be kicked out as provided in Rules 41 and 42.

Rule 52: When the ball has been touched down in the opponents' goal, none of the side in whose goal it has so been touched down shall touch it or in any way displace it or interfere with the player of the other side who may be taking it up or not.

Rule 53: The ball is dead whenever a goal has been obtained; but if a try at goal be not successful, the kick shall be considered as only an ordinary kick in the course of the game.

Rule 54: Charging, i.e. rushing forward to kick the ball or tackle a player, is lawful for the opposite side of the ball in all cases of a place kick after a fair catch, or upon a try at goal immediately the ball touches the ground or is placed on the ground; and in cases of drop kick or punt after a fair catch, as soon as the player having the ball commences to run or offers to kick, or the ball has touched the ground; but he may always draw back, and unless he has dropped the ball or actually touched it with his foot, they must retire again to his mark (see Rule 56). The opposite side in case of a punt-out or punt-in, and the kicker's side in all cases, may not charge until the ball has been kicked.

Rule 55: If a player having the ball, when about to punt it out goes outside of the goal-line, or when about to punt-on advances nearer to his own goal-line than his mark, made on making the fair catch, or if after the ball has been touched down in the opponents' goal, or a fair catch has been made, more than one player of the side which has so touched it down, or made the fair catch, touch the ball before it is again kicked, the opposite may charge at once.

Rule 56: In case of a fair catch the opposite side may come up to and charge from anywhere on or behind the line drawn through the mark made by the player who has made the catch and parallel to their own goal-line; but in the case of a fair catch from punt-out or punt-on, they may not advance further in the direction of the touch-line nearest to such mark than a line drawn through such mark to their goal-line and parallel to such touch-line. In all cases, except a punt-out and a punt-on, the kicker's side must be behind the ball when it is kicked, but may not charge until it has been kicked.

Rule 57: No hacking or hacking over or tripping up shall be allowed under any circumstances.

Rule 58: No one wearing projecting nails, iron plates, or gutta percha on any parts of his boots or shoes shall be allowed to play in a match.

Rule 59: There shall be two judges, one for each side, and also a referee, to whom disputed points shall be referred, and whose decision shall be final. *Under Rugby Union Code the captains acted as officials.

Rule 60: The grounds shall be 140 yards long and 70 yards wide.

Rule 61: The number of players shall be limited to fifteen upon a side.

BIBLIOGRAPHY

The Bibliography is organized by chapter, section, and topic. Unless noted, all newspaper articles were accessed through newspapers.com.

FOOTNOTES

1 Totten, Charles Adiel Lewis. Laws of Athletics and General Rules. San Francisco, The Presidio. 1881.

2 Stagg, Amos Alonzo. '*Football as I Played It,*' The Official National Collegiate Athletic Association Football Guide, 1941. New York: A.S. Barnes. 1941

3 Camp, Walter. *1893 Spalding's Official Football Guide: Foot-Ball Rules and Referee's Book.* Chicago: A.G. Spalding & Bros. 1893.

4 Christy Walsh Syndicate. Warner, Glenn S. "Pop," 'My Life in Football, Chapter 6.' *Pittsburgh Press*, December 10, 1927.

5 'Armor of Football Men,' *Anaconda Standard (MT),* December 12, 1897.

6 'Armor of Football Men,' *Anaconda Standard (MT),* December 12, 1897.

7 Roosevelt to Walter Camp, March 11, 1895, Walter Camp Papers, Yale University Archives, New Haven, Connecticut as cited in Perkelman, Michael and Vincent Portillo, 'The Brutal Legacy of the Muscular Christianity Movement,' *Counterpunch*, August 9, 2013. Accessed April 3, 2019. https://www.counterpunch.org/2013/08/09/the-brutal-legacy-of-the-muscular-christian-movement/

8 'Athletics at Harvard,' *Sun (New York)*, September 29, 1884.

9 'College Football,' *Sun (New York),* December 12, 1889.

10 'Rules Set Down for Football During the 1898 Season,' *Philadelphia Inquirer*, August 29, 1898.

11 'This Should be Removed Altogether, *Hartford Courant*, November 19, 1897.

12 Lester, Robin. *Stagg's University: The Rise, Decline & Fall of Big-Time Football at Chicago*. Urbana and Chicago: University of Illinois Press. Illini Books edition, 1999. p. 19

13 Davis, Parke H. *Football.* 1911.

14 *Constitution*. Southern Inter-Collegiate Athletic Association. Athens (GA): Stone. 1895.

15 'Football Rules Revised,' Was*hington Times*, August 22, 1898.

16 Elder, Samuel J., 'Change Football Rules,' *Boston Globe*, December 8, 1894.

17 'Athletics at the Colleges,' *Brooklyn Daily Eagle*, April 8, 1900.

18 Bushnell, Edward. 'Football Rules Committee Content to Let Game Alone,' *Pittsburgh Press*, February 12, 1911.

19 Heisman, J.W. 'Minor Colleges are Gaining Football Strength Rapidly,' *Tampa Tribune*, October 20, 1912.

20 Associated Press, 'Coach Wants New Markers,' *Salt Lake Telegram*, November 24, 1945.

21 Brooks, George H. 'How to Play Football Under the New Rules,' *New York Tribune*, September 23, 1906.

22 'New Game Spectacular, But is it Skillful?,' *New York Times*, October 29, 1906.

23 Dooley, Edwin B. 'Michigan Punt Formation Proves Success,' *Boston Globe*, September 28, 1934.

24 *Official Football Rules of the National Collegiate Athletic Association*. New York: American Sports Pub. Co. 1935.

25 Bible, Dana. *Championship Football: A Guide for Player, Coach and Fan*. New York: Prentice-Hall. 1947.

26 Casey, Eddie, 'The Forward Pass Defense,' *Charlotte News*, October 28, 1920.

27 Bible, Dana. *Championship Football: A Guide for Player, Coach and Fan*. New York: Prentice-Hall. 1947.

28 Freedman, Lew. *Illustrated History of the New York Giants*. Chicago: Triumph Books. 2012.

29 Monty, Gridiron Heroes are Rapidly Crowding to the Front – Close Contests Expected,' *Ogden Standard*, September 20, 1913.

30 Official Football Rules of the National Collegiate Athletic Association, 1930, Rule 5, Section 3.

31 Nelson. *Anatomy of a Game*. 1994.

32 'Blaik Knocks Coaches Who Send In All Plays,' *Raleigh Register*, November 17, 1964.

33 Lanham, Sean. *The Pro Football Historical Abstract: A Hardcore Fan's Guide to All-Time Player Rankings*. Lyons Press: Guilford, CT. 2008.

34 Eckersall, Walter, 'Penn State Drill Costs Star Lineman,' *Chicago Tribune*, December 27, 1922.

35 Dreyspool, Joan Flynn, 'Subject: Bud Wilkinson,' *Sports Illustrated*, September 12, 1955. Accessed February 26, 2019. https://www.si.com/vault/1955/09/12/604566/subject-bud-wilkinson

36 Cavanaugh, Maj. Frank W. *Inside Football*. Boston: Small, Maynard and Co. 1919.

37 Slutz, Don. 'Why Referees Wear 'Zebra' Shirts,' *Detroit Free Press*, April 24, 1971.

38 'The Game,' *Evening World (New York)*, November 30, 1893.

39 'A Football-Mad Throng,' *New York Times*, November 25, 1906.

40 United Press, 'Gives Pointers for Deciding Games,' *Vidette-Messenger of Porter County (Valparaiso, IN),* November 28, 1931.

41 Smith, Seymour S., 'Audibles Not Always Play,' *Baltimore Sun*, December 10, 1966.

42 Longman, Jere, 'Shoulder Pads Slim Down in Faster, Sleeker N.F.L.,' *New York Times*, January 30, 2014.

43 Ramirez, Steve, 'Colorado State Tackles Toughest Schedule,' *El Paso Times*, July 24, 1993.

44 Fuson, Wayne, 'Time Out",' *Indianapolis News*, October 1, 1993.

45 Grieve, Curly,' Sports Parade, *San Francisco Examiner*, October 25, 1958.

46 'Red Smith's Views on Sports, Sponsor's Time-Out,' *Honolulu Star-Bulletin*, October 22, 1958.

47 Sharnik, Morton, 'A Rough Day for the Bear,' *Sports Illustrated*, November 26, 1962. Accessed May 24, 2017. https://www.si.com/vault/1962/11/26/592367/a-rough-day-for-the-bear

INTRODUCTION

Nelson, Dave, 'NCAA, NFL Rule Changes Put Emphasis on Player Safety,' *News Journal (Wilmington, DE)*, August 24, 1979. / Oriard, Michael. *In the Beginning Was the Rule*, in Pope, S. W. The New American Sport History: Recent Approaches and Perspectives. Urbana: University of Illinois Press. 1997

CHAPTER 1: THE EMERGENCE OF THE GAME (1869-1905)

Origins of American Football

Bernstein, Mark F. *Football: The Ivy League Origins of an American Obsession.* Philadelphia: University of Pennsylvania Press. 2001. / Camp, Walter. *American Football.* New York: Harper and Brothers. 1891. / Welch, Lewis Sheldon and Walter Camp. *Yale, Her Campus, Class Rooms and Athletics*. Boston: L. C. Page and Co. 1899. / Davis, Parke H. *Football: The American Intercollegiate Game.* New York: Charles Scribner's Sons, 1911. / Revsine, Dave. *The Opening Kickoff, The Tumultuous Birth of A Football Nation.* Guilford, CT: Lyons Press, 2014. /Cunningham, John, 'Why Do Some People Call Football "Soccer"?,' *Britannica.com.* Accessed March 31, 2019. https://www.britannica.com/story/why-do-some-people-call-football-soccer

Eastern Domination

'Historical Scores - Alphabetically by Team, jhowell.net. Accessed June 10, 2019. http://www.jhowell.net/cf/scores/byname.htm / Nelson, David M. *Anatomy of a Game: Football, the Rules, and the Men Who Played the Game.* University of Delaware Press. 1994. / Hill, Dean. *Football Through the Years*. New York: Gridiron Publishing. 1940. / Camp, Walter. *1893 Spalding's Official Football Guide: Foot-Ball Rules and Referee's Book.* Chicago: A.G. Spalding & Bros. 1893. / 'Stagg Approves the New Rules,' *Chicago Tribune*, November 29, 1896.

A Fall Sport

Davis, Parke H. *Football.* 1911. / Bernstein. *Football.* 2001.

CHAPTER 2: THE BALL, THE FIELD, AND STADIUMS (1869-1905)

Brown, Timothy P. *Fields of Friendly Strife: The Doughboys and Sailors of the WWI Rose Bowls*. West Bloomfield, MI: Brown House Publishing. 2017. / Warner, Glenn S., *A Course in Football for Players and Coaches*, Carlisle, PA, 1912.

The Ball

Richard Lindon & Co. Rugby England. Accessed January 22, 2019. http://richardlindon.co.uk / 'Princeton Grad, 89, to See Game with Rutgers; Has Viewed More Than 560 Tilts,' *Central New Jersey Home News*, October 14, 1948.

The Field

Davis, Parke H. *Football.* 1911. / Nelson. *Anatomy of a Game.* 1994. / 'Camp on Football Rules,' *Davenport Morning Star*, June 9, 1903. / 'Camp on Football Rules,' *Record (Hackensack, NJ),* June 10, 1903. / 'What the Changes in Football Rules Mean,' *Minneapolis Journal*, June 25, 1904.

Goal Posts

Davis, Parke H. *Football.* 1911. / 'Goal Posts,' *Decatur Herald*, October 8, 1900.

Stadiums

College football national championship history. *NCAA.com.* Accessed March 21, 2018. https://www.ncaa.com/news/football/article/college-football-national-championship-history / Bernstein, 2001 / Hoover, Herbert. *Memoirs of Herbert Hoover, Years of Adventure, 1874-1920.* New York: Macmillan, 1951. / Harvard Stadium Football History. Accessed February 13, 2018. http://www.gocrimson.com/information/facilities/Harvard_Stadium_Football_History / Hall, Spencer, 'The Future of Football, *SBNation.com*, May 1, 2017. Accessed May 21, 2019. https://www.sbnation.com/a/future-of-football

Safety and Hospitality

Lottman, Michael S. 'Nation's Oldest Stadium Has Colorful Past,' *Harvard Crimson*, November 7, 1959. Accessed August 26, 2018. https://www.thecrimson.com/article/1959/11/7/nations-oldest-stadium-has-colorful-past/ / 'In Huge "Yale Bowl" 61,000 May See A Gridiron Battle, *New York Tribune*, June 15, 1913. / 'Gift by Trustees to Stanford Athletes,' San Francisco Call, January 28, 1907. / 'The Syracuse Stadium,' *New York Tribune*, December 3, 1905.

Reinforced Concrete Stadiums

'New Harvard Stadium Ready for Yale Game,' *Brooklyn Daily Eagle*, November 15, 1903. / Lottman, Michael S. 'Nation's Oldest Stadium Has Colorful Past,' *Harvard Crimson*, November 7, 1959. Accessed August 26, 2018. https://www.thecrimson.com/article/1959/11/7/nations-oldest-stadium-has-colorful-past/ / 'Gift by Trustees to Stanford Athletes,' *San Francisco Call*, January 28, 1907. / 'The Syracuse Stadium,' *New York Tribune*, December 3, 1905.

CHAPTER 3: PLAY AND TECHNIQUES (1869-1905)

'Football Rules of the American Intercollegiate Association,' *Postville Review (IA),* October 8, 1892.

Scrummage and Start of Play

Johnson, Alexander. "The American Game of Foot-Ball," *Century Illustrated Monthly Magazine*, Vol. XXXIV, No. 6, October 1887. / Heisman, J. W. 'Historical Development of American Rugby Football,' *Atlanta Constitution*, October 2, 1904. / Davis, Parke H. *Football.* 1911. / Danzig, Allison. *Oh, How They Played the Game: The Early Days of Football and the Heroes Who Made It Great.* New York: MacMillan. 1971. / Watterson, John Sayles. *College Football: History Spectacle Controversy.* Baltimore: Johns Hopkins University Press. 2009. / Bernstein. *Football.* 2001.

System of Downs

'Vain Work at Foot-Ball,' *New York Times*, November 26, 1880. / 'Football in the Snow,' *New York Sun*, November 26, 1880. / 'Princeton Faces Yale,' *New York Times*, November 25, 1881. / 'Yale and Princeton,' *Buffalo Commercial*, November 26, 1881. / 'Foot-ball Rules May Be Changed,' *Times (Philadelphia, PA)*, December 24, 1899. / 'What the Changes in Football Rules Mean,' *Minneapolis Journal*, June 25, 1904.

On Side and Interference

Warner, Glenn S. "Pop", 'My Life in Football,' *Pittsburgh Press*, December 23, 1927.

Signals and Huddles

'Penn Soldiers Spring Signals For First Time,' *Salt Lake Herald-Republican*, November 21, 1915. / 'Invention of Signals,' *Chicago Eagle*, November 18, 1916. / McGrane, Bert, 'Played Football 45 Years Ago,' *Des Moines Tribune*, January 23, 1931. / 'Yale is Most Advanced,' *Chicago Tribune*, October 24, 1998. / Paolantonio, Sal. *How Football Explains America.* Chicago: Triumph Books. 2015. / The Football Huddle: When Was It First Used? *America Comes Alive.* Accessed June 11, 2019. https://americacomesalive.com/2016/10/05/the-football-huddle-when-was-it-first-used/

Tackling and Forward Progress

'Radical Changes in Style of Play,' *Dispatch (Moline, IL)*, August 8, 1903. / Stagg, Amos Alonzo. '*Football as I Played It,*' The Official National Collegiate Athletic Association Football Guide, 1941. New York: A.S. Barnes. 1941 / 'Chicago is Victor; Leads the West,' *Chicago Tribune*, December 1, 1905.

Mass and Momentum Plays

'The New Football Rules,' *Sun (New York),* April 10, 1887. / Johnson, Alexander. "The American Game of Foot-Ball," *Century Illustrated Monthly Magazine*, Vol. XXXIV, No. 6, October 1887. / 'New Football Rules,' *Boston Globe*, March 11, 1888. / 'Changes in Football Rules,' *Philadelphia Inquirer*, May 13, 1894. / Yost, Fielding H. *Football for Player and Spectator.* Ann Arbor: University Publishing. 1905. / Christy Walsh Syndicate. Warner, Glenn S. "Pop," 'My Life in Football, Chapter 6.' *Pittsburgh Press*, December 10, 1927. / Camp, Walter and Lorin F. Deland. 'How the Game of Football is Now Played,' *Chicago Tribune*, September 20, 1896. / Nelson. *Anatomy of a Game*. 1994. / Heisman, John W., 'Heisman's Hundred in Hall of Fame,' *Philadelphia Inquirer*, December 7, 1928. / 'Camp on Football Rules,' *Record (Hackensack, NJ),* June 10, 1903.

In Touch (Out of Bounds)

'The New Football Rules,' *Sun (New York),* April 10, 1887. / 'Football Rules of the American Intercollegiate Association,' *Postville Review (IA),* October 8, 1892. / 'Chicago's Eleven,' San Francisco Call. December 24, 1894. / Eckersall, Walter. 'Changes Made in Grid Code are Explained', *Great Falls Tribune*, August 30, 1926.

Forward Progress and Maul-ins

Nelson. *Anatomy of a Game*. 1994. / 'Changes in Football Rules,' *Philadelphia Inquirer*, May 13, 1894. / 'Football Rules Changes in West,' *Pittsburgh Daily Post*, January 24, 1898. / 'Chicago is Victor; Leads the West,' *Chicago Tribune*, December 1, 1905. / Davis, Parke H. *Football.* 1911.

Scoring

'Changes in Gridiron Rules Ban Punt After Touchdown to Make Goal Kick Certain,' *Capital Times (Madison, WI)*, March 24, 1920

Kickoff

'A College Game,' *Morning Call (Paterson, NJ)*, April 28, 1887. / 'Flying Wedge,' *Boston Globe*, November 24, 1892. / 'Sporting Gossip,' *Los Angeles Herald*, May 22, 1894. / Christy Walsh Syndicate. Warner, Glenn S. "Pop," 'My Life in Football, Chapter 9,' *Pittsburgh Press*, December 14, 1927. / Georgia Wins Out,' *Atlanta Constitution*, November 27, 1896. / 'Camp Reviews Rules,' *Chicago Tribune*, September 4, 1898. / 'Gridiron Armor to Go,' *Detroit Free Press*, March 31, 1903.

Kick-outs

Davis, Parke H. *Football.* 1911. / Nelson. *Anatomy of a Game*. 1994.

Punting

Des Jardins, Julie. *Walter Camp, Football and the Modern Man.* New York: Oxford University Press. 2015. iBook / 'Will Make No Radical Changes,' *Times (Philadelphia, PA),* February 22, 1898. / United Press International, Winfrey, Lee, 'Football Rules Group Adopts Four Changes,' *Herald (Jasper, IN)*, January 18, 1962.

Fair Catch

'Walter Camp on Football,' *New York Times*, October 30, 1890. / Nelson. *Anatomy of a Game*. 1994.

Onside Kick from Scrimmage

'Harvard's Easy Win,' *Chicago Tribune*, December 1, 1893. / 'The Development of Strategic Foot-Ball,' *Times (Philadelphia)*, September 5, 1897.

Goal from Field (Field Goal)

'How Football is Played,' *Sun (New York),* October 17, 1886. / 'New Gridiron Stars Already Shooting in the Direction of Marks,' *Oregon Daily Journal*, November 12, 1916.

Goal After Touchdown (PATs) and Punt-out

'Inquirer Praised by Dr. Stauffer,' *Philadelphia Inquirer*, February 16, 1898. / Warner, Glenn S. *Football for Players and Coaches,* Carlisle, PA, 1912. / 'Changes in Gridiron Rules Ban Punt After Touchdown to Make Goal Kick Certain,' *Capital Times (Madison, WI)*, March 24, 1920 / 'Radical Changes Made by Football Rules Committee,' *Nebraska State Journal*, March 12, 1922. / Camp, Walter. *Spalding's Official Football Guide for 1915. New York: American Sports Publishing. 1915.*

CHAPTER 5: PLAYER EQUIPMENT (1869-1905)

'Armor of Football Men,' Anaconda Standard (MT), December 12, 1897.

Uniforms

'Yale Again Victorious,' *New York Times*, November 30, 1883. / Cook, Charles Emerson. 'Football in Armour,' *Strand*, March 1897. / 'Armor of Football Men,' *Anaconda Standard (MT),* December 12, 1897. / 'Startling New Football Play,' *World (New York),* October 24, 1897. / 'Yale Again Victorious,' New York Times, November 30, 1883.

Shoes and Cleats

Gallagher, Brendan, 'The Surprising and Unexpected Evolution of Football Cleats,' *complex.com*, September 13, 2012. Accessed October 4, 2019. https://www.complex.com/sneakers/2012/09/the-surprising-and-unexpected-evolution-of-the-football-cleat

Head and Facial Protection

'The Catcher's Mask,' *Wyandotte Gazette (Kansas City, KS),* June 4, 1886. / The Cumnock Nose Mask, *New York Times*, November 2, 1890.

CHAPTER 6: COACHES AND OFFICIALS (1869-1905)

Coaches and Coaching

'Athletics at Harvard,' *Sun (New York)*, September 29, 1884. / Hoover, Herbert. Memoirs of Herbert Hoover, Years of Adventure, 1874-1920. New York: Macmillan, 1951. / 'Training Big Teams,' *Washington Post*, December 3, 1905. / Christy Walsh Syndicate. Warner, Glenn S. "Pop," 'My Life in Football, Chapter 15.' *Pittsburgh Press*, December 21, 1927.

Coaching from the Sideline

'Sons of Eli Fall Before the Tigers,' *New York Times*, November 28, 1899. ./ 'Gridiron Gossip,' *Philadelphia Inquirer*, December 4, 1899. / 'Coaches on Sideline,' *Courier-Journal (Louisville, KY),* March 29, 1900. / 'Football Coach Should be Kept Off Side Lines,' *Philadelphia Inquirer*, December 6, 1908. / 'Football Coaches Barred from Sideline,' *Inter Ocean (Chicago),* February 8, 1914. / Christy Walsh Syndicate. Warner, Glenn S. "Pop," 'My Life in Football, Chapter 12,' *Pittsburgh Press*, December 17, 1927. / Christy Walsh Syndicate. Warner, Glenn S. "Pop," 'My Forty Years in Football, Chapter 34.' *Pittsburgh Press*, January 12, 1928.

Substitutions and Pace of Play

'Vain Work at Foot-Ball,' *New York Times*, November 26, 1880. / 'Coaches on Sideline,' *Courier-Journal (Louisville, KY),* March 29, 1900.

Tackling Dummies

'Between the Goals,' *Waterloo Courier (IA),* October 30, 1896

Charging Machines and Other Barbarities

'Practice at Cornell,' *New York Tribune*, November 25, 1900. / 'Things Talked in World of Sports,' *Star-Gazette (Elmira, NY),* November 7, 1902. / "Charging Machine" to Teach United Action in Football, *Caldwell Tribune (Caldwell, ID),* February 6, 1904. / 'Size Up of the Year', *Courier-Journal (Louisville, KY)*, September 18, 1904. / 'The Charging Machine at Shadyside Academy', *Pittsburgh Weekly Gazette*, September 26, 1904. / 'New Device to Develop Harvard Line,' *Anaconda Standard (Anaconda, MT),* October 8, 1911.

Film Study

Solnit, Rebecca. River of Shadows: *Eadweard Muybridge and the Technological Wild West*. New York: Penguin. 2003. iBook. / Camp, Walter and Lorin F. Leland. *Football*. Boston: Houghton, Mifflin. 1896. / 'Photos Aid in Coaching,' *Topeka State Journal*, September 20, 1905. / Carpenter, Kenneth J. 'The Nobel Prize and the Discovery of Vitamins.'

Accessed on March 26, 2018. https://www.nobelprize.org/nobel_prizes/themes/medicine/carpenter/ / 'College Football,' *Sun (New York),* December 12, 1889. / 'A Training Table,' *San Francisco Chronicle*, October 21, 1893.

Training Table and Diet

'A Training Table,' *San Francisco Chronicle*, October 21, 1893. / 'Football Eating,' *Lawrence Daily Gazette (KS)*, November 16, 1894. / 'Training the Giants,' *Chicago Tribune*, November 18, 1894. / 'Penn's Team East for 19 Cents, Oregon's Rivals Dieteticians,' *Oregon Daily Journal (Portland, OR)*, December 10, 1916. / Carpenter, Kenneth J. 'The Nobel Prize and the Discovery of Vitamins.' Accessed on March 26, 2018. https://www.nobelprize.org/nobel_prizes/themes/medicine/carpenter/

Officials

Totten, Charles Adiel Lewis. Laws of Athletics and General Rules. San Francisco, The Presidio. 1881. / Davis, Parke H. *Football.* 1911. / 'Football,' *New York Daily Herald*, November 17, 1878. / Johnson, Alexander. "The American Game of Foot-Ball," *Century Illustrated Monthly Magazine*, Vol. XXXIV, No. 6, October 1887.

The Clock

'Changes in Football Rules,' *Philadelphia Inquirer*, May 13, 1894. / Camp, Walter (Ed.). *Spalding's Official Foot Ball Guide for 1906.* New York: American Sports Publishing. 1906. / Davis, Parke H. *Football.* 1911

Whistles and Horns

'*The First Police Whistle*,' Accessed on March 11, 2018. https://www.acmewhistles.co.uk/since-1870/the-first-whistle / 'Yost Machine is at Work Again,' *St. Louis Post-Dispatch*, November 1, 1908.

CHAPTER 6: OFF THE FIELD (1869-1905)

Cheerleaders

'Yale Beats Harvard,' *Star-Gazette (New York),* June 19, 1894. / 'The Kiskimintas Club Celebration at Princeton College,' *Indian Democrat (Indiana, PA)*, October 31, 1895. / 'Sporting Chat of All Kinds,' *Times (Philadelphia)*, March 20, 1896. / 'Tigers are in Good Shape,' *Times (Philadelphia)*, November 17, 1897. / 'Columbia is Victorious,' *New York Times*, November 7, 1900.

Fans

'Fans Going En Masse,' *Minneapolis Journal*, November 18, 1904. / 'Sport at Princeton,' *Seattle Post-Intelligencer*, November 16, 1890. / 'Stanford's Big Football Rally,' *San Francisco Call*, November 18, 1898. / 'Rah Carolina,' *Daily Tar Heel*, November 7, 1900.

All America Teams

Bryan, Henry, 'The All-America Team,' *College Football Historical Society*, November 1998. / 'Plans All America Eleven,' *Sun (Leavenworth, KS),* December 31, 1887. / Bryan, Henry, 'The All-America Team,' *College Football Historical Society*, November 1998. / 'Princeton Football All-Americans.' Accessed on May 2, 2018. http://etcweb.princeton.edu/CampusWWW/Companion/football_allamericans.html

Management and Control

Chandler, Jr., Alfred D. *The Visible Hand: The Managerial Revolution in American Business*. Cambridge: Harvard University Press. 1977.

Commercialization of Football

'Harvard-Yale Boat Race turns 150,' *Harvard Magazine*, May-June 2002. Accessed July 30, 2018. https://harvardmagazine.com/2002/05/harvard-yale-boat-race-t.html

Amateurism and Eligibility

'Good for Varsity,' *Wheeling Democrat Intelligencer*, October 16, 1896. / 'Penn's Victorious Career Checked,' *Philadelphia Inquirer*, October 25, 1896.

Conferences

'Inter-Collegiate Football,' *Chicago Tribune*, Jun 16, 1892. / 'Given the Pennant, *Saint Paul Globe*, December 24, 1892. / 'A Foot-Ball Association,' *Baltimore Sun*, April 5, 1894. / *Constitution*. Southern Inter-Collegiate Athletic Association. Athens (GA): Stone. 1895. / 'The Grand Stand,' *Times-Democrat (New Orleans)*, April 13, 1895.

Racial Integration

Demas, Lane. *Integrating the Gridiron: Black Civil Rights and American College Football*. New Brunswick: Rutgers University Press. 2011. / 'Black Sporting Experience at Dartmouth,' Accessed October 4, 2019. https://journeys.dartmouth.edu/blacksportingexperience/matthew-bullock-04/ / 'Washington Ready for Lake Forest,' *St. Louis Republic*, October 25, 1901. / 'Washington Wins From Lake Forest,' *St. Louis Republic*, October 27, 1901. / 'Middies May Object to Harvard's Negro Player,' *Washington Times*, December 18, 1902. / 'Negro Player Caused Trouble,' *Buffalo Enquirer*, April 20, 1903. / 'No Negro Player,' *Dayton Daily News*, October 9, 1903. / 'Football Color Line,' *Evening Journal (Wilmington, DE)*, November 11, 1903. / 'Color Line in Football,' *Anaconda Standard (MT)*, December 3, 1904. / 'Knocked Out Negro Player,' *Gazette (Montreal, QC)*, November 14, 1905.

Rules Committee and the Looming Crisis

'College Football,' *Philadelphia Inquirer*, November 17, 1887. / 'Change in Football Rules,' *Brooklyn Daily Eagle*, February 26, 1900. / 'Foot-ball Rules May Be Changed,' *Times (Philadelphia, PA)*, December 24, 1899. / 'Football Suggestions,' *Pittsburgh Press*, December 24, 1894.

CHAPTER 7: FOOTBALL CRISIS AND ASCENDANCY (1906-1959)

Watterson, John Sayles. The Football Crisis of 1909-1910, The Response of the Eastern "Big Three." *Journal of Sports History*. Spring 1981. / 'Growing Interest in Game in This Community, *St. Louis Post-Dispatch*, October 30, 1898. / 'Eli Shatters Crimson Idols,' *Chicago Tribune*, November 25, 1900. / 'Pigskin's Fare Hangs on Rules,' *Los Angeles Times*, April 3, 1910.

The Test Game

'New Rules Are Not a Decided Success,' *Wichita Daily Eagle*, December 26, 1905. / 'It Will Not Do,' *Topeka State Journal*, December 26, 1905. / Camp, Walter (Ed.). *Spalding's Official Foot Ball Guide for 1906*. New York: American Sports Publishing. 1906. (See guides for 1908, 1909, 1910, and 1912 as well.) / 'New Football Rules by New Rules Committee,' *New York Times*, January 27, 1907. / 'New Football Rules are Made,' *Altoona Tribune*, May 3, 1910. / 'Retain the Pass,' *Butte Miner,* January 13, 1912. / Revision of Football Rules, *The Cincinnati Enquirer,* February 3, 1912. / 'Football Rules Shot to Pieces by Committee,' *Baltimore Sun*, February 4, 1912. / United States Census Bureau.

History, Urban and Rural Area. Accessed November 2, 2017. https://www.census.gov/history/www/programs/geography/urban_and_rural_areas.html

Onside Kick From Scrimmage

'Harvard's Easy Win,' *Chicago Tribune*, December 1, 1893. /'Football Rules Hamper Attack,' *Courier-Journal (Louisville, KY)*, June 3, 1906. / 'Quarterback Kick is Sure to be Prominent,' *Pittsburgh Press*, September 30, 1906. / Foster, John B., 'Forward Pass and Onside Kick the Greatest Ground Gainers,' *Evening Star (Washington, D.C.)*, October 18, 1908. / 'Onside Kick Has Come On Slowly,' *Evening Statesman (Walla Walla, WA)*, November 3, 1909. / 'Onside Kick in Football,' *Jackson Daily News (MS)*, September 9, 1910. / Camp, Walter (Ed.). *Spalding's Official Foot Ball Guide for 1912*. New York: American Sports Publishing. 1912. / 'Football Rules Shot to Pieces by Committee,' *Baltimore Sun*, February 4, 1912. / 'New Rule for Onside Kick is Being Studied,' *Anaconda Standard (MT)*, October 5, 1913. / Banks, M.B., 'Modern Football, No. 40 (The Onside Kick), *Des Moines Register*, November 23, 1920. / Associated Press, 'One Vital Grid Change Is Made,' *Baltimore Sun*, March 11, 1923. / 2018 CFL Rule Book: The Official Playing Rules of the Canadian Football League. Toronto: Canadian Football League. 2018.

CHAPTER 8: THE BALL, THE FIELD, AND STADIUMS (1906-1959)

The Ball

'Perfects New Inverted Valve,' Battle Creek Enquirer, May 5 1925. / Tice, Joyce M. 'It Happened One Night,' Tri-Counties Genealogy & History. Accessed May 25, 2018. http://www.joycetice.com/articles/1892foot.htm / Ross, Alan, 'The White, Night Football,' *Coffin Corner*, Vol. 21, No. 2, 1999. / Buechner, Frank A. U.S. Patent No. 1560657A. Washington, D.C.: United States Patent Office. / Ross, Alan, 'The White, Night Football,' *Coffin Corner*, Vol. 21, No. 2, 1999. / 'New Wrinkle,' *Buffalo Enquirer*, November 17, 1922 / 'Football at Night to be Played in Cincinnati,' *Dayton Daily News*, January 28, 1923. / 'They're Playing Football at Night Now So the Grid Stars Can Shine,' *Republic (Columbus, IN)*, October 3, 1923. / 'Corvallis Plays Washington Next, All Teams Busy,' *Medford Mail Tribune (OR)*, October 2, 1924. / McDonough, John and Paul T. Owens. *Don't Hit Him, He's Dead*. Millbrae, CA: Celestial Arts. 1978.

55-Yard Line and End Line

'Football Rules Shot to Pieces by Committee,' *Baltimore Sun*, February 4, 1912. / Eckersall, Walter, 'Better Football Under New Code,' *Chicago Tribune*, February 5, 1912. / Nelson. *Anatomy of a Game*. 1994.

Goal Posts

'Sportoscope,' *Stevens Point Daily Journal (WI)*, October 6, 1927. / Associated Press, 'Grid Teams Have New Grid Method,' *Ogden Standard-Examiner*, October 26, 1927. / 'Moving Posts Confused Fans,' *Baltimore Sun*, December 6, 1927.

Hash Marks and Lockney Lines

'Walkaway for Iowa,' *Inter Ocean (Chicago)*, November 4, 1900. / Klein, Christopher. 'The Bizarre History of the NFL's First Title Game,' *History.com*, January 29, 2015. Accessed February 9, 2018. http://www.history.com/news/the-bizarre-history-of-the-nfls-first-title-game / 'Bernie Bierman to Ask Big Ten Sideline Rule,' *Star Tribune (Minneapolis)*, January 21, 1933. / 'Football Sideline Rule Adopted, and Clipping Penalty Reduced,' *Star Tribune (Minneapolis)*, February 13, 1933. / 'To Experiment with Novel Football Field Layout Plan Tonight,' *Waukesha Daily Freeman*, September 17, 1954. / 'Unique Grid Layout at Waukesha Praised,' *Waukesha Freeman*, September 19, 1954. / 'Lockney's 'Lines' Get More Favorable Comments; Big Ten May Adopt Unique Marking System,' *Waukesha Freeman*,

October 30, 1954. / 'Memorial Has Largest Football Turnout Ever,' *Waukesha Freeman*, August 31, 1955. / 'Rules Confab Uneventful,' *Long Beach Independent*, January 14, 1956. / 'Marking System May be Seen on TV,' *Waukesha Freeman*, October 8, 1954. /. 'Lockney's 'Lines' Get More Favorable Comments; Big Ten May Adopt Unique Marking System,' *Waukesha Freeman*, October 30, 1954./ Christenson, Dave, 'Sport Chatter,' *Wausau Daily Herald,* September 30, 1955. / "Tech Backers Optimistic On Eve of Announcement,' *Abilene Reporter-News*, December 10, 1955. / 'College Football Rules to Remain As Is,' *Lake Charles American-Press (LA)*, January 15, 1956. / Personal communication. Thomas Lockney. April 1, 2019.

Stadiums

Schmidt, Raymond. *Shaping College Football: The Transformation of an American Sport, 1919-1930*. Syracuse: Syracuse University Press. 2007. / New Deal Category: Stadiums. *The Living New Deal*. Accessed May 24, 2018. https://livingnewdeal.org/new-deal-categories/parks-and-recreation/stadiums/

Loudspeaker Systems

'At the Coliseum,' *Los Angeles Times*, November 22, 1924. / 'Loud Speaker to Help Illini Fans,' *Journal Gazette (Mattoon, IL*), April 16, 1926.

Scoreboards

'The Season's Wind-Up,' *Times (Philadelphia),* November 24, 1892. / 'Pitt Second Line Outscores First,' *Pittsburgh Daily*, October 8, 1916. / 'Yale an Easy Winner Over Princeton Team,' *Brooklyn Daily Eagle*, November 14, 1909. / 'Stadium's Little Man in the Red Sweater Tells of his Signal System,' *Boston Globe*, October 15, 1926. / 'The Pacific Telephone and Telegraph Company,' *Plumas Independent (Quincy, CA),* November 17, 1927. / Associated Press, 'Clock, Crowd to Feature Opening Wisconsin Game,' *Chippewa Herald-Telegram (Chippewa Falls, WI)*, September 28, 1927. / 'Huge Electric Clock Tells Time for Football Games at Harvard,' *Pittson Gazette (PA)*, December 6, 1930. / 'Electric Scoreboard Clocks at California,' *Honolulu Star-Bulletin*, September 8, *1931.*

Field Markers

Associated Press, 'S.D. Judge Invents New Grid Yardage Marker,' *Star Tribune (Minneapolis)*, April 5, 1931. / Associated Press, 'Madigan Rigs Up Only New Football Play,' *Daily Press (Newport News, VA)*, November 21, 1939.

Amenities

Tutka, Patrick Michael. *An Ideal-Type through Innovation Diffusion, Recording the Construction History of Football Stadiums in the National Collegiate Athletic Association Division I Football Subdivision (FBS),* Doctoral Dissertation. Louisiana State University. 2016. / Seifried, Chad S. *An Analysis of the American Outdoor Sport Facility: Developing an Ideal Type on the Evolution of Professional Baseball and Football Structures*. Doctoral Dissertation. Ohio State University. 2005.

CH. 9: PLAY AND TECHNIQUES (1906-1959)

Forward Passing Techniques

Cochems, Edward B. 'Passing the Ball,' *Janesville Daily Gazette*, October 20, 1907. / 'Cornell Could Not Score on Weak Team,' *Minneapolis Journal*, September 30, 1906. / 'Smaller Ball Will give All Elevens Chance at Forward Pass,' *St. Louis Globe-Democrat*, December 6, 1906. / Morrison, Jim, The Early History of Football's Forward Pass, *Smithsonian*, December 28, 2010.

Single Wing

Warner, Glenn S. *A Course in Football for Players and Coaches.* Carlisle, PA. 1912. / United Press International. 'UCLA to Unveil Tailback,' *Capital Journal (Salem, OR)*, November 4, 1958. / Layden, Tim. *Blood, Sweat and Chalk: The Ultimate Football Playbook: How The Great Coaches Built Today's Game.* New York: Sports Illustrated Books. 2001.

Notre Dame Box

Warner, Glenn S.,' Heisman Is Likely To Discard It Soon,' *Pittsburgh Press*, November 1, 1919. / Rockne, Knute, 'Notre Dame System Credited to A.A. Stagg,' *Pittsburgh Press*, November 29, 1929. / Layden, Tim. *Blood, Sweat and Chalk: The Ultimate Football Playbook: How The Great Coaches Built Today's Game.* New York: Sports Illustrated Books. 2001. / Crist, John, 'Chalk Talk: The Notre Dame Box,' *247Sports*, June 28, 2007. Accessed June 10, 2019. https://247sports.com/nfl/chicago-bears/Article/Chalk-Talk-the-Notre-Dame-Box-104429461 / Cristl, Cliff, 'Lambeau's Notre Dame Box Offense Not a Simple Scheme,' *packers.com*, March 17, 2016. Accessed June 10, 2019. https://www.packers.com/news/lambeau-s-notre-dame-box-offense-not-a-simple-scheme-16940152

Signals and Huddles

"Versatile Attack Prominent in West,' *Washington Post*, November 20, 1921. / "Tea Party" was Zuppke's Invention, *Evening Public Ledger (Philadelphia),* October 17, 1922. / 'Rutgers Discards Huddle,' *Evening Public Ledger (Philadelphia),* November 6, 1922. / 'Huddle System is Fad, Declares Officials,' *Baltimore Sun*, October 31, 1924 / ''Huddle System,' Why It Is Used,' *Burlington Free Press (VT)*, November 9, 1926. / 'Midwest Coaches Please with Rule Changes, ' *Journal Times (Racine, WI),* March 8, 1927. ' 'Grid Mentors Discuss Rules, *Detroit Free Press*, September 11, 1927. / 'Football Rules Committee to Curb Practice of Beating Time on the Shift, *Sun (Baltimore),* March 26, 1930. / Rasmussen, Harry, 'Rule Changes Make Faster, Safer Game,' *Morning Post (Camden, NJ)*, September 13, 1939. / Reed, Herbert. *Football for Public and Player.* New York: Frederic A. Stokes. 1913. / 'New Game Spectacular, But is it Skillful?,' *New York Times*, October 29, 1906. / 'Harvard Lucky to Win,' *New York Times*, October 29, 1906.

Early Passing

Football Bowl Subdivision Records. Indianapolis: National Collegiate Athletic Association. 2017. / 'Statistics of Game,' *Oakland Tribune*, November 20, 1927. / Roberts, Jerry. *Pass Receiving in Early Professional Football: A History to 1960.* Jefferson, NC: McFarland. 2016. / Wright, Theon, 'Brawn and Bulk Decide Battle of Year,' *Oakland Tribune*, November 20, 1927. / 'Detailed Story of How the Warfare Raged at Palo Alto,' *Oakland Tribune*, November 20, 1927. / '2018 NFL Passing,' *Pro Football Reference.* Accessed June 10, 2019. https://www.pro-football-reference.com/years/2018/passing.htm / Murray, Peg, 'Football Fans Should Keep Their Eyes On These Babies; Early Games Give Evidence They're All-American Prospects,' *Courier (Waterloo, IA)*, October 17, 1928. / Carroll, Bob, 'Bronco Nagurski,' *Coffin Corner*, Vol. 4, No. 4, 1982. Accessed June 10, 2019. http://profootballresearchers.com/archives/Website_Files/Coffin_Corner/04-04-094.pdf / Blake, Randall W. 'Jump Pass Seen By Collegians as a Real Boon To Offensive Football,' *Akron Beacon*, September 3, 1945. / 'Football ABC's,' *Arizona Daily Star*, November 16, 1931. / Associated Press, 'Slow Whistle Out Under Gridiron Rules for '36,' *Montana Standard (Butte)*, February 18, 1936. / 'Shovels,' *Cincinnati Enquirer*, January 4, 1939. / Eckersall, Walter. 'Changes Made in Grid Code are Explained', *Great Falls Tribune*, August 30, 1926. / Eckersall, Walter, 'Onside Kick as Offense Weapon,' *Honolulu Advertiser*, October 17, 1926. / Associated Press. 'Football Rules Committee Lifts Barriers to Passes,' *Evening Herald (Klamath Falls, OR)*, February 12, 1934.

Screen Play

'Shovels,' *Cincinnati Enquirer*, January 4, 1939. / Haughton, Percy D. *Football, and How to Watch It*. Boston: Marshall Jones. 1922.

Roughing the Passer

'Radical Changes in Style of Play,' *Dispatch (Moline, IL)*, August 8, 1903. / Okeson, W. R. (Ed.) *1933 Official Intercollegiate Football Guide*, New York: American Sports Publishing. 1933. / Nelson, David M., 'The Rule Book,' *La Crosse Tribune*, August 24, 1979.

Short Punt Formation

Warner, Glenn S., 'How New Rules Change Football,' *Nebraska State Journal (Lincoln)*, October 9, 1927. / Haymore, Jeremy, 'A Short Punt Double Feature,' *Fear the Wing*, May 23, 2017. Accessed October 19, 2018. https://www.fearthewing.com/short-punt/

Modern T Formation

'Glen Warner, University of Pittsburgh Coach, Condemns Forward Pass,' *Pittsburgh Press*, October 26, 1916. / 'Kickoff and Passing Rules Revamped for College Play,' *Times Recorder (Zanesville, OH)*, April 3, 1945. / Football Bowl Subdivision Records, *National Collegiate Athletic Association*, 2017. / 'Scoring Summary League Averages Per Team Game,' *Pro Football Reference*. Accessed May 29, 2019. https://www.pro-football-reference.com/years/NFL/scoring.htm

Split T

Wright, Bart. *Football Revolution: The Rise of the Spread Offense and How It Transformed College Football*. Lincoln: University of Nebraska Press. 2013. / Faurot, Don. *Football: Secrets of the "Split T" Formation*. New York: Prentice Hall. 1950.

Kicking

Hamilion, H.C., 'Make Changes in Football Rules,' *Wisconsin State Journal (Madison)*, March 18, 1917. / 'Yost Interprets Football Rules,' *News-Palladium (Benton Harbor, MI)*, September 23, 1924. / Klosinski, Emil. 'Move over Gipp, Thorpe... make room for Bowser!,' *Coffin Corner*, Vol. 14, No. 4, 1992.

Kickoff

'Yost Interprets Football Rules,' *News-Palladium (Benton Harbor, MI)*, September 23, 1924. / *Official Collegiate Football Record Book*. New York: National Collegiate Athletic Bureau. 1959.

Field Goals

Taylor, James F. 'The Five-Man Kick – Football's Newest Play,' *Times (Shreveport, LA)*, December 3, 1916. / O'Neill, Harold E. 'Sporting Topics,' *Central New Jersey News (New Brunswick)*, October 27, 1917. / 'The Multiple Kick,' *Tampa Times*, October 24, 1923.

Try for Goal After Touchdown (PAT)

'Changes in Gridiron Rules Ban Punt After Touchdown to Make Goal Kick Certain,' *Capital Times (Madison, WI)*, March 24, 1920 / 'Touchdown Goal is Taken from Game,' *New York Times*, March 12, 1922. / Bailey, Spencer, 'Football Rule Change Poses Dilemma for Coaches,' *Tallahassee Democrat*, January 13, 1958. / Menton, Paul, 'Football Gets a One-Point Safety,' *Evening Sun (Baltimore, MD)*, February 5, 1958.

Safety

'No Limitation is Put on Forward Pass,' *New York Herald*, March 13, 1921. / Lamb, Al, 'Observed from Side Line and Bleachers,' *Press and Sun-Bulletin (Binghamton, NY)*, March 24, 1926.

Touchbacks and Kick-outs

'14 Changes to Football Rules,' *York Daily (PA),* September 30, 1914. / Associated Press. 'Football Rules Committee Lifts Barriers to Passes,' *Evening Herald (Klamath Falls, OR)*, February 12, 1934. / Associated Press. 'Two Rule Changes Aid Football Offenses, *Arizona Daily Star*, January 4, 1938.

Defensive Positions

Hannun, Max E. 'They are Versatile,' *Pittsburgh Press*, September 5, 1929.

Linebackers and Blitzing

Easton, Jerry, 'Ettinger Good Grid Prospector,' *Arizona Republic (Phoenix, AZ)*, June 2, 1965. / AP Wirephoto, 'Nice Floor Play,' *Lincoln Journal Star*, January 3, 1947. / United Press, 'Cards, Bears and Eagles Monopolize Star Team of National Grid League,' *Star Gazette (Elmira, NY)*, November 10, 1948.

New York Giants Defense

Yowell, Keith, '1950: Giants "Umbrella" Defense Shuts Down the Browns,' *Today in Pro Football History*, October 10, 2010. Accessed April 23, 2019. https://fs64sports.blogspot.com/2010/10/1950-giants-umbrella-defense-shuts-down.html / Zimmer, Ben, 'How Sam, Mike, and Will Became Football Positions,' *Boston Globe*, September 9, 2012. Accessed November 8, 2018. https://www.bostonglobe.com/ideas/2012/09/08/how-sam-mike-and-will-became-football-positions/URHq2XoAdviKJYZLQfbKNK/story.html / Geyer, Jerry, 'Geyerscope,' *Los Angeles Times*, November 22, 1957. / 'The Roster,' *Stevens Point Journal (WI),* July 18, 1955.

CHAPTER 10; PLAYER EQUIPMENT (1906-1959)

Clendening, M.D., Logan, 'Diet and Health, *Courier-News (Bridgewater, NJ)*, October 8, 1936. / Alderton, George, ''Man in the Iron Mask' has Coaches in Lather,' *Lansing State Journal*,' September 10, 1939. / Associated Press, 'Hard Football Helmets Assailed,' *Bee (Danville, VA),* December 17, 1947. / Associated Press. 'Prep Grid Injuries Suggest Return of Nose Guards,' *Times Herald (Port Huron, MI),* November 13, 1949.

Legs

Associated Press, 'Boilermakers Entrain Today,' *Star Press (Muncie, IN)*, September 30, 1926. / The Debris, 1927. West Lafayette (IN): Purdue University Class of 1927. / 'Cardinals to Don Silk Grid Pants,' *Oakland Tribune*, December 11, 1926. / 1928 Fall 1929 Winter Rawlings Football and Basketball Equipment Catalog / Snider, Steve, 'Rules Eliminate 'Tricks' in Modern Football Equipment,' *Greenville News (SC)*, January 8, 1946. / North, Jack, 'Grinnell and Ripon to Clash Saturday,' *Des Moines Tribune*, November 5, 1941. / Cromie, Robert, 'Why Athletes Can't Grow Too Big for Their Pants,' *Chicago Tribune*, March 8, 1951.

Head Harnesses and Helmets

American Football Helmet Classification Chart. *Antique Football*. Accessed June 9, 2019. http://www.antiquefootball.com/helmet_identification.htm / 'Getting in Gear,' *Tamp Bay Times (St. Petersburg, FL)*, October 20, 1996. / *Review of Department of Defense Test Protocols for Combat Helmets*. Washington, D.C.: National Academies Press. 2014. / Official Football Rules of the National Collegiate Athletic Association, 1930, Rule 5, Section 3. / 'Football Rules Committee to Curb Practice of Beating Time on the Shift, *Sun (Baltimore),* March 26, 1930. / 'Harvard Bans Plastic Helmets,' *Kingston Daily Freeman (NY),* November 10, 1948.

Uniform Numbers

'Stagg Favors a Changed System,' *Pittsburgh Press*, February 18, 1905. / 'Will Number the Football Players,' *Des Moines Register*, November 16, 1905. / 'Ames Defeats Drake in Great Battle,' *Des Moines Register*, December 1, 1905. / 'Eastern Football Gossip,' *Star Tribune (Minneapolis)*, September 29, 1907. / 'Comment on Football,' N*ew York Tribune*, November 30, 1908. /'Would Number Gridiron Men,' *Buffalo Commercial*, January 17, 1908. / 'Easy to Tell Indians from Pitt Players,' *Pittsburgh Press*, November 12, 1908. / 'Stagg Offers More Changes, *Chicago Tribune*, November 19, 1909. / 'Work Ahead for Football Coaches,' *Buffalo Evening News*, September 9, 1911. / 1911 Harvard-Dartmouth Scorecard / 'Numbering Football Men Would Help Very Little,' *Brooklyn Daily Eagle*, November 5, 1913. / 'Numbering Players is Popular Idea,' I*thaca Journal,* November 2, 1914. / 'Smart Football Won Game for Johnnies,' *Philadelphia Inquirer*, November 28, 1922. / Brown, Norman E., 'Removed for the Last Time,' *Atlanta Constitution*, November 22, 1925.

Friction Strips

'North Scores on Fumble by South Fullback,' *Evening Sun (Baltimore),* December 10, 1932. / Associated Press, 'Slow Whistle Out Under Gridiron Rules for '36,' *Montana Standard (Butte)*, February 18, 1936. / 'The UCLA football uniforms of 1934 — big changes . . .,' *Southern Branch*, June 11, 2018. Accessed April 3, 2019. https://thesouthernbranch.wordpress.com/2018/06/11/the-ucla-football-uniforms-of-1934-big-changes/

Standard Numbering Systems

'Lehigh Captain Plays Better with Odd Number, ' *Courier-News (Bridgewater, NJ)*, November 14, 1929. / Feder, Sid, 'Football Rules Group May Decide to Widen Goals Posts,' *Standard-Sentinel (Hazleton, PA)*, December 30, 1940. / Bible, Dana. *Championship Football: A Guide for Player, Coach and Fan*. New York: Prentice-Hall. 1947. / Snider, Steve, 'LSU to Glorify Offensive Lineman By Using Identifying Letters with Numbers,' *Arizona Republic (Phoenix, AZ)*, August 27, 1952. / NEA, 'New System Simplifies Football Identification,' *Daily Telegram (Eau Claire, WI)*, September 25, 1952. / Associated Press, Identification System to Help Fans, *Star-Herald (Kosciuscko, MS)*, September 25, 1952. / 'Signs of Grid Times,' *Lancaster Eagle-Gazette (OH),* November 1, 1952. / Lukas, Paul, 'You Sunk My Battleship!,' *UniWatch.com*, July 21, 2014. Access September 5, 2018. https://uni-watch.com/2014/07/21/several-college-football-teams-wore-letters-with-their-uniform-numbers/

White Road Uniforms

'Washburn at IT,' *Topeka State Journal*, September 24, 1910. / 'Stanford Rooters Thought Stanford Lost, Says Warner,' *Star Tribune (Minneapolis),* October 28, 1924. / 'Oregon Aggies to Wear White Jerseys in Stanford Game,' *New-Review (Roseburg, OR),* October 23, 1925. / 'Suggest Change in Grid Suits,' *St. Cloud Times*, November 6, 1929. / 'Favor Standard Attire,' *Tampa Tribune*, December 11, 1929. / 1867-1939 Michigan Uniform Timeline. *mvictors.com*. Accessed January 18, 2019. http://mvictors.com/1867-1939-michigan-uniform-timeline/

Spotter Numbers

Associated Press, Golden, Julies, 'Bug-Eyed Football Fan Gets Break With Numbers,' *Chillicothe Gazette*, October 28, 1954. / 'Spotter Numbers for Cotton Bowl,' *Albuquerque Journal*, January 1, 1958. / Solomon, Joe, 'NCAA Uniform Numbers Getting Harder to Read, Causing Problems,' *cbssports.com*, March 4, 2015. Accessed January 23,

2019. https://www.cbssports.com/college-football/news/ncaa-uniform-numbers-getting-harder-to-read-causing-problems/

TV Numbers

Howell, Fritz, 'Big Ten Football Officials Granted Pay Boost; Death, Disability Insurance Also Approved,' *Palladium-Item (Richmond, IN)*, May 26, 1955. / United Press Telephoto, 'Miami Beached by the Wrecks,' *St. Louis Post-Dispatch*, September 18, 1955. / Associated Press, 'Tech's Quick Strikes Clobber Miami, 14-6,' *Greenville News (SC)*, September 18, 1955. / 'Morgantown,' *St. Cloud Times*, October 18, 1955. / AP Photofax, 'And Down You Go, Gifford,' *Greenville News (SC)*, December 16, 1956. / Taylor, Sec, 'Sittin' In With the Athletes,' *Des Moines Register*, September 1, 1957. / 'Alabama, 1957-71 Crimson Tide,' Helmet Hut. Accessed November 6, 2018. http://www.helmethut.com/College/Alabama/ALUXUA5771.html

Helmet Logos

'Football Notes,' *Boston Globe*, October 15, 1914. / 'Giants From Coast Rip Up Aggies Line and Win, 20 to 0,' *Detroit Free Press*, October 31, 1915. / 'Black History Month: Football Player Had Higher Calling Than Just 'Phys Ed'.' From Woody's Couch, February 27, 2013. Accessed April 2, 2019. https://library.osu.edu/blogs/archives/category/football/page/3/ / 'Carter's Long Run Starts Purdue On Way to Victory Over Tartans,' *Indianapolis Star*, November 5, 1933. / Luka, Paul, 'Winging It: Helmet History Reconsidered' *Uni Watch*, December 29, 2019. Accessed June 9, 2019. https://uni-watch.com/2010/12/29/winging-it-helmet-history-reconsidered/ / Mandernach, Mark, 'Rembrandt of the Rams,' *Sports Illustrated*, September 4, 1994. Accessed June 9, 2019. https://www.si.com/vault/1994/09/05/131946/rembrandt-of-the-rams-fred-gehrke-got-out-his-brushes-and-changed-helmets-forever / Cushman, Tom, 'Gehrke Designed Broncos' Turnaround,' *Philadelphia Daily News*, December 21, 1977.

Mouth Guards

Priyadarshani G. Pawar, Mukesh M. Suryawanshi, Ashishkumar K. Patil, Pravin S. Purnale, and Fareedi Mukram Ali. "Importance of Mouth Guards in Sports: A Review". Journal of Evolution of Medical and Dental Sciences 2013; Vol. 2, Issue 46, November 18; Page: 8903-8908. / Nelson. *Anatomy of a Game*. 1994.

Socks

Thorn, John, 'Old News in Baseball, No9,' Our Game, June 26, 2015. Accessed April 9, 2019. https://ourgame.mlblogs.com/old-news-in-baseball-9-6f8037f0954c / Dyer, Bravin, 'Crimson Fans Rely on Great Backfield Star,' *Los Angeles Times*, December 27, 1925. / 'Alabama Grid Men Work Out,' *Los Angeles Times*, December 28, 1925. / Associated Press, Fullerton, Jr., Hugh, 'Newsreel of Sports in America, *Oshkosh Northwestern (WI)*, April 10, 1945. / Associated Press, Fullerton, Jr., Hugh, 'Newsreel of Sports in America,' *Oshkosh Northwestern (WI)*, July 24, 1947. / Football Bowl Subdivision Records, National Collegiate Athletic Association, 2017.

Knee Pads

'Harry Auckland on Trail of Players Says Ottawa's Line Prospects Good,' *Ottawa Journal*, September 11, 1919. / 'Specially Made Uniforms to be Issued Jackets Eleven,' *Atlanta Constitution*, March 13, 1924. / Bentley, John, 'I May Be Wrong,' *Lincoln Journal Star*, October 24, 1934.

CHAPTER 11: COACHES, OFFICIALS, AND OTHERS (1906-1959)

Brown. *Fields of Friendly Strife*. 2017. / Christy Walsh Syndicate. Warner, Glenn S. "Pop," My Forty Years in Football, Chapter 51,' *Pittsburgh Press*, February 1, 1928. / '1925: Spalding Sporting Goods Endorsement Proposal for Notre

Dame's Football Coach Knute Rockne,' *Tom and Kate Hickey Family History*, October 19, 2015. Accessed June 10, 2019. http://tomandkatehickeyfamilyhistory.blogspot.com/2015/10/1925-spalding-sporting-goods.html / Cantor, George. Paul Brown: *The Man Who Invented Modern Football*. Chicago: Triumph Books. 2008.

Coaching from the Sideline

Oriard, Michael. 'In the Beginning Was the Rule' in S.W. Pose (Ed.) The New American Sport History: Recent Approaches and Perspectives. Urbana: University of Illinois Press. 1997. / 'Football Coaches Barred from Sideline,' *Inter Ocean (Chicago)*, February 8, 1914. / 'Temple Can't Come to Coach Tigers,' *Evening Missourian (Columbia)*, September 14, 1914. / Schlemmer, Jim, 'Krieger Speaks, Official Blames Bob Voigts for Ill Times Substitution that Cost Wildcats Victory,' *Akron Beacon Journal*, November 12, 1947. / 'Waco Products Head Bear Athletic Teams,' *Austin American*, June 5, 1925. / 'Dual Captains,' *Evening News (Wilkes-Barre, PA)*, December 10, 1925. / 'Bobcats Names McCall and Willis Co-Captains of 1926 Grid Eleven,' *Austin American*, January 27, 1926. / 'Two Captains for St. Ambrose Football Team,' *Quad-City Times (Davenport, IA)*, February 26, 1926. / 'Austin Gridders Have 12 Letter Men for Squad,' *Times (Shreveport, LA)*, August 16, 1926. / 'Dawson Named Team Captain,' *Austin American-Statesman*, November 25, 1926.

Substitutions and Pace of Play

Leahy, Frank, 'Leahy's Football Review, *Indianapolis News*, October 27, 1941. / 'Three Major College Football Rules Changes Announced by Committee,' *Billings Gazette*, January 4, 1941. / Graham, Gordon, 'Graham Crackers,' *Journal and Courier (Lafayette, IN)*, November 5, 1952. / 'Two Platoons Named for AP Grid Honor,' *Arizona Daily Star*, December 7, 1950. / 'NCAA Football Rules Committee Ends Costly Two-Platoon System,' *Bee (Danville, VA)*, January 15, 1953. / 'Death of Platoons Was Sneak Blow, Is Claim,' *Dayton Daily News*, January 18, 1953. / United Press International. Opotowsky, Stan. ' Two-Platoon System Traced to Rockne's Use of Shock Troops,' *Pittsburgh Press*, January 20, 1953. / Associated Press. Hoobing, Bob, 'Lattner, Giel are Repeaters on AP All-America Football Team, *Index-Journal (Greenwood, SC)*, December 4, 1953. /United Press, 'Parker Raps Plan for All-Star Tilt,' *Holland Evening Sentinel (MI)*, May 4, 1954. / 'Football Rule Change Pose Dilemma for Coaches,' *Tallahassee Democrat*, January 13, 1958. / Terrell, Bob, 'Wanted: Free Substitution Within Platoon Football,' *Asheville Citizen-Times*, January 14, 1964. / Holland, Gerald, 'The Man Who Changed Football,' *Sports Illustrated*, February 3, 1964. /Associated Press. Smits, Ted, 'Butkus Lone AP All-America Vet,' *Progress-Index (Petersburg, VA)*, December 4, 1964. / 'NCAA Football Rules Committee Adopts Two-Platoon System for 1965 Campaign,' *Daily Press (Newport News, VA)*, January 18, 1965. / 'Three Little Words Changed the Game Overnight,' *Chicago Tribune*, May 19, 1968. / 'Two Platoons Named for AP Grid Honor,' *Arizona Daily Star*, December 7, 1950. / Associated Press. Smits, Ted, 'Butkus Lone AP *All-America Vet,' Progress-Index (Petersburg, VA), December 4, 1964.*

Film Study

'Moving Pictures Aid in Football,' *Daily Review (Decatur, IL)*, October 25, 1912. / 'Georgetown Coaches Switch Their Plans,' *Washington Post*, October 31, 1912. / 'Scrubs Hold Tiger Varsity,' *Sun (New York)*, November 13, 1912. / '"My Men Bunged Up; We'll Lose Sure"-Dobie,' *Morning Register (Eugene, OR)*, November 13, 1913. / 'Football Film at Star Monday,' *Evening Herald (Klamath Falls, OR)*, January 31, 1914. / Sutton, Phil. 'The Other Bill,' runnerspace.com, December 1, 2017. Accessed on June 16, 2018. www.runnerspace.com/download.php?file_id=5495 / Collier's Weekly, 'College Coaches Use Movies,' *Indianapolis Star*, October 15, 1915. / 'N.C.A.A. Delegates to Ban Camera From Football,' *Brooklyn Daily Eagle*, December 31, 1924. / 'Move to Abolish Football Scouting Likely to be Made at Meeting,' *Salt Lake Telegram*, December 18, 1925.

Practice and Practice Equipment

'Knibbs Describes Two Innovations,' *San Francisco Chronicle*, November 10, 1905. / Folsom, Fred Gorham. Foot-Ball Bucking-Strap. U.S. Patent 528,580 filed September 5, 1905 and issued August 28, 1906. Accessed June 9, 2019. https://patentimages.storage.googleapis.com/57/9d/d9/854e5d669cc424/US829580.pdf / 'Bucking Strap and Charging Fence Latest on Football Gridiron,' *Tennessean (Nashville),* October 3, 1912. / '"Bucking Strap" Latest in Football, *Dayton Herald,* October 29, 1921. / Brown, Maynard. 'Psychology in Football,' *Lincoln Star*, November 21, 1926. / 'Queer Gear is Utilized by Coaches,' *Akron Beacon Journal*, March 13, 1941. / 'Training Aid,' *Marion Star (OH)*, April 3, 1957. / Fogarty, Fred, 'Press Box,' *Times Recorder (Zanesville, OH)*, April 5, 1957.

Skeleton Drills

'University is Shy Veterans,' *Detroit Free Press*, September 17, 1915. / Associated Press, 'Harvard Coach Scouted Old Penn,' *Philadelphia Inquirer*, November 6, 1928.

Oklahoma Drill

Trotter, Jake, 'OU's Gift to Football,' *Daily Oklahoman (Oklahoma City, OK)*, August 22, 2010. / Fleming, David, 'Is Oklahoma Drill a Right of Passage or Everything to Fear About Football,' *ESPN.com*, August 19, 2015. Accessed February 26, 2019. http://www.espn.com/college-football/story/_/id/13348894/is-oklahoma-drill-just-rite-passage-everything-fear-football / Jones, Kyle, 'Film Study: The Evolution of 'Oklahoma,' Football's Most Famous Practice Drill,' *Eleven Warriors*, March 19, 2018. Accessed February 26, 2019. https://www.elevenwarriors.com/ohio-state-football/film-study/2018/03/91898/film-study-the-evolution-of-oklahoma-footballs-most-famous-practice-drill

Conditioning and Diet

Carpenter, Kenneth J. 'The Nobel Prize and the Discovery of Vitamins.' Accessed on March 26, 2018. https://www.nobelprize.org/nobel_prizes/themes/medicine/carpenter/ 'College Football,' *Sun (New York),* December 12, 1889. / 'A Training Table,' *San Francisco Chronicle*, October 21, 1893. / 'Must Obey Trainer,' *Inter Ocean (Chicago),* September 4, 1898. / 'Penn's Team East for 19 Cents, Oregon's Rivals Dieticians,' *Oregon Daily Journal (Portland, OR)*, December 10, 1916. / 'Football Training Table Proves a Big Hit in Big Ten,' *Chicago Tribune*, October 29, 1939. / 'Suggest Farmers Contribute Steers to Serve Iowa State Gridders at Training Table,' *Courier (Waterloo, IA)*, June 2, 1961. / Langmack, Holger Christian. *Football Conditioning: An Illustrated Hand Book for Coaches, Students and Players*. New York: A.S. Barnes. 1926. / 'Ike and the Pledge of Allegiance,' Presidential History Geeks, June 14, 2012. Accessed August `15, 2018. https://potus-geeks.livejournal.com/230948.html / Paupa, Joseph. *U.S. Patent No. 2354050A*. Washington, D.C.: United States Patent Office.

Isometrics

Rogin, Gilbert. "Get Strong," *Sports Illustrated*, October 30, 1961. / Broussard, Marty. 'Function Isometric Contraction Exercise,' *Journal of the National Athletic Trainers Association, 14th Annual Meeting.* August 1962./ Blodget, Bill, 'Isometric Contraction Builds Champions,' *Tampa Times*, September 1, 1962. / Fair, John D. 'Isometrics or Steroids? Exploring New Frontiers of Strength in the Early 1960s,' *Journal of Sports History*, Spring 1993. Accessed June 10, 2019. http://library.la84.org/SportsLibrary/JSH/JSH1993/JSH2001/jsh2001b.pdf

The Clock

'Farewell to Flying Tackle,' *Tennessean (Nashville, TN),* March 27, 1910. / Perry, Lawrence. 'Variety Lack of Team Play Will Result,' *Oakland Tribune*, March 11, 1927. / 'Football Periods to be Limited to 40 Plays, Under New Plan,' *St.*

Louis Post-Dispatch, February 17, 1920. / 'New Play System Proved Successful When Tried in Brown-Boston Contest,' *Honolulu Star-Bulletin*, November 21, 1925. / Johnson, Charles. 'Gophers Keep Jug, 16-14,' *Minneapolis Star*, October 25, 1942. / 'Big Ten Endorses Drastic Rules Revisions, *Eau Claire Leader*, December 10, 1944. / 'College Football Rules are OK as they are; Some of Nation's Coaches Ask for a Few Changes,' *Rushville Republican (IN)*, December 12, 1946.

Linesman and Chains

'Warren in Trim for Jamestown,' *Warren Tribune (PA)*, November 12, 1925. / 'Football Marker is Presented Tigers by Corsicana Fandom,' *Corsicana Daily Sun (TX)*, October 26, 1934. / Carroll, Tom. 'Local Scene,' *Dayton Daily News*, September 12, 1948. / 'Dubuque Tonight's Opponent,' *St. Louis Post-Dispatch*, September 17, 1948. / 'Down' Marker,' *Plain Speaker (Hazelton, PA)*, June 7, 1949. / 'Boosters to Give New 'Teledown' Marker to School,' *Lancaster Eagle-Gazette (OH)*, October 28, 1949.

Evolution of the Zebra

'Sturdy Explains Changes in Rules,' *Baltimore Sun*, December 1, 1923. / Zimmerman Jr., Eng. 'Brownies 'Off' on Free Shots; Score: 32-26,' *Vidette-Messenger of Porter County (Valparaiso, IN)*, February 9, 1929.

Whistles, Horns, Pistols, and Flags

Camp, Walter (Ed). *Spalding's Official Foot Ball Guide, 1915.* New York: American Sports Publishing. 1915. / 'Describes Penalties by Code of Signals,' *Washington Post*, November 8, 1917. / 'Football Fans to Find Rules Badly Changed,' *Iowa City Press-Citizen*, September 18, 1924. / Camp, Walter, 'Walter Camp Defines Rules,' *Harrisburg Telegraph (PA)*, April 4, 1924. / 'Changes Made in 'Dead Ball' Rule,' *Chicago Tribune*, January 28, 1911. / 'Wesleyan Smothers Mines in First Game Here in Years, Score 7 to 0,' *Independent-Record (Helena, MT)*, October 5, 1919. / 'Longhorns Celebrate First Real Victory,' *Austin American-Statesman*, October 26, 1919. / 'Changes in Football Rules Expected to Speed Up Game,' *Boston Globe*, September 18, 1924. / 'Important Changes in Football Rules by Conference Men,' *Daily Republican-Register (Mount Carmel, IL)*, October 6, 1924. / Jay, Mike, 'Navy Football Team Given Hairline Edge Over Townies Tomorrow,' *Honolulu Star-Bulletin*, November 15, 1924. / Hall, E.K. (Ed.). *Official Intercollegiate Football Guide.* New York: American Sports Publishing. 1930. / Bingham, W. J. (Ed.) *The Official National Collegiate Athletic Association Guide.* New York: A. S. Barnes. 1947. / Hatcher, J. C., 'Sports Lowdown,' *Daily Advertiser (Lafayette, LA)*, July 18, 1971. / Schultz, Mark, 'Officials Used to Use a Gunshot to Signal the End or a Quarter or Half,' *Football Zebras*, December 21, 2018. Accessed May 2, 2019. http://www.footballzebras.com/2018/12/officials-used-to-use-a-gunshot-to-signal-the-end-to-a-quarter-or-half/

Penalty Flag

Beck, Bill. 'Local Football Fan's Two-Flag Plan Earns Rules Group Scrutiny,' *Tampa Bay Times*, January 1953. / Mooney, John. 'Sports Mirror: Red, Green Penalty Flags Might Hike Grid Interest,' *Salt Lake Tribune*, January 2, 1967. / Perazich, Chuck of Youngstown Vindicator. 'Beede Initiated Penalty Flag,' *La Crosse Tribune*, August 17, 1969. / Scorecard, Footnote on Flags, *Sports Illustrated*, November 10, 1969. / 19th Hole, Flag Wave, *Sports Illustrated*, November 24, 1969. / 19th Hole, Flag Waver (Cont.), *Sports Illustrated*, December 15, 1969. / Allen, Phil. *The Penalty Flag in American Football: A 45th Anniversary Appreciation.* Berkeley: Ardgay Flag Service. 1985. / Guerrieri, Vince. 'How a College Coach and his Wife Changed Football Forever,' *The Daily Dose*, August 6, 2017. Accessed February 1, 2018. http://www.ozy.com/the-huddle/how-a-college-coach-and-his-wife-changed-football-forever/79276

Referee Signals

Smith, Lou. 'Sports Sparks,' *Cincinnati Enquirer*, October 22, 1929. / 'Describes Penalties by Code of Signals,' *Washington Post*, November 8, 1917. / Seton, Ernest Thompson. *Sign Talk: A Universal Signal Code, Without Apparatus, for Use in the Army, the Navy, Camping, Hunting, and Daily Life*. New York: Doubleday, Page & Co. 1918 / 'Complete List of Penalties,' *Honolulu Advertiser*, October 4, 1927. / 'New System of Signals for Referee to Let Fans Know What's Happening in Games This Fall,' *Sterling Daily Gazette (IL)*, September 16, 1929. / Solving the Fall's Big Gridiron Mystery, *Literary Digest*, September 21, 1929 / Ellwood A. Geigas, Profile Details, National Football Foundation. Accessed on March 1, 2018. http://www.footballfoundation.org/Biography.aspx?id=17291 / Signals Intelligence. Accessed on March 1, 2018. https://operations.nfl.com/the-rules/signals-intelligence/ / 'Football Coach Frame 11 Suggestions for Rules Committee,' *New York Herald*, December 28, 1922.

Game Statistics

Pickle, David, 'Numbers That Formed Legends,' *College Football Historian*, May 2010. / Jackson, Stewart, 'Game Settles Into Real Battle After "Home Run",' *Indianapolis Star*, October 31, 1915. / Associated Press, Neil, Edward J, 'Inconsistency of Statistics of Grid Lamented,' *Argus-Leader, (Sioux Falls, SD)*, November 12, 1934. / Fowler, Gail, 'Bureau Brings New Meaning to Muddled Grid Statistics,' *Capital Times (Madison, WI)*, December 5, 1939. / McElroy, Cheryl A., Statistics Figure Big in College Football Picture, *NCAA News*, September 2, 1987.

CHAPTER 12: OFF THE FIELD (1906-1959)

Snyder, Thomas O (Ed.). *120 Years of American Education: A Statistical Portrait.* Washington, D.C.: U.S. Department of Education, Center for Education Statistics. 1993.

Traveling to the Game

Brown. *Fields of Friendly Strife*. 2017. / 'College Teams to Use Planes for Long Distance Travel,' *Daily News (Mount Carmel, PA)*, July 25, 1929. / 'Lobo Team to Fly Here Today,' *Los Angeles Times*, October 10, 1929. / Associated Press, 'Gridders Travel by Airplane,' *Pottsville Republican (PA)*, November 9, 1929. / Associated Press, 'Big Nine Starts Season Saturday,' *Daily Times (Davenport, IA)*, September 20, 1946. / Associated Press, 'Faculty to Decide On Early Bowl Trip,' *Daily Tribune (Wisconsin Rapids, WI)*, December 1, 1952. / Associated Press, 'Omaha Students Whoop It Up,' *Orlando Sentinel*, November 15, 1954.

Simulated Games

'On Market Street,' *Philadelphia Inquirer*, November 10, 1995. / 'Crowds In Front of Inquirer Office,' *Philadelphia Inquirer*, November 8, 1903. / 'Crowds Watching Tribune's Electric Football Scoreboard, *Star Tribune (Minneapolis)*, December 26, 1912. / Covil, Eric C., 'Radio and Its Impact on the Sports World,' *American Sports Online*. Accessed July 5, 2018. http://www.americansportscastersonline.com/radiohistory.html / 'Radiophone to Keep State Folks Posted,' *Pittsburgh Post-Gazette*, November 24, 1921.

Tailgating

'Football Picnic Kit' advertisement, *Press and Sun-Bulletin (Binghamton, NY)*, October 29, 1931. / Greig, Dorothy. 'Rah! Rah! Rah! Siss, Boom, Bah! We're Off to the Game,' *Morning Herald (Hagerstown, MD)*, November 18, 1938. / Siegel, Arthur. 'Pre-Game Picnics Morale Builders,' *Boston Globe*, November 10, 1963. / 'George A. Stephen, 71; Invented Famous Grill,' *New York Times*, February 16, 1993. / Schiff, Judith. 'Tailgating: a century of feasting al fresco,' *Yale Alumni Magazine*, November/December 2011. Accessed August 8, 2018. https://yalealumnimagazine.com/articles/3300-tailgating-a-century-of-feasting-al-fresco

Fight Songs

Studwell, William E. and Bruce R. Scheuneman. *College Fight Songs: An Annotated Anthology*. New York: Haworth Press. 1998. / McGrann, Jeremiah W., 'Tune-full,' *Boston College Magazine*, Fall 2014. Accessed September 29, 2019. http://bcm.bc.edu/issues/fall_2014/linden_lane/tune-full.html / Kryk John. *Natural Enemies, Major College's Oldest, Fiercest Rivalry - Michigan vs. Notre Dame.* Lanham, MD: Taylor Trade Publishing, 2004.

Mascots

Blitz, Matt. 'Who -or What- was the First Sport Mascot and How Did the Practice Start?' *todayIfoundout.com*, September 29, 2016. Accessed June 10, 2019. http://www.todayifoundout.com/index.php/2016/09/first-sports-mascot/ / 'Battin a Mascot,' *Pittsburgh Press*, July 18, 1884. / 'Mascots on the Diamond,' *Critic (Washington, D.C.)*, July 17, 1886. / 'Harvard – 6 Yale – 0,' *Evening World (New York)*, November 19, 1892. / 'Harvard and Yale Tie,' *Sun (New York)*, November 14, 1897. / 'Basketball Notes,' *Pittsburgh Press*, February 18, 1899. / 'Sidelights on Panthers' Victory Over State,' *Pittsburgh Daily Post*, December 1, 1922. / Servey, Erin, 'Penn State History Lessons: The Nittany Lion Mascot,' *Onward State*, March 31, 2016. Accessed June 15, 2019. https://onwardstate.com/2016/03/31/penn-state-history-lessons-the-nittany-lion-mascot/

Cheerleaders

Friedman, Dick, 'The Football Industrial Complex,' Harvard Magazine, September-October 2018. Accessed April 5, 2019. https://harvardmagazine.com/2018/09/football-origins-america / 'University Women in Football Rally,' *Lawrence Daily Journal-World*, November 19, 1914. / 'K.U. Has First Woman Cheerleader in World,' *University Daily Kansan (Lawrence, KS)*, November 23, 1914. / 'November, November 18, 1914,' *1915 Jayhawker*. Lawrence, KS: University of Kansas. 1915. / 'Women. Too, Will Cheer,' *University Daily Kansan (Lawrence, KS)*, October 15, 1915. / Hanson, Mary Ellen. *Go! Fight! Win!: Cheerleading in American Culture*. Bowling Green University Popular Press. 1995. / 'Something New for Young Collegians," *Pittsburgh Press*, October 25, 1925. / 'First Feminine Cheerleader Dead; Organized Little Theater in L.C.,' *Town Talk (Alexandria, LA)*, June 8, 1964.

Card Stunts

'Stanford Wins Championship,' *Los Angeles Herald*, November 12, 1905. 'How to Turn a Stadium Full of People Into Thousand of Pixels,' *Priceonomics*, May 14, 2015. Accessed October 7, 2018. https://priceonomics.com/how-to-turn-a-stadium-full-of-people-into/ / 'History,' Card Stunts by Kivett Productions. Accessed October 8, 2018. http://www.cardstunts.com/about/history/

Serpentines

'Stanford Holds Her Football Rally,' *San Francisco Call*, November 7, 1909. / 'New Football is Superior,' *Los Angeles Times*, November 6, 1910. / Kryk John. *Natural Enemies, Major College's Oldest, Fiercest Rivalry - Michigan vs. Notre Dame.* Lanham, MD: Taylor Trade Publishing, 2004. / 'Brilliant Offensive of Cards Sweeps Bears Off Their Feet, *Oakland Tribune*, November 13, 1925.

Tearing Down Goal Posts

'Parsons Will Play Here Tomorrow,' *Chanute Daily Tribune (KS)*, November 16, 1922.

Playing the National Anthem

'Separating fact from fiction about 'The Star-Spangled Banner',' *Constitution Daily*, September 14, 2006. Accessed

January 28, 2018. https://constitutioncenter.org/blog/separating-fact-from-fiction-about-the-star-spangled-banner / Leeke, Jim. *From the Dugouts to the Trenches: Baseball During the Great War*, Lincoln and London: University of Nebraska Press. 2017. / 'Breaks Smiled Upon Boston,' *Illustrated Buffalo Express*, October 10, 1915. / 'Middies Game Fight to No Avail Against Army,' *Tampa Tribune*, November 28, 1915. / 'President Sees Senators Swat Donovans, 12-4,' *Chicago Tribune*, April 21, 1916. / 'World Series Weather Fine,' *Lansing State Journal*, October 6, 1917. / 'Big Show Sidelights,' *Los Angeles Times*, October 7, 1917. / '38,000 See New York and Chicago Start Third Game of Series,' *St. Louis Post-Dispatch*, October 10, 1917. / 'Giants and Sox Start 5th Game; N.Y. Wins Toss for Probable 7th,' *Wilkes-Barre Times Leader*, October 13, 1917. / 'How Sox Won World's Titular Honors, Play by Play,' *Detroit Free Press*, October 16, 1917. / 'Badgers Turns and Trample Gophers, 10-7,' *Chicago Tribune*, November 4, 1917. / Richardson, James J. 'Marines' Machine Wins From Oregon,' *Sunday Oregonian,* November 4, 1917. / Babwin, Bob. 'Roots of 'Star Spangled Banner' and Baseball have a Unique History,' *Associated Press*. July 4, 2017. Accessed January 28, 2018. https://constitutioncenter.org/blog/separating-fact-from-fiction-about-the-star-spangled-banner / 'Separating fact from fiction about 'The Star-Spangled Banner,'' *Constitution Daily*, September 14, 2006. Accessed January 28, 2018. https://constitutioncenter.org/blog/separating-fact-from-fiction-about-the-star-spangled-banner

Goodyear Blimp and Flyovers

Baldwin, Thomas Scott, The National Aviation Hall of Fame, *nationalaviation.org*. Accessed January 17, 2019 https://www.nationalaviation.org/our-enshrinees/baldwin-thomas/ / 'Dickinson Asks Airships for Army,' *Buffalo Evening News*, December 10, 1910. / 'The Game From Above,' *New York Times*, November 5, 1911. / 'Princeton Beating Harvard, The First Football Game Photographed from an Aeroplane,' *Collier's*, November 18, 1911. / 'Atwood Must Not Fly Over Gridiron,' *Bridgeport Times and Evening Farmer (CT)*, November 24, 1911. / 'Blimp Lands at Opa-Locka Before Crowd,' *Miami News*, December 6, 1929. / 'Warm Weather Slashes Hopes of Visitor Clan,' *Miami News*, December 7, 1929. / Felt, Truman T., 'Gators Smash Way to Victory Over Webfoots,' *Miami News*, December 8, 1929. / '25,000 Bask in Warm Sun at Grid Game,' *Miami News*, December 8, 1929. / United Press, 'Blimp Will Tote Camera for Rose Bowl Television,' *Boston Globe*, January 1, 1955. / Gowran, Clay, 'TV Today: Super Bowl Telecast Means Work, Dollars,' *Chicago Tribune*, January 14, 1968. / Williams, Doug, 'How Flyovers Hit Their Exact Marks at Games,' *espn.com*, July 23, 2012. / Personal conversation with Eddie Ogden, Airship PR Specialist & Historian, with Goodyear Tire and Rubber Company, March 30, 2020.

Bowl System and Post-Season Play

'Score,' *Tennessean (Nashville, TN),* December 12, 1896. / 'Yale Team Home,' *Topeka State Journal*, January 4, 1897. /
'Score,' *Tennessean (Nashville, TN),* December 12, 1896. / 'Yale Team Home,' *Topeka State Journal*, January 4, 1897. /
Wood, Michael T. 'American Football in Cuba: A Brief Introduction,' / *Sport in American History*. Accessed on May 2, 2018. https://ussporthistory.com/2015/07/30/american-football-in-cuba-a-brief-introduction/ / 'U.S.C. Wins Over Missouri, 20-7,' *Los Angeles Times*, December 26, 1924. / 'Brick Muller Makes Touchdown for Victory,' *Oakland Tribune*, December 27, 1925. / 'Bruins Will Not Play New Year's Game in the South', *Oakland Tribune,* November 9, 1922. / Florida. Population of Counties by Decennial Census: 1900 to 1900. U.S. Bureau of Census. Accessed on May 1, 2018. https://www.census.gov/population/cencounts/fl190090.txt / '85-Yard Drive Wins for Notre Dame All-Stars,' *Tampa Tribune*, January 2, 1926. / 'Revamped Hurricanes Trip Manhattan by 7-0,' *Miami News*, January 3, 1933 / Duquesne Superior to Scrappy Hurricane Eleven,' *Miami News*, January 1, 1934. / 'That First Orange Bowl,' *Pensacola News Journal*, December 8, 1963. / Wodrich, Andrew. Building Miami: Assessing Orange Bowl Festival's Effect on Tourism in Miami, 1933-1958. Working paper. / 'Warner Predicts Owls Will Baffle Wave With Passes,' *Times (Shreveport, LA),* December 31, 1934. / 'Bowl Beginning,' Accessed April 30, 2018. https://allstatesugarbowl.org/classic/origin-purpose/ / 'High Powered Grid Sets Clash in Dixie Classic,' *Lubbock Morning Avalanche*, December 27, 1930. / 'Dixie

Classic at Dallas New Years,' Big *Spring Daily Herald (TX),* December 22, 1933. / 'Cotton Bowl May Promote,' *Amarillo Globe-Times*, November 16, 1936. / 'Memphis Abandons Cotton Bowl Plans,' *Austin American (TX),* December 12, 1936.

Naming a National Champion

Whitney, Caspar, 'Ranking of the Elevens for 1902,' *Outing*, January 1903. / Whitney, Caspar, 'Football Ranking,' *Outing*, January 1904. / 'Propose New Scheme to End Grid Title Snarls,' *Decatur Herald*, February 11, 1925. / Associated Press. 'Michigan Takes Big Ten Honors by Point Table,' *Dispatch (Moline, IL)*, November 22, 1926.

Subsidies and Scholarships

Schmidt, Raymond. *Shaping College Football: The. Transformation of an American Sport, 1919-1930.* Syracuse University Press. 2007. / McGill, Ralph, 'Southeastern Meets Today in Nashville,' *Atlanta Constitution*, February 8, 1935. / 'Coaches Approve Southeastern Conference Football Scholarship Ruling,' *Miami News*, December 15, 1935. / Cavagnaro, Bob, 'Subsidization of Athletes Hit by NCAA,' *Messenger-Inquirer (Owensboro, KY),* December 29, 1935. / 'Villanova Head Call NCAA Purity Act 'Subterfuge',' *Philadelphia Inquirer*, January 20, 1950. / 'Subsidy Rule Tightened,' *Arizona Republic*, January 1, 1940. / Ward, Arch, 'Here's Plan to Save College Football,' *Chicago Tribune*, September 20, 1951. / Associated Press, 'Notre Dame, Purdue Praise Coach Rotation Plan,' *Chicago Tribune*, September 21, 1951. / Peeler, Ben, 'Talking to Myself,' *Odessa American*, October 9, 1951.

Dropping or Deemphasizing Football

Lester. *Stagg's University*. 1999. / Watterson, John Sayles. *College Football: History Spectacle Controversy.* Baltimore: Johns Hopkins University Press. 2009. / Dunnavant, Keith. *The 50 Year Seduction: How Television Manipulated College Football, from the Birth of the Modern NCAA to the Creation of the BCS.* New York: St. Martin's Press. 2004. / 'NCAA Football Rules Committee Ends Costly Two-Platoon System,' *Bee (Danville, VA),* January 15, 1953. / Fullerton, Jr., Hugh, '2 New Rules Passed By NCAA Committee,' *Palladium-Item (Richmond, IN)*, January 12, 1957.

Redshirting

'Putting on Speed for Cornell Game,' *Philadelphia Inquirer*, November 28, 1917. / 'Laval Continues to Rest Varsity,' *Greenville News*, November 14, 1923. / United Press, 'Warren Alfson Nears End Great Career as Cornhusker Lineman,' *Nebraska State Journal (Lincoln)*, November 30, 1940. / Emmert, Mark, ''Redshirt' Origin,' *Iowa City Press-Citizen*, November 5, 2009. / Hewitt, Purser, 'Sports,' *Clarion-Ledger (Jackson, MS)*, September 11, 1939. / 'FU Practice Set,' *Greenville News (SC)*, January 16, 1948. / Fullerton, Jr., Hugh, 'N.C.A.A. Seeks Solution to Football 'Redshirting',' *Terre Haute Star*, January 3, 1958. / 'NCAA Places Curb on Grid 'Red-Shirts',' *Lincoln Star*, January 12, 1961. / 'NFL Winning Fight to Sign Collegians,' *Cincinnati Enquirer*, January 12, 1964. / Trimble, Joe, 'Pros Outlaw In-Season Raids,' *Daily News (New York, NY)*, January 13, 1965. / 'This Year You Are Going To See Red,' *Sports Illustrated*, September 1, 1982. Accessed June 10, 2019. https://www.si.com/vault/1982/09/01/638013/this-year-youre-going-to-see-red] / Maisel, Ivan, 'Redshirting Colored By Assortment of Pros, Cons,' *Chicago Tribune*, October 22, 1989. / 'Bar to be Placed Upon Collegiate Gridiron Stars,' *Sedalia Democrat (MO)*, February 7, 1926. / Willis, Wally, '49ers Reach for Junior Gridders at Draft Meet,' *Oakland Tribune*, January 18, 1955. / 'NFL Winning Fight to Sign Collegians,' *Cincinnati Enquirer*, January 12, 1964. / Trimble, Joe, 'Pros Outlaw In-Season Raids,' *Daily News (New York, NY)*, January 13, 1965.

Role of the Media

'New Field of Communication Art Developed In Adapting Telephone Lines as Radio Link,' *Hancock Democrat (Green-*

field, IN), January 18, 1923. / 'Fifty Stations Will Broadcast Tournament of Roses,' *Palladium-Item (Richmond, IN)*, December 27, 1927. / 'Broadcast Rights to Army-Navy Game are Sold for $150,000,' *Dayton Herald*, November 22, 1930. / 'Local Store to Aid in Charity Football Tilt, *Pensacola News-Journal*, December 4, 1930. / 'Coast Conference School May Get Broadcast Money,' *Eugene Guard*, July 16, 1933. / '$20,000 Is Bid for Right to Broadcast Big Six Grid Games,' *St. Louis Post-Dispatch*, May 9, 1934. / Smith, Red, 'Will Colleges Be Forced to Change Their Policy on Football Television?,' *Boston Globe*, October 8, 1954. / Carter, Bill. 'Roone Arledge, 71, a Force in TV Sports and News, Dies,' *New York Times*, December 6, 2002. https://ww.nytimes.com/2002/12/06/business/roone-arledge-71-a-force-in-tv-sports-and-news-dies.html / Deford, Frank. 'Roone Arledge 1931-2002 in Presenting the Olympics, Wide World, Howard Cosell and Much More, This Visionary Revolutionized Sports Television,' *Sports Illustrated*, December 16, 2002. https://www.si.com/vault/2002/12/16/334171/roone-arledge-1931-2002-in-presenting-the-olympics-wide-world-howard-cosell-and-much-more-this-visionary-revolutionized-sports-television / Saunders, Patrick, 'A Look AT&T's Instant Replay Through the Years,' *Denver Post*, November 16, 2013. https://www.denverpost.com/2013/11/16/a-look-at-tvs-instant-replay-through-the-years/ / '"Marching On" for JFK,' *cbsnews.com*, 2013. Accessed February 21, 2019. https://www.cbsnews.com/video/jfk-tribute-1963-army-navy-football-game-honored-assassinated-president/

Racial Integration

'Puts Blame on Missouri,' *Topeka Daily Capital*, October 17, 1913. / Sherman, Shy, 'Brass Tacks, *Lincoln Star*, October 17, 1944. / Associated Press, 'Drake Can Play Negro, Says Aggies,' *Des Moines Register*, October 12, 1949. / 'Action Starts in Sugar Bowl, *Miami News*, December 25, 1955. / Miller, Patrick B. and David K. Wiggins (Eds.). *Sport and the Color Line: Black Athletes and Race Relations in Twentieth Century America*. New York: Routledge. 2004. / Drape, Joe. 'Changing the Face of Texas Football, *New York Times*, December 23, 2005. / Barra, Allen, 'Bigger, Stronger, More Complex: College Football, Then and Now,' *Atlantic*, October 4, 2012. Accessed March 31, 2019. https://www.theatlantic.com/entertainment/archive/2012/10/bigger-stronger-more-complex-college-football-then-and-now/263200/ / La Noue, George R. and Mark Bennett, 'The Impact of Desegregation on College Choice of Elite Athletes,' *International Journal of Higher Education*, 2014. / Sherman, Ed. 'How Michigan State's Duffy Daugherty Helped Integrate College Football,' *Chicago Tribune*, February 16, 2015. / Baker, S. Zebulon, '"To Help Foster Athletic Equality Here in the Midwest"- Defeating Jim Crow in the Big Seven Conference,' *Kansas History*. Summer 2016. Accessed August 13, 2018. https://www.kshs.org/publicat/history/2016summer_baker.pdf / Barra, Allen. 'The Integration of College Football Didn't Happen in One Game, *Atlantic*, November 13, 2013. / 'Black History at LSU,' LSU Office of Diversity. Accessed August 13, 2018. https://www.lsu.edu/diversity/aacc/history/lsublackhistoryinfo.php / The Reintegration of the NFL,' NFL Operations. Accessed May 7, 2019. https://operations.nfl.com/the-players/evolution-of-the-nfl-player/the-reintegration-of-the-nfl/

Summary

Staples, Andy, 'How Television Changed College Football -- and How It Will Again,' *Sports Illustrated*, August 6, 2012. Accessed August 8, 2018. https://www.si.com/college-football/2012/08/06/tv-college-football

CHAPTER 13:TELEVISION BECOMES KING (1960 to 2018)

Television and Revenues in 1960

United Press International, 'Iowa State Football Lost Money in Fiscal 1958-59, *Globe-Gazette (Mason City, IA)*, January 26, 1960. / Associated Press. 'NCAA Football Goes to ABC for 2 Years,' *Springfield Leader and Press (MO)*, March 16, 1960. / Associated Press, 'Indiana Faced by Loss of Revenues,' *Muncie Evening Press*, August 5, 1960. / Becker, Dick, 'NU Athletics Costly; Football Makes Lone Profit,' *Lincoln Journal Star*, September 11, 1960. / 'Sports Schedule This

Week,' *Oneonta Star (NY)*, October 29, 1960. / Carter, Bill, 'Sports Talk,' *Town Talk (Alexandria, LA)*, March 21, 1969. / Smith, Ronald A. *Play-by-Play: Radio, Television, and Big-Time College Sport*. Baltimore: Johns Hopkins. 2001. / Dunnavant, Keith. *The 50 Year Seduction: How Television Manipulated College Football, from the Birth of the Modern NCAA to the Creation of the BCS*. New York: St. Martin's Press. 2004. / Hinnen, Jerry, 'ESPN Reaches 12-Year Deal to Air College Football Playoffs,' *cbssports.com*, November 21, 2012. Accessed February 15, 2019. https://www.cbssports.com/college-football/news/espn-reaches-12-year-deal-to-air-college-football-playoffs/ / Staples, Andy, 'How Television Changed College Football -- and How It Will Again,' *Sports Illustrated*, August 6, 2012. Accessed August 8, 2018. https://www.si.com/college-football/2012/08/06/tv-college-football / Chengelis, Angelique S., Michigan Athletics Projects $2.5M Surplus,' *Detroit News*, June 22, 2018. / Berkowitz, Steve, 'The SEC Has Record Revenue in 2018, But Big Ten Schools Rake In More Pre-School Distribution,' *USA Today*, February 1, 2019. Accessed March 31, 2020. https://www.usatoday.com/story/sports/ncaaf/2019/02/01/sec-passed-big-ten-per-school-distribution-after-record-revenue/2743885002/

NCAA Structure and Stratification

Watterson, John Sayles. *College Football: History Spectacle Controversy.* Baltimore: Johns Hopkins University Press. 2009. / Myers, Bob, 'NCAA Members Vote to Retain TV Curb and Then Adjourn,' *Alabama Journal (Montgomery)*, January 12, 1956. / Associated Press, 'Major Bowl Games Begin Saturday,' *Alton Evening Telegraph*, December 14, 1964. / Attner, Paul, 'Divisions Setup Pleases Major College Powers,' *Cincinnati Enquirer*, July 31, 1973. / Lawrence, Mitch, 'Reclassification to I-AA Hasn't Hurt Cornell or Colgate,' *Democrat and Chronicle (Rochester, NY)*, August 22, 1982. / Associated Press, 'Florida A&M Moves Up,' *Ithaca Journal*, August 31, 1978. / Associated Press, 'NCAA Reclassified 39 Grid Teams to I-AA Division,' *Sante Fe New Mexican*, February 3, 1982.

Conferences

Writes, Tobi, 'The Real Killer of the Southwest Conference,' *BleacherReport.com*, April 22, 2010. Accessed November 15, 2018. https://bleacherreport.com/articles/382576-the-real-killer-of-the-southwest-conference / https://en.wikipedia.org/wiki/1960_NCAA_University_Division_football_season / https://en.wikipedia.org/wiki /List_of_NCAA_Division_I_FBS_football_programs / Forde, Pat, 'SEC Head Avoids Obvious: League Expansion is Here,' *Courier-Journal*, August 1, 2000. / Smith, Chris, The First SEC Championship Game Changed College Football Forever,' *Saturday Down South*, 2015. Accessed May 1, 2019. https://www.saturdaydownsouth.com/sec-football/first-sec-championship-game-changed-college-football-forever/ / Bostock, Mike, Shan Carter, and Kevin Quealy, 'Tracing the History of N.C.A.A. Conferences, *New York Times*, November 30, 2013. Access November 15, 2018. http://www.nytimes.com/newsgraphics/2013/11/30/football-conferences/index.html / Townsend, Brad, 'SW's Dying Days, *Dallas Morning News*, September 4, 1915. Accessed November 15, 2018. http://interactives.dallasnews.com/2015/swc-anniversary/

CHAPTER 14: THE BALL, THE FIELD, AND THE STADIUM (1960-2018)

Midfield Decorations and Team Areas

Associated Press, 'NCAA Rules Group Outlaws Grabbing Face Masks in College Football,' *Times and Democrats (Orangeburg, SC)*, January 17, 1957. / '1966 Kansas City Chiefs,' *YouTube*, January 14, 2016. Accessed April 29. https://www.youtube.com/watch?v=s6LFeSeOGkk / 'Packers vs. Cowboys – NFL Championship – 1966,' *YouTube*, November 6, 2017. Accessed April 29, 2019. https://www.youtube.com/watch?v=1dPEvB0EHws / 'Photo Collection – November 22, 1967 – Kansas City Chiefs vs. Oakland Raiders,' *Tales from the American Football League*, November 3, 2014. Accessed April 29, 2019. http://talesfromtheamericanfootballleague.com/photo-collection-november-22-1967-kansas-city-chiefs-vs-oakland-raiders/ / 'Super Bowl I: The First AFL-NFL Championship Game | Chiefs vs. Packers |

NFL,' *YouTube*, January 12, 2016. Accessed April 29, 2019. https://www.youtube.com/watch?v=-ihLXZ2-l7A / 'It's His Turf,' *Times Leader (Wilkes-Barre, PA)*, February 3, 2013. / Associated Press, 'New NCAA Rule Changes Punt Return Procedure,' *Colorado Springs Gazette-Telegraph*, January 21, 1973. / Associated Press, 'NCAA Ponders Changes,' *Times Recorder (Zanesburg, OH)*, January 10, 1978. / Nelson, Dave, 'NCAA, NFL Rule Changes Put Emphasis on Player Safety,' *News Journal (Wilmington, DE)*, September 5, 1979. / Associated Press, 'NCAA Rules Committee OKs 44 Changes,' *Tampa Tribune*, January 20, 1983. / Associated Press, 'New NCAA Rule Changes Stress Safety,' *News Journal (Wilmington, DE)*, January 20, 1984. / Nelson. *Anatomy of a Game*. 1994.

Artificial Turf

'Tennis Under Cover,' *San Francisco Chronicle*, December 14, 1892. / 'Gigantic Sports Club for London,' *Minneapolis Journal*, October 29, 1905. / Associated Press. 'Dome to Have Artificial Turf,' *Progress-Index (Petersburg, VA)*, March 13, 1966. / 'Bug in the Astrodome,' *Tyrone Daily Herald (PA)*, April 2, 1966. / Fuson, Wayne, 'AstroTurf, Sycamores Are 'Ready' for Butler,' *Indianapolis News*, September 18, 1967. / Steinbach, Paul, 'A Majority of Division I-A Football Programs Now Use Synthetic Turf, *Athletic Business*, October 2006. Accessed September 26, 2018. https://www.athleticbusiness.com/Outdoor/a-majority-of-division-i-a-football-programs-now-use-synthetic-turf.html / Jiggens, Mike. 'Know the facts before investing in a synthetic turf sports field,' *Turf&Rec*, December 2, 2013. Accessed August 20, 2018. https://www.turfandrec.com/news/know-the-facts-before-investing-in-a-synthetic-turf-sports-field-3164

Goal Posts

Henneman, Jim, 'Referee: Kick That Sank '65 Colts was Good,' *Washington Examiner*, September 14, 2007. / McLemore, Morris, 'Wishbone Goal Posts,' *Miami News*, October 13, 1966. / United Press International, 'Field Goal 'Needle' Invades Grid Game, *Daily Independent (Kannapolis, NC)*, November 15, 1966. / McNeil, Al, 'Goose-neck Goalpost in Use Saturday,' *Ottawa Citizen*, November 17, 1966. / Mastronardi, Pete, 'Bridgeport Native Invents Goal Post Designed to Improve play, Cut Injuries,' *Bridgeport Post*, August 6, 1967. / Fialkov, Harvey, 'Boynton Inventor Put Slingshot in the NFL,' *South Floridan Sun Sentinel (Ft. Lauderdale, FL)*, February 6, 2010. / Associated Press,' NCAA Committee Votes to Reduce Goal-Post Width,' *Courier-Journal (Louisville, KY)*, January 19, 1990.

Goal Post Nets

Associated Press, 'NCAA Football Committee Liberalizes Rules, *News Leader (Staunton, VA)*, January 25, 1985. / 'Live Tips and Topics,' *Boston Globe*, November 17, 1939. / 'Bears Score Record 73-0 Rout in Title Game with Redskins,' *Alton Evening Telegraph*, December 9, 1940. / 'Cotton Bowl Fans Can Keep Kicks Going in Stands,' *Rapid City Journal (SD)*, February 21, 1953. / 'Camp Randall Adds Screen – For Football,' *Wisconsin State Journal (Madison)*, October 16, 1959. / ''Nets to You,' Say Chiefs to End Zone Fans,' *Des Moines Register*, October 11, 1970. / Lefton, Terry and Michael Smith. 'Allstate's new gain,' *SportsBusiness Journal*, May 5, 2014. Accessed August 19, 2018. https://www.sportsbusinessdaily.com/Journal/Issues/2014/05/26/In-Depth/Allstate.aspx

Stadiums

Siegfried, John and Andrew Zimbalist. *The Economics of Sports Facilities and Their Communities*. Journal of Economic Perspectives. Summer 2000. / Cohen, Andrew. "How Stadium Construction Costs Reached the Billions,' *Athletic Business*. July 2012. Accessed April 19, 2019. https://www.athleticbusiness.com/stadium-arena/how-stadium-construction-costs-reached-the-billions.html

Domes

Rosen, Rebecca J. 'Keepin' It Cool: How the Air Conditioner Made Modern America,' *Atlantic*, July 14, 2011. / Chandler, Adam. 'The Sad Fate (but Historic Legacy) of the Houston Astrodome,' *Atlantic*, November 8, 2013. / List of covered stadiums by capacity. Accessed August 20, 2018. https://en.wikipedia.org/wiki/List_of_covered_stadiums_by_capacity

Luxury Seating

Associated Press. 'Astrodome Opens This Weekend, *West Palm Beach Post*, April 4, 1965. / Tutka, Patrick Michael. *An Ideal-Type through Innovation Diffusion, Recording the Construction History of Football Stadiums in the National Collegiate Athletic Association Division I Football Subdivision (FBS),* Doctoral Dissertation. Louisiana State University, 2016. / Lawrence, Heather J., James Kahler, and Ron T. Contorno. An Examination of Luxury Suite Ownership in Professional Sports. 2016. Accessed September 20, 2018. https://www.sc.edu/study/colleges_schools/hrsm/research/journal_venue_and_event_management_archives/jvem_pdfs/vol1_no1/luxury_suites.pdf

Concessions

'Why Sports Stadiums Have Morphed into Entertainment Centers,' *Knowledge@Wharton podcast,* September 20, 2017. Accessed September 19, 2018. http://knowledge.wharton.upenn.edu/article/professional-sports-invest-much-stadiums/ / Smith, Annabelle K. 'The History of Baseball Stadium Nachos,' *Smithsonian*. May 7, 2013.

Scoreboards

Associated Press, 'Details Told of Houston's New Scoreboard,' *Decatur Herald*, December 21, 1964. / 'New Scoreboards for Iowa Stadium,' *Iowa City Press-Citizen*, July 18, 1967. / 'Dodgers Installing $3 Million Video System in Scoreboard,' *Los Angeles Times*, February 27, 1980. / 'Not The Same Old 'Stick,' *San Francisco Examiner*, February 16, 1987. / Associated Press, 'Reds Unveil JumboTRON,' *Newark Advocate (OH)*, May 25, 1987. / Greenberg, Jay, 'Sky's The Limit,' *Philadelphia Daily News*, August 25, 1989. / Morgan, Jon, 'Scores Courtesy of Space Age,' *Baltimore Sun*, November 1, 1997.

CHAPTER 15: PLAY AND TECHNIQUE (1960-2018)

Sucker Shifts and Offensive Line Stances

Perry, Lawrence, 'Old Stuff, Says Dick,' *Evening Sun (Baltimore)*, October 8, 1942. / Associated Press, 'Seven Changes Made For 1947 Football Code,' *Chicago Tribune*, February 3, 1947. / Associated Press, 'Sucker Shift: New Term, Old Problem Gets Airing Today, *Chicago Tribune*, November 12, 1953. / Associated Press, 'Evashevski Defends His Iowa Shift,' *Mt. Vernon Register-News (IL)*, September 10, 1955. / Associated Press, 'NCAA Outlaws The Sucker Shift, Alters Punting In Rule Changes,' *Burlington Free-Press (VT)*, January 18, 1968. / United Press International. 'Rule Changes Are Minor,' *Hartford Courant*, September 18, 1977.

Spread

Layden, Tim. *Blood, Sweat and Chalk: The Ultimate Football Playbook: How The Great Coaches Built Today's Game*. New York: Sports Illustrated Books. 2001. / 'Heisman Tells Inside Story or Strupper's Play,' *Atlanta Constitution*, November 9, 1924. / 'Football ABC's, Spread Formations, Weapons of Desperate Tea, Good Only for Passer,' *St. Louis Star and Times*, December 4, 1931. / Bohne, Bob, 'Looking 'Em Over,' *Cincinnati Enquirer*, October 22, 1937. / Zimmerman, Paul, ''Gloomy Gus' Henderson, Ex-USC Grid Coach, Dies,' *Los Angeles Times*, December 18, 1965. / Fite, Ed, 'TCU Will Use 7 Formations in Delta Bowl,' *Tampa Tribune*, December 22, 1947. / '49ers Fall Off Pace With Loss,' *Eugene Guard*, December 11, 1960. / Associated Press, 'Cowboys Plan to Use Shotgun Formation,' *Amarillo Globe-Times*, May 26, 1975. / Hermsmeyer, Josh. "The Secret to the Rams' Blocking Success Isn't the Linemen. It's

Sean McVay," fivethirtyeight.com, January 30, 2019. Accessed February 3, 2019. https://fivethirtyeight.com/features/the-secret-to-the-rams-blocking-success-isnt-the-linemen-its-sean-mcvay/?ex_cid=story-twitter

Option Routes

Associated Press, 'Domres Passes Colts To 31-0 Rout of Pats,' *Hartford Courant*, November 21, 1972. / *Seminole Football, Florida State Outlook*. Tallahassee: Florida State University. 2011. / Kelly, Danny. 'Don Coryell, The Man Who Created the Modern NFL,' *sbnation.com*, July 17, 2014. Accessed March 30, 2020. https://www.sbnation.com/2014/7/17/5900675/don-coryell-offense-nfl-chargers-dan-fouts-passing-league

Personnel Groupings

Dodd, Mike, 'Bengals Mix and Match Linebackers,' *Cincinnati Enquirer*, November 8, 1985. / Associated Press, 'Neither Cincinnati, Houston Can Afford Setback Tonight,' *Sioux City Journal*, November 13, 1989. / Adams, John R. (Ed.) *2005 NCAA Football Rules and Interpretations*. Indianapolis: National Collegiate Athletic Association. 2005.

Blocking Rules

Originally in New York Times, White, Jr., Gordon S., 'Passing for First Time Dominates College Football, *News Journal (Wilmington, NJ)*, December 26, 1982. / Associated Press, 'NCAA Football Committee Liberalizes Rules, *News Leader (Staunton, VA)*, January 25, 1985.

Kicking

Associated Press, 'Kickoffs Moved to the 35,' *Manhattan Mercury (KS)*, January 23, 1986. / 'NCAA Panel Alters Several Rules for Football,' *Orlando Sentinel*, April 13, 2007. / 'NCAA Proposal Tweaks Touchbacks,' *Austin American Statesman*, March 3, 2018.

Return Kicks

Smith, Wilfrid, 'Football for the Fan, *Chicago Tribune*, September 23, 1931. / Strickler, George, Football – A to Z,' *Chicago Tribune*, November 1, 1963. / United Press International, 'Committee Change 5 Grid Rules,' *Indianapolis Star*, January 19, 1967. / Higgins, Tom, 'Kicking the Ball Back Out of the End Zone,' *cfl.ca*, November 13, 2008. Accessed November 26, 2018. https://www.cfl.ca/2008/11/13/kicking-the-ball-back-out-of-the-end-zone/

Rugby-Style Punters

Hall, Tommy, 'Spectacular Kickers of American Game,' *San Francisco Chronicle*, November 11, 1906. / Gimino, Anthony, 'Punts' Good Rolls Help UA Remain On Its Roll,' *Arizona Daily Star*, October 18, 1993. / Associated Press, 'Punter From Down Under Just May Stick,' *Sante Fe New Mexican*, July 28, 1995. / Covitz, Randy, 'Rugby-Style Kicking Helps Colquitt Take Punting to Another Level,' *Wichita Eagle*, November 7, 2014. Accessed October 8, 2018. https://www.kansas.com/sports/nfl/kansas-city-chiefs/article3651384.html

Soccer-Style Kickers

Williams, Doug. 'How European soccer-style kickers started a revolution 50 years ago,' *ABC News*, October 12, 2016. / Daly, Dan. 'A Soccer-Style Kicker for the Giants in 1953!,' *Pro Football Daly*, August 20, 2015. Accessed August 31, 2018. http://profootballdaly.com/a-soccer-style-kicker-for-the-giants-in-1953/ / Gaines, Harry E. 'Short Shots on Sports,' *Journal Gazette (Mattoon, IL)*, November 3, 1950. / 'Giants Ready to Break Out a Revamped Umbrella Defense,' *Des Moines Register*, August 16, 1953. / Associated Press. 'New York Giants Beat Bears, 14-7,' *Baltimore Sun*, September 4, 1953. / United Press International. 'Badger Kickoff Artist Uses Unusual Method,'

Sheboygan Press, October 2, 1957. / Stirling, Scott. 'Raiders Bow, Cotton Hurt, *Oakland Tribune*, October 6, 1962. / 'Baughan Names Defensive Line Coach,' *Ithaca Journal*, March 2, 1983. / Rice, Jack. 'Western Michigan's Late Tally Spoils Bears' Homecoming,' *St. Louis Post-Dispatch*, October 24, 1954. / Sarno, Phil. 'Sideline Chatter, ' *Plain Speaker (Hazelton, PA)*, November 14, 1956. / United Press International, 'Longhorns Beat Arkansas Eleven in 17-0 Contest, *Anniston Star (AL)*, October 20, 1957. / Clark, Bob, 'Off the Record,' *Pocono Record (Stroudsburg, PA)*, November 18, 1958. / Taylor, Sec. 'Officials Agree Jack Pence Drop Kicked 59 Yards,' *Des Moines Register*, November 26, 1923.

Field Goals

White, Jr., Gordon S. 'Are There Too Many Field Goals,' *Quad-City Times (Davenport, IA)*, October 24, 1985. (Originally published in the New York Times) / United Press International, Hendel, John, 'NCAA Bans Use of Tees,' *Tyrone Daily Record (PA)*, January 19, 1988. / *Football Bowl Subdivision Records*, National Collegiate Athletic Association, 2017.

Icing the Kicker

Associated Press, Meredith, Luke, 'Icing the Kickers May Not Pay Off in Fourth Quarter,' *Florida Today (Cocoa, FL)*, September 20, 2014. / Needell, Paul. 'League Might Look at Icing Timeout Treachery on Kicks,' *Austin American*, October 11, 2007. / VanHeel, Jim, 'Looking It Over, *Globe-Gazette (Mason, IA)*, October 27, 1969.

Tie Games

'Championship Pennant Flies Today From Conning Tower of Wyoming,' *Brooklyn Daily Eagle*, December 2, 1915. / Henry, William, 'Balboa Would Play Marines,' Los Angeles Time, December 16, 1918. / Gridder, 'Yes, Mr. Moore! We Do Not Like Your New Fangled Tie Football Playoff System,' *Santa Ana Register*, November 29, 1926. / Holaday, Jeremy, 'Breaking the Tie,' *Kansas State High School Activities Association*. Accessed November 11, 2018. http://www.kshsaa.org/Public/PDF/BreakingtheTie.pdf / Associated Press, 'NCAA May Abolish Ties,' *Times (Munster, IN)*, January 14, 1976. / 'NCAA Changes Tiebreaker,' *Reno Gazette-Journal*, February 25, 1995. / 'NCAA Approved Overtime for Bowls,' *Star-Gazette (Elmira, NY)*, May 18, 1995. / 'Overtime Approved for I-A Football, *Billings Gazette*, February 16, 1996. / Associated Press, 'NCAA Changes Football Overtime Rules,' *Indiana Gazette (Indiana, PA)*, February 12, 1997.

Signals and Huddles

'St. Mary's-Marquette Game in Chicago on Friday is Grid Feature,' *Greeley Daily Tribune (CO)*, October 27, 1936. / 'Cas Plans 'No Huddle' Attack,' *Capital Journal*, August 2, 1958. / 'Geneva's 'No Huddle' Offense Begins Fifth Season Tomorrow,' *New Castle News (PA)*, September 22, 1961. / Klobuchar, Jim, 'Ram Defense Snags Vikings,' *Star Tribune (Minneapolis, MN)*, September 28, 1964. / 'No Huddle for Gophers,' *Globe-Gazette (Mason City, IA)*, October 16, 1973. /Meyer, Ed, 'Browns Will Try New Wrinkle Against, Broncos,' *Akron Beacon Journal*, November 6, 1981.

Scoring

United Press International, 'Rules Changed,' *Daily Republican-Register (Mount Carmel, IL)*, January 21, 1988. / McKeever, Curt, 'College Rule Change Allows Some Fumble Returns, *Lincoln Journal Star*, August 31, 1990.

Disguising Defenses and Coverage

Corum, Bill, 'Navy's Newest Weapon of Attack Fatal to Army, Has Others Guessing,' *Journal News (White Plains, NY)*, December 3, 1957. / Associated Press, Thompson, Herb 'Middies 'Jitterbug' Defense Could Slow Rice to Waltz,' *Rapid City Journal (SD)*, December 22, 1957. / Wallis, Wally, 'Navy Plans New Defense for Rice,' *Daily*

Oklahoman (Oklahoma City), December 31, 1957. / Rice Institute Football Video, 1958 Rice vs. Navy, Cotton Bowl Highlight,' *Rice Digital Scholarship Archive.* Accessed May 22, 2019. https://scholarship.rice.edu/handle/1911/76461

Nickel and Dime Defenses

Larson, Al. 'Rams Unbeaten – Only 18 to Go!,' *Independent (Long Beach, CA)*, August 14, 1967. / Boice, Chuck, 'Gibson's New Book Shows Cardinal Ace Bitter Man,' *Capitol Journal (Salem, OR)*, October 8, 1968. / Oates, Bob, 'Allen's Switches Leave Foes Short-Changed,' *Los Angeles Times*, October 15, 1969. / Cross, Irv with Clifton Brown. *Bearing the Cross: My Inspiring Journey From Poverty to the NFL and Sports Television*. New York: Sports Publishing. 2017.

Bump and Run

'Cage Star Jones Given Good Chance to Land Berth with Rams,' *Los Angeles Times*, July 26, 1958. / United Press International, 'Los Angeles Chargers Name Noll Assistant,' *Hartford Courant*, February 3, 1960. / Kendle, Joe, 'Bump and Run, or Just Boxing Out? K.C. Jones Left Impact on NFL,' *Pro Football Hall of Fame*, November 17, 2017. Accessed October 29, 2018. https://www.profootballhof.com/blogs/stories-from-the-pro-football-hall-of-fame-archives/ / 'Training Camp Tales – The Amazing and the Absurd Are Normal in an NFL Camp,' *GoUpstate.com*, July 16, 1995. Accessed October 29, 2018. https://www.goupstate.com/news/19950716/training-camp-tales---the-amazing-and-the-absurd-are-normal-in-an-nfl-camp

Zone Blitz

Whittingham, Richard. *Illustrated History of the New York Giants.* Chicago: Triumph Books. 2005. / Bedard, Greg, 'Zoned In On Each Other,' *Boston Globe*, February 4, 2011. / Dudko, James, 'Bill Arnsparger: Remembering the Godfather of the Zone Blitz and Hybrid Defense,' *Bleacher Report*, July 19, 2015. Accessed June 9, 2019. https://bleacherreport.com/articles/2526034-bill-arnsparger-remembering-the-godfather-of-the-zone-blitz-and-hybrid-defense

CHAPTER 16: PLAYER EQUIPMENT (1960-2018)

Associated Press, 'Devaney Questions Cleat Rule,' *Argus-Leader (Sioux Falls, SD)*, November 7, 1972. / Sports World Specials, *New York Times*, December 25, 1978. / Nelson, Dave, 'Coaches' Ingenuity Leads to Many Rules Changes, *News Journal (Wilmington, DE)*, September 30, 1980.

Arm Pads

Marz, Ron, 'Football Man of Today Are Well-Padded,' *Tampa Bay Times (St. Petersburg, FL)*, October 15, 1976. / Rhoden, William, 'Deacon Jones's Deep Impact on the N.F.L.,' *New York Times*, June 5, 2013.

Pants

Chapman, Scooter, 'Spotlight on Sports,' *Daily News (Port Angeles, WA)*, July 16, 1975. / McIntyre, Bill, 'The Thundering Heard by Highsmith,' *Times (Shreveport, LA)*, July 26, 1975.

Flak Jackets

'Miner Eleven Rated Highly,' *Billings Gazette*, October 16, 1931. / 'Rib-Protectors Given M'Kinney High Grid Team,' *Courier-Gazette (McKinney, MT)*, September 1, 1936. / Mlynczak, Larry, 'Medical Gadgets Figure in Pastorini Resurgence,' *Palm Beach Post*, December 25, 1978. / Hevesi, Dennis, 'Byron Donzis, Inventor of Football Flak Jacket, Dies at 79,' *New York Times*, January 19, 2012. Accessed October 18, 2018. https://www.nytimes.com/2012/01/19/sports/football/byron-donzis-inventor-of-football-flak-jacket-dies-at-79.html / Sandoval, Rick, 'Easton Seeks to Bang a Niche,

United Press International, December 4, 1988. Access October 18, 2018. https://www.upi.com/Archives/1988/12/04/Easton-seeks-to-bang-a-niche/7790597214800/

Shoulder Pads

Personal conversation with Nelson Kraemer, Director Engineering, Riddell Inc., July 12, 2019.

Neck Rolls

'Grid Fatalities May Doom Present Helmets,' *Morning Herald (Uniontown, PA)*, November 24, 1961. / Bromberg, Bill, 'Former Pit OL Bill Fralic, the Inspiration for the Term, 'Pancake Block,' Dies at 56,' *Yahoo Sports*, December 14, 2018. Accessed March 27, 2019. https://sports.yahoo.com/former-pitt-ol-bill-fralic-inspiration-term-pancake-block-dies-56-171738958.html / 'Sypult Gets Second WVU Football Star,' *Beckley Post-Herald* (WV), October 27, 1966. / 'Panthers' May Enjoys Like In 'Pits',' *Indiana Gazette (PA)*, October 24, 1979.

Knee Braces

'Danger in Football,' *Boston Globe*, November 21, 1903. / 'Mike Charles Murphy, Athletic Training,' *Athlos*. Accessed October 18, 2018. http://www.athletics-archive.com/books/athletictraining.htm / 'In The Football World,' *Sun (New York, NY)*, November 22, 1999. / Castator, Katie, 'Residue of an NFL Career – Pain,' *San Bernardino Sun*, July 19, 1981. / Borden, Sam, 'Colleges Swear by Football Knee Braces. Not All Players and Experts Do,' *New York Times*, January 8, 2017. Accessed October 18, 2018. https://www.nytimes.com/2017/01/08/sports/ncaafootball/college-football-playoff-alabama-clemson-knee-braces.html. / Pietrosimone, Brian G., MEd, ATC; Terry L. Grindstaff, DPT, PT, ATC, CSCS; Shelley W. Linens, MEd, ATC; Elizabeth Uczekaj, MEd, ATC; Jay Hertel, PhD, ATC, FNATA, FACSM, 'A Systematic Review of Prophylactic Braces in the Prevention of Knee Ligament Injuries in Collegiate Football Players,' *Journal of Athletic Training*, 2008. Accessed October 18, 2018. https://www.ncbi.nlm.nih.gov/pmc/articles/PMC2474821/

Helmets

'History,' NOCSAE.org. Accessed October 18, 2018. https://nocsae.org/about-nocsae/history/ / Sherman, Ed, 'The Search For the 'Perfect' Football Helmet,' *Chicago Tribune*, October 16, 1983. / Kram, Mark, 'Making Some Head-way?,' *Philadelphia Daily News*, January 26, 2000. / Associated Press, 'Redesigned Football Helmets Tackle Head Injuries,' *Quad-City Times (Davenport, IA)*, August 13, 2002. / Lukas, Paul, 'Uni Watch: New F7 Design is Latest Round in Helmet Arms Race,' *ESPN.com*, January 18, 2017. Accessed October 18, 2018. http://www.espn.com/nfl/story/_/id/18495409/uni-watch-aesthetics-new-schutt-f7-helmet / Channick, Robert, ''Sense of Urgency' On Helmet Safety,' *Chicago Tribune*, October 15, 2017.

Face Masks

Ward, Gene, 'Ward to the Wise,' *Daily News (New York, NY)*, November 12, 1963. / McDonald, Tommy, 'The Monsters and Me,' *Sports Illustrated*, July 27, 1964. Accessed September 18, 2018. https://www.si.com/vault/1964/07/27/608021/the-monsters-and-me / Bak, Richard, 'Helmets and Facemasks Once Were Optional Gear,' *Detroit Athletic*, October 21, 2013. Accessed September 18, 2018. https://www.detroitathletic.com/blog/2013/10/21/helmets-and-facemasks-once-were-optional-nfl-gear/ / Adams, John (Ed.). *1993 NCAA Football Rules and Interpretations*. Indianapolis: National Collegiate Athletic Association, 1993. / Ramirez, Steve, 'Colorado State Tackles Toughest Schedule,' *El Paso Times*, July 24, 1993. / Fuson, Wayne, 'Time Out",' *Indianapolis News*, October 1, 1993.

Playbook Wristbands

McEwen, Tom, 'Sportniks,' *Tampa Times*, November 3, 1960. / Litsky, Frank, 'Paul Dietzel, Coach Who Led L.S.U. to

First National Title, Dies at 89,' *New York Times*, September 24, 2013. / Boeck, Larry, 'It Takes Three Hats for Woolum -But He Has Head to Wear Them,' *Courier-Journal (Louisville, KY)*, September 16, 1962. / Ledord, Cawood, 'Cawood Calls Football,' *Interior-Journal (Stanford, KY),* December 5, 1963. / Associated Press. 'Colts to Carry Playoff Hopes on Wristband,' *Bee (Danville, VA)*, December 21, 1965. / Dombonvissuto, 'Tom Matte's Playbook Wristband,' *Sports Illustrated*, May 27, 2014.

Stickum and Gloves

'All About Those Leather Suits,' Boston Globe, *November 26*, 189. / 'How Yale Team Upset Plans,' *Harrisburg Telegraph*, December 27, 1932. / Walton, Bob, 'BOB-ing Along,' *San Bernardino County Sun*, October 2, 1937. / 'Spartan Coach Now Leary of Fumble Cures,' *Detroit Free Press*, November 2, 1939. / Farmer, Sam, 'Gloves in NFL Have Gained Popularity But Use is Largely Unregulated,' *Los Angeles Times*, August 30, 2015. Accessed January 2, 2016. https://www.latimes.com/sports/nfl/la-sp-nfl-receiver-gloves-20150830-column.html / Pompei, Dan, 'How the NFL Cheats,' *Bleacher Report*, September 9, 2016. Accessed January 2, 2016. https://bleacherreport.com/articles/2656747-how-the-nfl-cheats-foreign-substances

Helmet Visors and Eye Shields

'Vandeweghe Visor Newest Grid Idea,' *Daily Press (Newport News, VA)*, October 10, 1954. / 'Neeld's Helmet Wins Approval,' *Vancouver Sun*, June 16, 1975. / 'Report on Eye Injuries Released,' *Leader-Post (Regina, SK)*, June 18, 1975. / 'Defensive Breakdowns Hurt Vikings, *Star Tribune (Minneapolis)*, October 8, 1984. / Selman, Jim, 'Green Returns to Buc Workouts, Team Meetings,' *Tampa Tribune*, October 23, 1984. / Turner, Gus, 'The 10 Dumbest Rule Changes in NFL History,' *Complex.com*, September 5, 2013. Accessed April 10, 2019. https://www.complex.com/sports/2013/09/nfl-rule-changes/tinted-visors-are-banned / Wogenrich, Mark, 'Ill Winds of Change Blowin',' *Morning Call (Allentown, PA)*, August 19, 1906.

Helmet Award Decals

'Pete Elliott,' *Husker Max*. Accessed April 2, 2019. https://en.wikipedia.org/wiki/Helmet_sticker / Lukacs, John D. 'Buckeye Stickers a Tradition 40 Years In the Making,' *ESPN.com*, September 12, 2008. Accessed April 2, 2019. http://www.espn.com/college-football/news/story?id=3583496 / Lukas, Paul, 'A Close Look at College Football Merit Decal History,' *uni-watch.com*, October 3, 2017. Accessed June 8, 2018. https://uni-watch.com/2017/10/03/a-closer-look-at-college-football-merit-decal-history/ / 'Pete Elliott,' *Husker Max*. Accessed April 2, 2019. https://www.huskermax.com/interviews/Pete_Elliott.html / 'Decals on Skin Helmets? Yup! Denotes Interceptions,' *Daily Utah Chronicle (Salt Lake City)*, November 26, 1962. / Dunleavy, Ryan, 'Did Rutgers, not Ohio State, start helmet stickers in college football? Here's proof, ' *nj.com*, September 28, 2017. Accessed June 8, 2018. http://www.nj.com/rutgersfootball/index.ssf/2017/09/did_rutgers_not_ohio_state_start_helmet_stickers_i.html#incart_river_mobileshort_index

Logos

Underwood, John, 'No Goody Two-Shoes,' *Sports Illustrated*, March 10, 1969. / 'Ask The Globe,' *Boston Globe*, March 3, 1985. / Macnow, Glen. 'NCAA Shoe Rule May Cost Millions,' *Daily Press (Newport News, VA)*, December 16, 1987. / Knight-Ridder, 'NCAA's Logo Policy Gets Court Challenge,' *Greenville News (SC)*, February 23, 1999. / *2000 NCAA Football Rules And Interpretations*. Indianapolis: National Collegiate Athletic Association. 2000. / 'NCAA Sacks Use of Eye-Black Messages,' *Daily Oklahoman*, May 5, 2010. / Barker, Jeff, 'Under Armour Has College 'Zebras' On Its Side,' *Santa Maria Times*, October 2, 2016. / Shaw, Steve (Secretary, NCAA Football Rules Committee). *2018 NCAA Football Rules and Interpretations*. Indianapolis: National Collegiate Athletic Association. 2018.

Tearaway Jerseys

Smith, Chester, 'The Village Smithy,' *Pittsburgh Press*, November 20, 1934. / Geier, Leo, 'The Firing Line,' *Lincoln Star*, July 27, 1949. / Associated Press, 'Gridders' Torn Jerseys Part of Touchdown Act,' *Akron Beacon Journal*, September 30, 1951. / Johnson, Charlie, 'Lowdown on Sports, *Minneapolis Star*, January 11, 1956. / Associated Press. 'College Football Rules to Remain As Is,' *Lake Charles American-Press*, January 15, 1956. / Associated Press, 'League Group Hears Report on New Rules, *Marshall News Messenger (TX)*, August 19, 1956. / Cushman, Tom, 'Sooner Said, Done: Huskers No. 1,' *Philadelphia Daily News*, November 26, 1971. / 'Ask Them Yourself,' *Sunday News and Tribune (Jefferson City, MO)*, October 27, 1974. / Newcomb, Tim, '10 Technological Innovations That Changed the NFL,' *Popular Mechanics*, September 7, 2017. Accessed May 3, 2017. https://www.popularmechanics.com/adventure/sports/g1094/10-tech-innovations-that-changed-the-nfl/ / Associated Press, 'Tearaway Jerseys Banned,' *Lansing State Journal*, October 5, 1978. / Grett, Wayne, 'New Face Mask, Holding Rules for '82 College Football,' *Des Moines Tribune*, September 4, 1982.

Player Names on Jerseys

'Players on This Quint to Have Their Name on Back of Jerseys,' *Democrat and Chronicle (Rochester, NY)*, December 17, 1916. / Associated Press, 'Santa Clara Cage Men Wear Names on Backs of Jersey,' *Times Herald (Port Huron, MI)*, January 3, 1930. / United Press International, 'Player's Name on AFL Jerseys,' *Courier-Post (Camden, NJ)*, August 26, 1960. / Associated Press, 'Coach Nugent's Latest Idea: Terp Names on Jerseys,' *Baltimore Sun*, September 15, 1961.

Shoes and Cleats

'Rules Remove Oldtime Hideout From High School Football Fields,' *Iola Register (KS)*, January 22, 1954. / Kazy, Ted, 'Coaches Find Grid 'Knees' Pet Topic,' *Arizona Republic (Phoenix, AZ)*, September 25, 1957. / Associated Press, 'Devaney Questions Cleat Rule,' *Argus-Leader (Sioux Falls, SD)*, November 7, 1972. / Sports World Specials, *New York Times*, December 25, 1978. / Nelson, Dave, 'Coaches' Ingenuity Leads to Many Rules Changes, *News Journal (Wilmington, DE)*, September 30, 1980. / Butler, Guy, 'Topics of the Tropics,' *Miami News*, October 1, 1946. / Marlowe, Dick 'On Upness,' *Orlando Evening Star*, December 12, 1962. / Young, Dick, 'Young Ideas,' *Daily News (New York, NY)*, November 17, 1965. / Cimini, Rich, 'The Man Behind Joe Namath's White Shoes Deserves a Tribute from the Jets,' *ESPN.com*, November 15, 2015. Accessed November 7, 2018. http://www.espn.com/blog/new-york-jets/post/_/id/56154/the-man-behind-joe-namaths-white-shoes-deserves-a-tribute-from-the-jets / Nike Football Illustrated: A Timeline of Game-Changing Innovations, *Nike News*, January 29, 2015.

Throwbacks, Third Jerseys and Oregon

'Tigers Err, Flints Win, 9-1,' *Dispatch (Moline, IL)*, July 24, 1952. / 'Dukes Go Old Fashioned For 250th Celebration,' *Albuquerque Journal*, July 4, 1956. / Petersen, Randy, 'Razing History Floors Veeck, *Des Moines Register*, June 22, 1990. / Strauss, Joe, 'NFL Envisions History, Profit in 'Throwbacks',' *Atlanta Constitution*, August 28, 1994. / Ismail, 'The Green Machine: A History of Notre Dame's Green Jerseys,' *Bleacher Report*, March 9, 2010.

CHAPTER 17: COACHES AND OFFICIALS (1960-2018)

Coaching Specialization

Finucane, Bob, 'Bob's Tales,' *Delaware County Daily Times (Chester, PA)*, November 29, 1954. / United Press, 'Tennessee Vols Name Captains,' *Panama City News-Herald*, January 7, 1952. / Cordaro, Tony, 'Double Success Story,' *Des Moines Tribune*, November 13, 1957. / 'Schmakel Quits Huskers for Rutgers Post,' *Lincoln Star Journal*, December 28,

1959. / Associated Press, 'Cornell Grid Staff Adds 2,' *Clarion-Ledger (Jackson, MS)*, May 24, 1962. / Dodd, Dennis, 'As NCAA Zeroes In On College Football Staff Sizes, Survey Shows Inconsistencies,' *cbssports.com*, May 15, 2017.

Coaching from the Sideline

'Blaik Knocks Coaches Who Send In All Plays,' *Raleigh Register*, November 17, 1964. / 'A Radio Signals Change,' NFL Operations. Accessed October 23, 2018. https://operations.nfl.com/the-game/technology/ / Burick, Si, 'Si-ings,' *Dayton Daily News*, August 31, 1967. / 'Who Should Call the Plays?,' *Quad-City Times (Davenport, IA)*, October 10, 1978. / Kadish, Paige. Email message to author. May 5, 2018. / Associated Press, Peterson, Anne M., 'Amusing Sideline Signs Convey Plays for Oregon,' *Anniston Star (AL)*, November 5, 2010. / Associated Press, Brunt, Cliff, 'Funny Photo Boards Used to Call Signals From Sideline,' *Seattle Times*, October 10, 2015. Accessed October 23, 2018. https://www.seattletimes.com/sports/funny-photo-boards-used-to-call-signals-from-sideline/

Coaches' Compensation and Contracts

'Legendary Notre Dame Football Coach Ara Parseghian Dies at 94, *South Bend Tribune*, August 2, 2017. Accessed September 3, 2018. https://www.southbendtribune.com/news/local/legendary-notre-dame-football-coach-ara-parseghian-dies-at/article_affde563-1edb-5bc1-a86d-655ebc55345f.html / Johnson, Richard, 'A History of Skyrocketing College Football Coach Salaries, From Walter Camp to Nick Saban,' sbnation.com, June 4, 2018. Accessed on September 2, 2018. https://www.sbnation.com/college-football/,2018/6/4/17390394/college-football-coach-salary-history-highest / 'Powers Departs,' *Missoulian (Missoula, MT)*, December 14, 1977. / 'Bitter WSU Reacts Harshly,' *Missoulian (Missoula, MT)*, December 14, 1977. / Hobson, Will, 'As NCAA Money Trickles Down, Even Tennis Coaches are Outearning Professors,' *Washington Post*, March 13, 2017. Accessed October 8, 2018. https://www.washingtonpost.com/sports/colleges/as-ncaa-money-trickles-down-even-tennis-coaches-are-outearning-professors/2017/03/13/d40d448e-043b-11e7-b9fa-ed727b644a0b_story.html?utm_term=.8a2394e19014 / 'NCAA Salaries, 2018 NCAAF Coaches Salaries,' *USA Today*. Accessed October 8, 2018. http://sports.usatoday.com/ncaa/salaries/

Game Clock and Game Length

Associated Press, 'College Football Rules to Allow More Scoring,' *Vernon Daily Record (TX)*, August 11, 1968. / Langan, Phil, 'College TV Policy Criticized,' *Ithaca Journal*, August 7, 1969. / Vince, Joe, 'How Much Time Do You Spend Watching Commercials During a College Football Game?,' *Upvoted*, October 30, 2015. Accessed January 4, 2019. https://redditblog.com/2015/10/30/how-much-time-do-you-spend-watching-commercials-during-a-college-football-game/ / Harris, Doug, 'Rule Changes Won't Speed Up Game Much,' *Springfield News-Sun (OH)*, April 27, 2006. /*Football Bowl Subdivision Records*. National Collegiate Athletic Association, 2017. / 'NCAA Panel Alters Several Rules for Football,' *Orlando Sentinel*, April 13, 2007. Galveston Daily News, January 31, 1982. /McKeever, Curt, 'College Rule Change Allows Some Fumble Returns, *Lincoln Journal Star*, August 31, 1990.

Limiting Contact in Practice

'Scrimmage Work Is Not In Favor At Pennsylvania U.,' *St. Louis Star and Times*, October 18, 1919. / Associated Press, 'Collegiate Grid Drill Roundup,' *Troy Record (NY)*, September 7, 1950. / Blyth, Carl S. and Frederick O. Mueller, '*An Epidemiologic Study of High School Football Injuries in North Carolina – 1968 – 1972*,' Chapel Hill: North Carolina University, Department of Physical Education, 1972. / 'NCAA Shortens Basketball Season,' *San Bernardino County Sun (CA)*, January 10, 1990. / Crumpacker, John and Frank Cooney, 'Limited-contact Practices Copied by Rest of the League,' *San Francisco Examiner*, August 23, 1990. / 'NCAA Shortens Basketball Season,' *San Bernardino County Sun (CA)*, January 10, 1990. / Associated Press, 'Avoiding Danger,' *Poughkeepsie Journal*, August 20, 2003. / McKee, Ann C. et al. "Chronic Traumatic Encephalopathy in Athletes: Progressive Tauopathy After Repetitive Head Injury." *Journal of Neuropathology and Experimental Neurology*. 2009. / Ledbetter, D. Orlando, 'Look at NFL's New Practice Rules,' *Atlanta Journal-Constitution*, July 31, 2011. Accessed June 9, 2019. https://www.ajc.com/sports/football/look-nfl-new-practice-rules/ZLKiNsjADuSDy8uHzsvYoN/ / Associated Press, 'NCAA Suggests Limiting Contact Football Practices, *Courier-Journal (Louisville, KY)*, July 9, 2014. / Belson, Ken, 'Keeping a Clear Head,' *Santa Fe New Mexican*, March 3, 2016. / Belson, Ken, 'Canadian Football Big Steps to Reduce Hits, a Contrast to the N.F.L., *New York Times*, November 24, 2017. Accessed June 6, 2019. https://www.nytimes.com/2017/11/24/sports/football/canadian-footballs-big-steps-to-reduce-hits-a-contrast-to-the-nfl.html / Parks, Brad, 'How Buddy Teevens '79 Transformed Football Forever,' *Dartmouth Alumni Magazine*, September-October 2018. Accessed April 26, 2019. https://dartmouthalumnimagazine.com/articles/how-buddy-teevens-79-transformed-football-forever

Year-Round Conditioning

Rockafield, Bob, 'Tar Heel Track Coach Urges Cubs' Better Conditioning,' *Arizona Republic (Phoenix, AZ)*, February 27, 1962. / Associated Press, 'Athletes Need Year-Round Conditioning, Says Official,' *Post-Crescent (Appleton, WI)*, May 22, 1962. / Coleman, MD, Lester L. 'Speaking of Your Health…, Year-Round Physical Training,' *Daily Journal (Franklin, IN)*, December 31, 1963. / 'AMA Prescribed Total Training to Win Olympics,' *Daily Item (Sunbury, PA)*, April 28, 1964. / Veltman, Noah, 'NFL Players: Height and Weigh Over Time.' Accessed May 21, 2019. https://noahveltman.com/nflplayers/ / Anzell, Anthony, Jeffrey A. Potteiger, William Kraemer, and Sango, Otieno, 'Changes in Height, Body Weight, and Body Composition in American Football Players from 1942 to 2011,' *Journal of Strength and Conditioning Research*, February 2013.

Drugs and Drug Testing

United Press International, 'Drug Traffic Worries NFL,' *Daily Herald (Provo, UT)*, June 12, 1973. / Quinn, T. J.,' Pumped Up Pioneers: The '63 Chargers,' *ESPN.com*, February 1, 2009. Accessed April 26, 2019. http://www.espn.com/espn/otl/news/story?id=3866837 / David J. Sisson and Brian D. Trexell, 'The National Football League's Substance Abuse Policy: Is Further Conflict Between Players and Management Inevitable?,' *Marquette Sports Law Review*, 1991. / Associated Press. 'Unlimited Substitution Is Permitted By NCAA Football Rules Committee,' *Morning Call, Allentown, PA)*, January 20, 1973. / United Press International. 'NCAA Takes First Swipe At Tackling Drug Woes,' *Republic (Columbus, IN)*, January 15, 1986.

Gatorade

Rovell, Darren. *First in Thirst: How Gatorade Turned the Science of Sweat Into a Cultural Phenomenon.* New York: American Management Association. 2006. / Amdur, Neil, 'Gatorade The Key to UF Success?,' *Tallahassee Democrat*, November 30, 1966. / Dale, Dick, 'G-G-G-Gatorade Give Gators Their Go,' *Pensacola News Journal*, April 23, 1967. / Borden, Sam, 'A Splashy Tradition, Gatorade-Style,' *New York Times*, January 20, 2012. / Roberts, Daniel, 'The History of an Iconic Sports Beverage: Gatorade Turns 50,' *Fortune*. October 1, 2015.

The 40-Yard Dash, Scouting, and the Combine

Snyder, Cameron C., "Gino Marchetti Belies Age, Outrunning Some Backs,' *Baltimore Sun*, July 28, 1962. / 'Gino Marchetti: An End of All-Time,' *Victoria Advocate (TX)*, December 11, 1981. / Jones, Jonathan, "The Longest 40 Yards: How a Short Sprint Became the Combine's Marquee Event," *Sports Illustrated*, February 23, 2017. / Byrod, Fred, '4 Dip Into One Pool for New Players,' *Philadelphia Inquirer*, September 9, 1965. / Vasilogambros, Matt, 'The Roots of NFL Draft Obession,' *Atlantic*, April 28, 2016. / Gabriel, Greg, 'Greg Gabriel: A Look At the NFL Scouting Process in the Fall,' *profootballweekly.com*, October 17, 2016. Accessed February 3, 2019. https://www.profootballweekly.com/2016/10/17/greg-gabriel-a-look-at-the-nfl-scouting-process-in-the-fall/aq6vs8w/ / Tinsman, Brian, 'Cal Rossi: The Redskins

Star Who Got Away (Twice),' *CBS DC*, April 27, 2017. Accessed February 4, 2019. https://washington.cbslocal.com/2017/04/26/cal-rossi-the-redskins-star-who-got-away-twice/ / Landry, Chris, "A Look at the History of the NFL Draft," *LandryFootball.com*, April 19, 2018. Accessed February 3, 2019. https://landryfootball.com/nfl-draft-history-free/ / Orr, Conor, 'The History of NFL Scouting, *NFL.com*. Accessed February 3, 2019. http://www.nfl.com/historyofscouting

Officials' Compensation

'To Act As An Advisory Board,' *Democrat and Chronicle (Rochester, NY)*, April 5, 1906. / Bushnell, E. R., 'Great Crowd Will See Track Stars,' *Pittsburgh Press*, January 14, 1917. / Howell, Fritz, 'Big Ten Football Officials Granted Pay Boost; Death, Disability Insurance Also Approved,' *Palladium-Item (Richmond, IN)*, May 26, 1955. / Wallis, David, 'Earning Their Stripes as Umpires and Referees,' *New York Times*, March 17, 2014. Accessed May 14, 2019. https://www.nytimes.com/2014/03/18/education/earning-their-stripes-as-umpires-and-referees.html / 'A Tougher NFL Job to Get Than Becoming a Player,' *cbsnews.com*, September 18, 2014. Accessed May 14, 2019. https://www.cbsnews.com/news/a-tougher-nfl-job-to-get-than-becoming-a-player/

Officiating Crew Growth

Nelson, David M. *Anatomy of a Game: Football, the Rules, and the Men Who Played the Game.* University of Delaware Press. 1994. / Fullerton Jr., Hugh S., Sports Roundup, *Ithaca Journal*, November 20, 1950. / Associated Press, 'NFL Adds 6th Man to Officials Teams, New Line Judge Expected to Help,' *Montgomery Advertiser (AL)*, July 25, 1965. / Associated Press, 'NFL Bids to Open Up Offense,' *News Journal (Wilmington, DE)*, March 14, 1978. / Solomon, Jon, 'SEC to Experiment With 8 Football Officials, But What's Right Number?,' *CBS Sports*, April 29, 2014. Accessed May 3, 2019. https://www.cbssports.com/college-football/news/sec-to-experiment-with-8-football-officials-but-whats-right-number/ / Associated Press, 'Colts Want Umpires to Pick Up the Pace,' *Cincinnati Enquirer*, August 28, 2010. / Associated Press, 'League Adds First Female Replay Official,' *Orlando Sentinel*, June 30, 2017.

Electronics and Officials

Miller, Norm 'Live-Wire Refs in Offing for Jets-Pats, Giants-Colts,' *Daily News (New York)*, December 6, 1975. / Padecky, Bob, 'Sticky Games Trigger Abuse of Officials,' *Fort Lauderdale News*, January 16, 1976. / Pope, Larry, ''Whatsisname' is Unmasked,' *Asheville Citizen-Times*, February 1, 1976. / Maysel, Lou, 'Whodunit? Naming Penalized Players Not Against College Rules,' *Austin American-Statesman*, December 9, 1987. / Jones, David, 'College Officials to Name Penalized Players,' *Chillicothe Gazette*, July 29, 2004. / Associated Press, 'NFL Officials Will Use Instant Replay,' *Town Talk (Alexandria, LA)*, March 12, 1986. / Associated Press, 'College Football,' *Indiana Gazette (Indiana, PA)*, March 7, 1991. / Bennett, Bruce, 'After Further Review, Instant Replay Is Gone,' *Honolulu Advertiser*, August 16, 1992. / 'Follow the Rules,' *Detroit Free Press*, September 2, 1999. / Spencer, Jon, 'Big Ten To Use Instant Replay,' *News-Journal (Mansfield, OH)*, August 5, 2004. / Schmadtke, Alan, 'Eager Lift Off,' *Orlando Sentinel*, August 28, 2006. / 'History of Instant Replay,' *NFL Operations*. Accessed October 16, 2018. https://operations.nfl.com/the-game/history-of-instant-replay/

Split Officiating Crews

'Powerful New Valley Conference to Start in Fall,' *Iowa City Press-Citizen*, April 3, 1957. / 'Romanowski, Steinman Represent Region on Big-Time College Grid,' *Scrantonian (Scranton, PA)*, September 14, 1969. / 'College Football and Officials,' *Call-Leader (Ellwood, IN)*, October 17, 1984. / 'Big Ten Officiating Crew Accompanies Illinois to Game,' *Pittsburgh Press*, September 14, 1986. / Lambert, Jr. Butch, 'Like Players, Officials Look Forward to Bowl Assignments,' *Clarion-Ledger (Jackson, MS)*, November 22, 1986. / Nelson. *Anatomy of a Game*. 1994.

CHAPTER 18: OFF THE FIELD (1960-2018)

Pre-Game and Studio Shows

'Evolution of a Pregame', *cbspressexpress.com*. Accessed February 17, 2019. https://www.cbspressexpress.com/cbs-sports/media-guides/the-nfl-on-cbs-2012/document?id=32 / 'ESPN's College Football GameDay to Premier Sept. 5,' *Rayne Acadian-Tribune (Rayne, LA)*, August 30, 1987. / Siroky, Mike, 'NBC May Have Telecast, but ESPN Will Be Here Too,' *South Bend Tribune,* November 11, 1993. https://en.wikipedia.org/wiki/List_of_Super_Bowl_halftime_shows

Instant Replay

'"Marching On" for JFK,' *cbsnews.com*, 2013. Accessed February 21, 2019. https://www.cbsnews.com/video/jfk-tribute-1963-army-navy-football-game-honored-assassinated-president/ / Saunders, Patrick, 'A Look ATT's Instant Replay Through the Years,' *Denver Post*, November 16, 2013. / NPR Morning Edition. 'He Invented Instant Replay, The TV Trick We Now Take for Granted,' January 20, 2015

Cameras and Shots

'Impact of Television,' *NFL Ops*. Accessed February 25, 2019. https://operations.nfl.com/the-game/impact-of-television/ / Grossman John ''goalpost' Brown's Amazing Flying Camera, *Inc*., January 1, 1985. Accessed February 18, 2019. https://www.inc.com/magazine/19850101/4162.html / Giardina, Carolyn, 'Steadicam Inventor Garrett Brown to Receive Lifetime Achievement Award at Engineering Emmys,' *Hollywood Reporter*, September 29, 2015. Accessed February 20, 2019. https://www.hollywoodreporter.com/behind-screen/engineering-emmys-steadicam-inventor-receive-828053

On-Screen Graphics

Bass, Rudi, 'The Development of Vidifont,' *Journal of Typographical Research*, 1971. / Sandomir, Richard, 'The Innovation That Grew,' *New York Times*, June 12, 2014. / Barber, Scott, 'The Story of TV Graphics,' *LinkedIn*, March 29, 2016. Accessed February 21, 2019. https://www.linkedin.com/pulse/story-tv-graphics-scott-barber/ / Wirth, Richard, 'Television's On Screen Graphics,' *Provideo Coalition*, October 27, 2018. Accessed February 21, 2019. https://www.provideocoalition.com/televisions-on-screen-graphics/

Television Timeouts

Young, Dick, 'Young Ideas,' *Daily News (New York, NY)*, September 19, 1958. / Associated Press, 'Television Breaks Raise Spectator Ire,' *Daily Oklahoman (Oklahoma City)*, December 12, 1967.

Crowd Behavior

Associated Press, 'Anti-Booing Order Poses Some Humorous Sabotage,' *Herald and New (Klamath Falls, OR)*, November 8, 1946. / Johnson, Charlie, 'Lowdown on Sports,' *Minneapolis Star*, May 7, 1947. / Associated Press, 'Sportswriters Desire Better Crowd Behavior, *Times and Democrat (Orangeburg, SC)*, March 8, 1958. / United Press International, 'Lot of Noise About Southern Bells,' *Honolulu Advertiser*, March 8, 1975. / Cowbell, *Mississippi State University Alumni Association*. Accessed April 12, 2019. https://www.alumni.msstate.edu/s/811/alumni/interior.aspx?sid=811&gid=1&pgid=761 / White, Danny, 'Arizona's Boisterous Football Crowds Drawing Penalties Against Wildcats,' *Arizona Daily Star (Tucson)*, October 17, 1978. / Associated Press, 'NCAA Noise Rule Hits Tigers Hard,' *Ashville Citizen-Times (NC)*, July 27, 1981. / Pressgrove, Andy, Bruce Moak and Jack Vaughn, '1989 Football Rule Changes,' *Star-Herald (Kosciusko, MS)*, August 31, 1989. / 'NCAA: SEC Can Assess Penalties for Noisemakers,' *Anniston Star (AL)*, August 27, 2006.

The Wave

Rohrer, Finio, 'Who Invented the Mexican Wave?, *BBC.com*, June 16, 2010. Accessed September 25, 2018. http://news.bbc.co.uk/2/hi/8742454.stm / Williams, Doug, 'It's Settled: Where The Wave First Started,' *ESPN.com*, March 1, 2013. Accessed September 25, 2018. http://www.espn.com/blog/playbook/fandom/post/_/id/18888/its-settled-where-the-wave-first-started

Licensed Team Apparel

Warbington, Lauren T. 'Crossing the Line: The Collegiate Licensing Company's Overindulgent Attempt to Limit Small Businesses' Online Marketing Techniques Based on Frivolous Claims of Trademark Infringement.' *University of Georgia, Journal on Intellectual Property Law*. March 2012. / Layden, Tim. 'We Are What We Wear: How Sports Jerseys Became Ubiquitous in the U.S.,' *Sports Illustrated*. February 1, 2016. Accessed June 10, 2019. https://www.si.com/nfl/2016/02/01/mlb-nba-nhl-sports-jersys-rise-popularity / Tanklefsky, David and Nathan Rothstein. 'What Happened to Nutmeg Mills? The Forgotten Story of a Sports Apparel Pioneer,' *Vice Sports*, August 8, 2016. Accessed June 10, 2019. https://sports.vice.com/en_au/article/d7m7ay/what-happened-to-nutmeg-mills-the-forgotten-story-of-a-sports-apparel-pioneer

Whiteouts and Their Cousins

Branch, John. 'When Spotlight is On, The Clothes Turn Black,' *New York Times*, October 4, 2008. / Branch, John, 'Fans' Uniform Look is a Team Effort, *New York Times*, May 18, 2015. Accessed August 28, 2018. https://www.nytimes.com/2015/05/19/sports/basketball/in-sea-of-t-shirts-nba-hits-all-of-its-marketing-notes.html / O'Connor-Clarke, Charlie, 'A History of the Hockey Sweater: From Eaton's Catalogue to the C of Red,' *Last Word On Hockey*, April 17, 2017. Accessed November 17, 2018. https://lastwordonhockey.com/2017/04/17/8895/ / Faris, Nick, 'The Whiteout Returns: How It Started and What It Means to Winnipeg and Those Early Jets Players,' *National Post (Toronto, ON)*, April 20, 2018. Accessed June 10, 2019. https://nationalpost.com/sports/hockey/nhl/winnipeg-jets-enter-playoffs-as-canadas-top-stanley-cup-hope-and-their-citys-best-team-in-decades / Yarnell, Maggie, 'History of the Penn State White Out,' *Last Word on College Football*, September 26, 2018. Accessed June 10, 2019. https://lastwordoncollegefootball.com/2018/09/26/history-of-the-penn-state-white-out-game/

The NFL and Antitrust Legislation

Rand, Jack, 'Why Pro Football's Popularity,' *Times (Shreveport, LA)*, February 8, 1959. / Shoemaker, Whitney, 'Supreme Court Hears Arguments on NFL Anti-Trust Violations,' *Ashville Citizen-Times (NC)*, January 18, 1957. / Associated Press 'Bell, Congressman Discuss NFL's Anti-Trust Legislation,' *Troy Record (NY)*, March 21, 1957. / Associated Press, 'Grid Loop Settles Anti-Trust Suit Out of Court,' *Bee (Danville, VA)*, April 16, 1958. / Associated Press, 'AFL's Television Plan Will Give Fans More Games,' *Miami News*, February 7, 1960. / Associated Press, 'NFL's Television Pact Violates Antitrust Laws,' *Wausau Daily Herald*, July 21, 1961. / 'Kennedy Signs Pro Sports TV Pool Bill,' *Green Bay Press-Gazette*, October 1, 1961.

Eligibility

United Press, 'Freshmen Eligible for Boxing Tournament,' *Pittsburgh Press*, March 13, 1932. / Weekes, William, 'Olympic Aspirants to Receive Tests at Chicago,' *Argus-Leader (Sioux Falls, SD)*, June 10, 1932. / 'NCAA Makes Freshmen Eligible for Compete,' *Lincoln Star*, January 9, 1972. / Smith, Ronald A. *Pay for Play: A History of Big-Time Athletic Reform*. Urbana: University of Illinois Press. 2011.

Racial Integration

Pennington, Richard. Racial Integration of College Football. *Richardpennington.com*. November 8, 2010. Accessed My 6, 2019. https://www.richardpennington.com/2010/11/racial-integration-college-football/. / Sherman, Ed. 'How Michigan State's Duffy Daugherty Helped Integrate College Football,' *Chicago Tribune*, February 16, 2015. / Rittenberg, Adam, 'Spartans Blended Race in 1960s,' *ESPN*, February 21, 2013. Accessed May 8, 2018. / Drape, Joe. 'Changing the Face of Texas Football, *New York Times*, December 23, 2005. http://www.espn.com/college-football/story/_/id/8970293/segregation-led-star-players-michigan-state-spartans-1960s-college-football / Vaught, Larry, 'Brother's Book Offers Insights to Greg Page,' *Advocate-Messenger (Danville, KY)*, December 4, 2013. / Coclanis, Peter A., 'Southern Football, African American Athletics, and the Relative Decline of the Big Ten,' *Southern Spaces*, December 17, 2014. / Gosselin, Rick, 'The Once-Great HBCU Pipeline Now Just a Trickle,' *Football Maven*, July 27, 2017. Accessed May8, 2019. https://footballmaven.io/talkoffame/nfl/the-once-great-hbcu-pipeline-now-just-a-trickle-twOYVU450UyfXIIy13syeQ/ / Associated Press, 'Macalaster Names Black Grid Coach,' *Winona Daily News (MN)*, December 23, 1971. / 'S.C. State's Jeffries Goes To Wichita State,' *Tallahassee Democrat*, December 29, 1978. / Associated Press, 'NU Coach Vows to Be Competitive,' *Journal Times (Racine, WI)*, December 24, 1980. / Associated Press, 'Raiders Name Shell Head Coach,' *Battle Creek Enquirer*, October 4, 1989.

Early Entry

Associated Press, 'College Football Officials Seek Truce with USFL,' *Star-Gazette (Elmira, NY)*, March 3, 1983. / Janofsky, Michael, 'U.S.F.L. Loses Antitrust Suit On Eligibility,' *New York Times*, March 1, 1984. Accessed November 15, 2018. https://www.nytimes.com/1984/03/01/sports/usfl-loses-antitrust-suit-on-eligibility.html / United Press International, 'Dupree Become $6 Million Man,' *Dispatch (Moline, IL)*, March 4, 1984. / Myers, Gary, 'Is NFL's Happy Marriage With Colleges In Trouble,' *Austin American-Statesman*, August 27, 1987. / Shelton, Gary, 'Three Years Or Less,' *St. Petersburg Times*, February 18, 1990.

Player Safety

United Press International, 'NCAA Football Rule Changes Made for '72,' *Tennessean (Nashville, TN)*, January 17, 1972. / Kucera, Kristen L. and David Klossner, Bob Colgate and Robert C. Cantu, *Annual Survey of Football Injury Research, 1931-2014*, National Center for Catastrophic Sport Injury Research, 2015. Accessed May 30, 2019. https://nccsir.unc.edu/files/2013/10/Annual-Football-2014-Fatalities-Final.pdf / Rapaport, Daniel, 'New Study Says Repeated Hits to Head, Not Just Concussions, Can Cause CTE,' *Sports Illustrated*, January 18, 2018. Accessed May 12, 2019. https://www.si.com/nfl/2018/01/18/study-repeated-head-hits-concussions-cte / Rapaport, Daniel, 'Timeline: Six Studies of Head Trauma in Football That Helped Establish Link to CTE,' *Sports Illustrated*, July 26, 2017. Accessed May 30, 2019. https://www.si.com/nfl/2017/07/26/nfl-concussion-head-trauma-studies-football-timeline

EPILOGUE

Bernstein. Football. 2001. / 'How They Coach," *Boston Post*, October 29, 1893. / Schultz, Mark, 'Is A Wider Field Coming to NFL Stadiums?,' *Football Zebras*, February 11, 2013. Accessed May 18, 2019. http://www.footballzebras.com/2013/02/is-a-wider-field-coming-to-a-nfl-stadium-near-you/ / Nussbaum, Jeff, 'Three Simple Fixes That Could Save Pro Football,' *Washington Monthly*, January-February 2015. Accessed May 18, 2019. https://washingtonmonthly.com/magazine/janfeb-2015/three-simple-fixes-that-could-save-pro-football/ / Washchyshyn, Marika, 'Is The Canadian Football League Safer Than The NFL?,' *Complex*, January 25, 2015. Accessed May 18, 2019. https://www.complex.com/sports/2015/11/cfl-concussions / Kubota, Taylor. 'The Science of Football: Which Positions Take the Hardest Hots?,' *Scientific American*, June 7, 2016. Accessed March 31, 2020. https://www.scientificamerican.com/article/the-science-of-football-which-positions-take-the-hardest-hits/ / Auerbach, Paul S. and William H. Waggoner, 'It's Time to Change the Rules,' *Journal of the American Medical Association*, 2016. Accessed April 1, 2020. https://www.

semanticscholar.org/paper/It's-Time-to-Change-the-Rules.-Auerbach-Waggoner/c4a9c4b0e9609fe016982993b1b933d114c1e74f / Popplewell, Bret, 'Inside the Controversial Concussion Lab That Could Save Football,' *thewalrus.ca*, September 17, 2017. Accessed June 6, 2019. https://thewalrus.ca/inside-the-controversial-concussion-lab-that-could-save-football/ / Belson, Ken, 'Canadian Football Big Steps to Reduce Hits, a Contrast to the N.F.L., *New York Times*, November 24, 2017. Accessed June 6, 2019. https://www.nytimes.com/2017/11/24/sports/football/canadian-footballs-big-steps-to-reduce-hits-a-contrast-to-the-nfl.html / Geier, David, 'Nine Ways to Make Football Safer Without Drastically Changing the Game, *Post and Courier (Charleston, SC)*, February 1, 2018. Accessed September 6, 2019. https://www.postandcourier.com/sports/nine-ways-to-make-football-safer-without-drastically-changing-the/article_a80fe9d2-004c-11e8-a146-af76db0619c5.html / University of Pennsylvania School of Medicine, 'How Can We Reduce Concussions in Football? Change Kickoffs, Experts Say,' *ScienceDaily*, October 1, 2018. Accessed September 6, 2019. www.sciencedaily.com/releases/2018/10/181001114220.htm. / Wollan, Mali, 'Safer Tackling,' *New York Times*, February 26, 2019. Accessed June 6, 2019. https://www.nytimes.com/2019/02/26/magazine/how-to-tackle-someone.html/

ILLUSTRATION CREDITS

MJ Brown created all tables and play illustrations included in this book.

Some images in the book are snapshots or other photographs taken by unknown individuals. Most of those are "Real Photograph Post Cards" or RPPCs. RPPCs were popular from the early 1900s through the 1930s. Commercial and personal photographers commonly printed images on post card stock either for sale or to send to family and friends. Attributing these images to specific photographers can be difficult, even in those instances in which commercial photographers added their names to the images.

Illustration credits are noted throughout the book. Full citations follow for those instances in which the body of the book includes abbreviated credits.

COVER

Harris & Ewing, photographer. *Jim Thorpe,* [Between 1910 and 1920]. *Library of Congress.*

INTRODUCTION

Trade card for Massasoit House, corner of Main and Rail Road Streets, Springfield, Mass., undated. Courtesy of *Historic New England.*

CHAPTER 1: THE EMERGENCE OF THE GAME (1869-1905)

Harvard versus McGill. Davis, Parke H. *Football: The American Intercollegiate Game.* New York: Charles Scribner's Sons, 1911.

Walter Camp at Yale. Edwards, William H. *Football Days: Memories of the Game and of the Men Behind the Ball.* New York: Moffat, Yard and Company. 1916.

CHAPTER 2: THE BALL, THE FIELD, AND STADIUMS (1869-1905)

N/A

CHAPTER 3: PLAY AND TECHNIQUES (1869-1905)

Rushers shielding defense. Johnson, Alexander. "The American Game of Foot-Ball," *Century Illustrated Monthly Magazine*, Vol. XXXIV, No. 6, October 1887.

Placekick holder demonstrating over-under technique in 1902. *Wilfred B. Shaw Papers, Bentley Historical Library, University of Michigan.*

CHAPTER 4: PLAYER EQUIPMENT (1869-1905)

Cleat design. Camp, Walter. Intercollegiate Foot-Ball in America. *St. Nicholas*, January 1890.

Nose guard. Cook, Charles Emerson. 'Football in Armour,' *Strand*, March 1897.

CHAPTER 5: COACHES AND OFFICIALS (1869-1905)

1895 Auburn-Georgia. https://commons.wikimedia.org/wiki/File:1895_Auburn_-_Georgia_football_game_at_Piedmont_Park_in_Atlanta_Georgia.jpg. This file is licensed under the Creative Commons Attribution-Share Alike 4.0 International license. https://creativecommons.org/licenses/by-sa/4.0/deed.en

Referee's Horn advertisement. Camp, Walter (Ed.). *Spalding's Official Football Guide, 1904*. New York: American Sports Publishing. 1904.

CHAPTER 6: OFF THE FIELD (1869-1905)

N/A

CHAPTER 7: FROM CRISIS TO ASCENDANCY (1906-1959)

N/A

CHAPTER 8: THE BALL, THE FIELD, AND STADIUMS (1906-1959)

In goal at Polo Grounds. *Leslie's Weekly*, November 5, 1903.

Program cover with end zone flag. September 28, 1946 Wisconsin-California game. Harry Bonath (artist), Associated Students, University of California. Personal Collection.

CHAPTER 9: PLAY AND TECHNIQUES (1906-1959)

Center-quarterback exchange. Camp, Walter (Ed.). *Spalding's Official Football Guide, 1908*. New York: American Sports Publishing. 1908.

Bradbury Robinson. Saint Louis University Libraries Digital Collections, Saint Louis University Football player, Bradley Robinson, throwing a forward pass. The Blue and White Yearbook 1907, p. 190 - SLU Photo Collection - Archives. Saint Louis University Libraries. Saint Louis University, Saint Louis, Missouri. *http://cdm.slu.edu/cdm/singleitem/collection/photos/id/1553/rec/3*

Harvard screen pass. Houghton, Percy D. *Football and How to Watch It*. Boston: Marshall Jones. 1922.

Pete Gogolak kicking. 1964 Cornellian, Division of Rare and Manuscript Collections, Cornell University Library.

CHAPTER 10: PLAYER EQUIPMENT (1906-1959)

Shoulder pad and head harness advertisements. Reach Athletic Goods for Fall and Winter. A.J. Reach and Co. 1918.

Harry Eielson. *Great Lakes Recruit, A Pictoral Naval Magazine*. Great Lakes, IL: Great Lakes Athletic Association. January 1919.

Football pants advertisement. Hall, E. K. (Ed.). *National Collegiate Athletic Association Foot Ball Rules 1926*. New York: American Sports Publishing. 1926.

Football pants. 1928-1929 Rawlings Catalog of Foot Ball, Basket Ball, Athletic Equipment. Fall and Winter.

c. 1950 Purdue players with missing teeth. Purdue University Athletics, Courtesy of Purdue University Libraries, Karnes Archives & Special Collections.

Jack Banta, Bob Waterfield, and Bob Hoffman of 1948 Los Angeles Rams. https://commons.wikimedia.org/wiki/File:Jack_Banta--Bob_Watterfield--Bob_Hoffman--1948_Los_Angeles_Rams.jpg#file This file is licensed under the Creative Commons Attribution-Share Alike 4.0 International license. https://creativecommons.org/licenses/by-sa/4.0/deed.en

Duke players wearing low cut shoes. Unidentified Football Game Photo, 1937 (UA13020018-N-05743). Sports Information Office: Photographic Negatives Collection.

Drake-Iowa State game. *'Drake Surprises Ames at the Start,' Des Moines Register, December 1, 1905. Accessed via newspapers.com*

CHAPTER 11: COACHES AND OFFICIALS (1906-1959)

Bucking Strap. Folsom, Fred Gorham. Foot-Ball Bucking Strap. U.S. Patent 528,580 filed September 5, 1905 and issued August 28, 1906. Accessed June 9, 2019. https://patentimages.storage.googleapis.com/57/9d/d9/854e5d669cc424/US829580.pdf

Harvard players practicing in dark and light jerseys. HUPSF Football (278), olvwork401856. Harvard University Archives.

Coin toss at UNC-Texas football game held at the University of North Carolina at Chapel Hill, in the Hugh Morton Photographs and Films #P0081, copyright, 1948, North Carolina Collection, University of North Carolina at Chapel Hill Library.

Frank Birch Signals. Seton, Ernest Thompson. *Sign Talk: A Universal Signal Code, Without Apparatus, for Use in the Army, the Navy, Camping, Hunting, and Daily Life*. New York: Doubleday, Page & Co. 1918.

CHAPTER 12: OFF THE FIELD (1906-1959)

Oregon State Electric Scoreboard. *Ball Studio, Harriett's Photograph Collection (1886-1996), Historical Images of Oregon State University, OSU Libraries Special Collections &morning Archives Research Center).*

Pittsburgh Golden Panther. *Nice Kitty (PANTHER02), University of Pittsburgh Historic Photographs, 1884-present, Archives & Special Collections, University of Pittsburgh Library System.*

Duke University Blue Devil mascot. *Duke University Blue Devil, ca. 1929-1930. University Archives Photograph Collection.*

Purdue Military Band. *The Debris 1923, West Lafayette (IN): Class of 1923, Purdue University.*

Carriages on sideline at 1902 Rose Bowl. *University of Michigan Photographs, Bentley Historical Library, University of Michigan.*

Tulane cheerleaders. *University Archives, Special Collections, Howard-Tilton Memorial Library, Tulane University, New Orleans, LA.*

Aerial View of Game. 'Princeton Beating Harvard, The First Football Game Photographed from an Aeroplane,' *Collier's*, November 18, 1911.

Blimp over Cleveland Stadium. *The Goodyear Tire & Rubber Company Records, The University of Akron, University Libraries, Archival Services.*

CHAPTER 13: TELEVISION BECOMES KING (1960-2018)

N/A

CHAPTER 14: THE BALL, THE FIELD, AND STADIUMS (1960-2018)

Super Bowl I halftime show. Jimberg13, https://commons.wikimedia.org/wiki/File:SuperBowl_I_-_Los_Angeles_Coliseum_(cropped).jpg. This file is licensed under the Creative Commons Attribution-Share Alike 4.0 International license. https://creativecommons.org/licenses/by-sa/4.0/deed.en

CHAPTER 15: PLAY AND TECHNIQUES (1960-2018)

N/A

CHAPTER 16: PLAYER EQUIPMENT (1960-2018)

Bill Fralic. Bill Fralic (FTBL44.UA), University of Pittsburgh Historic Photographs, 1884-present, Archives & Special Collections, University of Pittsburgh Library System.

Tom Harmon, UM Football, with torn jersey, autographed to Fritz Crisler. Collection: Athletic Department, Bentley Historical Library, University of Michigan.

Army wearing white shoes in 1962 Army-Navy game. The Lucky Bag V415.J1L9. Special Collections & Archives Department, Nimitz Library, United States Naval Academy

CHAPTER 17: COACHES AND OFFICIALS (1960-2018)

Dan Marino consults with Jackie Sherrill. Dan Marino Consults with Coaches (FTBL05.UA), University of Pittsburgh Historic Photographs, 1884-present, Archives & Special Collections, University of Pittsburgh Library System

Charging Fence. 'Bucking Strap and Charging Fence Latest on Football Gridiron,' *Tennessean (Nashville),* October 3, 1912.

Olson, Clarence E., 'New Training Devices Listed, Bruhn 'Chutes' Works', Capital Times (Madison, WI), August 21, 1956.

Paul Brown Bowman card. https://commons.wikimedia.org/wiki/File:Paul_Brown,_American_football_head_-coach.png. This file is licensed under the Creative Commons Attribution-Share Alike 4.0 International license. https://creativecommons.org/licenses/by-sa/4.0/deed.en

CHAPTER 18: OFF THE FIELD (1960-2018)

Stichweh touchdown run. *Photo by U.S. Army Signal Corps in Walter, Frank, 'Down the Field,' Assembly, West Point, NY: West Point Alumni Association, Winter 1964.*

EPILOGUE

N/A

INDEX

The pages numbers in the Index are based on the print version of the book. Those reading the book in electronic format can use the search function to find key words.

1.0

ALSO BY TIMOTHY P. BROWN

Fields of Friendly Strife: The Doughboys and Sailors of the WWI Rose Bowls

Available through Amazon in paperback and Kindle versions

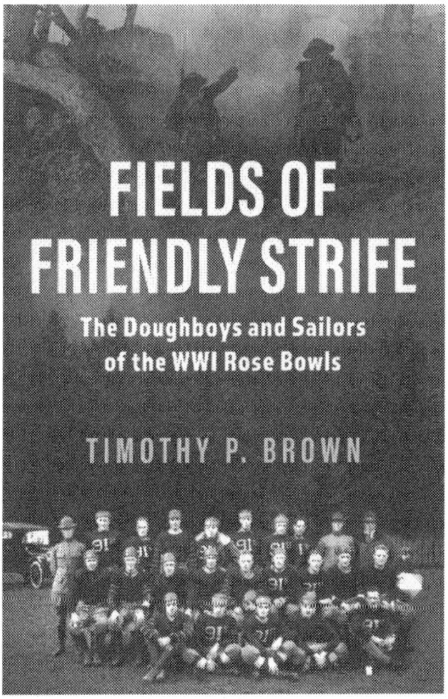

Made in the USA
Columbia, SC
05 June 2020

98298250R00259